SAS/GRAPH® Software: Reference

Version 8
Volume 2

The Power to Know™

 SAS Publishing

The correct bibliographic citation for this manual is as follows: SAS Institute Inc., *SAS/GRAPH® Software: Reference, Version 8*, Cary, NC: SAS Institute Inc., 1999. 1240 pp.

SAS/GRAPH® Software: Reference, Version 8

Copyright © 1999 by SAS Institute Inc., Cary, NC, USA.

ISBN 1–58025–525–6

Contents

Chapter 6 △ SAS/GRAPH Fonts 125

Chapter 7 △ SAS/GRAPH Colors 139

Chapter 8 △ SAS/GRAPH Statements 159

CHAPTER

14

The GCONTOUR Procedure

Overview

The GCONTOUR procedure produces plots that represent three-dimensional relationships in two dimensions. Lines or areas in a contour plot represent levels of magnitude (z) corresponding to a position (x, y) on a plane.

Use the GCONTOUR procedure to

- examine trends in your data when they contain too many peaks and valleys to be accurately observed using the G3D procedure
- examine data in which the levels, not the shape, of the data are important.
- identify contour levels using lines or patterns.

Note: The GCONTOUR procedure produces rectangular contour plots, not irregular contour maps. △

About Contour Plots

Contour plots represent the levels of magnitude of a variable z, called the *contour variable*, for a position on a plane given by the values of two variables x and y. Contour lines of different colors and line types show different levels of magnitude of z for locations of x and y.

Figure 14.1 on page 626 shows a simple contour plot that illustrates the percentage of clay found in soil samples at various locations of a testing site. The x and y axes on the plot represent a graph of surface height at various *x-y* locations. The contour lines within the plot represent the locations on the plane that have the clay percentages specified in the legend. The program for this plot is in Example 1 on page 641.

By default, the GCONTOUR procedure automatically scales the axes to include the maximum and minimum data values, labels each axis with the name of its variable or an associated label, and draws a frame around the plot. In addition, it plots values using seven contour levels of the contour variable, representing those levels with default colors and line types. Finally, it generates a legend that is labeled with the contour variable's name.

Figure 14.1   Sample Contour Plot (GR14N01)

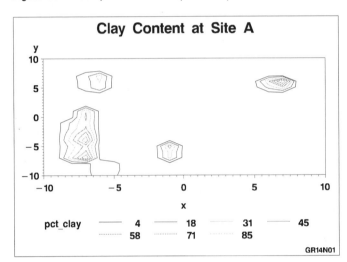

Concepts

Parts of a Contour Plot

Some terms used in the discussion of the GCONTOUR procedure are illustrated in Figure 14.2 on page 627.

Figure 14.2   GCONTOUR Procedure Terms

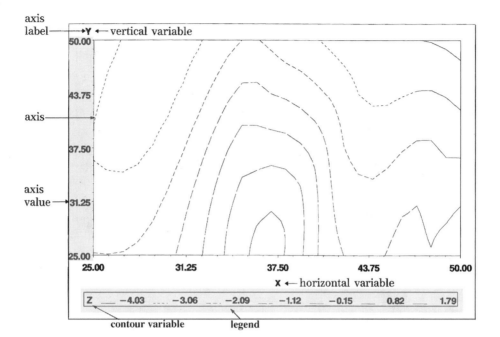

About the Input Data Set

The GCONTOUR procedure requires data sets that include three numeric variables: x and y for the horizontal and vertical axes, respectively, and z for the contour level. The observations in the input data set should form a rectangular grid of x and y values and exactly one z value for each x, y combination. For example, data that contain 5 distinct values of x and 10 distinct values for y should be part of a data set that contains 50 observations with values for x, y, and z. If a single x, y grid location has more than one associated z value, only the last such observation is used.

Interpolating Additional Values

Data sets often contain so few combinations of x, y, and z values that the GCONTOUR procedure cannot produce a contour plot. By default, the data set must contain nonmissing z values for at least 50 percent of the grid in order for the GCONTOUR procedure to produce a satisfactory plot. If your data are clustered in relatively small patches over a larger study area, you can use the PROC GCONTOUR statement's INCOMPLETE option, which allows plotting of data when over 50 percent of the plot grid contains missing data.

When the GCONTOUR procedure cannot produce a satisfactory contour plot because of missing x, y, or z values, SAS/GRAPH software issues an error message, and no graph is produced. To correct this problem, you can use the G3GRID procedure to process data sets to be used by the GCONTOUR procedure. The G3GRID procedure interpolates the necessary values to produce a data set with nonmissing z values for every combination of the x and y variables. The G3GRID procedure can also smooth data for use with the GCONTOUR procedure. You can use the output data set from the G3GRID procedure as the input data set for the GCONTOUR procedure. For an example of using PROC G3GRID to interpolate values, see Example 1 on page 641.

Procedure Syntax

Requirements: At least one PLOT statement is required.

Global statements: AXIS, FOOTNOTE, LEGEND, PATTERN, SYMBOL, TITLE

Reminder: The procedure can include the BY, FORMAT, LABEL, NOTE, and WHERE statements.

Supports: Output Delivery System (ODS)

PROC GCONTOUR <DATA=*input-data-set*>
    <ANNOTATE=*Annotate-data-set*>
    <GOUT=<*libref.*>*output-catalog*>
    <INCOMPLETE>;
    PLOT *plot-request* </*option(s)*>;

PROC GCONTOUR Statement

Identifies the data set that contains the plot variables. Optionally specifies annotation and an output catalog.

Requirements: An input data set is required.

Syntax

PROC GCONTOUR <DATA=*input-data-set*>
    <ANNOTATE=*Annotate-data-set*>
    <GOUT=<*libref.*>*output-catalog*>
    <INCOMPLETE>;

Options

ANNOTATE=*Annotate-data-set*
ANNO=*Annotate-data-set*
    specifies a data set to annotate all graphs produced by the GCONTOUR procedure. To annotate individual graphs, use ANNOTATE= in the action statement.

    See also: Chapter 10, "The Annotate Data Set," on page 403

DATA=*input-data-set*
    specifies the SAS data set that contains the variables to plot. By default, the procedure uses the most recently created SAS data set.

    See also: "SAS Data Sets" on page 25 and "About the Input Data Set" on page 627

GOUT=< *libref.* >*output-catalog*
    specifies the SAS catalog in which to save the graphics output produced by the GCONTOUR procedure. If you omit the libref, SAS/GRAPH looks for the catalog in the temporary library called WORK and creates the catalog if it does not exist.

    See also: "Creating and Specifying Catalogs" on page 50

INCOMPLETE
allows plotting of data when over 50 percent of the plot grid contains missing data.

PLOT Statement

Creates contour plots using values of three numeric variables from the input data set as the source of the contour coordinates.

Requirements: A plot request is required.

Global statements: AXIS, FOOTNOTE, LEGEND, PATTERN, SYMBOL, TITLE

Description The PLOT statement specifies the three variables to plot. Optionally, it controls the contour levels, labels the plot lines, and modifies axes as well as the general appearance of the graph. Only one plot request can be specified in a PLOT statement. To specify multiple plots for a single PROC GCONTOUR statement, use multiple PLOT statements.

The PLOT statement automatically

- □ plots the values using seven contour levels of the z variable
- □ scales the axes to include the maximum and minimum data values
- □ labels the x and y axes and displays the contour levels in the plot's legend
- □ draws a frame around the plot.

Note: You cannot produce overlaid contour plots with PROC GCONTOUR alone. △

You can use global statements to modify the axes, the legend, the contour lines and contour line labels, and the fill patterns and pattern colors for contour areas. You can also add titles, footnotes, and notes to the chart, and you can use an Annotate data set to enhance the chart.

Syntax

PLOT *plot-request* <*/option(s)*>;

plot-request must be

$y*x=z$

option(s) can be one or more options from any or all of the following categories:

- □ appearance options:
    - ANNOTATE=*Annotate-data-set*
    - CAXIS=*axis-color*
    - CFRAME=*background-color*
    - COUTLINE=*outline-color*

CTEXT=*text-color*

GRID

NOAXIS | NOAXES

NOFRAME

☐ horizontal axis options:

AUTOHREF

CHREF=*reference-line-color*

HAXIS=AXIS<1...99>

HMINOR=*number-of-minor-ticks*

HREF=*value-list*

HREVERSE

LHREF=*line-type*

XTICKNUM=*number-of-ticks*

☐ vertical axis options:

AUTOVREF

CVREF=*reference-line-color*

LVREF=*line-type*

VAXIS=AXIS<1...99>

VMINOR=*number-of-minor-ticks*

VREF=*value-list*

VREVERSE

YTICKNUM=*number-of-ticks*

☐ contour options:

CLEVELS=*color(s)*

JOIN

LEGEND=LEGEND<1...99>

LEVELS=*value-list*

LLEVELS=*line-type-list*

NLEVELS=*number-of-levels*

NOLEGEND

PATTERN

☐ labeling options:

AUTOLABEL | AUTOLABEL=(*autolabel-suboptions*)

where *autolabel-suboptions* can be one or more of these:

CHECK=*checking-factor* | NONE

MAXHIDE=*amount<units>*

REVEAL

TOLANGLE=*angle*

☐ catalog entry description options:

DESCRIPTION='*entry-description*'

NAME='*entry-name*'

Required Arguments

y*x=z

specifies three numeric variables from the input data set:

y   is the variable that is plotted on the vertical (y) axis.

x   is the variable that is plotted on the horizontal (x) axis.

z   is the variable that is plotted as contour lines.

Options

You can specify as many PLOT options as you want, and you can list them in any order. If you use a BY statement on the procedure, the options in each PLOT statement affect all graphs produced by that BY statement.

ANNOTATE=*Annotate-data-set*
ANNO=*Annotate-data-set*

specifies a data set to annotate charts produced by the PLOT statement.

See also: Chapter 10, "The Annotate Data Set," on page 403

AUTOHREF

draws reference lines at all major tick marks on the horizontal axis.

AUTOLABEL | AUTOLABEL=(*autolabel_suboptions*)

automatically labels the contour lines. *Autolabel-suboptions* can be one or more of the suboptions described in "Autolabel Suboptions" on page 636.

The label for each contour line is the z value for that contour level. By default, labels are displayed in BEST format. To change the format, use a FORMAT statement.

When AUTOLABEL is used, the LLEVELS= and CLEVELS= options are ignored and the SYMBOL statement controls label text and contour-line attributes. For more information on the SYMBOL statement, see "Modifying Contour Lines and Labels with the SYMBOL Statement" on page 640.

Even though AUTOLABEL labels the contour lines, a default legend is still generated. To suppress the legend, use the NOLEGEND option.

Featured in: Example 2 on page 643

AUTOVREF

draws reference lines at all major tick marks on the vertical axis.

CAXIS=*axis-color*

specifies a color for axis lines and all major and minor tick marks. By default, axes are displayed in the second color in the colors list.

If you use the CAXIS= option, it may be overridden by the COLOR= suboption of the MAJOR= or MINOR= option in an AXIS definition.

CFRAME=*background-color*
CFR=*background-color*

fills the axis area with the specified color and automatically draws a frame around the axis area.

CHREF=*reference-line-color*
CH=*reference-line-color*

specifies the color for reference lines that are requested by the HREF= option. By default, these lines are displayed in the axis color.

CLEVELS=*color(s)*

specifies a list of colors for plot contour levels. The number of specified colors should correspond to the number of contour levels since one color represents each level of contour. If fewer colors are specified than the number of levels in the plot, the procedure provides default colors from the current colors list. The procedure default is to rotate through the current colors list for each line type.

This option is ignored if AUTOLABEL is used.

COUTLINE=*outline-color*

specifies a color for outlining filled areas. This option is ignored unless the PATTERN option is also used. By default, the outline color is the same as the color of the filled area.

Note: The outline color is the only distinction between empty patterns. Use of this option makes the patterns look the same when VALUE=EMPTY in PATTERN definitions. △

Featured in: Example 4 on page 647

CTEXT=*text-color*

specifies a color for all text on the axes and legend, including axis labels, tick mark values, legend labels, and legend value descriptions.

If you omit the CTEXT= option, a color specification is searched for in this order:

1   specified colors on assigned AXIS and LEGEND statements

2   the CTEXT= option in a GOPTIONS statement

3   the default, the first color in the colors list.

For legend text, colors that you specify on an assigned LEGEND statement override CTEXT=. Thus, a LEGEND statement's VALUE= color is used for legend values, and its LABEL= color is used for legend labels.

For axes text, colors that you explicitly specify for values and labels on an assigned AXIS statement override CTEXT=. Thus, an AXIS statement's VALUE= color is used for axis values, and its LABEL= color is used for axis labels. However, if the AXIS statement specifies only general axis colors with its COLOR= option, the CTEXT= color overrides that general specification and is used for axis labels and values; the COLOR= color is still used for all other axis colors, such as tick marks.

If you use a BY statement in the procedure, the color of the BY variable labels is controlled by the CBY= option in the GOPTIONS statement.

Featured in: Example 4 on page 647

CVREF=*reference-line-color*
CV=*reference-line-color*

specifies the color for reference lines that are requested by the VREF= option. By default, these lines are displayed in the axis color.

DESCRIPTION='*entry-description*'
DES='*entry-description*'

specifies the description of the catalog entry for the chart. The maximum length for *entry-description* is 40 characters. The description does not appear on the chart. By default, the GCONTOUR procedure assigns a description of the form PLOT OF $y*x=z$, where $y*x=z$ is the request specified in the PLOT statement.

GRID

draws reference lines at all major tick marks on both axes. This is the same as specifying both AUTOHREF and AUTOVREF.

HAXIS=AXIS<1...99>

assigns axis characteristics from the corresponding AXIS definition to the horizontal (*x*) axis.

See also: "AXIS Statement" on page 162

Featured in: Example 2 on page 643

HMINOR=*number-of-minor-ticks*
HM=*number-of-minor-ticks*

specifies the number of minor tick marks to use between each major tick mark on the horizontal (*x*) axis. No values are displayed for minor tick marks. HMINOR= overrides the MINOR= option in an AXIS definition assigned to the horizontal (*x*) axis.

HREF=*value-list*

draws one or more reference lines perpendicular to the horizontal axis at points specified by *value-list*. See the LEVELS= option on page 633 for a description of *value-list*.

HREVERSE

specifies that the order of the values on the horizontal axis be reversed.

JOIN

combines adjacent grid cells with the same pattern to form a single pattern area. This option is ignored unless the PATTERN option is also used.

Featured in: Example 4 on page 647

LEGEND=LEGEND<1...99>

assigns legend characteristics to the legend to adjust the location, text, and appearance of axes on the plots. The option value indicates which LEGEND definition to use. To suppress the legend, use the NOLEGEND option. The LEGEND= option is ignored if the specified LEGEND definition is not currently in effect.

If you use the SHAPE= option in a LEGEND statement, the value LINE is valid. If you use the PATTERN option, SHAPE=BAR is also valid.

See also: "LEGEND Statement" on page 187

Featured in: Example 2 on page 643

LEVELS=*value-list*

specifies values of *z* for plot contour levels and therefore changes the number of contour levels. You can specify up to 100 values. By default, the GCONTOUR procedure plots seven contour levels for *z*. These levels occur at every 15th percent of the range between the 5th and 95th percentiles.

For numeric variables, *value-list* can be an explicit list of values, a starting and an ending value with an interval increment, or a combination of both forms:

□ *n* <...*n*>

□ *n* TO *n* <BY *increment*>

□ *n* <...*n*> TO *n* <BY *increment* > <*n* <...*n*> >

If a numeric variable has an associated format, the specified values must be the *unformatted* values.

By default, the GCONTOUR procedure selects colors and line types for the contour levels by rotating through the colors list for each line type (1 through 46) until all the levels have been represented. The level lines on the plot represent the intersection of a plane, parallel to the *x-y* plane, and the surface that is formed by the data at the *z* value. See "Selecting Contour Levels" on page 636 for more information.

You can specify the colors and line types for contour levels. The way to do this depends on whether AUTOLABEL is used:

□ If AUTOLABEL is used, the SYMBOL statement controls colors and line types for contour levels. See "Modifying Contour Lines and Labels with the SYMBOL Statement" on page 640 for more information.

□ If AUTOLABEL is not used, the CLEVELS= and LLEVELS= options control colors and line types for contour levels.

As an alternative to representing contour levels with contour lines, you can use the PATTERN option to fill each level with a solid pattern or with the colors and patterns specified in PATTERN statements.

Featured in: Example 2 on page 643 and Example 3 on page 645

LHREF=*line-type*
LH=*line-type*
>   specifies the line type for drawing reference lines that are requested by the HREF=
>   option. *Line-type* is a number from 1 to 46. The default is LHREF=1, a solid line.
>   See "Specifying Line Types" on page 248 for available line types.

LLEVELS=*line-type-list*
>   lists numbers for line types for plot contour lines. Each line type represents one
>   contour level, so the number of line types listed should correspond to the number of
>   contour levels. Thus, for a contour plot that uses the default seven levels, specify
>   seven line types.
>
>   If fewer line types are specified than the number of levels in the plot, the
>   procedure provides default line types. With the default, contour levels rotate through
>   line types 1 through 46, displaying each line type in all of the colors in the colors list
>   before moving to the next line type. See "Specifying Line Types" on page 248 for
>   available line types.
>
>   For colors and lines specified with both the CLEVELS= and LLEVELS= options,
>   the first contour level is displayed in the first color in the CLEVELS= color list and
>   in the first line type specified with the LLEVELS= option. The second level is
>   displayed in the second color and the second line type, and so on.
>
>   This option is ignored if AUTOLABEL is used.

Featured in: Example 3 on page 645

LVREF=*line-type*
LV=*line-type*
>   specifies the line type for drawing reference lines that are requested by the VREF=
>   option. *Line-type* is a number from 1 to 46. The default is LVREF=1, a solid line. See
>   "Specifying Line Types" on page 248 for available line types.

NAME=*'entry-name'*
>   specifies the name of the catalog entry for the graph. The maximum length for
>   *entry-name* is 8 characters. The default name is GCONTOUR. If the specified name
>   duplicates the name of an existing entry, SAS/GRAPH software adds a number to the
>   duplicate name to create a unique entry, for example, GCONTOU1.

NLEVELS=*number-of-levels*
>   specifies the number of contour levels to plot. Values can be integers from 1 to 100,
>   inclusive. The contour levels are computed as follows, where **L** represents an array of
>   levels:
>
>   □   If the value of NLEVELS= is less than 7, then
>
>    ```
>    D = (Zmax - Zmin) / NLEVELS
>    d = 0.5 * D
>    L[0]  = Zmin + d, L[i]  = L[i-1]  + D
>    ```
>
>   In this case, each level is the midpoint of a number of ranges equal to the
>   value of the NLEVELS= option. These ranges exactly cover the range of the *z*
>   variable.
>
>   □   If the value of NLEVELS= is greater than or equal to 7, then
>
>    ```
>    e = 0.05 * (100 - NLEVELS) / 93
>    d = (Zmax - Zmin) * e
>    D = ((Zmax - Zmin - 2*d) / (NLEVELS - 1)
>    ```

```
L[0]  = Zmin + d, L[i]  = L[i-1]  + D
```

In this case, the first and last midpoints are set closer to the minimum and maximum *z* values as the values of NLEVELS= gets closer to 100, and the remaining midpoints are equally spaced between them.

NOAXIS
NOAXES

specifies that a plot have no axes, axis values, or axis labels. The frame is displayed around the plot unless you use the NOFRAME option.

NOFRAME

suppresses the frame that is drawn by default around the plot area.

NOLEGEND

suppresses the plot legend that describes contour levels and their line types or fill patterns and colors.

PATTERN

specifies the fill pattern and pattern colors for contour areas. The plot contour levels are represented by rectangles filled with patterns. The pattern for each rectangle is determined by calculating the mean of the values of the *z* variable for the four corners of the rectangle and assigning the pattern for the level closest to the mean.

By default, the procedure uses a solid pattern for the levels and rotates the pattern through the colors list. If the V6COMP option is in effect for the GOPTIONS statement, cross-hatch patterns are used instead of solid patterns. To explicitly define patterns, use PATTERN definitions for map/plot patterns.

See also: "Selecting Contour Levels" on page 636

Featured in: Example 4 on page 647

VAXIS=AXIS<1...99>

assigns axis characteristics from the corresponding AXIS definition to the vertical (*y*) axis.

See also: "AXIS Statement" on page 162

Featured in: Example 2 on page 643

VMINOR=*number-of-minor-ticks*
VM=*number-of-minor-ticks*

specifies the number of minor tick marks located between each major tick mark on the vertical (*y*) axis. No values are displayed for minor tick marks. The VMINOR= option overrides the MINOR= option in an AXIS definition that is assigned to the vertical (*y*) axis.

VREF=*value-list*

draws one or more reference lines perpendicular to the vertical axis at points specified by *value-list*. See the LEVELS= option on page 633 for a description of *value-list*.

VREVERSE

specifies that the order of the values on the vertical axis be reversed.

XTICKNUM=*number-of-ticks*
YTICKNUM=*number-of-ticks*

specify the number of major tick marks located on a plot's *x* or *y* axis, respectively. The value of *n* must be 2 or greater. The defaults are XTICKNUM=5 and YTICKNUM=5.

The MAJOR= or ORDER= option in an AXIS definition that is assigned to the *x* axis overrides the XTICKNUM= option. The MAJOR= or ORDER= option in an AXIS definition that is assigned to the *y* axis overrides the YTICKNUM= option.

Autolabel Suboptions

In the AUTOLABEL= option, *autolabel-suboptions* can be one or more of the suboptions described here.

CHECK=*checking-factor* | NONE
> specifies a collision checking factor that controls collisions between contour label text and other contour lines or other labels. Values can be integers from 0 to 100, inclusive, where 0 provides minimal collision checking and 100 provides maximal collision checking. Fractional values are permitted. The default is CHECK=75.
>
> CHECK=NONE suppresses contour label collision checking and may substantially lessen the time needed to compute the contour graph.
>
> Specifying a checking factor can slow the graph procedure. Generally, CPU time required to fit all the labels increases in direct proportion to the size of the CHECK= number.

MAXHIDE=*amount<units>*
> specifies the maximum amount of contour line that can be hidden by contour labels. The value of *amount* must be greater than zero.
>
> Valid *units* are CELLS (horizontal character cell positions), CM (centimeters), IN (inches), or PCT (percentage of the width of the graphics output area). The default is MAXHIDE=100PCT. If you omit *units*, a unit specification is searched for in this order:
>
> 1 the GUNIT= option in a GOPTIONS statement
>
> 2 the default unit, CELLS.
>
> If you specify units of PCT or CELLS, the MAXHIDE= suboption calculates the amount of contour line that can be hidden based on the width of the graphics output area. For example, if you specify MAXHIDE=50PCT and if the graphics output area is 9 inches wide, the maximum amount of the contour line that can be hidden by labels is 4.5 inches.
>
> This option maintains data integrity. It provides a check for overly small increments in the STEP= option in the SYMBOL statement. Additionally, it can prevent small contours from being significantly hidden even when the value of STEP= is sufficiently large.

REVEAL
> specifies that the contour lines are visible through the label text as dashed lines. Line style 33 is used. This option provides a simple way to see all portions of labeled contours and can be used to inspect the label positions with respect to the contour lines. It is primarily used for debugging. Occasionally, single-character contour labels can be placed off center from the clipped portion of the contour line when the contour line is irregular or jagged.

TOLANGLE=*angle*
> specifies the maximum angle (the tolerance angle) between any two adjacent characters of a contour label. The value of *angle* must be between 1 and 85 degrees, inclusive. The default is TOLANGLE=30. To force contour labels to fall on very smooth sections, specify a small tolerance angle.

Selecting Contour Levels

You can use the LEVELS= option to select the contour levels for your plot. You use LEVELS= values differently, depending on whether you specify the PATTERN option in the PLOT statement.

When you do not use the PATTERN option, the levels represent the intersection of a plane (parallel to the *x-y* plane at the *z* value) and the surface formed by the data. That is, if you use the data to create a surface plot with the G3D procedure, the contour lines in a GCONTOUR procedure plot represent the intersection of the plane and the surface.

For example, suppose that you use the G3D procedure, and your data produces a surface plot like the one shown in Figure 14.3 on page 637. The same data used with this PLOT statement in the GCONTOUR procedure produces a contour plot like the one in Figure 14.4 on page 637:

```
plot y*x=z / levels=-7.5 to 7.5 by 2.5;
```

The contour lines in Figure 14.4 on page 637 represent the intersection of the surface in Figure 14.3 on page 637 with planes parallel to the plane formed by the variables x and y and located at z values of -7.5, -5.0, -2.5, and so on.

Figure 14.3 Surface Plot

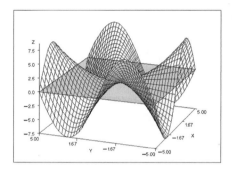

Figure 14.4 Line Contour Levels

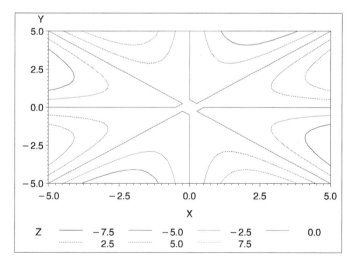

When you use the PATTERN option, contour levels are represented by rectangles filled with patterns. The rectangles are formed by points in the x-y grid. The contour pattern of a rectangle, or grid cell, is determined by the mean or average value of the z variable for the four corners of the rectangle. The grid cell is assigned the pattern for the level closest to the calculated mean. For example, if you have specified contour levels of 0, 5, and 10, and the plot contains a grid cell with a mean of 100, it is assigned the pattern for the nearest level: 10. A grid cell with a mean of 7.6 will also be assigned the pattern for the 10 level.

Figure 14.5 on page 638 shows a contour plot with the PATTERN option that uses the same data and contour levels as Figure 14.4 on page 637. The pattern for the rectangle is assigned depending on the mean of the grid values at the four corners. As a result, two contour plots using the same contour levels can present your data differently if one plot uses a pattern and the other does not. The contour pattern boundaries do not correspond to the contour lines shown in Figure 14.4 on page 637.

Figure 14.5 Pattern Contour Levels

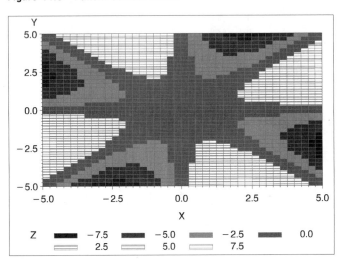

Specifying Axis Order

You can use AXIS statements to modify the text and appearance of plot axes, and then you can assign the axes to the contour plot with the PLOT statement's HAXIS= and VAXIS= options. If the AXIS statement uses an ORDER= option, there are special considerations for using that AXIS definition with the GCONTOUR procedure.

A list of variable values that are specified with the AXIS statement's ORDER= option must contain numbers listed in ascending or descending order; these numbers are treated as a continuous data range for an axis. Thus, for a contour line or pattern to span the entire specified range, it is not necessary for the maximum and minimum values of the list to match exactly with the maximum and minimum data values of the corresponding x or y variable. For example, suppose that you assign this AXIS definition to the horizontal (x) axis:

```
axis1 order=-2.5 to 2.5 by .5
```

Suppose also that the horizontal axis variable has these values: –5, –4, –3, –2, –1, 0, 1, 2, 3, 4, 5. Depending on the data, contours could extend through the full range of the ORDER= list rather than from –2 to 2, which are the actual values of the variable assigned to the horizontal (x) axis. In this case, values are interpolated for the x variable at any point where the y variable intersects the minimum axis value (–2.5) or the maximum axis value (2.5). Data values that are outside of the axis range (in this case, –5, –4, –3, 3, 4, and 5) are clipped from the plot.

When ORDER= lists cause data clipping, internal plotting grids are modified according to these rules:

  □ If an ORDER= list causes data clipping on a single axis, linear interpolation generates the z values of the starting and/or ending column of the plotting grid.

For example, in the previous example, the value of z is interpolated for -2.5 and 2.5 on the horizontal (x) axis.

□ If ORDER= lists cause data clipping on both axes, the response variable values of the new corners are derived by fitting the new x, y location on a plane formed by three of the original four points of the corresponding grid square.

In addition, if you assign the following AXIS definition to a plot of the same data, the contour levels on the plot will not extend beyond the range of the data:

```
axis1 order=-10 to 10 by 1;
```

To see the effects of the ORDER= option:

□ Figure 14.6 on page 639 shows the effects when the range of ORDER= values matches the range of values for the variables assigned to the horizontal (x) and vertical (y) axes.

□ Figure 14.7 on page 640 shows the effects when the range of ORDER= values is smaller than the range of data values.

□ Figure 14.8 on page 640 shows the effects when the range of ORDER= values is larger than the range of data values.

Figure 14.6 Effects of the AXIS Statement's ORDER= Option: ORDER= values match variable values

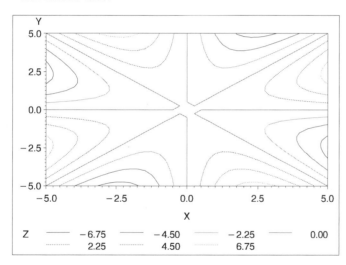

Figure 14.7 Effects of the AXIS Statement's ORDER= Option: ORDER= range is smaller than variable range

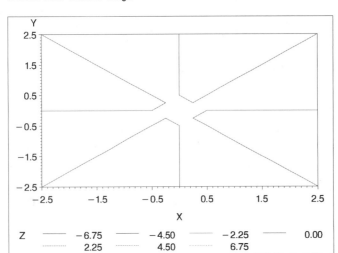

Figure 14.8 Effects of the AXIS Statement's ORDER= Option: ORDER= range is larger than variable range

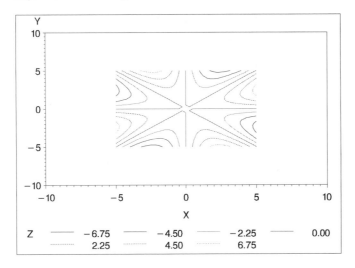

Modifying Contour Lines and Labels with the SYMBOL Statement

When you use the AUTOLABEL option, the LLEVELS= and CLEVELS= options are ignored, and contour-line and label attributes are controlled by the SYMBOL statement. Defaults are used if not enough SYMBOL statements are specified to match the number of contour levels.

If a SYMBOL statement does not include a color option, that statement may be applied to more than one contour level. In this case, the SYMBOL statement is used once with every color in the colors list and generates more than one SYMBOL definition. See "SYMBOL Statement" on page 226 for details.

Table 14.1 on page 641 describes how SYMBOL statement options affect contour plot lines and labels.

Table 14.1 The Effect of SYMBOL Statement Options on Contour Lines and Labels

SYMBOL Statement Option	Contour Line or Label Element Affected
LINE=*line-type*	Contour line style
WIDTH=*n*	Contour line thickness
CI=*line-color* or COLOR=*color*	Contour line color
FONT=*font*	Contour label font
HEIGHT=*height*	Contour label height
CV=*color* or COLOR=*color*	Contour label color
STEP=*distance<units>*	Minimum distance between labels on the same contour line
VALUE='*text*'	Contour label text
VALUE=NONE	Suppresses the contour label text

The SYMBOL statement option INTERPOL= is not supported by the GCONTOUR procedure.

The STEP= option specifies the minimum distance between contour labels. The lower the value, the more labels the procedure uses. A STEP= value of less than 10 percent is ignored by the GCONTOUR procedure and a value of 10 percent is substituted.

See STEP= on page 240 for more information.

Specifying Text for Contour Labels To override the default labels that are displayed by the AUTOLABEL option, you can specify label text for one or more contour lines. To do so, use both the FONT= and VALUE= options on the SYMBOL statement that is assigned to the contour level. Default labels are used for contour levels that you do not label.

For example, this SYMBOL1 statement displays the text string **Highest** in the Swiss font on the contour line that it modifies:

```
symbol1 font=swiss value='Highest';
```

You must specify both FONT= and VALUE= or the text is not used. For an example, see Example 2 on page 643.

Examples

Example 1: Generating a Simple Contour Plot

Procedure features:
    PLOT statement
Other features:
    FORMAT statement
    G3GRID procedure
Sample library member: GR14N01

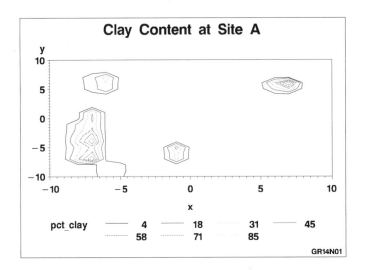

This example shows a simple contour plot that describes the percentage of clay found in soil samples at various locations of a testing site. By default, the axes are scaled to include all data values and are labeled with the names of the axes variables. Values are plotted with seven contour levels, which are represented by contour lines with default colors and line types. The default contour levels occur at every 15th percent of the range between the contour variable's 5th and 95th percentile. The legend is labeled with the contour variable's name and identifies the contour levels that are included in the plot.

This example uses the G3GRID procedure to interpolate clay percentages for grid cells that do not have percentages in the data. Without the G3GRID procedure, there are too many missing values for the percentages, and the GCONTOUR procedure cannot produce a satisfactory contour plot.

Assign the libref and set the graphics environment.

```
libname reflib 'SAS-data-library';
goptions reset=global gunit=pct border cback=white
         colors=(black blue green red)
         ftext=swiss ftitle=swissb htitle=6 htext=4;
```

Create the data set. REFLIB.CLAY contains the percent of clay at various locations of a test site.

```
data reflib.clay;
   input x y pct_clay;
   datalines;
-10    -10      2.316
-10    -9       1.816
-10    -8       2.427
...more data lines...
 10     8        .
 10     9        .
 10     10       .
;
```

Interpolate values for the contour plot. The interpolated data set is stored in REFLIB.CLAY2.

```
proc g3grid data=reflib.clay out=reflib.clay2;
   grid y*x=pct_clay / naxis1=21
                       naxis2=21
                       join;
run;
```

Define title and footnote.

```
title1 'Clay Content at Site A';
footnote1 j=r 'GR14N01 ';
```

Generate a simple contour plot. The procedure uses REFLIB.CLAY2, the output data set from PROC G3GRID. To simplify the legend labels, clay percentages are formatted with no decimal positions.

```
proc gcontour data=reflib.clay2;
   format pct_clay 2.0;
   plot y*x=pct_clay;
run;
quit;
```

Example 2: Labeling Contour Lines

Procedure features:
    PLOT statement options:

        AUTOLABEL=
        HAXIS=
        LEGEND=
        LEVELS=
        VAXIS=

Other features:
    AXIS statement

    LEGEND statement

    SYMBOL statement

Data set: REFLIB.CLAY2 on page 643

Sample library member: GR14N02

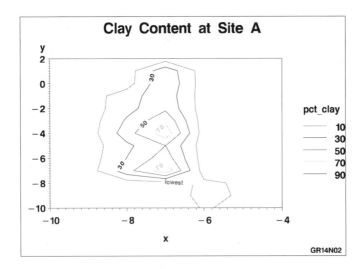

This example modifies Example 1 on page 641 to label contour levels with the AUTOLABEL option. When AUTOLABEL is used, the SYMBOL statement controls the labels and attributes of contour lines. In this example, SYMBOL1 defines a text label for the lowest contour level. Each remaining contour line gets the default label, which is the contour variable's value at that contour level. All the contour lines are solid, which is the default line type for the SYMBOL statement.

This example also uses AXIS statements to limit the plot to one of the contour areas from the output of Example 1 on page 641, and it uses a LEGEND statement to move the legend so the procedure has more room for displaying the *y* axis.

Assign the libref and set the graphics environment.

```
libname reflib 'SAS-data-library';
goptions reset=global gunit=pct border cback=white
         colors=(black blue green red)
         ftext=swiss ftitle=swissb htitle=6 htext=4;
```

Define title and footnote.

```
title1 'Clay Content at Site A';
footnote1 j=r 'GR14N02 ';
```

Define axes characteristics. AXIS1 uses ORDER= to set major tick marks at 2-unit intervals from -10 to -4. AXIS2 uses ORDER= to specify 2-unit intervals from -10 to 2. These axes ranges effectively zoom in on one of the contour areas from Example 1 on page 641.

```
axis1 order=(-10 to -4 by 2);
axis2 order=(-10 to 2 by 2);
```

Define legend characteristics. POSITION= centers the legend to the right of the graphics area, and LABEL= positions the legend label above the legend entries. ACROSS= places legend entries in rows 1 entry wide.

```
legend1 position=(right middle)
        label=(position=top)
```

```
across=1;
```

Define symbol characteristics. SYMBOL1 specifies a font and text string to label the lowest-level contour lines. COLOR= ensures that each SYMBOL definition is used only once. In SYMBOL2, STEP= increases the number of contour labels by placing the labels closer together than the default distance of 65 percent.

```
symbol1 height=2.5
        font=swissb
        value='lowest'
        color=red;
symbol2 height=2.5
        step=25pct
        color=black;
symbol3 height=2.5
        color=blue;
symbol4 height=2.5
        color=green;
```

Generate the contour plot. LEVELS= specifies contour levels from 10 to 90 at 20-unit intervals. AUTOLABEL= turns on labeling, and CHECK=NONE turns off collision checking so the maximum number of contour labels can be displayed. HAXIS= and VAXIS= assign AXIS definitions to the plot. LEGEND= assigns the LEGEND1 definition to the plot.

```
proc gcontour data=reflib.clay2;
   plot y*x=pct_clay / levels=10 to 90 by 20
                       autolabel=(check=none)
                       haxis=axis1
                       vaxis=axis2
                       legend=legend1;
run;
quit;
```

Example 3: Specifying Contour Levels

Procedure features:
  PLOT statement options:

    LEVELS=
    LLEVELS=

Sample library member: GR14N03

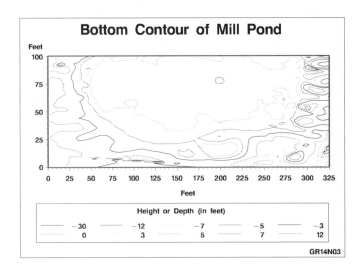

This example generates a contour plot that shows the height or depth of a pond and its surrounding land. In the example, the PLOT statement uses the LEVELS= and LLEVELS= options to specify explicit contour levels and line types for the contour plot. It also uses a LEGEND statement to modify the plot's default legend.

This example uses the G3GRID procedure to interpolate points for grid cells that do not have a needed dimension in the data. Without the G3GRID procedure, there are too many missing values for the point locations, and the GCONTOUR procedure cannot produce a satisfactory contour plot.

Assign the libref and set the graphics environment.

```
libname reflib 'SAS-data-library';
goptions reset=global gunit=pct border cback=white
         colors=(black blue green red)
         ftext=swiss ftitle=swissb htitle=6 htext=3;
```

Create the data set. REFLIB.POND contains the raw data for a pond floor and surrounding land.

```
data reflib.pond;
   input vdist hdist height;
   datalines;
10     88        0
18     55       -1
24     22.5     -1.67
...more data lines...
64     272.5   -6.25
60     277.5   -6.5
62     277.5   -6.5
;
```

Define title and footnote.

```
title 'Bottom Contour of Mill Pond';
footnote j=r 'GR14N03 ';
```

Define axis characteristics.

```
axis1 order=(0 to 325 by 25) width=3 minor=(n=4)
      label=('Feet');
axis2 order=(0 to 100 by 25) width=3 minor=(n=4)
      label=(' Feet');
```

Define legend characteristics.

```
legend1 frame shape=line(7)
        label=(position=top j=c 'Height or Depth (in feet)');
```

Interpolate points for the contour plot.

```
proc g3grid data=reflib.pond out=reflib.pondgrid;
   grid vdist*hdist=height / naxis1=100 naxis2=100;
run;
```

Generate the contour plot. LEVELS= specifies the values of the contour levels. LLEVELS= sets the line types for the contour lines. Solid lines identify negative contour levels, and dashed lines identify positive contour levels.

```
proc gcontour data=reflib.pondgrid;
   plot vdist*hdist=height /levels= -30 -12 -7  -3 0 3 5 7 12
                            llevels=  1   1  1  1 1 2 2 2  2
                            legend=legend1
                            coutline=
                            haxis=axis1
                            vaxis=axis2;
run;
quit;
```

Example 4: Using Patterns and Joins

Procedure features:

PLOT statement options:

COUTLINE=
CTEXT=
JOIN
PATTERN

Sample library member: GR14N04

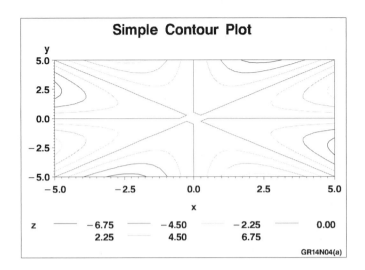

This example demonstrates the differences between using lines and patterns to represent contour levels. It first uses a simple PLOT statement to generate the default output, which uses lines to represent contour levels.

As shown in the following output, the example then modifies the PLOT statement by specifying the PATTERN option, which uses patterns to distinguish between contour levels. Additional PLOT statement options outline filled areas in gray and specify green text for all text on the axes and in the legend.

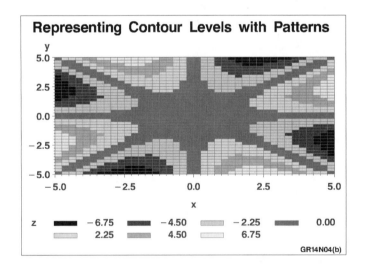

Finally, as shown by the following output, the example uses the JOIN option to combine the patterns in grid cells for the same contour level. Additional options enhance the plot by modifying the axes and framing the legend.

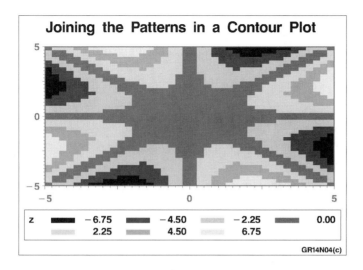

Joining the Patterns in a Contour Plot

Assign the libref and set the graphics environment.

```
libname reflib 'SAS-data-library';
goptions reset=global gunit=pct border cback=white
         colors=(black blue green red)
         ftext=swiss ftitle=swissb htitle=6 htext=4;
```

Create the data set. REFLIB.SWIRL is generated data that produces a symmetric contour pattern, which is useful for illustrating the PATTERN option.

```
data reflib.swirl;
   do x= -5 to 5 by 0.25;
      do y= -5 to 5 by 0.25;
         if x+y=0 then z=0;
         else z=(x*y)*((x*x-y*y)/(x*x+y*y));
         output;
      end;
   end;
run;
```

Define title and footnote for the default output.

```
title 'Simple Contour Plot';
footnote j=r 'GR14N04(a) ';
```

Generate a simple contour plot.

```
proc gcontour data=reflib.swirl;
   plot y*x=z;
run;
```

Define title and footnote for second plot.

```
title 'Representing Contour Levels with Patterns';
footnote j=r 'GR14N04(b) ';
```

Generate the contour plot. PATTERN fills the contour levels with solid patterns. COUTLINE= names the color that outlines the grid cells. CTEXT= names a color for axes and legend text.

```
proc gcontour data=reflib.swirl;
   plot y*x=z / pattern
                coutline=gray
                ctext=green;
run;
```

Define title and footnote for last plot.

```
title 'Joining the Patterns in a Contour Plot';
footnote j=r 'GR14N04(c) ';
```

Define axis and legend characteristics for last plot. Blanks are used to suppress tick labels at positions -2.5 and 2.5.

```
axis1 label=none value=('' ' ' '0' ' ' '5')
      color=red width=3;
axis2 label=none value=('' ' ' '0' ' ' '5')
      color=red width=3;

legend frame;
```

Generate the last contour plot. JOIN combines grid cells for the same contour levels.

```
proc gcontour data=reflib.swirl;
   plot y*x=z / pattern
                join
                haxis=axis1
                vaxis=axis2
                legend=legend1;
run;
quit;
```

References

Snyder, W.V. (1978), "Contour Plotting [J6] ," *ACM Transactions on Mathematical Software*, 4, 290–294.

CHAPTER

15

The GDEVICE Procedure

Overview

The GDEVICE procedure is a tool for examining and changing the parameters of the graphics device driver catalog entries used with SAS/GRAPH software. With the GDEVICE procedure, you can use either the GDEVICE windows or GDEVICE procedure statements to

☐ list the device entries stored in any DEVICES catalog

☐ view the parameters for any device entry

☐ create and modify new device entries

☐ copy, modify, rename, or delete existing device entries.

See Chapter 3, "Device Drivers," on page 37 for a discussion of device drivers and device entries, as well directions for selecting device drivers and changing the settings of device parameters.

For a complete list of Institute-supplied device entries supported by your operating environment, see the SASHELP.DEVICES catalog that is supplied with SAS/GRAPH software.

Concepts

About Device Catalogs

Device entries are stored in SAS catalogs that are named *libref*.DEVICES. Device entries for your operating environment that are supplied with SAS/GRAPH software are stored in the Institute-supplied catalog, SASHELP.DEVICES.

Custom device entries are typically stored in a catalog named GDEVICE*n*.DEVICES (where *n* can be any number from 0 to 9). However, device entries that have been created or modified by a system administrator specifically for your site also may be stored in SASHELP.DEVICES. (On multi-user systems, the SAS Support Consultant is usually the person who has write access to the SASHELP.DEVICES catalog and makes any changes.)

About the Current Catalog

When the GDEVICE procedure determines which catalog it should use, it searches for the catalog in the following order:

1 the catalog name specified in the CATALOG= option in the PROC GDEVICE statement

2 the catalog associated with the GDEVICE0 libref, if the libref has been assigned

3 the Institute-supplied catalog, SASHELP.DEVICES. (SASHELP.DEVICES is usually write-protected and is opened in browse mode.)

The first catalog it finds becomes the current catalog.
You can specify the current catalog by

☐ using the CATALOG= option in the PROC GDEVICE statement (this is required to open a driver entry in update mode)

☐ assigning the GDEVICE0 libref to the appropriate catalog.

Search Order of Device Catalogs

When you specify a device driver, SAS/GRAPH software looks only into catalogs with certain librefs and names to find a device entry for that driver. It searches these catalogs sequentially in the following order:

1 If the libref GDEVICE0 has been assigned to a SAS library, SAS/GRAPH software looks in that library for a catalog named DEVICES. If the GDEVICE0.DEVICES catalog exists, it is checked for the specified device entry. If the device entry is not there, SAS/GRAPH software looks next for a library with the libref GDEVICE1 and for a catalog named DEVICES in that library. The search is repeated for the sequence of librefs through GDEVICE9.

2 If SAS/GRAPH fails to find the specified device entry in any DEVICES catalog in the libraries GDEVICE0 through GDEVICE9, or if before locating the specified device entry it encounters in that sequence an undefined libref or a library that does not contain a DEVICES catalog, it jumps to SASHELP.DEVICES to search for the device entry. For example, if a GDEVICE0 libref is allocated but this library does not contain a DEVICES catalog, SAS/GRAPH software jumps to the SASHELP.DEVICES catalog, without searching for a GDEVICE1.DEVICES catalog, even if it exists. (SASHELP.DEVICES is the device catalog supplied with SAS/GRAPH software. SASHELP is one of the standard librefs defined automatically whenever you start your SAS session; you do not need to issue a LIBNAME statement to define it.)

3 If the specified device entry is not found in the SASHELP.DEVICES catalog, you receive an error message.

Since the GDEVICE0.DEVICES catalog is the first place that SAS/GRAPH software looks, you always should assign that libref to the library containing your personal catalog of device entries, if you have one. If for some reason you have personal device catalogs in more than one SAS data library, assign them librefs in the sequence GDEVICE0, GDEVICE1, GDEVICE2, and so on.

Note: As stated above, the search for entries terminates if there is a break in the sequence; the catalog GDEVICE1.DEVICES is not checked if the libref GDEVICE0 is undefined, or if GDEVICE0 does not contain a catalog named DEVICES. △

To cancel or redefine the libref GDEVICE*n*, first clear the current graphics options:

```
goptions reset=all;
```

You can then redefine the libref with another LIBNAME statement. To cancel a libref, use a null LIBNAME statement.

Ways to Use the GDEVICE Procedure

There are two ways to use the GDEVICE procedure:

☐ browse or edit the fields in the GDEVICE procedure windows (windowing mode)

☐ submit GDEVICE procedure statements in a SAS program (program mode).

If you run SAS software in a windowing environment (the SAS Display Manager System, for example), you can use either the GDEVICE procedure windows or the GDEVICE procedure statements. In a windowing environment, the GDEVICE procedure automatically opens the GDEVICE procedure windows.

If you run SAS software in a non-windowing environment (such as line-mode or batch), you can use only GDEVICE procedure statements. In a non-windowing environment, the GDEVICE procedure automatically uses program mode.

Both methods provide identical functionality and allow you to display or modify device parameters, or create new device entries.

Windowing Mode

In a windowing environment, open the GDEVICE windows by submitting the PROC GDEVICE statement without the NOFS option:

```
proc gdevice;
```

This opens the DIRECTORY window in browse mode. This window lists all of the device entries in the current catalog. (See "About the Current Catalog" on page 652.)

To open the DIRECTORY window in edit mode, or to specify a different catalog, include the CATALOG= option in the PROC GDEVICE statement.

From the DIRECTORY window you can select the device entry you want to work with and open other GDEVICE windows in which you can view or modify device parameters. For more information, see "Using the GDEVICE Windows" on page 664.

In a windowing environment, you can switch between the GDEVICE windows and program statements while you are running the procedure. See the "FS Statement" on page 661 and the NOFS window command in the SAS Help facility for SAS/GRAPH.

To exit the GDEVICE windows, submit the End command or close the window.

Program Mode

If you are in a non-windowing or batch environment, the GDEVICE procedure automatically starts in program mode. If you are in a windowing environment, specify the NOFS option to start the GDEVICE procedure in program mode:

```
proc gdevice nofs;
```

By default, the GDEVICE procedure accesses the current catalog in browse mode and prompts you in the LOG to enter additional program statements. (See "About the Current Catalog" on page 652.) To specify the current catalog, include the CATALOG= option in the PROC GDEVICE statement.

Once you start the GDEVICE procedure, you can enter and run additional statements without re-entering the PROC GDEVICE statement. For example, the following statement generates a listing of the device parameters for the PSCOLOR device entry that is stored in the Institute-supplied catalog, SASHELP.DEVICES:

```
list pscolor;
```

PROC GDEVICE procedure output is displayed in the Output window. Output 15.1 on page 654 shows the listing generated by the LIST statement.

Output 15.1   Sample Device Entry Listing Generated in Program Mode

```
                        GDEVICE procedure
             Listing from SASHELP.DEVICES - Entry PSCOLOR

Orig Driver: PSCOLOR          Module:  SASGDPSL  Model:    1251
Description: PostScript color--RGB color defs        Type: PRINTER
*** Institute-supplied ***
Lrows:   0  Xmax:   8.500 IN   Hsize:    8.000 IN  Xpixels:       2550
Lcols:   0  Ymax:  11.000 IN   Vsize:    8.500 IN  Ypixels:       3300
Prows:  68                     Horigin:  0.218 IN
Pcols:  80                     Vorigin:  1.496 IN
Aspect:   0.000                Rotate:
Driver query: Y                Queued messages: N
                               Paperfeed:   0.000 IN


OPTIONS

Erase:                Autofeed:       Y      Chartype:    1
Swap:                 Cell:                   Maxcolors: 256
Autocopy:             Characters:             Repaint:     0
Handshake:   XONXOFF  Circlearc:              Gcopies:     0
                      Dash:                   Gsize:       0
Prompt - startup:     Fill:                   Speed:       0
        end graph:    Piefill:                Fillinc:     0
        mount pen:    Polyfill:               Maxpoly:  1450
        chg paper:    Symbol:                 Lfactor:     0
                      Pensort:        N
Promptchars:  '000A010D05000000'X
Devopts:      'FD9230402C130000'X
UCC:      '0001'X

Cback:     WHITE
Color list:

   BLACK     RED       GREEN     BLUE      CYAN
   MAGENTA   YELLOW    GRAY

CHARTYPE RECORDS

Chartype Rows  Cols              Font Name              Scalable
    1     89    85   Courier                               Y
    2     89    85   Courier-Oblique                       Y
    .
    {ob ...more hardware fonts...}
    .
   34     89    85   Bookman-LightItalic                   Y
   35     89    85   Bookman-DemiItalic                    Y
Gend:     '0A'X

FILE INFORMATION

Gaccess:   sasgastd>sasgraph.ps
Gsfname:                       Gsfmode:  PORT    Gsflen:       0
Trantab:                       Devmap:
Devtype:   DISK
Gprotocol:
Fileclose: DRIVERTERM
Hostspec:

HOST INFORMATION
```

You can exit the GDEVICE procedure in these three ways:

□ Submit the END, QUIT, or STOP statement.

□ Submit another PROC statement or DATA step.

□ Exit your SAS session.

Procedure Syntax

Requirements: Statements other than the PROC GDEVICE statement can be used only in a non-windowing or batch environment. In these environments, at least one statement is required to give GDEVICE an action to perform. In a windowing environment, only the PROC GDEVICE statement is required. In program mode, at least one additional statement is required, and you can submit as many of each statement as you want.

Note: You must have write access to the device catalog in order to modify, add, or delete entries.

Supports: Output Delivery System (ODS LISTING).

PROC GDEVICE <CATALOG=<*libref.*>*SAS-catalog*>
   <BROWSE>
   <NOFS>;

ADD*new-device-entry*
   required-parameters
   <*optional-parameters*>;
COPY*device-entry*
   <FROM=<*libref.*>*SAS-catalog*>
   <NEWNAME=*new-device-entry*>;
DELETE *device-entry*;
FS;
LIST *device-entry* | _ALL_ | _NEXT_ | _PREV_ | DUMP>;
MODIFY *device-entry*
   parameter(s)
QUIT | *END* | *STOP*;
RENAME *device-entry* NEWNAME=*new-entry-name*;

PROC GDEVICE Statement

Starts the procedure and determines whether it runs in windowing mode or program mode. Optionally identifies a device catalog and determines how that catalog is opened.

PROC GDEVICE <CATALOG=<*libref.*>*SAS-catalog*>
   <BROWSE>
   <NOFS>;

Options

Options used in the PROC GDEVICE statement affect the way you use the procedure.

BROWSE
   opens a catalog in browse mode. You cannot modify a catalog when you open it with the BROWSE option. If you are running in program mode when you use BROWSE, you can use only the FS, LIST, QUIT, END, or STOP statements.

CATALOG=<*libref.*>*SAS-catalog*
CAT=<*libref.*>*SAS-catalog*
C=<*libref.*>*SAS-catalog*
>   specifies the catalog containing device information. If you do not specify a catalog,
>   the procedure opens the first catalog found in the search order of catalogs in browse
>   mode. (See "About the Current Catalog" on page 652.)
>
>   To edit the device entries in a catalog, you must use the CATALOG= option.

NOFS
>   specifies that you are using program mode. In windowing environments, the
>   GDEVICE windows are the default and you must specify NOFS to start GDEVICE in
>   program mode.

ADD Statement

**Adds a new device entry to the catalog selected by the CATALOG= option in the PROC GDEVICE
statement. The device entry is initialized with NULL values for most parameters.**

Requirements: You must have write access to the device catalog in order to add entries,
and use CATALOG= in the PROC GDEVICE statement.

Restriction: Not valid in browse mode.

ADD *new-device-entry*
>   *required-parameters*
>   <*optional-parameters*>;

>   *required-parameters* are all of the following:
>   MODULE=*driver-module*
>   XMAX=*width* <IN | CM>
>   YMAX=*height* <IN | CM>
>   XPIXELS=*width-in-pixels*
>   YPIXELS=*height-in-pixels*
>   plus one or both of the following parameter pairs:
>   LCOLS=*landscape-columns*
>   LROWS=*landscape-rows*
>   or
>   PCOLS=*portrait-columns*
>   PROWS=*portrait-rows*
>   *optional-parameters* can be one or more of the following:
>   ASPECT=*scaling-factor*
>   AUTOCOPY=Y | N
>   AUTOFEED=Y | N
>   CBACK=*background-color*
>   CELL=Y | N
>   CHARACTERS=Y | N

CHARREC=(*charrec-list(s)*)

CHARTYPE=*hardware-font-chartype*

CIRCLEARC=Y | N

CMAP=('*from-color : to-color*' <...,'*from-color-n : to-color-n*'>)

COLORS=(<*colors-list*>)

COLORTYPE=NAME | RGB | HLS | GRAY | CMY | CMYK | HSV | HSB

DASH=Y | N

DASHLINE='*dashed-line-hex-string*'X

DESCRIPTION='*text-string*'

DEVMAP=*device-map-name* | NONE

DEVOPTS='*hardware-capabilities-hex-string*'X

DEVTYPE=*device-type*

DRVINIT1='*system-command(s)*'

DRVINIT2='*system-command(s)*'

DRVQRY | NODRVQRY

DRVTERM1='*system-command(s)*'

DRVTERM2='*system-command(s)*'

ERASE=Y | N

FILECLOSE=DRIVERTERM | GRAPHEND

FILL=Y | N

FILLINC=0...9999

FORMAT=CHARACTER | BINARY

GACCESS=*output-format* | '*output-format > destination*'

GCOPIES=*current-copies*

GEND='*string*' <...'*string-n*'>

GEPILOG='*string*' <...'*string-n*'>

GPROLOG='*string*' <...'*string-n*'>

GPROTOCOL=*module-name*

GSFLEN=*record-length*

GSFMODE=APPEND | REPLACE | PORT

SFNAME=*fileref*

GSIZE=*lines*

GSTART='*string*' <...'*string-n*'>

HANDSHAKE=HARDWARE | NONE | SOFTWARE | XONXOFF

HEADER='*command*'

HEADERFILE=*fileref*

ORIGIN=*horizontal-offset* <IN | CM>

HOSTSPEC='*text string*'

HSIZE=*horizontal-size* <IN | CM>

ID='*description*'

INTERACTIVE=USER | GRAPH | PROC

LFACTOR=*line-thickness-factor*

MAXCOLORS=*number-of-colors*

MAXPOLY=*number-of-vertices*

MODEL=*model-number*

NAK='*negative-handshake-response*'X

PAPERFEED=*feed-increment* <IN | CM>

PATH=*angle-increment*

PENSORT=Y | N

PIEFILL=Y | N

POLYGONFILL=Y | N

POSTGRAPH1='*system-command(s)*'

POSTGRAPH2='*system-command(s)*'

PREGRAPH1='*system-command(s)*'

PREGRAPH2='*system-command(s)*'

PROCESS='*command*'

PROCESSINPUT=*fileref*

PROCESSOUTPUT=*fileref*

PROMPT=0...7

PROMPTCHARS='*prompt-chars-hex-string*'X

QMSG | NOQMSG

RECTFILL='*rectangle-fill-hex-string*'X

REPAINT=*redraw-factor*

ROTATE=LANDSCAPE | PORTRAIT

ROTATION=*angle-increment*

SPEED=*pen-speed*

SWAP=Y | N

SYMBOL=Y | N

SYMBOLS='*hardware-symbols-hex-string*'X

TRAILER='*command*'

TRAILERFILE=*fileref*

TRANTAB=*table* | *user-defined-table*

TYPE= CAMERA | CRT | EXPORT | PLOTTER | PRINTER

UCC='*control-characters-hex-string*'X

VORIGIN=*vertical-offset* <IN | CM>

VSIZE=*vertical-size* <IN | CM>

Required Arguments

new-device-entry
specifies the one-level name of the new device entry. *New-device-entry* must be a valid name for a SAS catalog entry for your operating environment and cannot already exist in the current catalog.

required-parameters
all required parameters for the ADD statement correspond to device parameters of the same name. Refer to Chapter 9, "Graphics Options and Device Parameters Dictionary," on page 301 for a description of each parameter.

Options

All optional parameters for the ADD statement correspond to device parameters of the same name. Refer to Chapter 9, "Graphics Options and Device Parameters Dictionary," on page 301 for a description of each parameter.

Note: The COLORS= device parameter is not required; the device entry will be created if you do not use it. However, the GDEVICE procedure issues an error message if you do not specify at least one color for COLORS=. △

Details

The ADD statement is rarely used because it initializes parameter values to NULL and you have to set values for all the parameters. The best way to add a new driver is to copy an existing driver and modify it.

COPY Statement

Copies a device entry and places the copy in the current catalog. The original device entry can be either in the current catalog or in a different catalog.

Requirements: You must have write access to the catalog to which the device entry is being copied.

Restriction: Not valid in browse mode.

See also: "Creating or Modifying Device Entries" on page 670

Featured in: Example 1 on page 671

COPY *device-entry where*;

Where *where* must be one or both of the following:
  FROM=*<libref.>SAS-catalog*
  NEWNAME=*new-device-entry*

Required Arguments

device-entry
  specifies the one-level name of the device entry to copy. The entry must exist in either the current catalog (the default) or the catalog specified by FROM=.

FROM=*<libref.>SAS-catalog*
  names the catalog from which to copy *device-entry*.

NEWNAME=*new-device-entry*
  specifies a name for the copy of the device entry that is placed in the current catalog. *New-device-entry* must be a valid name for a SAS catalog entry and cannot already exist in the current catalog.

  If you copy device entries across catalogs and you do not specify a new name, the GDEVICE procedure uses the original name for the new device entry.

DELETE Statement

Deletes the device entry from the current catalog.

Requirements: You must have write access to the current catalog to delete a device entry from it, and use CATALOG= in the PROC GDEVICE statement.

Restriction: Not valid in browse mode.

Caution: A device entry cannot be restored once it has been deleted. Depending on the environment in which you are using the GDEVICE procedure, you may be asked to verify that you really want to delete the entry.

DELETE *device-entry*;

Required Arguments

device-entry
> specifies the one-level name of device entry to delete. The entry must exist in the current catalog.

FS Statement

Switches from program mode to the GDEVICE windows.

Requirements: You must be running SAS software in a windowing environment.

FS;

Options

No options.

LIST Statement

Lists all of the parameters of the specified device entry in the Output window.

Default: _ALL_
See also: "Program Mode" on page 654

LIST <*device-entry*>
    <_ALL_>
    <_NEXT_>

```
<_PREV_>
<DUMP>;
```

Options

device-entry

specifies the one-level name of the device entry whose contents you want to list. The entry must exist in the current catalog.

ALL

lists only the name, description, and creation date of all device entries in the current catalog. This is the default. If no entries exist in the catalog, the GDEVICE procedure issues a message.

NEXT

lists the contents of the next device entry. The GDEVICE procedure lists the first entry in the catalog if no entries have been previously listed.

PREV

lists the contents of the previous device entry. If you have not previously listed the contents of a device entry, the GDEVICE procedure issues the following message:

```
No objects preceding current object.
```

DUMP

lists detailed information on *all* device entries in the current catalog. Depending on the number of device entries in the catalog, the DUMP option can create a *large* amount of output.

MODIFY Statement

Changes the values in a device entry.

Requirements: You must have write access to the current catalog to modify a device entry, and use CATALOG= in the PROC GDEVICE statement.

Restriction: Not valid in browse mode.

See also: "Creating or Modifying Device Entries" on page 670

Featured in: Example 1 on page 671

MODIFY *device-entry*
    parameter(s);

Required Arguments

device-entry

specifies the one-level name of the device entry that you want to modify. The entry must exist in the current catalog.

parameter(s)

are the parameters you want to modify. These can be any of the parameters listed in the ADD statement, whether listed as required or optional for ADD. See "ADD Statement" on page 657 for a complete list. Refer to Chapter 9, "Graphics Options and Device Parameters Dictionary," on page 301 for a description of each parameter.

Details

To modify a device entry, create your own catalog and then copy the device entries you need into it. You can then change your personal copies of the device entries without affecting the original drivers in SASHELP.DEVICES. (To copy device entries, use the COPY statement, the COPY command available after you choose Import Device Entry from the DIRECTORY window's File menu, or the CATALOG procedure, which is part of base SAS.

CAUTION:

Be careful when modifying device entries in program mode. In program mode, you cannot cancel any modifications you have just made. To change a value you have modified, you must use another MODIFY statement to replace the original value or reset it to its default. (In the GDEVICE windows, you can type the CANCEL command in the command line to cancel changes you have made to the fields.) △

QUIT Statement

Saves all modifications made to device entries during the procedure and exits the GDEVICE procedure.

QUIT | *END* | *STOP*;

Options

No options.

RENAME Statement

Changes the name of the device entry to the name specified in the statement.

Requirements: You must have write access to the current catalog to rename a device entry, and use CATALOG= in the PROC GDEVICE statement.

Restriction: Not valid in browse mode.

RENAME *device-entry*
    NEWNAME=*new-entry-name*;

Required Arguments

device-entry

specifies the one-level name of the device entry that you want to rename. The entry must exist in the current catalog.

NEWNAME=*new-entry-name*

specifies the new entry name. *New-entry-name* must be a valid name for a SAS catalog entry and cannot already exist in the current catalog. If the name already exists, the GDEVICE procedure issues an error message.

Using the GDEVICE Procedure

Using the GDEVICE Windows

You can use the GDEVICE windows instead of program mode to view, modify, copy, create, or delete device entries. You perform tasks in the GDEVICE windows by entering values in the fields, by using the pulldown menus, and by issuing commands from the command line.

These are the thirteen GDEVICE windows in order of appearance:

- □ Directory Window
- □ Detail Window
- □ Parameters Window
- □ Gcolors Window
- □ Chartype Window
- □ Colormap Window
- □ Metagraphics Window
- □ Gprolog Window
- □ Gepilog Window
- □ Gstart Window
- □ Gend Window
- □ Host File Options Window
- □ Host Commands Window

The fields in these windows represent device entry parameters. The GDEVICE windows group the device parameters by topic, to make it easy for you to review or modify the entry. If you open the device entry in edit mode, you can modify the fields directly. For a description of each field, see the corresponding parameter in Chapter 9, "Graphics Options and Device Parameters Dictionary," on page 301 or refer to the SAS Help facility. For a complete list of device parameters, see "ADD Statement" on page 657.

Note: The parameters are sometimes an abbreviation of the field names, but the correspondence should be clear. For example, in the Detail window, the "Driver query" field corresponds to the DRVQRY parameter, and the "Queued messages" field corresponds to the QMSG parameter. △

This section briefly describes the GDEVICE windows; for a complete description of each window and its fields, refer to the SAS Help facility.

GDEVICE Window Commands

You can navigate and manipulate the GDEVICE windows by entering commands on the command line or selecting them from the menus. For a complete description of all the GDEVICE window commands, refer to the SAS Help facility.

GDEVICE Window Descriptions

DIRECTORY Window

This window appears when you start the GDEVICE procedure in window mode. It lists all the device entries in the default catalog or the catalog you specified in the PROC GDEVICE statement. You can use it to

☐ copy, rename, or delete device entries in the catalog

☐ select a device entry whose parameters you want to browse or edit.

You can enter these commands in the Directory window selection field:

B | S

open the Detail window and browse (B) or, if you are in edit mode, edit (S) the selected device entry.

D

delete the selected device entry. You cannot restore a device entry once it has been deleted.

E

open the Detail window and edit the selected device entry.

R

rename the device entry and/or description.

You cannot edit the TYPE and UPDATED fields in the Directory Window.

Figure 15.1 The DIRECTORY Window

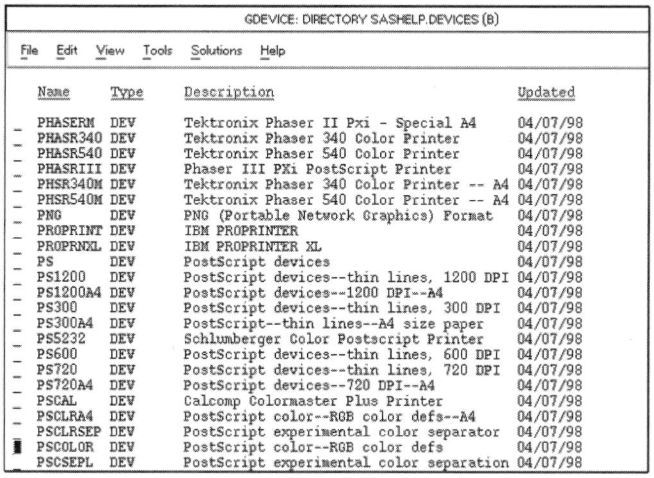

```
                        GDEVICE: DIRECTORY SASHELP.DEVICES (B)

   File   Edit   View   Tools   Solutions   Help


     Name       Type    Description                              Updated

_    PHASERM    DEV     Tektronix Phaser II Pxi - Special A4      04/07/98
_    PHASR340   DEV     Tektronix Phaser 340 Color Printer        04/07/98
_    PHASR540   DEV     Tektronix Phaser 540 Color Printer        04/07/98
_    PHASRIII   DEV     Phaser III PXi PostScript Printer         04/07/98
_    PHSR340M   DEV     Tektronix Phaser 340 Color Printer -- A4  04/07/98
_    PHSR540M   DEV     Tektronix Phaser 540 Color Printer -- A4  04/07/98
_    PNG        DEV     PNG (Portable Network Graphics) Format    04/07/98
_    PROPRINT   DEV     IBM PROPRINTER                            04/07/98
_    PROPRNXL   DEV     IBM PROPRINTER XL                         04/07/98
_    PS         DEV     PostScript devices                        04/07/98
_    PS1200     DEV     PostScript devices--thin lines, 1200 DPI  04/07/98
_    PS1200A4   DEV     PostScript devices--1200 DPI--A4          04/07/98
_    PS300      DEV     PostScript devices--thin lines, 300 DPI   04/07/98
_    PS300A4    DEV     PostScript--thin lines--A4 size paper     04/07/98
_    PS5232     DEV     Schlumberger Color Postscript Printer     04/07/98
_    PS600      DEV     PostScript devices--thin lines, 600 DPI   04/07/98
_    PS720      DEV     PostScript devices--thin lines, 720 DPI   04/07/98
_    PS720A4    DEV     PostScript devices--720 DPI--A4           04/07/98
_    PSCAL      DEV     Calcomp Colormaster Plus Printer          04/07/98
_    PSCLRA4    DEV     PostScript color--RGB color defs--A4      04/07/98
_    PSCLRSEP   DEV     PostScript experimental color separator   04/07/98
▮    PSCOLOR    DEV     PostScript color--RGB color defs          04/07/98
     PSCSEPL    DEV     PostScript experimental color separation  04/07/98
```

Detail window

This window contains device parameters that control basic characteristics of the device, for example, the size of the graphics output area.

Figure 15.2 The Detail Window

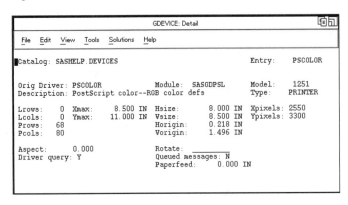

From this window you can access any of the subsidiary GDEVICE windows by

☐ entering the name of the window on the command line

☐ selecting the window from the Tools pulldown

☐ opening the subsidiary windows in order of appearance by using the View pulldown and choosing Next Screen, or using the NEXTSCR command on the command line.

Parameters window

This window includes additional device parameters that affect the way graphs are drawn. For example, you choose whether certain graphics primitives are drawn by your hardware or by SAS/GRAPH software, whether to feed paper to printers or plotters automatically, and whether to have SAS/GRAPH software prompt you with messages under certain conditions.

Note: If the device does not support a hardware characteristic, the catalog entry cannot enable the support. △

Figure 15.3 The Parameters Window

```
┌──────────────────────────────────────────────────────────────────────┐
│                          GDEVICE: Parameters                    ⌐⊡ ⌐⊟ │
├──────────────────────────────────────────────────────────────────────┤
│   File    Edit    View    Tools    Solutions    Help                   │
│                                                                        │
│ ▮Catalog: SASHELP.DEVICES                        Entry:    PSCOLOR     │
│                                                                        │
│  Erase:        _         Autofeed:    Y       Chartype:      1         │
│  Swap:         _         Cell:        _       Maxcolors:   256         │
│  Autocopy:     _         Characters:  _       Repaint:       0         │
│  Handshake: XONXOFF      Circlearc:   _       Gcopies:       0         │
│                          Dash:        _       Gsize:         0         │
│  Prompt:   start up:     _   Fill:    _       Speed:         0         │
│            end of graph: _   Piefill: _       Fillinc:       0         │
│            mount pens:   _   Polyfill:_       Maxpoly:    1450         │
│            change paper: _   Symbol:  _       Lfactor:       0         │
│                              Pensort: N                                │
│                                                                        │
│  Promptchars: 000A010D05000000       Dashline: _____           │
│  Rectfill:                           Symbols:  _____           │
│  Devopts:     FD9230402C130000                                        │
│  UCC:         0001                                                     │
└──────────────────────────────────────────────────────────────────────┘
```

Gcolors window

This window lists the colors that the device driver uses by default. When you do not explicitly specify the color of a graphics feature in your program or in a GOPTIONS statement, SAS/GRAPH software uses this list to determine what color to use.

Figure 15.4 The Gcolors Window (partial view)

```
┌──────────────────────────────────────────────────────────────────────┐
│                        GDEVICE: GColors                             ▣  │
├──────────────────────────────────────────────────────────────────────┤
│  File   Edit   View   Tools   Solutions   Help                         │
│                                                                        │
│ Catalog: SASHELP.DEVICES                    Entry:    PSCOLOR          │
│ Cback: WHITE                                                           │
│ Colors:                                                                │
│                                                                        │
│      BLACK          RED         GREEN        BLUE         CYAN          │
│      MAGENTA        YELLOW      GRAY                                    │
│      ──────        ──────      ──────       ──────       ──────        │
│      ──────        ──────      ──────       ──────       ──────        │
│      ──────        ──────      ──────       ──────       ──────        │
│      ──────        ──────      ──────       ──────       ──────        │
└──────────────────────────────────────────────────────────────────────┘
```

Chartype window

This window lists the hardware fonts that the device can use, along with information about the size of the characters. The Chartype value is the value you can use to reference a font in another window. For example, you would enter a Chartype number in the Parameters window's Chartype field.

Figure 15.5 The Chartype Window (partial view)

```
┌──────────────────────────────────────────────────────────────────────┐
│                        GDEVICE: Chartype                           ▣  │
├──────────────────────────────────────────────────────────────────────┤
│  File   Edit   View   Tools   Solutions   Help                         │
│                                                                        │
│ Catalog: SASHELP.DEVICES                 Entry:    PSCOLOR             │
│                                                                        │
│ Chartype  Rows  Cols            Font Name           Scalable           │
│     1      89    85    Courier                          Y              │
│     2      89    85    Courier-Oblique                  Y              │
│     3      89    85    Courier-Bold                     Y              │
│     4      89    85    Courier-BoldOblique              Y              │
│     5      89    85    Times-Roman                      Y              │
│     6      89    85    Times-Italic                     Y              │
│     7      89    85    Times-Bold                       Y              │
│     8      89    85    Times-BoldItalic                 Y              │
│     9      89    85    Helvetica                        Y              │
│    10      89    85    Helvetica-Oblique                Y              │
│    11      89    85    Helvetica-Bold                   Y              │
│    12      89    85    Helvetica-BoldOblique            Y              │
└──────────────────────────────────────────────────────────────────────┘
```

Colormap window

This window allows you to specify a color map for the device. The FROM field specifies the name to assign to the color designated by the *color* value, and the TO field specifies a SAS/GRAPH color name up to eight characters long. Once you have defined the color mapping, you can use the new color name in any color option. For example, if your device entry maps the color name DAFFODIL to the SAS color value PAOY, you can specify COLOR=DAFFODIL on any statement that supports a COLOR= option, and the driver will map this to the color value PAOY.

Figure 15.6 The Colormap Window (partial view)

Metagraphics window

This window is used by all drivers that support multiple color spaces, for example, RGB or CMYK. It is also used if the device entry is a Metagraphics (user-written) driver. Metagraphics drivers are created when an Institute-supplied device entry cannot be adapted to support your graphics device. For information about Metagraphics drivers, contact Technical Support.

Do not alter the fields in the Metagraphics window unless you are changing the color scheme (colortype), or building a Metagraphics driver.

Figure 15.7 The Metagraphics Window

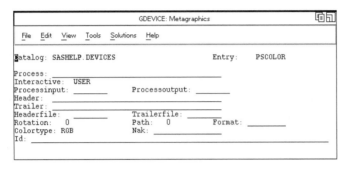

Gprolog window

This window enables you to specify one or more hexadecimal strings that are sent to the device just before graphics commands are sent. Additional commands can be sent with the PREGPROLOG= and POSTGPROLOG= graphics options. See Chapter 9, "Graphics Options and Device Parameters Dictionary," on page 301 for details.

Figure 15.8 The Gprolog Window (partial view)

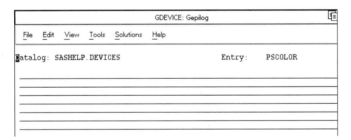

Gepilog window

This window enables you to specify one or more hexadecimal strings that are sent to the device just after graphics commands are sent. Additional commands can be sent with the PREGEPILOG= and POSTGEPILOG= graphics options. See Chapter 9, "Graphics Options and Device Parameters Dictionary," on page 301 for details.

Figure 15.9 The Gepilog Window (partial view)

Gstart window

This window enables you to specify one or more hexadecimal strings that are placed at the beginning of each record of graphics data.

Figure 15.10   The Gstart Window (partial view)

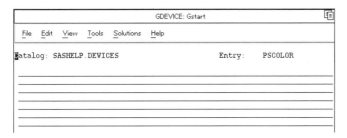

Gend window

This window enables you to specify one or more hexadecimal strings that are placed at the end of each record of graphics data.

Figure 15.11   The Gend Window (partial view)

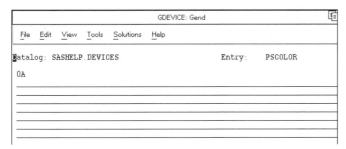

Host File Options window

This window controls the output destination and formatting of the data stream produced by the driver. (Most of these values can also be specified with the GOPTIONS statement and with the FILENAME statement. See also "Exporting SAS/GRAPH Output with Program Statements" on page 58.)

Figure 15.12   The Host File Options Window

```
┌──────────────────────────────────────────────────────────┐
│              GDEVICE:  Host File Options            ▣▣    │
│  File  Edit  View  Tools  Solutions  Help                 │
│                                                           │
│ ■           Catalog: SASHELP.DEVICES     Entry: PSCOLOR   │
│                                                           │
│ Gaccess: sasgastd>sasgraph.ps                             │
│ Gsfname: _____    Gsfmode: PORT        Gsflen:     0   │
│ Trantab: _____    Devmap: _____     Devtype: DISK   │
│ Gprotocol: _____                                       │
│                                                           │
│ Host file options:                                        │
│ _____  │
│ _____  │
│ ◆ Close file at end of driver or procedure termination    │
│ ◇ Close file at end of each graph                         │
└──────────────────────────────────────────────────────────┘
```

Host Commands window

This window stores the host commands issued at driver initialization, before and after each graph is produced, and at driver termination. These commands are typically used to send graphics output to a hardcopy device such as a printer or a plotter.

Figure 15.13 The Host Commands Window

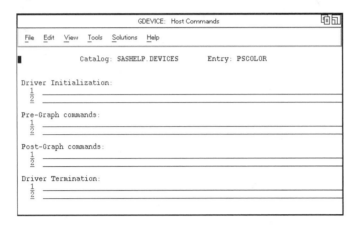

Creating or Modifying Device Entries

In order to add, modify, or delete device entries, you must have write access to the catalog. On multi-user systems, the SAS support consultant is usually the only person who has write access to the SASHELP.DEVICES catalog and can make any changes. Therefore, when creating new entries or modifying existing ones, individual users usually work in a personal catalog. Be sure the catalog in which you store new or modified device entries is named DEVICES.

To use a device entry stored in a personal catalog, you must assign the GDEVICE*n* libref to the library that contains the device catalog. See "About Device Catalogs" on page 652.

It is a good idea to give a new or modified device entry a name that is different from the original. Then, if you want to use the original device, SAS/GRAPH can find that device when it searches the device catalogs. Remember that SAS/GRAPH searches the GDEVICE*n* libraries *before* it searches SASHELP.DEVICES and uses the first device it finds whose name matches the one you have specified. (See "Search Order of Device Catalogs" on page 653.)

For example, suppose there is a customized copy of PSCOLOR in your GDEVICE0.DEVICES catalog as well as the original in SASHELP.DEVICES. If you specify DEV=PSCOLOR and if the libref GDEVICE0 is assigned, SAS/GRAPH will search GDEVICE0.DEVICES first and use the copy of PSCOLOR stored there. Unless you cancel the GDEVICE0 libref, SAS/GRAPH will never find the original in SASHELP.DEVICES.

Creating a New Device Entry

Typically you create a new device entry by copying an existing device and modifying its parameters to suit your needs. You can copy and modify a device entry in two ways:

☐ Use the DIR command on the command line to open the DIRECTORY window, and then use the COPY command to make a copy of an existing device entry. Then edit the new entry and modify its parameters. The existing device entry can be from any catalog. (See the SAS Help facility for information on using GDEVICE windows and commands.)

    □ In program mode, use the COPY statement to make a copy of the device entry and use the MODIFY statement to change the parameters (see Example 1 on page 671).

If you want to start with a blank device entry and fill in values for the parameters, use the EDIT command from the DIRECTORY window or use the ADD statement with program mode PROC GDEVICE.

With either method, you must provide values for the parameters listed in "Required Arguments" on page 659. If you copy and modify an existing entry, all the required parameters will already have values. If you create a new entry with GDEVICE windows, you are prompted to fill in the appropriate fields.

Note: When you change a field in an Institute-supplied device entry (either the original device entry in SASHELP.DEVICES or a copy), SAS/GRAPH software asks whether you really want to change the entry. Answer Y to change the entry or N to cancel the operation. △

Modifying an Existing Device Entry

Typically, you modify an existing device entry when you want to change the device parameters permanently in order to customize a device entry. The process is similar to creating a new entry in that you usually begin by copying the entry you want to modify into your personal catalog and making the changes there. See Example 1 on page 671 for an example of creating a custom device entry.

Changing Device Parameters Temporarily

You can change some device parameters temporarily by overriding their settings with graphics options in a GOPTIONS statement. In this case, the settings remain in effect until you change them or end your SAS session. For details, see "Overriding Device Parameters Temporarily" on page 41.

Examples

The following examples illustrate major features of the GDEVICE procedure.

Example 1: Creating a Custom Device Entry with Program Statements

Procedure features:
    COPY statement
    MODIFY statement

Other features:
    PROC GTESTIT

Sample library member: GR15N01

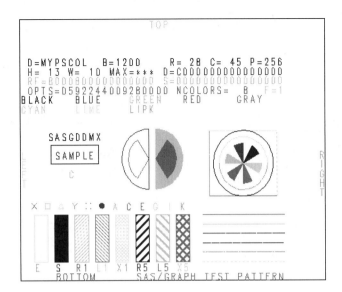

This example shows how to use GDEVICE procedure statements to modify a device entry by copying the original entry into a personal catalog and changing the device parameters. You can submit these statements one at a time or together.

This example permanently changes the default colors list for the PSCOLOR device entry. The contents of the original PSCOLOR entry are shown in Output 15.1 on page 654. The new device entry is illustrated in the PROC GTESTIT output above.

Assign the libref GDEVICE0. The LIBNAME statement assigns the libref to the aggregate file storage location that contains (or will contain) the DEVICES catalog.

```
libname gdevice0 'SAS-data-library';
```

Start the GDEVICE procedure. NOFS causes GDEVICE to use program mode. CATALOG= assigns GDEVICE0.DEVICES as the current catalog. If the DEVICES catalog does not already exist in the library, it is automatically created.

```
proc gdevice nofs catalog=gdevice0.devices;
```

Copy the original device entry from SASHELP.DEVICES to the current catalog. NEWNAME= specifies a name for the copy of PSCOLOR that is placed in GDEVICE0.DEVICES. The name of a catalog entry cannot exceed eight characters.

```
copy pscolor from=sashelp.devices newname=mypscol;
```

Modify the new entry. DESCRIPTION= specifies a new device description that appears in the catalog listing. COLORS= defines a new colors list.

```
modify mypscol
   description='PSCOLOR with new colors list'
   colors=(black blue green red gray cyan
        lime lipk);
```

Exit the procedure.

```
quit;
```

Test the new device entry. The TARGET= graphics option specifies the new device. Since GDEVICE0 is already defined, SAS/GRAPH looks first in that catalog for the specified device entry. The GTESTIT procedure produces a test picture that show the new colors list and a listing in the LOG.

```
goptions target=mypscol;
proc gtestit pic=1;
run;
```

CHAPTER

16

The GFONT Procedure

Overview

The GFONT procedure displays new or existing fonts and creates user-generated fonts for use in SAS/GRAPH programs. These fonts can contain standard Roman alphabet characters, foreign language characters, symbols, logos, or figures.

The GFONT procedure

- displays SAS/GRAPH software fonts

- displays fonts that were previously generated with the GFONT procedure (user-generated fonts)

- displays the character codes or hexadecimal values that are associated with the characters in a font

- creates stroked fonts or polygon fonts.

Each of these activities has its own requirements, its own process, and its own options (although some options are valid for either process). In this chapter, each topic to which this distinction applies is divided into two sections: "Displaying Fonts" and "Creating Fonts."

About Displaying Fonts

You can use the GFONT procedure to display a font when you want to do one of the following:

- □ review the characters that are available in either Institute-supplied fonts or user-generated fonts
- □ see the character codes or the hexadecimal values that are associated with the characters in a font.

When you display a font, you can modify the color and height of displayed font characters, draw reference lines around the characters, or display the associated character codes or hexadecimal values. See Example 1 on page 698.

About Creating Fonts

You can use the GFONT procedure to create and store fonts of your own design. The GFONT procedure is not limited to creating alphabet fonts. You can use it to create and store any series of figures that you can draw using X and Y coordinates or that you can digitize. The characters or figures in a font can be displayed with any SAS/GRAPH statement or option that allows for font specification and a text string (for example, a TITLE statement). See "Creating a Font" on page 687 for details.

Concepts

About Fonts

Some specialized terms are associated with font characteristics. The *capline* of a font is the highest point of a normal uppercase letter. The *baseline* is the line upon which the characters rest. The *font maximum* is the highest vertical coordinate in a font. The *font minimum* is the lowest vertical coordinate in a font. Figure 16.1 on page 676 illustrates these GFONT procedure terms:

Figure 16.1   Parts of a Font

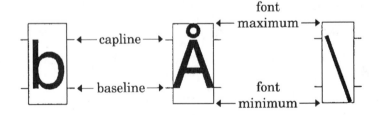

Specialized terms also exist for types of fonts. The term *uniform font* refers to a font in which all of the characters occupy exactly the same amount of space, even though the characters themselves are different sizes. Each character in a uniform font is placed in the center of its space, and a fixed amount of space is added between characters. A *proportional font* is a font in which each character occupies a space that is proportional to its actual width (for example, m occupies more space than i). The characters in a *stroked font* are drawn with discrete line segments or circular arcs. Figure 16.2 on page 677 illustrates a stroked font with several characters from the Simplex font.

Figure 16.2 Characters from a Stroked Font

Figure 16.3 on page 677 illustrates two types of *polygon fonts*: filled (CENTBI) and outline (CENTBIE). A *filled font* is a polygon font in which the areas between the lines are solid. An *outline font* is a polygon font in which the areas are empty.

Figure 16.3 Filled and Outline Characters from Polygon Fonts

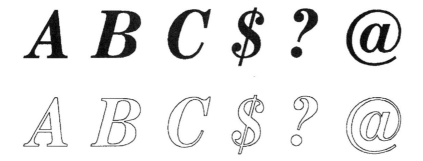

All font characters, regardless of whether they are stroked or polygon, are drawn with line segments. In the GFONT procedure, the term *line segment* means a continuous line that can change direction. For example, the letter C in Figure 16.2 on page 677 is drawn with one line segment, while the letter A can be drawn with two.

Polygon characters can also be drawn with one or more line segments. In a polygon font, one character can be made up of a single polygon, multiple polygons, or polygons with holes. For example, the letter C in Figure 16.3 on page 677 is a single polygon with one line segment. The question mark (?) is made up of two polygons, each drawn with a separate line segment. The letter A is one polygon with a hole in it. It is drawn with one line segment that is broken to form the outer boundary of the figure and the boundary of the hole.

About the Libref GFONT0

The GFONT procedure stores user-generated fonts in the location that is associated with the libref GFONT0. Therefore, before you create a font or display a user-generated font, you must submit a LIBNAME statement that associates the libref GFONT0 with the location where the font is to be stored, as follows:

```
libname gfont0 'SAS-data-library';
```

Since the GFONT0 library is the first place that SAS/GRAPH software looks for fonts, you should always assign that libref to the library that contains your personal fonts. If for some reason you have personal fonts in more than one SAS data library, assign them librefs in the sequence GFONT0, GFONT1, GFONT2, and so forth. The search for entries terminates if there is a break in the sequence; the catalog GFONT1.FONTS is not checked if the libref GFONT0 is undefined. If the libref GFONT0 is not defined, by default SAS/GRAPH software begins searching for fonts in SASHELP.FONTS.

To cancel or redefine the libref GFONT*n*, submit the following statement:

```
goptions reset=all fcache=0;
```

Note that when you specify RESET=ALL, all graphics options are reset to their default values. Once you have cleared the font cache, you can redefine the libref with another LIBNAME statement.

Procedure Syntax

Requirements: A font name is required. To display a font, include NOBUILD. To create a font, include DATA=.

Global statements: FOOTNOTE, TITLE

Reminder: The procedure can include the SAS/GRAPH NOTE statement.

Supports: Output Delivery System (ODS)

PROC GFONT NAME=*font-name*
    mode
    <*display-option(s)*>
    <*creation-option(s)*>;

PROC GFONT Statement

The PROC GFONT statement can either create user-defined fonts or display existing software fonts. Therefore, it names the font to be created or displayed. If the procedure creates a font it names the input data set. Optionally, the procedure modifies the design and appearance of the fonts that you create or display, and specifies a destination catalog for graphics output.

Syntax

PROC GFONT NAME=*font-name*
    mode
    <*display-option(s)*>
    <*creation-option(s)*>;

□ *mode* must be one of the following:

    DATA=*font-data-set*
    NOBUILD

□ *display-option(s)* can be one or more of the following:

     CTEXT=*text-color*

     GOUT=*<libref.>output-catalog*

     HEIGHT=*character-height<units>*

     NOKEYMAP

     NOROMAN

     NOROMHEX

     REFCOL=*reference-line-color*

     REFLINES

     ROMCOL=*code-color*

     ROMFONT=*font*

     ROMHEX

     ROMHT=*height<units>*

     SHOWALL

     SHOWROMAN

□ *creation-option(s)* can be one or more of the following:

     BASELINE=*y*

     CAPLINE=*y*

     CHARSPACETYPE=DATA | FIXED | NONE | UNIFORM

     CODELEN=1 | 2

     FILLED

     KERNDATA=*kern-data-set*

     MWIDTH=*character-width*

     NODISPLAY

     NOKEYMAP

     RESOL=1...4

     ROMHEX

     SHOWROMAN

     SPACEDATA=*space-data-set*

     UNIFORM

For more detail on using the GFONT syntax, see "Displaying Fonts: Required Arguments, Options" on page 679 and "Creating Fonts: Required Arguments, Options" on page 682.

Displaying Fonts: Required Arguments, Options

Required Arguments for Displaying Fonts

NAME=*font-name*
N=*font-name*

specifies the font to be displayed. *Font-name* can be the name of a SAS software font or a font you previously created.

See also: Chapter 6, "SAS/GRAPH Fonts," on page 125

NOBUILD
NB

specifies that the GFONT procedure is to display an existing font. The NOBUILD argument tells the procedure that no font is being generated and not to look for an input data set.

Featured in: Example 1 on page 698

To display a user-generated font, you must define libref GFONT0. See "About the Libref GFONT0" on page 677 for details.

Options for Displaying Fonts

Options that can be used for either font display or font creation are described here and in "Options for Creating Fonts" on page 683.

Options that display a font can be used when you create a font if you also display it (that is, the NODISPLAY option is not used in the PROC GFONT statement). However, none of the display options affect the design and appearance of the stored font except the NOKEYMAP, SHOWROMAN, and ROMHEX options.

When the syntax of an option includes *units*, use one of these:

CELLS	character cells
CM	centimeters
IN	inches
PCT	percentage of the graphics output area
PT	points

If you omit *units*, a unit specification is searched for in this order:

1 the value of GUNIT= in a GOPTIONS statement

2 the default unit, CELLS.

CTEXT=*text-color*
CT=*text-color*

specifies a color for the body of the characters. If you do not use the CTEXT= option, a color specification is searched for in the following order:

1 the CTEXT= option in a GOPTIONS statement

2 the default, the first color in the colors list.

The CTEXT= value is not stored as part of the font.

Featured in: Example 2 on page 700

GOUT=<*libref.*>*output-catalog*

specifies the SAS catalog in which to save the graphics output produced by the display of the font. The GOUT option is ignored if you use the NODISPLAY option in the PROC GFONT statement. You can use the GREPLAY procedure to view the output that is stored in the catalog. If you omit the libref, SAS/GRAPH looks for the catalog in the temporary library called WORK and creates the catalog if it does not exist.

See also: "Storing Graphics Output in SAS Catalogs" on page 49

HEIGHT=*character-height*<*units*>
H=*character-height*<*units*>

specifies the height of the font characters in number of units, *n*. Height is measured from the minimum font measurement to the capline. By default, HEIGHT=2.

Featured in: Example 1 on page 698

NOKEYMAP

specifies that the current key map is ignored when displaying the font and its character codes or hexadecimal values. If you do not use the NOKEYMAP option when you display a font, the current key map remains in effect. If any characters in the font are not available through the current key map, they are not displayed and a warning is issued in the SAS log. This happens when the key map is asymmetrical, that is, not all characters in the font are mapped into the current key map.

Displaying a font using the NOKEYMAP option enables you to see all of the characters in the font, including those that are not mapped into your current key map. Note that only those characters that are mapped into your current key map are available (that is, those that are displayed when you display the font without the NOKEYMAP option).

See also: Chapter 6, "SAS/GRAPH Fonts," on page 125 Chapter 18, "The GKEYMAP Procedure," on page 719 and the NOKEYMAP option on page 685 for Creating Fonts

NOROMAN
NR

turns off the automatic display of character codes that are produced when you use the SHOWROMAN option during font creation.

NOROMHEX
NOHEX

turns off the automatic display of hexadecimal values that are produced when you use the ROMHEX option during font creation.

REFCOL=*reference-line-color*

specifies a color for reference lines. By default, the first color in the colors list is used.

REFLINES

draws reference lines around each displayed character. Vertical reference lines show the width of the character. Horizontal reference lines show the font maximum and the font minimum, as well as the baseline and the capline. See Figure 16.1 on page 676 for an illustration of the placement of reference lines.

ROMCOL=*code-color*
RC=*code-color*

specifies the color of the character codes or hexadecimal values that are displayed with the SHOWROMAN and ROMHEX options. If you do not use the ROMCOL= option, a color specification is searched for in the following order:

1 the CTEXT= option in a GOPTIONS statement

2 the default, the first color in the colors list.
The ROMCOL= value is not stored as part of the font.

Featured in: Example 1 on page 698

ROMFONT=*font*
RF=*font*

specifies the font for character codes and hexadecimal values that are displayed by the SHOWROMAN and ROMHEX options. If you do not use the ROMFONT= option, a font specification is searched for in the following order:

1 the FTEXT= option in a GOPTIONS statement

2 the default hardware font, NONE.

Featured in: Example 1 on page 698

ROMHEX
HEX

displays hexadecimal values below the font characters. If you use both the ROMHEX and SHOWROMAN options, both the character codes and the hexadecimal values are displayed. You also can use the ROMHEX option when you create a font.

See also: the ROMHEX option on page 686

ROMHT=*height<units>*
RH=*height<units >*

specifies the height of the character codes and the hexadecimal values that are displayed with the SHOWROMAN and ROMHEX options in number of units, n. If you do not use the ROMHT= option, a height specification is searched for in the following order:

1 the HTEXT= option in a GOPTIONS statement

2 the default, ROMHT=1.

Featured in: Example 1 on page 698

SHOWALL

displays the font with a space for every possible character position whether or not a font character exists for that position. The characters that are displayed are those available under your current key map, unless you use the NOKEYMAP option. The SHOWALL option usually is used in conjunction with the ROMHEX option, in which case all possible hexadecimal values are displayed. If, under your current key map, a font character is available for a position, it displays above the hexadecimal value. If no character is available for a position, the space above the hexadecimal value is blank. You can use the SHOWALL option to show where undefined character positions fall in the font.

SHOWROMAN
SR

displays character codes below the font characters even if they are not displayed automatically with the font. If you use both the SHOWROMAN and ROMHEX options, both the character codes and the hexadecimal values are displayed. You can also use the SHOWROMAN option when you create a font.

See also: the SHOWROMAN option on page 686 for Creating Fonts.

Featured in: Example 1 on page 698

Details

To display a font, you must specify the name of the font with the NAME= argument and include the NOBUILD argument. For example, to display the Weather font with character codes that are displayed in the Swiss font, use the following statement:

```
proc gfont name=weather nobuild romfont=swiss;
```

Creating Fonts: Required Arguments, Options

Required Arguments for Creating Fonts

NAME=*font-name*
N=*font-name*

assigns a name to the font that you create. *Font-name* is the name of a catalog entry and must be a valid SAS name of no more than eight characters. Do not use the name of an Institute-supplied font or NONE for the name of a font.

Featured in: Example 2 on page 700

DATA=*font-data-set*

specifies the SAS data set that the GFONT procedure uses to build the font. The
data set must be sorted by the variables CHAR and SEGMENT. By default, the
procedure uses the most recently created data set as the font data set.

See also: "SAS Data Sets" on page 25

Featured in: Example 2 on page 700

When you create a font, you must define the libref GFONT0. See "About the Libref
GFONT0" on page 677 for details.

Note: If a user-generated font has the same name as an Institute-supplied font and
if the libref GFONT0 has been defined, the user-generated font is used because
GFONT0 is searched first. △

Options for Creating Fonts

Options that can be used for either font display or font creation are described here
and in "Options for Displaying Fonts" on page 680.

Options that display a font can be used when you create a font if you also display it
(that is, the NODISPLAY option is not used in the PROC GFONT statement). However,
none of the display options affect the design and appearance of the stored font except
the NOKEYMAP, SHOWROMAN, and ROMHEX options.

When the syntax of an option includes *units*, use one of these:

CELLS   character cells

CM   centimeters

IN   inches

PCT   percentage of the graphics output area

PT   points

If you omit *units*, a unit specification is searched for in this order:

1 the value of GUNIT= in a GOPTIONS statement

2 the default unit, CELLS.

BASELINE=*y*

B=*y*

specifies the vertical coordinate in the font data set that is the baseline of the
characters. The baseline is the line upon which the letters rest. If you do not use the
BASELINE= option, the GFONT procedure uses the lowest vertical coordinate of the
first character in the font data set.

CAPLINE=*y*

C=*y*

specifies the vertical coordinate in the font data set that is the capline of the
characters. The capline is the highest point of normal Roman capitals. If you do not
use the CAPLINE= option, the GFONT procedure uses the highest vertical coordinate
in the font data set, in which case the capline and the font maximum are the same.
See Figure 16.1 on page 676 for an illustration of capline and font maximum.

If you use the CAPLINE= option, then when the GFONT procedure calculates the
height of a character, any parts of the character that project above the capline are
ignored in the calculation.

You can use this option to prevent an accented capital like A from being shortened
to accommodate the accent. For example, if you do not use the CAPLINE= option,

the capline and the font maximum are the same and the A is shortened to make room for the accent below the capline. However, if CAPLINE= is used, the top of the letter A is at the capline, and the accent is drawn above the capline and below the font maximum.

CHARSPACETYPE=DATA | FIXED | NONE | UNIFORM
CSP=DATA | FIXED | NONE | UNIFORM

specifies the type of intercharacter spacing. The following are valid values:

DATA

specifies that the first observation for each character sets the width of that character. When CHARSPACETYPE=DATA, the PTYPE variable is required, and the observation that specifies the width of the character must have a PTYPE value of W. See "The Font Data Set" on page 687 for details on the PTYPE variable.

Intercharacter spacing is included in the character's width. For example, if the first observation for the letter A specifies a character width of 10 units and the A itself occupies only 8 units, the remaining 2 units serve as intercharacter spacing.

Note: The character can extend beyond the width that you specified in the first observation if desired. △

FIXED

adds a fixed amount of space between characters based on the font size. The width of the individual character is determined by the data that generate the character.

NONE

specifies that no space is added between characters. The width of the individual character is determined by the data that generate the character. This type of spacing is useful for script fonts in which the characters should appear connected.

UNIFORM

specifies that the amount of space that is used for each character is uniform rather than proportional. This means that each character occupies the same amount of space. For example, in uniform spacing the letters m and i occupy the same amount of space, whereas in proportional spacing m occupies more space than i. In uniform spacing, the character is always centered in the space and a fixed space is added between characters.

When UNIFORM is specified, the amount of space that is used for each character is one of the following:

□ by default, the width of the widest character in the font.

□ the width specified by the MWIDTH= option. See the MWIDTH= option on page 685 for details.

Specifying CHARSPACETYPE=UNIFORM is the same as using the UNIFORM option.

Note: By default, CHARSPACETYPE=FIXED. △

CODELEN=1 | 2

specifies the length in bytes of the CHAR variable. By default, CODELEN=1. To specify double-byte character sets for languages such as Chinese, Japanese, or Korean, use CODELEN=2. If you specify a double-byte character set, you cannot specify kerning or space adjustment with the KERNDATA= or SPACEDATA= options.

FILLED
F

specifies that the characters in a user-generated polygon font are filled.

Featured in: Example 2 on page 700

KERNDATA=*kern-data-set*
KERN=*kern-data-set*
specifies the SAS data set that contains kerning information. When the KERNDATA= option is used during font creation, the data that are contained in the kern data set are applied to the font and stored with it. You cannot specify kerning for a double-byte character set that is created by using the option CODELEN=2.

See also: "The Kern Data Set" on page 694

MWIDTH=*character-width*
specifies the width of a character in a uniform font, where *character-width* is the number of font units. The MWIDTH= option is only valid when you specify uniform spacing by using the UNIFORM option or when you specify CHARSPACETYPE=UNIFORM. If you do not use MWIDTH=, the default is the width of the widest character in the font (usually the letter m).

Typically, you use the MWIDTH= option to tighten the spacing between characters. To do this, specify a smaller value (narrower width) for *character-width*. Figure 16.4 on page 685 shows the effect of decreasing the space that is allowed for uniformly spaced characters.

Figure 16.4   Using the MWIDTH= Option to Modify Spacing

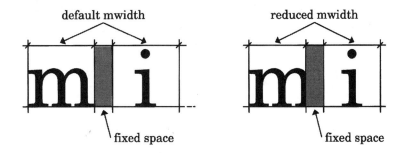

See also: the CHARSPACETYPE= option on page 684 and the UNIFORM option on page 687

NODISPLAY
ND
specifies that the GFONT procedure is not to display the font that it is creating.

NOKEYMAP
specifies that the current key map is ignored when you generate and use the font that is being created, and that the character codes you enter are not mapped in any way before being displayed. As a result, the generated font is *never* affected by any setting of the KEYMAP= graphics option.

CAUTION:
Fonts generated with the NOKEYMAP option are never affected by any setting of the KEYMAP= graphics option. △

By default, the NOKEYMAP option is *not* used; in which case, when you build a font, the current key map is applied to the values in the CHAR variable.

However, your current key map may not be symmetrical; that is, two or more input character codes may be mapped to the same output character. For example, if A is mapped to B, then both A and B map to B, but nothing maps to A. In this case, more than one code in your input data set can map to the same character in the resulting font. For example, if A and B are values of CHAR, both map to B. If this happens, a message that indicates the problem characters is displayed in the SAS log. To solve this problem, you can do one of the following:

- □ change the character code of one of the characters
- □ eliminate one of the characters
- □ use the NOKEYMAP option.

When you use the NOKEYMAP option, your font works correctly only if the end user's host or controller encoding is the same as the encoding used to create the input data set.

See also: the NOKEYMAP option on page 681 for Displaying Fonts and Chapter 18, "The GKEYMAP Procedure," on page 719

RESOL=1...4

R=1...4

controls the resolution of the fonts by specifying the number of bytes (1 through 4) for storing coordinates in the font. The GFONT procedure provides three resolution levels (RESOL=3 produces the same resolution level as RESOL=4). By default, RESOL=1.

The higher the number, the closer together the points that define the character can be spaced. A high value specifies a denser set of points for each character so that the characters approximate smooth curved lines at very large sizes. RESOL=2 works well for most applications; RESOL=3 or 4 may be too dense to be practical.

The table below shows the resolution number and the maximum number of distinct points that can be defined horizontally or vertically.

Resolution	Number of Distinct Points
2	32,766
3	2,147,483,646
4	2,147,483,646

Featured in: Example 2 on page 700

ROMHEX

HEX

specifies that hexadecimal values display automatically below the font characters when the GFONT procedure displays the font. If you use the ROMHEX option for a font that you create, you can later use the NOROMHEX option to suppress display of the hexadecimal values.

See also: the SHOWROMAN option on page 686, the ROMHEX option on page 682 for Displaying Fonts, and the NOROMHEX option on page 681

SHOWROMAN

SR

specifies that character codes display automatically below the font characters when the GFONT procedure displays the font. If you use the SHOWROMAN option for a font you create, you can later use the NOROMAN option to suppress display of the character codes.

See also: the ROMHEX option on page 686, the SHOWROMAN option on page 682 for Displaying Fonts, and the NOROMAN option on page 681

SPACEDATA=*space-data-set*

SPACE=*space-data-set*

specifies the SAS data set that contains font spacing information. When you use the SPACEDATA= option during font creation, the data contained in the space data set are applied to the font and stored with it. You cannot specify space adjustment for a double-byte character set that is created by using the option CODELEN=2.

See also: "The Space Data Set" on page 696

UNIFORM
U

specifies that characters are spaced uniformly rather than proportionately. Using the UNIFORM option is the same as specifying CHARSPACETYPE=UNIFORM.

See also: the CHARSPACETYPE= option on page 684 and the MWIDTH= option on page 685

Creating a Font

To create a font, you must create a data set that contains font information. Typically, you use a DATA step to create a SAS data set from which the GFONT procedure generates the font. The data set is referred to as the *font data set* and you can specify it with the DATA= argument.

To produce the font, invoke the GFONT procedure and specify the data set that contains the font information. In addition you can include options to modify the design and appearance of the font. For example, the following statement uses the data set FONTDATA to generate the font MYLOGO:

```
proc gfont data=fontdata name=mylogo;
```

For a demonstration of the font creation process, see Example 2 on page 700.

The GFONT procedure uses three types of data sets: the font data set, the kern data set, and the space data set. Each type of data set must contain certain variables and meet certain requirements. The following sections explain what each data set contains, how it is built, and what the requirements of the variables are.

The Font Data Set

The font data set consists of a series of observations that include the horizontal and vertical coordinate values and line segment numbers that the GFONT procedure uses to generate each character. In addition, each observation must include a character code that is associated with the font character and is used to specify the font character in a text string. The font data set also determines whether the font is stroked or polygon. A font data set that generates a polygon font produces an outline font by default. You can use the FILLED option with the same data set to generate a filled font.

The variables in the font data set must be assigned certain names and types. The table below summarizes the characteristics of the variables which are described further in "Font Data Set Variables" on page 688.

Table 16.1   Font Data Set Variables

Variable	Description	Type	Length	Valid Values	With Stroked Fonts	With Polygon Fonts
CHAR	the character code associated with the font character	character	1 or 2	keyboard characters or hexadecimal values	required	required
LP	the type of line segment being drawn, either a line or a polygon	character	1	L or P	optional	required
PTYPE	the type of data in the observation	character	1	V or C or W	optional	optional
SEGMENT	the number of the line segment or polygon being drawn	numeric		number	required	required
X	the horizontal coordinate	numeric		number	required	required
Y	the vertical coordinate	numeric		number	required	required

Font Data Set Variables

CHAR
> provides a code for the character or figure that you are creating. CHAR is a character variable with a length of 1 or 2 and is required for all fonts.

> ### CAUTION:
> **Using reserved or undefined hexadecimal codes as CHAR values may require the use of the NOKEYMAP option.** △

The CHAR variable takes any character as its value, including characters that you can enter from your keyboard and hexadecimal values from '00'x to 'FF'x. (If you use hexadecimal values as CHAR values, your font may not work correctly under a key map that is different from the one under which the font was created because positions that are not defined in one key map may be defined in another.)

When you specify the code character in a text string, the associated font character is drawn. For example, if you create a Roman alphabet font, typically the characters you specify for CHAR are keyboard characters that match the character in the font. All of the observations that build the letter A have a CHAR value of A. When you specify 'A' in a text string this produces A in the output.

However, if you build a symbol font, the symbols may not have corresponding keyboard characters. In that case, you select a character or hexadecimal value to represent each symbol in the font and assign it to CHAR. For example, in the Special font, the letter G is assigned as the code for the fleur-de-lis symbol. When you specify the code in a text string, the associated symbol displays.

If the CODELEN= option is set to 2, the values for CHAR represent two characters, such as AA, or a four-digit hexadecimal value, such as '00A5'x.

LP

tells the GFONT procedure whether the coordinates of each segment form a line or a polygon. LP is a character variable with a length of 1. It is required for polygon fonts but optional for stroked fonts. You can assign the LP variable either of the following values:

L   lines

P   polygons.

Every group of line segments with an LP value of P is designated as a polygon; if the observations do not draw a completely closed figure, the program closes the figure automatically. For example, the following observations do not contain an LP variable. They produce a shape like the one in Figure 16.5 on page 689.

OBS	CHAR	SEG	X	Y
1	b	1	1	1
2	b	1	1	3
3	b	1	3	3
4	b	1	3	1

Figure 16.5 Using an LP Value of Line

LP (continued)

An LP variable with a value of P for all observations added to the data set produces a complete box like the one in Figure 16.6 on page 690.

OBS	CHAR	SEG	X	Y	LP
1	b	1	1	1	P
2	b	1	1	3	P
3	b	1	3	3	P
4	b	1	3	1	P

Figure 16.6 Using an LP Value of Polygon

LP (continued)
 The LP variable allows you to mix lines and polygons when you create characters in a font. For example, the following observations produce the single figure that is composed of a polygon and a line segment, as shown in Figure 16.7 on page 690:

OBS	CHAR	SEG	X	Y	LP
1	b	1	1	1	P
2	b	1	1	3	P
3	b	1	3	3	P
4	b	1	3	1	P
5	b	2	0	0	L
6	b	2	2	4	L
7	b	2	4	0	L

Figure 16.7 Mixing LP Values of Line and Polygon

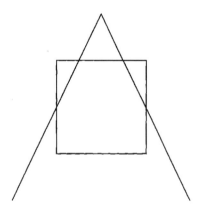

PTYPE
 tells the GFONT procedure what type of data are in the observation. PTYPE is a character variable of length 1 that is optional for both stroked and polygon fonts. For each observation, the PTYPE variable assigns a characteristic to the point

that is determined by the X and Y values. You can assign the PTYPE variable any of the following values:

V	normal point in the line segment
C	center of a circular arc joining two V points
W	width value for CHARSPACETYPE=DATA.

   If the GFONT procedure encounters the sequence V-C-V in consecutive observations, it draws an arc that connects the two V points and has its center at the C point. If a circle cannot be centered at C and pass through both V points, the results are unpredictable. Arcs are limited to 106 degrees or less.

   If you specify an observation with a PTYPE value of W, it must always be the first observation for a character. Instead of providing digitizing data to the procedure, the observation gives the minimum and maximum X values for the character. Note that in this case, the Y variable observation actually contains the maximum X value. Usually, these values include a little extra space for intercharacter spacing. Use a PTYPE of W only if you have specified CHARSPACETYPE=DATA; otherwise, the points are ignored. For more information on intercharacter spacing, see the description of the CHARSPACETYPE= option on page 684.

   If you do not specify a PTYPE variable in the font data set, all points are assumed to be V-type points.

   The following observations illustrate how the PTYPE variable is used to draw an arc similar to Figure 16.8 on page 692. (After the figure was generated, a grid was overlaid on it to show the location of the points.) A comment following each observation explains its function.

OBS	CHAR	SEG	X	Y	LP	PTYPE	Comment
1	a	1	40	60	P	W	define width of character as 20 font units, which is the number of units from left margin, 40, to right margin, 60
2	a	1	45	40	P	V	start line segment at position 45,40
3	a	1	45	50	P	V	draw a line to position 45,50, which is start point of arc
4	a	1	45	40	P	C	draw an arc whose center is at 45,40
5	a	1	55	40	P	V	finish drawing the arc at 55,40

Figure 16.8   Using the PTYPE Variable to Create an Arc

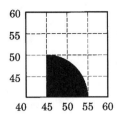

Note the following:

- ☐ Three observations are required to draw the arc: observation 3 and observation 5 denote the start point and endpoint of the arc, respectively, and observation 4 locates the center of the arc.
- ☐ The figure is closed because the line segments have an LP value of P (polygon).
- ☐ The font that contains the figure of the arc was generated with a PROC GFONT statement like the following:

```
proc gfont data=arc name=arcfig charspacetype=data filled ;
```

Note that the GFONT procedure uses the CHARSPACETYPE= option with a value of DATA to specify that the first observation sets the width of the character. The FILLED option fills the area of the arc.

SEGMENT

numbers the line segments that compose a character or symbol. SEGMENT is a numeric variable that is required for both polygon and stroked fonts. All the observations for a given line segment have the same segment number. The segment number changes when a new line segment starts.

When the GFONT procedure draws a stroked character with more than one line segment (for example, the letter E), or a polygon character with a hole (for example, the letter A), it needs to know when one line stops and where the next line begins. There are two ways to do this, as follows:

1 Change the segment number when a new line segment starts. If the value of LP is L (line), a change in segment numbers tells the GFONT procedure not to connect the last point in line segment 1 and the first point in line segment 2. If the value of LP is P (polygon), a change in segment numbers causes both of the following:

  - ☐ The last point in line segment 1 is joined to the first point in line segment 1, thus closing the polygon.
  - ☐ The program starts a new polygon. If the value of CHAR has not changed, the new polygon is part of the same character.

  Use this method for characters that are composed of two polygons, such as a question mark (?). If you draw a polygon with a hole in it, such as the letter A, use the second method.

2 Keep the same segment number for all lines, but insert an observation with missing values for X and Y between the observation that marks the end of the first line and the observation that begins the next line. For example, if you are drawing the letter O, insert an observation with a missing value between the line that draws the outer circle and the beginning of the line that draws the inner circle.

The first method is preferred, unless you are creating a polygon character with a hole in it. In this case, you should separate the lines with a missing value and keep the same segment numbers. (Note that if you use separate line segments when you create a polygon with a hole, the results may be unpredictable.) For example, observations such as the following from a data set called BOXES were used to draw the hollow square in Figure 16.9 on page 693. The data points that form the figure are laid out on a grid shown next to the square.

OBS	CHAR	SEG	X	Y	LP
1	b	1	1	1	P
2	b	1	1	3	P
3	b	1	3	3	P
4	b	1	3	1	P
5	b	1	-	-	P
6	b	1	0	0	P
7	b	1	0	4	P
8	b	1	4	4	P
9	b	1	4	0	P

Note that observation 5, which has missing values for X and Y, separates the observations that draw the inner box from those that draw the outer box and that the segment number is the same for all the observations. Figure 16.9 on page 693 was generated with a GFONT statement like the following:

```
proc gfont data=boxes name=boxes filled;
```

Note that the FILLED option is included and that only the space between the two squares is filled.

Figure 16.9 Drawing Nested Polygons

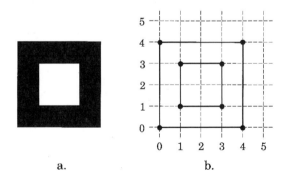

a.   b.

X Y

specify the horizontal and vertical coordinates of the points for each character. These variables must be numeric, and they must be named X and Y for the horizontal and vertical coordinates, respectively. Their values describe the position of the points on the character. These values can be in any range that you choose, but both variables must describe the character in the same scale or font units. In other words, 10 horizontal units must be the same distance as 10 vertical units. You should define vertical coordinates for all characters on the same baseline.

Note: When you specify PTYPE=W, both X and Y contain horizontal coordinate values. △

Creating a Font Data Set

You can create a font data set by digitizing the shape of the characters or figures either manually or with special digitizing equipment. To create a font data set by digitizing the characters manually, follow these steps:

1 Determine the coordinate points for each line segment by drawing the characters on a grid.

2 Lay out the observations for each character. Each observation describes a move from one point to another along a line segment. For each line segment, enter the coordinate points in the order in which they are drawn. For a stroked font, when you start a new line segment, change the segment number. For a polygon font, when you start a new polygon, change the line segment number.

If the polygon has a hole in it, as in the letter O, keep the line segment number and separate the lines with a missing value. Use the same value for CHAR for all of the observations that describe one character.

3 Create a SAS data set that contains the variables CHAR, SEGMENT, X, and Y, and read in the data for each observation. Include the variables LP and PTYPE if necessary.

4 Sort the data set by CHAR and SEGMENT.

5 Assign the font data set with the DATA= argument.

This process is illustrated in Example 2 on page 700.

The Kern Data Set

The kern data set consists of observations that specify how much space to add or remove between any two characters when they appear in combination. This process, called *kerning*, increases or decreases space between the characters. Kerning usually is applied to certain pairs of characters that, because of their shape, have too much space between them. Reducing the space between characters may allow part of one character to extend over the body of the next. Examples of some combinations that should be kerned are AT, AV, AW, TA, VA, and WA.

You can apply kerning to the intercharacter spacing that you specify with the CHARSPACETYPE= option (except for uniform fonts). You can refine the kerning of your characters as little or as much as you like. You assign the kern data set with the KERNDATA= option.

Kern Data Set Variables

The kern data set must contain these variables:

CHAR1
 specifies the first character in the pair to be kerned. CHAR1 is a character variable with a length of 1.

CHAR2
 specifies the second character in the pair to be kerned. CHAR2 is a character variable with a length of 1.

XADJ

> specifies the amount of space to add or remove between the two characters. XADJ is a numeric variable that uses the same font units as the font data set. The value of XADJ specifies the horizontal adjustment to be applied to CHAR2 whenever CHAR1 is followed immediately by CHAR2. Negative numbers decrease the spacing, and positive numbers increase the spacing.

Creating a Kern Data Set

Each observation in a kern data set names the pair of characters to be kerned and the amount of space to be added or deleted between them. To create a kern data set, follow these steps:

1 Select the pairs of characters to be kerned, and specify the space adjustment (in font units) for each pair as a positive number (more space) or negative number (less space).

2 Create a SAS data set that contains the variables CHAR1, CHAR2, and XADJ; produce one observation for each pair of characters and the corresponding space adjustment.

```
data kern1;
    input char1 $ char2 $ xadj;
    datalines;
A T -4
D A -3
T A -4
;
```

3 Assign the kern data set with the KERNDATA= option.

```
proc gfont data=fontdata
            name=font2
            charspacetype=data
            kerndata=kern1
            nodisplay;
run;
```

Figure 16.10 on page 696 illustrates how you can use the KERNDATA= option to create a font in which the space between specified pairs of letters is reduced. The characters A, D, and T are shown as the word DATA. The first line uses the unkerned font, FONT1, and the second line uses the kerned font, FONT2. Note that the characters in FONT2 are spaced more closely than the characters in FONT1.

The following title statements specify the kerned and unkerned fonts and are used with the GSLIDE procedure to produce Figure 16.10 on page 696:

```
title2 lspace=6 f=font1 h=10 j=l 'DATA';
title3 lspace=4 f=font2 h=10 j=l 'DATA';
```

Figure 16.10 Comparison of Kerned and Unkerned Text

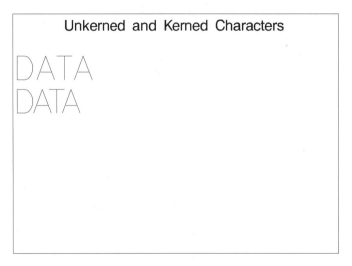

The Space Data Set

As the height (point size) of a font increases, less space is required between letters in relation to their height. If the point size decreases, more space may be needed. The space data set tells the GFONT procedure how much to increase or decrease the intercharacter spacing for a given point size. Like kerning, spacing is added to or subtracted from the intercharacter spacing that is specified by the CHARSPACETYPE= option. However, kerning applies the adjustment to specified pairs of characters, while spacing is applied uniformly to all characters.

Values that are specified in the space data set are added to the normal intercharacter spacing and any kerning data. Normal intercharacter spacing is determined by the CHARSPACETYPE= option.

Space Data Set Variables

The space data set must contain these variables:

SIZE
    specifies the point size of the font. SIZE is a numeric variable.

ADJ
    specifies the spacing adjustment for the point size in hundredths (1/100) of a point. (A point is equal to 1/72 of an inch.) ADJ is a numeric variable. Positive values for the ADJ variable increase the spacing between characters; negative values reduce the space.

Creating a Space Data Set

Each observation in a space data set specifies a point size (SIZE) and the amount of space (ADJ) to be added or subtracted between characters when a font of that point size is requested. When you specify a point size that is not in the space data set, the adjustment for the next smaller size is used. To create a space data set, follow these steps:

1 Determine the amount of adjustment that is required for typical point sizes; positive numbers increase spacing, and negative numbers decrease spacing.

2 Create a SAS data set that contains the variables SIZE and ADJ; produce one observation for each point size and corresponding space adjustment.

```
data space1;
   input size adj;
   datalines;
 6    40
12     0
18   -40
24   -90
30  -150
36  -300
42  -620
;
```

3 Assign the space data set with the SPACEDATA= option.

```
proc gfont data=reflib.fontdata
           name=font3
           charspacetype=data
           spacedata=space1
           nodisplay;
run;
```

Figure 16.11 on page 698 illustrates how to use the SPACEDATA= option to
generate a font in which intercharacter spacing is adjusted according to the height of
the characters. The characters A, D, and T are shown as the word DATA. Each pair of
lines displays the word DATA and at the same size uses first the font with spacing
adjustment (FONT3) and then the original font (FONT1). Note that as the size of the
characters increases, the space between them decreases.

The following title statements are used with the GSLIDE procedure to produce
Figure 16.11 on page 698:

```
title2;
title3 f=font3 h=.25in j=l 'DATA'; /* 18 points */
title4 f=font1 h=.25in j=l 'DATA';
title5;
title6 f=font3 h=.50in j=l 'DATA'; /* 36 points */
title7 f=font1 h=.50in j=l 'DATA';
title8;
title9 f=font3 h=1.0in j=l 'DATA'; /* 72 points */
title10 f=font1 h=1.0in j=l 'DATA';
```

Figure 16.11 Comparison of Text with and without Spacing Adjustments

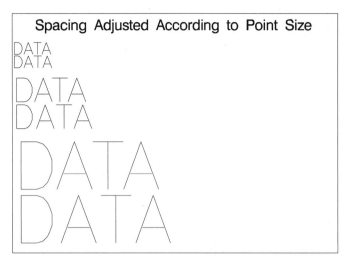

Examples

The following examples illustrate major features of the GFONT procedure.

Example 1: Displaying Fonts and Character Codes

Procedure features:
GFONT statement options:

HEIGHT=
NOBUILD
ROMCOL=
ROMFONT=
ROMHT=
SHOWROMAN

Sample library member: GR16N01

Figure 16.12 Display of the Greek Font with Character Codes (GR16N01)

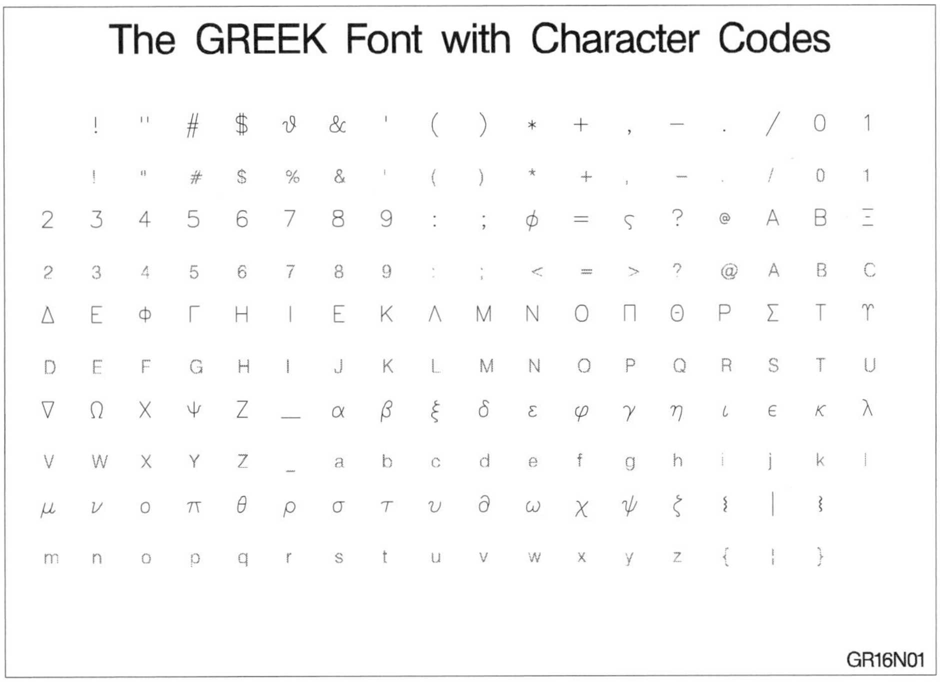

This example illustrates the SHOWROMAN option, which displays the character codes that are associated with the font characters that are being displayed. A display such as this one shows which keyboard character you enter to produce the Greek character you want. In addition, this example shows how to modify the appearance of both the font characters and the character codes when they are displayed.

Set the graphics environment.

```
goptions reset=global gunit=pct border cback=white
        colors=(black blue green red)
        ftext=swiss htitle=6 htext=3;
```

Define title and footnote.

```
title 'The GREEK Font with Character Codes';
footnote j=r 'GR16N01 ';
```

Display the GREEK font with character codes. NOBUILD indicates that the font specified in the NAME= argument is an existing font. HEIGHT= specifies the height of the Greek characters. ROMCOL=, ROMFONT=, and ROMHT= assign the color, type style, and height of the character codes. SHOWROMAN displays the character codes.

```
proc gfont name=greek
        nobuild
        height=3.7
        romcol=red
        romfont=swissl
        romht=2.7
```

```
                    showroman;
    run;
    quit;
```

Example 2: Creating Figures for a Symbol Font

Procedure features:
    GFONT statement options:

        CTEXT=
        DATA=
        FILLED
        NAME=
        RESOL=

Other features:
    LIBNAME statement

Sample library member: GR16N02

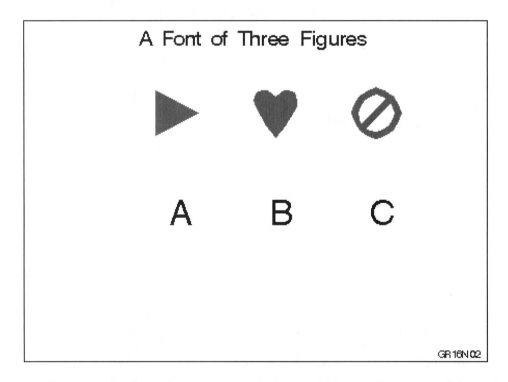

This example shows how to create three simple figures for a symbol font. Each figure is laid out on a grid that is 64 font units square. The third figure is a circle with a slash through it. Figure 16.13 on page 701 shows the figure and some of its coordinate points laid out on a grid.

Figure 16.13 Diagram of Circle with Slash Figure

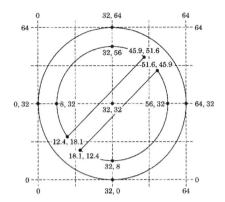

Assign the librefs and set the graphics environment. REFLIB is the permanent library that is used to store the data set. The second LIBNAME statement associates the libref GFONT0 with the SAS data library in which the font catalog is stored.

```
libname reflib 'SAS-data-library';
libname gfont0 'SAS-data-library';
goptions reset=global gunit=pct border cback=white
         colors=(black blue green red)
         ftext=swiss htitle=6 htext=3;
```

Create the font data set REFLIB.FIGURES for a triangle, a heart, and a circle with slash. The first figure, a right-pointing triangle that is assigned the character code A, is a polygon drawn with three straight lines.

```
data reflib.figures;
   input char $ ptype $ x y segment lp $;
   datalines;
A    W    0    64    0    P  /* triangle pointing right */
A    V    4     4    1    P
A    V    60   32    1    P
A    V    4    60    1    P
A    V    4     4    1    P
```

The second figure, a heart that is assigned the character code B, uses the PTYPE variable combination V-C-V to draw the arcs that make up the top of the heart. Each side requires two arcs. Since the arcs are continuous, the observation that marks the end of one arc is also the beginning of the next arc. The heart drawing begins at the bottom point and continues counterclockwise.

```
B    W    0    64    0    P  /* heart */
B    V    32    2    1    P
B    V    44   17    1    P
B    V    58   40    1    P
B    C    46   47    1    P
```

```
B      V     56    58    1    P
B      C     46    47    1    P
B      V     32    52    1    P
B      C     18    47    1    P
B      V      8    58    1    P
B      C     18    47    1    P
B      V      6    40    1    P
B      V     20    17    1    P
B      V     32     2    1    P
```

The third figure, a circle with a slash through it that is assigned the character code C, is composed of three polygons: a circle and two empty arcs. An observation with missing values separates the observations defining each of the three polygons. The outer circle is defined by the first group of observations. The empty arcs are drawn with three continuous arcs using the PTYPE variable pattern V-C-V-C-V-C-V. The straight line that closes the arc is drawn automatically by the GFONT procedure in order to complete the polygon. Because all the polygons are part of one character, the continuous space they define is filled.

```
C      W      0    64    0    P    /* circle with slash */
C      V     32    64    1    P
C      C     32    32    1    P
C      V     64    32    1    P
C      C     32    32    1    P
C      V     32     0    1    P
C      C     32    32    1    P
C      V      0    32    1    P
C      C     32    32    1    P
C      V     32    64    1    P
C      V      .     .    1    P
C      V   12.4  18.1    1    P
C      C     32    32    1    P
C      V      8    32    1    P
C      C     32    32    1    P
C      V     32    56    1    P
C      C     32    32    1    P
C      V   45.9  51.6    1    P
C      V      .     .    1    P
C      V   51.6  45.9    1    P
C      C     32    32    1    P
C      V     56    32    1    P
C      C     32    32    1    P
C      V     32     8    1    P
C      C     32    32    1    P
C      V   18.1  12.4    1    P
;
```

Define the title and footnote.

```
title 'A Font of Three Figures';
footnote j=r 'GR16N02 ';
```

Generate and display the font FIGURES. The DATA= argument names the input data set
that is used to generate the font. The NAME= argument names the font that the procedure
generates and automatically stores it in the GFONT0 catalog. (Note that you do not need to
specify GFONT0.) FILLED specifies a filled polygon font. CTEXT= specifies the color of the
figures in the font display. The color specification is not stored with the font. RESOL= is set to 2
to improve the resolution of the lines. By default, the newly generated font is displayed (the
NODISPLAY option is not used).

```
proc gfont data=reflib.figures
           name=figures
           filled
           height=.75in
           ctext=red
           showroman
           romht=.5in
           resol=2;
run;
quit;
```

CHAPTER

17

The GIMPORT Procedure

Overview

The GIMPORT procedure enables you to import into SAS/GRAPH software graphics output that is produced with other software applications, graphics output that is produced by SAS/GRAPH software, or graphics output that is produced on other machines. The GIMPORT procedure takes as its input a computer graphics metafile (CGM) and produces graphics output that can be displayed in your SAS/GRAPH session and stored in a SAS catalog. This graphics output can be reviewed and played like any other SAS/GRAPH output using the GREPLAY procedure. The GIMPORT procedure may also write any of the following information to the log:

□ any elements used in the CGM that the procedure cannot process

□ color mapping information when a color in a CGM is not available on the destination device

□ a list of fonts that are used by the application that produced the CGM.

Note: In addition to the GIMPORT procedure, you can use commands in the File pull-down menu in the Image Editor, Graph Editor, and Graph window to import other graphic formats such as GIF, TIFF, and WMF. △

Concepts

About Importing Graphics

A computer graphics metafile (CGM) is a graphics output file that is created according to a standard (ANSI X3.122). Since many graphics applications, including SAS/GRAPH software, can generate and import CGMs, these files can be read by different applications programs or used on different machines.

The GIMPORT procedure imports a CGM with which a fileref has been associated. Using the CGM as input, the procedure displays the graphics output and creates a catalog entry. The following sections address how to assign the fileref to the external file (CGM) and how to import the file.

Specifying a Fileref

You must assign a fileref to the external file that contains the CGM that you want to use as input so that the GIMPORT procedure can locate it. You can do this with a FILENAME statement that has the following form:

```
FILENAMEcgm-fileref'external-file';
```

Replace *cgm-fileref* with any fileref name that you want. Replace *'external-file'* with the complete file name of the CGM. You can omit the FILENAME statement if you have already defined the fileref. You can also specify a fileref with a host command in some operating environments. See "FILENAME Statement" on page 24 for additional information.

Importing the File

The PROC GIMPORT statement reads the input CGM and displays the graphics output. When the CGM is displayed using only the PROC GIMPORT statement, the resulting graphics output may not be sized or positioned correctly for the device on which it is displayed. In these cases, you can use the SCALE and TRANSLATE statements to adjust the size and location of the new graphics output.

In addition, if the CGM contains the FONT LIST element, the procedure lists in the log the fonts used in the CGM. You can change these fonts to SAS software fonts using the MAP statement. If you do not change these fonts to SAS software fonts, the GIMPORT procedure uses a default font.

Because it is easier to determine what adjustments the graphics output needs after it has been displayed, you may want to follow these steps:

1 Import the CGM and display the graphics output using only the PROC GIMPORT statement.

2 Decide what adjustments you want to make to the size and position of the graphics output.

3 If the procedure lists the fonts that are used by the CGM, decide what font substitutions you want to make.

4 Run the procedure again with the appropriate MAP, SCALE, or TRANSLATE statements.

Note: Once you have determined the correct values for the SCALE and TRANSLATE statements for the graphics output produced by a particular CGM, you can use the same values for all other graphics output that is generated by the same software application. △

CGM Elements Not Supported

The GIMPORT procedure does not support certain CGM elements. If the input CGM contains any of the following elements, the GIMPORT procedure writes a message to the log noting that the procedure cannot process them:

☐ the CELL ARRAY primitive element (a bitmap CGM file)

☐ the CHARACTER SPACING attribute element

☐ the APPLICATION DATA element

☐ the ESCAPE element.

These elements are rarely used and their absence should not affect the graphics output produced by the GIMPORT procedure.

About Color Mapping

If the CGM specifies colors for the graphics elements that it generates, you may or may not be able to map them to the color that you want in your SAS/GRAPH output, depending on the way these colors are specified in the CGM.

You cannot change the color mapping if, in the CGM, the COLOUR SELECTION MODE element is set to DIRECT. In this case, the colors are explicitly defined by the CGM and you cannot change them. However, if the CGM was created with a SAS/GRAPH CGM device driver, you can control the colors by specifying the appropriate colors when you create the graphics output or by changing the colors in the CGM device entry and re-creating the CGM. See Chapter 15, "The GDEVICE Procedure," on page 651 for details. In addition, you can use a color map with the GREPLAY procedure to remap the colors. In the color map, the FROM color must be specified in RGB format, but the TO color can be any valid color name. See Chapter 26, "The GREPLAY Procedure," on page 919 for details on color maps.

You can change the color mapping if the COLOUR SELECTION MODE element is set to INDEXED and there is no color table defined in the CGM file. In this case, you can map the colors from the CGM to the colors of your choice by using the COLORS= graphics option when you run the GIMPORT procedure. The CGM colors are mapped to match the order of the colors in the colors list. If the procedure cannot reproduce the colors specified in the CGM, the following message is written to the log:

```
WARNING: Invalid color index n encountered.
         It has been mapped to color-name.
```

Note: The color name from the CGM is converted to the RGB format for SAS/GRAPH color names; that is, WHITE is converted to CXFFFFFF, and so on. See Chapter 7, "SAS/GRAPH Colors," on page 139 for details. △

About Pattern Mapping

If the CGM contains pattern specifications, you may be able to map them to patterns of your choice using SAS/GRAPH PATTERN definitions.

If the CGM defines a PATTERN TABLE, then the patterns defined by this table are the patterns that are used and you cannot change them.

If a PATTERN TABLE is not defined in the CGM, under certain conditions you may be able to use SAS/GRAPH PATTERN definitions to control the patterns that are used. If INTERIOR STYLE is set to PATTERN and if a PATTERN TABLE INDEX has been specified, then the GIMPORT procedure uses the PATTERN TABLE INDEX to look up SAS/GRAPH PATTERN definitions. If patterns are defined, the procedure uses the first available pattern. For example, if the PATTERN TABLE INDEX *n* has been defined, the procedure uses SAS/GRAPH PATTERN definition *n*. If the SAS/GRAPH PATTERN definition is not the correct pattern type, the procedure modifies the pattern as necessary. If no PATTERN definitions are currently in effect, an INVALID PATTERN TABLE INDEX warning is issued and no pattern is used.

About Font Mapping

By default, the GIMPORT procedure maps all of the fonts in the CGM to the font that is specified by the FTEXT= graphics option. If the FTEXT= graphics option is not used, the default is the hardware font NONE. However, you may be able to specify a different font either by mapping the fonts or by using a graphics option.

When the CGM is imported, a numbered list of the fonts that are used in the CGM may be displayed in the LOG window. These are the fonts that were available to the application that originally generated the CGM. Depending on how the fonts are represented in the CGM, you may be able to map these fonts to fonts of your choice.

If the font and text in the imported graphics output are produced with move and draw commands that are included in the CGM, then no font name appears in the LOG window and the font cannot be mapped to a different one.

If the fonts used in the imported graphics output are represented in the CGM as a font name accompanied by a text string, they can be mapped to SAS/GRAPH fonts using the MAP statement. You can use the MAP statement if the message "WARNING: Invalid font index *n*. Font has been mapped to *font-name*" appears in the LOG window after the list of fonts. This means that font *n* in the list could not be reproduced and was mapped to the font specified in the FTEXT= graphics option or to the hardware font. You can map this font to a SAS/GRAPH software font of your choice using the MAP statement. See "MAP Statement" on page 710 for more information on mapping fonts.

You can also specify a font with the FTEXT= or CHARTYPE= graphics options if both of the following conditions are true:

□ The font has not been mapped with a MAP statement.

□ The CGM font contains a font name and text rather than the move and draw commands that draw the text in the specified font. In the latter case, the font name is not included in FONT LIST.

However, using a graphics option causes all fonts to be mapped to the one that is specified. See Chapter 6, "SAS/GRAPH Fonts," on page 125 for details of font specification and Example 2 on page 715.

Procedure Syntax

Supports: Output Delivery System (ODS)

PROC GIMPORT FILEREF=*cgm-fileref* | *'external-file'*
       FILETYPE=CGM
       FORMAT=BINARY | CHARACTER | CLEARTEXT
       <GOUT=<*libref.*>*output-catalog*>;

MAP *'cgm-font'* TO *font* ;
SCALE X=*factor* | Y=*factor* | X=*factor* Y=*factor*;
TRANSLATE X=*offset* | Y=*offset* | X=*offset* Y=*offset*;

PROC GIMPORT Statement

Identifies the input file to be processed, and specifies its file type and format. Optionally specifies an output catalog.

Syntax

PROC GIMPORT FILEREF=*cgm-fileref* | *'external-file'*
    FILETYPE=CGM
    FORMAT=BINARY | CHARACTER | CLEARTEXT
    <GOUT=<*libref.*>*output-catalog*>;

Required Arguments

FILEREF=*cgm-fileref* | *'external-file'*
  specifies the computer graphics metafile (CGM) that is input for PROC GIMPORT. Following are the possible values for FILEREF=:

cgm-fileref
  a fileref that is associated with the CGM and that has been previously defined using a FILENAME statement or host command.

'external-file'
  the complete file name of the CGM that you want to import. See the operating system companion for your system for valid values for *external-file*.

  Featured in: Example 2 on page 715

FILETYPE=CGM
  specifies the type of the input file, that is, the graphics standard to which the file conforms. CGM is the only valid value for the FILETYPE= argument. If the FILETYPE= argument is omitted, an error is issued and the procedure stops.

  Featured in: Example 2 on page 715

FORMAT=BINARY | CHARACTER | CLEARTEXT
  specifies the format of the input file. CGMs can be encoded in one of the following three formats:

BINARY
  specifies binary encoding. It is not printable.

CHARACTER
  specifies an encoding suitable for transfer through networks that cannot support binary transfers. It is printable but not readable.

CLEARTEXT
  specifies a text format that can be read using a standard text editor.
  Most graphics packages use BINARY format. If you specify the wrong format, an "ERROR: Unable to interpret the CGM file" message is issued and the procedure stops. If this occurs, try a different format.

Featured in: Example 2 on page 715

Options

GOUT=<*libref.*>*output-catalog*
specifies the SAS catalog in which to save the graphics output produced by the GIMPORT procedure. If you omit the libref, SAS/GRAPH looks for the catalog in the temporary library called WORK and creates the catalog if it does not exist.

See also: "Storing Graphics Output in SAS Catalogs" on page 49

MAP Statement

Substitutes a SAS/GRAPH software font for a font in the CGM.

Requirements: Submit a separate MAP statement for each CGM font that you want to map.

Tip: You can submit multiple MAP statements with the procedure.

Featured in: Example 2 on page 715

Syntax

MAP *'cgm-font'* TO *font*;

Required Arguments

'*cgm-font*'
identifies a font in the CGM. The name of the font must be enclosed in single quotation marks and written exactly as it appears in the font list; *cgm-font* is case sensitive. Do not include the font list number in *cgm-font*.

font
specifies the SAS/GRAPH font to which the CGM font is mapped. You can specify software fonts or hardware fonts for the destination device. You can also use fonts that are created by the GFONT procedure.

Note: Remember to specify the libref GFONT0 with a LIBNAME statement if *font* is a user-generated font. △
By default, the GIMPORT procedure maps all of the CGM fonts to the font specified by the FTEXT= graphics option or, if the FTEXT= graphics option is not used, to the default hardware font, NONE.

Details

If the CGM includes the FONT LIST element, the GIMPORT procedure automatically lists the CGM font names in the log. Use this list to select the fonts for mapping. For example, suppose the font list includes the following entry:
3. Times Roman

If the LOG window displays the message "WARNING: Invalid font index *n*," you can map the Times Roman font to the SAS/GRAPH font CENTX with the following statement:

```
map 'Times Roman' to centx;
```

SCALE Statement

Enlarges or reduces the graphics output by increasing or decreasing the values of the *x* and *y* coordinates.

Requirements: You can submit only one SCALE statement.

Tip: You can submit the SCALE statement alone or in conjunction with the TRANSLATE statement, but the SCALE statement is always processed first.

Featured in: Example 2 on page 715

Syntax

SCALE X=*factor* | Y=*factor* | X=*factor* Y=*factor*;

Required Arguments

At least one of the following arguments is required; both may be used and can be listed in either order:

X=*factor*

specifies the enlargement or reduction of the values of the *x* coordinates. *Factor* is the number by which these values are multiplied and cannot be less than or equal to 0. By default, X=1. Values less than 1 reduce the size of the graphics output while values greater than 1 increase the size of the graphics output. There is no limit on the size of *factor*.

Y=*factor*

specifies the enlargement or reduction of the values of the *y* coordinates. *Factor* is the number by which these values are multiplied and cannot be less than or equal to 0. By default, Y=1. Values less than 1 reduce the size of the graphics output while values greater than 1 increase the size of the graphics output. There is no limit on the size of *factor*.

Details

If the shapes in the imported graphics output are too narrow, you can make them wider by increasing the values of the *x* coordinate. To make the elements in the graphics output twice as wide, specify X=2. To make them half as high, specify Y=.5.

For example, if the values of the *x* coordinates range from 5 to 50 and if in the SCALE statement the factor for X= is specified as 2, then the values of all of the *x* coordinates are multiplied by 2 and the range of these values increases. The new range is 10 to 100. And if the values of the *y* coordinates range from 0 to 25 and if in the SCALE statement the factor for Y= is specified as .5, then the values of all of the *y* coordinates are multiplied by .5 and the range of these values decreases. The new range is 0 to 12.5.

If you specify a factor that causes the graphics output to exceed the size of the graphics output area, the procedure draws as much of the graphics output as will fit in the available space.

TRANSLATE Statement

Adjusts the location on the display of the graphics output imported by the procedure. Graphics output can be shifted left or right by offsetting the *x* values or shifted up or down by offsetting the *y* values.

Requirements: You can submit only one TRANSLATE statement.

Tip: You can submit the TRANSLATE statement alone or in conjunction with the SCALE statement but the SCALE statement is always processed first.

Featured in: Example 2 on page 715

Syntax

TRANSLATE X=*offset* | Y=*offset* | X=*offset* Y=*offset* ;

Required Arguments

 At least one of the following arguments is required; both may be used and can be listed in either order:

X=*offset*

specifies the number of units in percent of the display area to move the graphics output right (positive numbers) or left (negative numbers). The value of *offset* is added to the value of the *x* coordinate. By default, X=0.

Y=*offset*

specifies the number of units in percent of the display area to move the graphics output up (positive numbers) or down (negative numbers). The value of *offset* is added to the value of the *y* coordinate. By default, Y=0.

Details

The TRANSLATE statement adjusts the position of the graphics output without changing its size. The amount of the *offset* that is specified for X= or Y= in the TRANSLATE statement is the amount that the graphics output is moved.

For example, suppose your imported graphics output is positioned in the upper-left corner of the display. To move it right 10% and down 5%, use the following statement:

```
translate x=10 y=-5;
```

Examples

The following examples illustrate major features of the GIMPORT procedure. For illustration purposes, these examples create a CGM using SAS/GRAPH software and import the resulting CGM by using the GIMPORT procedure. Ordinarily, you would use the GIMPORT procedure to import graphics output that is generated by another software package.

Note: Because this example uses a CGM device driver to produce a graphics stream file, you may need to respecify a device driver for your output device. In addition, these examples use the HSIZE= and VSIZE= graphics options to set a specific size for the graphics output area for the CGM so that the second example can illustrate the use of the SCALE and TRANSLATE statements. Depending on the output device that you are using, you may need to adjust the HSIZE= and VSIZE= values in this example and the values in the SCALE and TRANSLATE statements in the second example. △

Example 1: Creating and Importing a CGM

Procedure features:
    GIMPORT statement options:
        FILEREF=
        FILETYPE=
        FORMAT=

Other features:
    FILENAME statement
    GOPTIONS stratement

Sample library member: GR17N01

Title One is SCRIPT Font
Title Two is CENTB Font
Title Three is ZAPF Font

This example creates a CGM in binary format by directing SAS/GRAPH output to a graphics stream file (GSF) and using a CGM device driver. It uses the GIMPORT procedure to import the resulting CGM into SAS/GRAPH where it can be viewed and stored in a catalog. (See Chapter 2, "SAS/GRAPH Programs," on page 21 for additional information on catalog entries and graphics stream files.) The output shows the imported version of the graphic. Note that the output uses the default font because the specified fonts are unavailable. Example 2 on page 715 shows how to map these fonts to get the output that you want. Also see "About Font Mapping" on page 708 for additional information.

Assign the fileref for a graphics stream file and set the graphics environment. Set graphics stream file characteristics, and select CGMCRT device drive for binary CGM.

```
filename gsasfile 'external-file';
goptions reset=global gunit=pct border cback=white
```

```
colors=(black)
gaccess=gsasfile gsfmode=replace
noprompt device=cgmcrt
hsize=5 in vsize=5 in;
```

Define titles and footnote for slide.

```
title1 f=script h=7 'Title One is SCRIPT Font';
title2 f=centb h=5 'Title Two is CENTB Font';
title3 f=zapf h=5 'Title Three is ZAPF Font';
footnote h=3 f=swiss j=r 'GR17N01 ';
```

Generate a slide. The graphics output is stored in the GSF file that was specified with the fileref and in the GOPTIONS statement.

```
proc gslide;
run;
quit;
```

Reset the graphics environment.

```
goptions reset=goptions border cback=white
         colors=(black);
```

Import the GSF file created by the CGMCRT device driver. FILEREF= specifies the fileref where the CGM is located. FILETYPE= specifies the type of file to be imported. FORMAT= specifies the format of the CGM being imported.

```
proc gimport fileref=gsasfile
             filetype=cgm
             format=binary;
run;
```

Output 17.1 on page 714 shows the font list that is displayed in the log file. The font list contains all of the fonts that are used by the CGM. The warning messages following the font list indicate which fonts can be remapped using the MAP statement.

Output 17.1   Font List

```
.
.
.
NOTE: These fonts are used in this CGM file. You may use the MAP statement
      to map these fonts to  SAS/GRAPH
fonts.
 1. SIMPLEX
 2. BRUSH
 3. CENTB
 4. CENTBE
 5. CENTBI
 6. CENTBIE
 7. CENTX
 8. CENTXE
 9. CENTXI
10. CENTXIE
11. GERMAN
12. GITALIC
13. DUPLEX
14. COMPLEX
15. TRIPLEX
16. TITALIC
17. ITALIC
18. OLDENG
19. SCRIPT
20. CSCRIPT
21. SWISS
22. SWISSE
23. SWISSB
24. SWISSBE
25. SWISSBI
26. SWISSBIE
27. SWISSX
28. SWISSXE
29. SWISSXB
30. SWISSXB
31. SWISSXBE
32. SWISSI
33. SWISSIE
34. SWISSL
35. SWISSLE
36. ZAPF
37. ZAPFE
38. ZAPFB
39. ZAPFBE
40. ZAPFBI
41. ZAPFBIE
42. ZAPFI
43. ZAPFIE
WARNING: Unspecified font index 19. Font has been mapped to the default font.
WARNING: Unspecified font index 3. Font has been mapped to the default font.
WARNING: Unspecified font index 36. Font has been mapped to the default font.
WARNING: Unspecified font index 21. Font has been mapped to the default font.
.
.
.
```

Example 2: Adjusting the Graphics Output

Procedure features:

SCALE statement

TRANSLATE statement

MAP statement

Sample library member: GR17N02

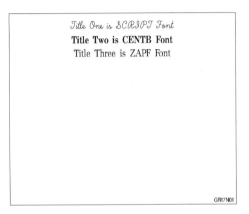

This example imports the CGM file that was created in the earlier example and modifies the output. This example uses the SCALE and TRANSLATE statements to correct the size and position of the imported CGM. The MAP statement is also used to substitute a SAS/GRAPH software font for a font in the CGM.

Assign the fileref for a GSF file and set the graphics environment.

```
filename gsasfile 'external-file';
goptions reset=goptions gunit=pct border cback=white
         colors=(black) htitle=6 htext=3;
```

Import the GSF file created by the CGMCRT device driver. The SCALE statement specifies the scale factor for the values of the x and y coordinates. The TRANSLATE statement specifies the amount that the imported graphics output should be moved horizontally and vertically. The MAP statements remap the fonts shown in the first example.

```
proc gimport fileref=gsasfile filetype=cgm format=binary;
   scale x=.7 y=.8;
   translate x=3.5 y=10;
   map 'SCRIPT' to script;
   map 'CENTB' to centb;
   map 'ZAPF' to zapf;
   map 'SWISS' to swiss;
run;
```

Output 17.2 on page 717 shows the font list that is displayed in the log file. Note that no warning messages follow the font list because all of the fonts that are used in the CGM have been remapped.

Output 17.2 Font List

```
  .
  .
  .

  NOTE: These fonts are used in this CGM file. You may use the MAP statement
        to map these fonts to  SAS/GRAPH
fonts.
  1. SIMPLEX
  2. BRUSH
  3. CENTB
  4. CENTBE
  5. CENTBI
  6. CENTBIE
  7. CENTX
  8. CENTXE
  9. CENTXI
 10. CENTXIE
 11. GERMAN
 12. GITALIC
 13. DUPLEX
 14. COMPLEX
 15. TRIPLEX
 16. TITALIC
 17. ITALIC
 18. OLDENG
 19. SCRIPT
 20. CSCRIPT
 21. SWISS
 22. SWISSE
 23. SWISSB
 24. SWISSBE
 25. SWISSBI
 26. SWISSBIE
 27. SWISSX
 28. SWISSXE
 29. SWISSXB
 30. SWISSXB
 31. SWISSXBE
 32. SWISSI
 33. SWISSIE
 34. SWISSL
 35. SWISSLE
 36. ZAPF
 37. ZAPFE
 38. ZAPFB
 39. ZAPFBE
 40. ZAPFBI
 41. ZAPFBIE
 42. ZAPFI
 43. ZAPFIE
  .
  .
  .
```

References

ANSI X3.122–1986, *Computer Graphics Metafile for the Storage and Transfer of Picture Description Information*.

Arnold, D.B. and Bono, P.R. (1988), *CGM and CGI: Metafile Interface Standards for Computer Graphics*, New York: Springer-Verlag.

CHAPTER

18

The GKEYMAP Procedure

Overview

The GKEYMAP procedure creates key maps and device maps that compensate for differences between the way that characters are encoded internally bySAS/GRAPH software and the way that they are encoded by different operating environments and output devices.

In addition, the GKEYMAP procedure can create SAS data sets from existing key maps and device maps, either Institute-supplied or user-generated. This capability is useful when you want to make minor alterations in a large key map or device map and you do not want to or cannot re-create the original data set with a DATA step.

The Institute supplies key maps for many keyboard configurations and operating-environment character representations. Your SAS Software Consultant should have selected the appropriate key map for your site. If the Institute-supplied device maps and key maps do not meet your needs, you can use this procedure to modify an existing map or create a new one.

Concepts

About Key Maps and Device Maps

The characters A through Z (upper- and lowercase), 0 through 9, and many symbols and national characters are represented by a set of hexadecimal codes. However, a character may be represented by one code for the keyboard, another code for the operating environment, and yet another for the output device. To resolve these differences, SAS/GRAPH software stores all characters using its own internal encoding scheme, which is a set of hexadecimal values that are associated with all supported characters. Figure 18.1 on page 721 shows these internal character encoding (ICE) codes.

To accommodate differences in the encoding of characters, you must be able to translate the hexadecimal codes generated by your keyboard or operating environment into the corresponding SAS/GRAPH internal encoding. A key map gives you this ability.

You also must be able to convert the internal encoding that is used by SAS/GRAPHsoftware to the codes required to produce the corresponding hardware characters on your output device. A device map gives you this ability.

Key maps and device maps are SAS catalog entries. Institute-supplied key maps and device maps are stored in the catalog SASHELP.FONTS. User-generated key maps and device maps are stored in the catalog GFONT0.FONTS. Key maps are stored with the extension KEYMAP (for example, GERMAN.KEYMAP), and device maps are stored with the extension DEVMAP (for example, DEFAULT.DEVMAP).

Figure 18.1 SAS/GRAPH Internal Character Encoding

00	© 01	® 02	■ 03	TM 04	° 05	´ 06	¨ 07	08	Œ 09	œ 0A	' 0B	' 0C	" 0D	" 0E	¤ 0F
10	11	↕ 12	« 13	¶ 14	§ 15	Ø 16	ø 17	↑ 18	↓ 19	→ 1A	← 1B	» 1C	↔ 1D	1E	1F
20	! 21	‖ 22	# 23	$ 24	% 25	& 26	' 27	(28	) 29	* 2A	+ 2B	, 2C	– 2D	. 2E	/ 2F
0 30	1 31	2 32	3 33	4 34	5 35	6 36	7 37	8 38	9 39	: 3A	; 3B	< 3C	= 3D	> 3E	? 3F
@ 40	A 41	B 42	C 43	D 44	E 45	F 46	G 47	H 48	I 49	J 4A	K 4B	L 4C	M 4D	N 4E	O 4F
P 50	Q 51	R 52	S 53	T 54	U 55	V 56	W 57	X 58	Y 59	Z 5A	[5B	\ 5C	] 5D	^ 5E	_ 5F
` 60	a 61	b 62	c 63	d 64	e 65	f 66	g 67	h 68	i 69	j 6A	k 6B	l 6C	m 6D	n 6E	o 6F
p 70	q 71	r 72	s 73	t 74	u 75	v 76	w 77	x 78	y 79	z 7A	{ 7B		7C	} 7D	~ 7E	7F
Ç 80	ü 81	é 82	â 83	ä 84	à 85	å 86	ç 87	ê 88	ë 89	è 8A	ï 8B	î 8C	ì 8D	Ä 8E	Å 8F
É 90	æ 91	Æ 92	ô 93	ö 94	ò 95	û 96	ù 97	ÿ 98	Ö 99	Ü 9A	¢ 9B	£ 9C	¥ 9D	Pt 9E	ƒ 9F
á A0	í A1	ó A2	ú A3	ñ A4	Ñ A5	ª A6	º A7	¿ A8	✗ A9	¬ AA	½ AB	¼ AC	¡ AD	‹ AE	› AF
´ B0	` B1	¨ B2	˝ B3	^ B4	° B5	˛ B6	¯ B7	ß B8	˘ B9	ˇ BA	BB	Ğ BC	† BD	‡ BE		BF
C0	C1	C2	C3	C4	C5	C6	C7	C8	C9	CA	CB	CC	CD	CE	CF
¦ D0	⌡ D1	´ D2	` D3	¨ D4	˝ D5	^ D6	• D7	˛ D8	˘ D9	ˇ DA	˘ DB	ğ DC	Ş DD	ş DE	DF
⌂ E0	◻ E1	• E2	◻ E3	µ E4	Đ E5	Þ E6	đ E7	þ E8	⅛ E9	⅜ EA	⅝ EB	¾ EC	⅞ ED	⅓ EE	⅔ EF
Č F0	± F1	≥ F2	≤ F3	Ć F4	Š F5	÷ F6	Ž F7	č F8	ć F9	š FA	ž FB	≠ FC	FD	FE	FF

Note: Positions 00-1F are reserved.
Note: SAS Institute reserves the right to change, at any time, the character displayed and the hexadecimal code returned for all undefined codes.

What Key Maps Do

A key map changes the code generated by a keyboard key to the value corresponding to the SAS/GRAPH internal character encoding. Otherwise, a different character (or no character) may be drawn when the character is requested in a SAS/GRAPH software font.

Key maps are required when the code that is sent to the operating environment does not match the SAS/GRAPH internal encoding for the character corresponding to the key that is pressed. They are useful for generating a character in a software font that is not available on your keyboard or when the same key on different keyboards sends a different character to the operating environment. They are also useful for creating new characters by combining existing characters with accent characters (called *diacritics*).

Note: In Figure 18.1 on page 721, the diacritic characters specified by the codes D2 through DB are backspaced before being drawn and can be used to create new characters (characters resulting from codes B0 through B7, B9, and BA are not backspaced before being drawn). See Example 1 on page 726 for an example of using a diacritic character as an accent. Two commonly used characters have already been created for you: the character located in position F0 of the ICE table could be created by combining DA with an uppercase C, and the character located in position BC could be created by combining DB with an uppercase G. △

What Device Maps Do

A device map maps the code stored in the SAS/GRAPH internal encoding to the code required to reproduce the character on the output device when a particular hardware character is requested in a SAS/GRAPH program.

You usually use device maps in these two situations:

□ reversing the translation performed by key maps (if needed). To display the proper hardware character, you must use a device map to convert the SAS/GRAPH internal encoding of the character back to the encoding that the device expects.

□ accounting for differences between the code that represents a character on the operating environment and the code or codes required to generate the same character as a hardware character on an output device. The problem can be further complicated if you have multiple output devices, each with its own way of generating a particular character using hardware text.

Using Key Maps and Device Maps

You use key maps and device maps by specifying them with the KEYMAP= or DEVMAP= options in a GOPTIONS statement. You also can specify a device map by filling in the DEVMAP field in the Detail window of the device entry for the device driver that you are using.

For example, if you use the GKEYMAP procedure to generate a key map called MYKEYMAP, you can specify it with a statement like this:

```
goptions keymap=mykeymap;
```

Once you specify MYKEYMAP as your current key map, you can press a key and the code it generates is translated by MYKEYMAP into the ICE code that is specified by the key map.

When you specify a device map with the DEVMAP= graphics option and you use a hardware character set, mapped characters are converted from their SAS/GRAPH internal encoding to the codes required to display the corresponding characters on your device. See Chapter 9, "Graphics Options and Device Parameters Dictionary," on page 301 for more information on the KEYMAP= and DEVMAP= graphics options.

Asymmetrical Maps

It is possible, and sometimes necessary, to define a key map or device map that is not symmetrical (that is, two or more input character codes map to the same output character code). For example, if you define a key map to map the keyed character A to the internal encoding for B, the keyed characters A and B both map to the internal encoding for B, but no code maps to A. This situation may make it impossible for you to display certain characters defined in software fonts.

Seeing What Characters in a Font are Available

To see what characters in a font can be displayed if a particular key map is used, do the following:

1 Use the KEYMAP= option in a GOPTIONS statement to specify the key map that you are interested in.

2 Then, use the GFONT procedure with the ROMHEX option to display the font that you want to use.

The hexadecimal values and corresponding font characters that are displayed are the ones available under the specified map. If the map is not symmetrical, a warning is issued. See Chapter 16, "The GFONT Procedure," on page 675 for more information on using hexadecimal values to display special characters.

About the GKEYMAP Data Set

To generate a key map or device map, you must create a data set that contains the mapping information and use that data set as input for the GKEYMAP procedure. The mapping information is specified as values for the variables in the data set, which should contain one observation for each character or key to be mapped. Any characters not specified in the data set are passed through the map unchanged.

GKEYMAP Data Set Variables

To provide information on the character mapping that is to be performed for a key map or a device map, you must use a variable named FROM to specify the character that you are mapping from, and a variable named TO to specify the character to map to. For key maps, these are the only variables in the data set. For device maps, you may also need variables named CHARTYPE and TOLEN.

Here are definitions for these variables:

CHARTYPE
specifies which hardware character set to use when a device requires that you select an alternate character set in order to display certain characters. CHARTYPE is a numeric variable.

All of the characters in the TO string for a particular FROM value must use the same character set. The CHARTYPE variable is required if you use the MULTFONT option in the PROC GKEYMAP statement; otherwise, it is ignored. (The CHARTYPE variable is always ignored when you are creating a key map.) The CHARTYPE value must match a value listed in the Chartype field in the Chartype window of the device entry for the device to which the map is applied. However, you can set the CHARTYPE variable to a missing value to specify that the character can be drawn in any hardware character set.

FROM
specifies the character you are mapping from. FROM is a character variable. For each observation, the FROM variable should contain a single character value. Any characters after the first are ignored. The data set must be sorted by the FROM variable.

Featured in: Example 1 on page 726

TO
specifies the string that the character in the FROM variable is mapped to. TO is a character variable.

For device maps, if the TO variable contains more than one character, you must also specify TYPE=MAP1N in the PROC GKEYMAP statement to indicate that a single FROM character is being mapped to multiple TO characters. In addition, you must include the TOLEN variable in the data set to specify the length of each TO string. If you specify TYPE=MAP11 in the PROC GKEYMAP statement or if you do not use the TYPE= option, only the first byte of the TO string is recognized.

Featured in: Example 1 on page 726

TOLEN
specifies the length of the string in the TO variable. TOLEN is a numeric variable. The TOLEN variable is used only with device maps and is required if you specify TYPE=MAP1N in the PROC GKEYMAP statement; otherwise, it is ignored.

Procedure Syntax

Requirements: The NAME= argument is always required. To create a key map or device map, the DATA= argument is required. To output a data set, the OUT= argument is required.

PROC GKEYMAP NAME=*map-name*
 data-set-argument
 <option(s)>;

PROC GKEYMAP Statement

The PROC GKEYMAP Statement names the key map or device map to be created or output as a data set. If the procedure creates a key map or a device map, it identifies the data set that is used as input. If it outputs a map, it identifies the data set to which the map is written.

Syntax

PROC GKEYMAP NAME=*map-name*
 data-set-argument
 <option(s)>;

data-set-argument must be one or more of the following:

DATA=*keymap-data-set*

OUT=*output-data-set*

option(s) can be one or more of the following:

DEVICE=*device-name*

DEVMAP | KEYMAP

TYPE=MAP11 | MAP1N

MULTFONT

Required Arguments

NAME=*map-name*
identifies the map that is to be created or converted to a SAS data set. Key maps are stored as *map-name*.KEYMAP, and device maps are stored as *map-name*.DEVMAP. The value of the KEYMAP or DEVMAP option determines the type of map and the

extension added to *map-name*. It is possible to use the same *map-name* value for both a key map and a device map.

If you create a key map or device map, the map is stored as an entry in the catalog GFONT*n*.FONTS where *n* is a number from 1 to 9, and you must use a LIBNAME statement to specify a libref for GFONT*n*. See "About the Libref GFONT0" on page 677 for details.

If you specify an existing key map or device map, SAS/GRAPH software searches for the map using the same search path that it uses to search for fonts. See "Font Locations" on page 127 for details.

Featured in: Example 1 on page 726

DATA=*keymap-data-set*

identifies the input data set for the GKEYMAP procedure. Used only when you are creating a key map or device map.

See also: "SAS Data Sets" on page 25 and "About the GKEYMAP Data Set" on page 723

Featured in: Example 1 on page 726

OUT=*output-data-set*

identifies the output data set to which the data from a key map or device map are to be written. Used only when you output an existing key map or device map as a SAS data set.

Featured in: Example 1 on page 726

Options

You can specify as many options as you want and list them in any order.

DEVICE=*device-name*

specifies the device driver that a device map is associated with, where *device-name* is the name of an entry in a device catalog. DEVICE= is not required when creating a device map, but it can be used if you want to limit the use of the device map to one particular driver. If you do not use DEVICE=, the device map can be used with any device. DEVICE= is valid only if you are creating a device map.

DEVMAP | KEYMAP

specifies whether you are working with a device map or a key map. The default is KEYMAP unless you use an option that can be used only with DEVMAP. This option also specifies the type of map you are outputting as a data set.

Featured in: Example 1 on page 726

TYPE=MAP11 | MAP1N

specifies whether you are mapping characters in a device map one-to-one or one-to-many. If you specify TYPE=MAP11 (the default), each character in a graphics text string is mapped to only one character on the output device. If you specify TYPE=MAP1N, a single character in a graphics text string can be mapped to multiple characters on the output device. For example, if two characters have to be sent to the graphics output device to display a single hardware character, specify TYPE=MAP1N. Specify TYPE=MAP1N only when you create a device map.

MULTFONT

specifies that an alternate hardware character set is required to display one or more characters in the device map. Specify the MULTFONT option only when you create a device map.

Creating a Data Set from an Existing Key Map or Device Map

To generate a data set from an existing key map or device map, follow these steps:

1 Specify the name of the key map or device map with the NAME= argument. If the map is user generated, you must first submit a LIBNAME statement to associate the libref GFONT0 with the location where the map is stored, and NAME= must specify the name that was specified for the key map or device map when it was created. If the map is an Institute-supplied map, it is located in the catalog SASHELP.FONTS, and you do not need to submit a LIBNAME statement to access it.

2 In the OUT= argument, specify the name of the data set to which the data are to be written. By default, the data set is written to the temporary library WORK.

3 Use the DEVMAP option if a device map is selected.

4 Optionally, use the PRINT procedure to display the newly created data set (most values will be unprintable, so you should use a $HEX2. format for the FROM and TO variables).

Creating and Using Key Maps and Device Maps

To create and use a key map or device map, follow these steps:

1 Submit a LIBNAME statement that associates the libref GFONT0 with the location where your map is to be stored.

2 Create a data set that contains the mapping information you need. You can use a DATA step to create all of the mapping information for the key map or device map, or you can create a data set from an existing key map or device map, then update that data set with the mappings that you need. This process is illustrated in Example 1 on page 726.

3 Use the GKEYMAP procedure to create the key map or device map, using as input the data set that contains the mapping information. The GKEYMAP procedure stores the map in the catalog GFONT0.FONTS.

4 Use the KEYMAP= or DEVMAP= option in a GOPTIONS statement to assign the key map or device map in your SAS session. The specified map is used automatically in your SAS/GRAPH programs. (The device map is used only when you use a hardware character set.)

Examples

Example 1: Modifying a Key Map

Procedure features:
GKEYMAP options:

DATA=
KEYMAP
NAME=
OUT=

Other features:
DATA step
GOPTIONS procedure
GOPTIONS statement
LIBNAME statement

SORT procedure
Sample library member: GR18N01

This example shows how to change multiple characters in an existing key map. It assumes that the national characters ß and ã are not on your keyboard, so you want to create a key map that provides them.

To provide the ß character, this example's key map converts the @ character into the SAS/GRAPH internal encoding for ('B8'x). Whenever the @ character is typed in text that is displayed with a software font, the character ß is drawn instead. In this case, the replacement character uses the text position that would have been used by the typed character.

Note: Once you have modified your key map so that @ is mapped to ß, you can no longer generate @ in a software font from your keyboard when the key map is in effect. △

To provide the ã character, which is not on the keyboard or in the ICE table, this example's key map converts the asterisk (*) into the SAS/GRAPH internal encoding for the accent character 'D5'x (a tilde). In this case, when the character * is typed, the resulting tilde does not take up a text position but is backspaced and used as an accent over the character preceding it in the text. To create the ã character, therefore, the text must contain the two characters a*.

Note: The example updates the current key map rather than creating a new key map so that all of the other character mapping in the key map remains in effect. △

Assign the libref and set the graphics environment. LIBNAME associates the libref GFONT0 with the location of the SAS data library where your device maps and key maps are stored.

```
libname gfont0 'SAS-data-library';
goptions reset=global gunit=pct border cback=white
        colors=(black blue green red)
        ftext=swiss ftitle=swissb htext=6;
```

Determine the name of the current key map. The SAS log in Output 18.1 on page 729 shows that the keymap name is DEFAULT.

```
proc goptions
   option=keymap;
run;
```

Copy the DEFAULT key map to a temporary SAS data set. NAME= specifies the DEFAULT key map as input to the procedure. OUT= specifies the data set TEMP, which is created from the specified key map.

```
proc gkeymap name=default
   out=temp;
run;
```

Create data set NEW. NEW will be used to create the key map for the character conversions. Values for the FROM variable are the keyboard characters to be converted. Values for the TO variable are hexadecimal codes from the SAS ICE table. OUTPUT is required to write a separate observation for each character to be mapped.

```
data new;
   from='@';
   to='b8'x;
   output;
   from='*';
   to='d5'x;
   output;
run;
```

Sort data set NEW and update data set TEMP with the mapping information. The data set NEW must be sorted by the FROM variable before its observations can be used to update data set TEMP.

```
proc sort data=new;
   by from;
data temp;
   update temp new;
   by from;
run;
```

Create a new key map from the modified data set. NAME= assigns a name to the new key map. DATA= specifies the data set TEMP as input to the procedure. KEYMAP specifies that the map being generated is a key map (the default).

```
proc gkeymap name=mykeymap
             data=temp
             keymap;
run;
```

Specify the new key map in a GOPTIONS statement. KEYMAP= specifies the name of the new key map so that when the characters @ and a* are specified in TITLE statements, the characters ß and ã are displayed in the output.

```
goptions keymap=mykeymap;
```

Print two titles with the special characters. The character @ is typed where the character ß should print, and the character * is typed after the character it will accent.

```
title1 'Kaiserstra@e';
title2 'Sa*o Paulo';
footnote j=r 'GR18N01 ';
proc gslide;
run;
quit;.
'
```

Output 18.1   Log from GOPTIONS Procedure

```
                SAS/GRAPH software options and parameters
                   (executing in DMS Process environment)
KEYMAP=DEFAULT                Input character map for hardware and software
                             text
```

CHAPTER

19

The GMAP Procedure

Overview

The GMAP procedure produces two-dimensional (choropleth) or three-dimensional (block, prism, and surface) color maps that show variations of a variable value with respect to an area. A wide assortment of geographic maps are available with SAS/GRAPH software, and you also can create your own geographic or spatial maps.
Use the GMAP procedure to

□ summarize data that vary by physical area

□ show trends and variations of data between geographic areas

□ highlight regional differences or extremes

□ produce maps.

About Block Maps

Block maps display a block at the approximate center of each map area to convey information about response variable values. The height of each block represents a response level. The height of the blocks is not directly proportional to the value of the response variable. Instead, the block heights increase in order of the response levels.

Figure 19.1 on page 732 shows a simple block map of hazardous waste sites that are installed in each state. Each state is a midpoint. The number of sites in each state (the response value) is represented by the height of the block.

Figure 19.1   Block Map (GR19N01)

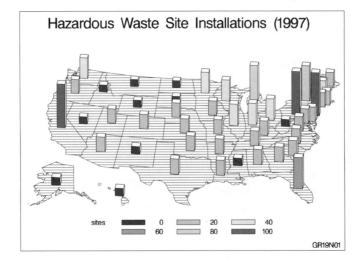

The program for this map is in Example 1 on page 771. For more information on producing block maps, see "BLOCK Statement" on page 742.

About Choropleth Maps

Two-dimensional (choropleth) maps indicate levels of magnitude or response levels of the corresponding response variable by filling map areas with different colors and patterns.

Figure 19.2 on page 733 shows a choropleth map of hazardous waste sites that are installed in each state. Each state is a midpoint. The number of sites in each state (the response value) is represented by the pattern that is assigned to the state.

Figure 19.2 Two-dimensional (Choropleth) Map (GR19N04)

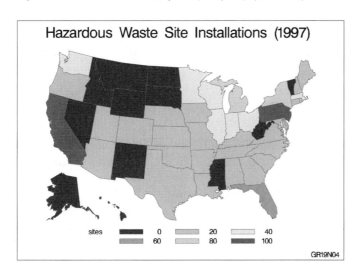

The program for this map is in Example 4 on page 778.

You can also produce a simple choropleth map that shows an outline of a map's areas by specifying your map data set as both the map data set and the response data set in a GMAP statement. For more information on producing choropleth maps, see "CHORO Statement" on page 748.

About Prism Maps

Prism maps use polyhedrons (raised polygons) in the shape of each map area to convey information about response variable values. The height of each polyhedron, or prism, represents an ordinal level of the response variable. Prism heights increase in order of response levels. That is, the lowest prisms correspond to the first level, and the tallest prisms correspond to the last level.

You can alter the perspective of the map by selecting a viewing position (the point in space from which you view the map). You can also change the position of the light source so that the shadowing on the prisms enhances the illusion of height.

Figure 19.3 on page 734 shows a prism map of hazardous waste sites installed in each state. Each state is a midpoint. The number of sites in each state (the response value) is represented by the height of the state.

Figure 19.3 Prism Map (GR19N07)

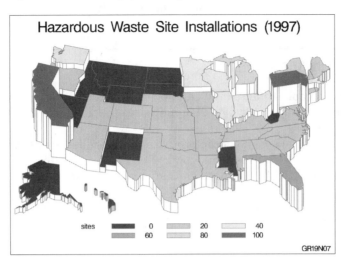

The program for this map is in Example 7 on page 788. For more information on producing prism maps, see "PRISM Statement" on page 753.

About Surface Maps

Surface maps display a spike at the approximate center of each map area to convey information about response variable values. The height of the spike corresponds to the relative value of the response variable, not to the actual value of the response variable. Thus, a spike that represents a value of 100 may not be exactly 10 times higher than a spike that represents a value of 10. Map area boundaries are not drawn.

Surface maps provide no clear map area boundaries and no legend. Thus, surface maps provide a simple way to judge relative trends in the response data but are an inappropriate way to represent specific response values.

Figure 19.4 on page 734 shows a surface map of hazardous waste sites that are installed in each state. Each state is a midpoint. The number of sites in each state (the response value) is represented by the height of the spike.

Figure 19.4 Surface Map (GR19N09)

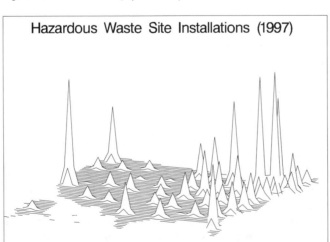

The program for this map is in Example 9 on page 791. For more information on producing surface maps, see "SURFACE Statement" on page 759.

Concepts

The GMAP procedure requires a map data set and a response data set. These two data sets must contain the required variables or the procedure stops with an error message. You can use the same data set as both the map data set and the response data set, as long as the requirements are met. If a different data set is used as the response data set, it must contain an ID variable that is identical to the ID variable in the map data set.

About Map Data Sets

A *map data set* is a SAS data set that contains coordinates that define the boundaries of map areas, such as states or counties. A map data set must contain at least these variables:

- □ a numeric variable named X that contains the horizontal coordinates of the boundary points. The value of this variable could be either projected or unprojected. If unprojected, X represents longitude.

- □ a numeric variable named Y that contains the vertical coordinates of the boundary points. The value of this variable could be either projected or unprojected. If unprojected, Y represents latitude.

- □ one or more variables that uniquely identify the areas in the map. Map area identification variables can be either character or numeric and are indicated in the ID statement.

The X and Y variable values in the map data set do not have to be in any specific units because they are rescaled by the GMAP procedure based on the minimum and maximum values in the data set. The minimum X and Y values are in the lower-left corner of the map, and the maximum X and Y values are in the upper-right corner.

Map data sets in which the X and Y variables contain longitude and latitude should be projected before you use them with PROC GMAP. See Chapter 23, "The GPROJECT Procedure," on page 873 for details.

Optionally, the map data set also can contain a variable named SEGMENT to identify map areas that comprise noncontiguous polygons. Each unique value of the SEGMENT variable within a single map area defines a distinct polygon. If the SEGMENT variable is not present, each map area is drawn as a separate closed polygon that indicates a single segment.

The observations for each segment of a map area in the map data set must occur in the order in which the points are to be joined. The GMAP procedure forms map area outlines by connecting the boundary points of each segment in the order in which they appear in the data set, eventually joining the last point to the first point to complete the polygon.

Any variables in the map data set other than the ones mentioned above are ignored for the purpose of determining map boundaries.

About SAS/GRAPH Map Data Sets

In addition to the variables described in "About Map Data Sets" on page 735, the SAS/GRAPH map data sets may also contain the following variables:

□ a numeric variable named LONG containing the unprojected longitude in radians of the boundary points.

□ a numeric variable named LAT containing the unprojected latitude in radians of the boundary points.

The GMAP procedure uses the values of the X and Y variables to draw the map. Therefore, if you want to produce an unprojected map by using the values in LONG and LAT, you would have to rename LONG and LAT to X and Y first.

SAS/GRAPH includes a number of predefined map data sets. These data sets are described in "SAS/GRAPH Map Data Sets" on page 761.

Map Data Sets Containing X, Y, LONG, and LAT

Most Institute-supplied map data sets contain four coordinate variables (X, Y, LONG, and LAT). In this case, X and Y are always projected values that will be used by the GRAPH procedures (by default). If you need to use the unprojected values that are contained in the LONG and LAT variables, you will need to rename the LONG and LAT variables to X and Y since the GMAP procedure automatically uses X and Y. See "Input Map Data Sets that Contain Both Projected and Unprojected Values" on page 875 for more details.

Map Data Sets Containing Only X and Y

The Institute-supplied map data sets that contain X and Y variables (and no LONG and LAT variables), are usually projected maps. However, there are a few map data sets for the US and Canada that contain X and Y values that are unprojected longitude and latitude. In this case, you will need to use the GPROJECT procedure to project the map (see Chapter 23, "The GPROJECT Procedure," on page 873).

Note: You can determine whether a SAS map data set is projected or unprojected by looking at the description of each variable that is displayed when you use the CONTENTS procedure or by browsing the MAPS.METAMAPS data set. △

Specialty Map Data Sets

There are several map data sets available with SAS/GRAPH that allow you to easily label maps:

MAPS.USCENTER
  contains the X and Y coordinates of the visual center of each state in the U.S. and Washington, D.C., as well as points in the ocean for states that are too small to contain a label. You can use MAPS.USCENTER with the MAPS.US, MAPS.USCOUNTY, MAPS.COUNTIES, and MAPS.COUNTY data sets.

MAPS.USCITY
  contains the X and Y coordinates of selected cities in the U.S. Many city names occur in more than one state, so you may have to subset by state to avoid duplication. You can use MAPS.USCITY with the MAPS.US, MAPS.USCOUNTY, MAPS.COUNTIES, and MAPS.COUNTY data sets.

MAPS.CANCENS
  contains the names of the Canadian census divisions. You can use MAPS.CANCENS with the MAPS.CANADA and MAPS.CANADA3 data sets.

See the MAPS.METAMAPS data set for details on each of the Institute-supplied map data sets.

About Response Data Sets

A *response data set* is a SAS data set that contains

☐ one or more response variables that contain data values that are associated with map areas. Each value of the response variable is associated with a map area in the map data set.

☐ identification variables that identify the map area to which a response value belongs. These variables must be the same as those that are contained in the map data set.

The response data set can contain other variables in addition to these required variables.

The values of the map area identification variables in the response data set determine the map areas to be included on the map unless you use the ALL option in the PROC GMAP statement. That is, unless you use ALL in the PROC GMAP statement, only the map areas with response values are shown on the map. As a result, you do not need to subset your map data set if you are mapping only a small section of the map. However, if you map the same small section frequently, create a subset of the map data set for efficiency.

For choropleth, block, and prism maps, the response variables can be either character or numeric. For surface maps, the response variables must be numeric with only positive values.

About Response Variables

The GMAP procedure can produce block, choropleth, and prism maps for both numeric and character response variables. Numeric variables fall into two categories: discrete and continuous.

☐ *Discrete variables* contain a finite number of specific numeric values that are to be represented on the map. For example, a variable that contains only the values 1989 or 1990 is a discrete variable.

☐ *Continuous variables* contain a range of numeric values that are to be represented on the map. For example, a variable that contains any real value between 0 and 100 is a continuous variable.

Numeric response variables are always treated as continuous variables unless the DISCRETE option is used in the action statement.

About Response Levels

Response levels are the values that identify categories of data on the graph. The categories that are shown on the graph are based on the values of the response variable. Based on the type of the response variable, a response level can represent these values:

☐ a specific character value. If the response variable is character type, the GMAP procedure treats each unique value of the variable as a response level. For example, if the response variable contains the names of ten regions, each region will be a response level, resulting in ten response levels.

The exception to this is that the MIDPOINTS= option chooses specific response level values. Any response variable values that do not match one of the specified response level values are ignored. For example, if the response variable contains the names of ten regions and you specify these midpoints, only the observations for **Midwest**, **Northeast**, and **Northwest** are included on the map:

```
midpoints='Midwest' 'Northeast' 'Northwest'
```

□ a range of numeric values. If the response variable is numeric, the GMAP procedure determines the number of response levels for the response variable. Each response level then represents the median of a range of values.

These options are exceptions to this:

□ The LEVELS= option specifies the number of response levels to be used on the map.

□ The DISCRETE option causes the numeric variable to be treated as a discrete variable.

□ The MIDPOINTS= option chooses specific response level values as medians of the value ranges.

If the response variable values are continuous, the GMAP procedure assigns response level intervals automatically unless you specify otherwise. The response levels represent a range of values rather than a single value.

□ a specific numeric value. If the response variable is numeric and you use the DISCRETE option, the GMAP procedure treats the variable much the same way as it treats a character response variable. That is, the procedure creates a response level for each unique value of the response variable. If you use DISCRETE with a numeric response variable that has an associated format, each formatted value is represented by a different response level. Formatted values are truncated to 16 characters.

The BLOCK, CHORO, and PRISM statements assign patterns to response levels. In CHORO and PRISM maps, response levels are shown as map areas. However, in BLOCK maps, response levels are shown as blocks. The default fill pattern for the response level is solid.

PATTERN statements can define the fill patterns and colors for both blocks and map areas. PATTERN definitions that define valid block patterns are applied to the blocks (response levels), and PATTERN definitions that define valid map patterns are applied to map areas.

See "PATTERN Statement" on page 211 for more information on fill pattern values and default pattern rotation.

About Identification Variables

Identification (ID) variables are common to both the map data set and the response data set. They identify the map areas (for example, counties, states, or provinces) that make up the map. A *unit area* or *map area* is a group of observations with the same ID value. The GMAP procedure matches the value of the response variables for each map area in the response data set to the corresponding map area in the map data set to create the output graphs.

Displaying Map Areas and Response Data

Whether the GMAP procedure draws a map area and whether it displays patterns for response values depends on the contents of the response data set and on the ALL and MISSING options. describes the conditions under which the procedure does or does not display map areas and response data.

If the response data set...	And if...	Then the procedure...
includes the map area	the map area has a response value	draws the map area and displays the response data
includes the map area	the map area has no response value (that is, the value is missing)	draws the map area but leaves it empty
includes the map area	the map area has no response value and the MISSING option is used in the map statement	draws the map area and displays a response level for the missing value
does not include the map area	the ALL option is used in the PROC GMAP statement	draws the map area but leaves it empty
does not include the map area	the ALL option is not used	does not draw the map area

Summary of Use

To use the GMAP procedure, you must do the following:

1 If necessary, issue a LIBNAME statement for the SAS data library that contains the map data set that you want to display.

2 Determine what processing needs to be done to the map data set before it is displayed. Use the GPROJECT, GREDUCE, and GREMOVE procedures or a DATA step to perform the necessary processing.

3 Issue a LIBNAME statement for the SAS data set that contains the response data set, or use a DATA step to create a response data set.

4 Use the PROC GMAP statement to identify the map and response data sets.

5 Use the ID statement to name the identification variable(s).

6 Use a BLOCK, CHORO, PRISM, or SURFACE statement to identify the response variable and generate the map.

Procedure Syntax

Requirements: One ID statement and at least one CHORO, BLOCK, PRISM, or SURFACE statement are required.

Global statements: FOOTNOTE, LEGEND, PATTERN, TITLE

Reminder: The procedure can include the BY, FORMAT, LABEL, and WHERE statements as well as the SAS/GRAPH NOTE statement.

Supports: RUN-group processing Output Delivery System (ODS)

PROC GMAP MAP=*map-data-set*
    <DATA=*response-data-set*>
    <ALL>
    <ANNOTATE=*Annotate-data-set*>
    <GOUT=<*libref.*>*output-catalog*>
    <IMAGEMAP=*output-data-set*>;

    ID*id-variable(s)*;
        BLOCK *response-variable(s)* </ *option(s)*>;
        CHORO *response-variable(s)* </ *option(s)*>;

PRISM *response-variable(s)</ option(s)>*; **SURFACE** *response-variable(s) </ option(s)>*;

PROC GMAP Statement

Identifies the map data set and the response data set that contains the variables associated with the map. Optionally causes the procedure to display all map areas and specifies annotation and an output catalog.

Requirements: Both a map data set and a response data set are required.

PROC GMAP MAP=*map-data-set*
  <DATA=*response-data-set*>
  <ALL>
  <ANNOTATE=*Annotate-data-set*>
  <GOUT=<*libref.*>*output-catalog*>
  <IMAGEMAP=*output-data-set*>;

Required Arguments

MAP=*map-data-set*
  names a SAS map data set that contains the Cartesian coordinates for the boundary points of each map area. The map data set also must contain the same identification variable or variables as the response data set.

  See also: "About Map Data Sets" on page 735

Options

  PROC GMAP statement options affect all of the graphs that are produced by the procedure.

ALL
  specifies that all maps generated by the procedure should include every map area from the map data set, even if the response data set does not include an observation for the map area. When ALL is used, the map areas that are not in the response data set are empty (no pattern fill) and are outlined in the foreground color. To change the outline color of an empty area, use the CEMPTY= option in the MAP statement.

  If you omit this option, the GMAP procedure does not draw those map areas in the map data set that have no corresponding observations in the response data set. This is the default behavior.

  When you use the ALL option with BY-group processing, the maps that are generated for each BY group include every map area from the map data set.

  See also: "Displaying Map Areas and Response Data" on page 738

ANNOTATE=*Annotate-data-set*
ANNO=*Annotate-data-set*
  specifies a data set to annotate all of the maps that are produced by the GMAP procedure. To annotate individual maps, use ANNOTATE= in the action statement.

  See also: Chapter 10, "The Annotate Data Set," on page 403

DATA=*response-data-set*
identifies the SAS data set that contains the response values that are evaluated and represented on the map. By default, the procedure uses the most recently created SAS data set.

See also: "About Response Data Sets" on page 737 and "SAS Data Sets" on page 25

GOUT=*<libref.>output-catalog*
specifies the SAS catalog in which to save the graphics output that is produced by the GMAP procedure. If you omit the libref, SAS/GRAPH looks for the catalog in the temporary library called WORK and creates the catalog if it does not exist.

See also: "Storing Graphics Output in SAS Catalogs" on page 49

IMAGEMAP=*output-data-set*
creates a SAS data set that contains information about the graph and about areas in the graph. This information includes the shape and coordinates of the areas, and is used to build an HTML file that links the graph areas to other files or images. This linking provides drill-down functionality on the graph. The Imagemap data set also contains the information that is stored in the variables referenced by the HTML= and HTML_LEGEND= options. Therefore, in order to use IMAGEMAP= to create an HTML file, you must also use the HTML= option or the HTML_LEGEND= option or both.

See also: "Customizing Web Pages for Drill-down Graphs" on page 100

ID Statement

Identifies the variable or variables in both the map data set and the response data set that define map areas.

Requirements: At least one *id-variable* is required.

ID *id-variable(s)*;

Required Arguments

id-variable(s)
identifies one or more variables in the input data sets that define map areas. Every variable that is listed in the ID statement must appear in both the map and response data sets. *Id-variable* can be either numeric or character and should have the same name, type, and length in both the response and map data sets.

See also: "About Identification Variables" on page 738

Featured in: Example 1 on page 771, Example 3 on page 775 and Example 4 on page 778

BLOCK Statement

Creates three-dimensional block maps on which levels of magnitude of the specified response variables are represented by blocks of varying height, pattern, and color.

Requirements: At least one response variable is required. The ID statement must be used in conjunction with the BLOCK statement.

Global statements: FOOTNOTE, LEGEND, PATTERN, TITLE

Description

The BLOCK statement specifies the variable or variables that contain the data that are represented on the map by blocks of varying height, pattern, and color. This statement automatically

- □ determines the midpoints
- □ scales the blocks
- □ assigns patterns to the block faces and map areas. (See "About Block Maps and Patterns" on page 748 for more information.)

You can use statement options to enhance the appearance of the map. For example, you can specify the width of the blocks, the outline colors for the blocks and the map areas, and the angle of view. Other statement options control the response levels.

In addition, you can use global statements to modify the block patterns, the map patterns, and the legend, as well as to add titles and footnotes to the map. You can also use an Annotate data set to enhance the map.

BLOCK*response-variable(s) </ option(s)>*;

option(s) can be one or more options from any or all of the following categories:

- □ appearance options:

  ANNOTATE=*Annotate-data-set*

  BLOCKSIZE=*size*

  CBLKOUT=*block-outline-color* I SAME

  CEMPTY=*empty-area-outline-color*

  COUTLINE=*nonempty-area-outline-color* I SAME

  SHAPE=*3D-block-shape*

  XSIZE=*map-width <units>*

  YSIZE=*map-height <units>*

  XVIEW=*x*

  YVIEW=*y*

  ZVIEW=*z*

- □ mapping options:

  AREA=*n*

  DISCRETE

  LEVELS=*number-of-response-levels*

  MIDPOINTS=*value-list*

  MISSING

- □ legend options:

      CTEXT=*text-color*

      LEGEND=LEGEND<1...99>

      NOLEGEND

□ description options:

      DESCRIPTION='*entry-description*'

      NAME='*entry-name*'

□ ODS options

      HTML=*variable*

      HTML_LEGEND=*variable*

Required Arguments

response-variable(s)

    specifies one or more variables in the response data set that contains response values that are represented on the map. Each response variable produces a separate map. All variables must be in the input data set. Separate multiple response variables with blanks.

    Blocks are not drawn for missing values for the response variable unless you use the MISSING option in the BLOCK statement.

See also: "About Response Variables" on page 737

Options

    Options in a BLOCK statement affect all of the maps that are produced by that statement. You can specify as many options as you want and list them in any order.

ANNOTATE=*Annotate-data-set*
ANNO=*Annotate-data-set*

    specifies a data set to annotate maps that are produced by the BLOCK statement.

    Note: Annotate coordinate systems 1, 2, 7, and 8 are not valid with block maps. △

    See also: Chapter 10, "The Annotate Data Set," on page 403

AREA=*n*

    specifies that a different map pattern be used for the surface of each map area or group of map areas on the map. The value of *n* indicates which variable in the ID statement determines the groups that are distinguished by a surface pattern. If your ID statement has only one map area identification variable, use AREA=1 to indicate that each map area surface uses a different pattern. If you have more than one variable in your ID statement, use *n* to indicate the position of the variable that defines groups that will share a pattern. When you use AREA=, the map data set should be sorted in order of the variables in the ID statement.

    By default, AREA= fills map areas by rotating the default hatch patterns through the colors list, beginning with the M2N0 pattern. Unless specified otherwise, the outline color is the first color in the colors list. If the V6COMP graphics option or a PATTERN statement is specified, then the value of COUTLINE= defaults to SAME.

    You can specify pattern fills and/or colors with PATTERN statements that specify map/plot patterns. A separate PATTERN definition is needed for each specified area. For more information about default pattern behavior or pattern specifications, see "PATTERN Statement" on page 211.

    Featured in: Example 3 on page 775

BLOCKSIZE=*size*

specifies the width of the blocks. The unit for *size* is the character cell width for the selected output device. By default, BLOCKSIZE=2.

Featured in: Example 5 on page 779

CBLKOUT=*block-outline-color* **| SAME**

outlines all blocks in the specified color. SAME specifies that the outline color of a block or a block segment or a legend value is the same as the interior pattern color.

The default outline color depends on the PATTERN statement:

☐ If no PATTERN statements are specified, the default outline color is the foreground color (the first color in the colors list).

☐ If a PATTERN statement or the V6COMP graphics option is specified, the default is CBLKOUT=SAME.

CBLKOUT= is not valid when SHAPE=CYLINDER.

Note: If you specify empty block patterns, (VALUE=EMPTY in a PATTERN statement) you should not change the outline color from the default value, SAME, to a single color. Otherwise all the outlines will be one color and you will not be able to distinguish between the empty areas. △

Featured in: Example 1 on page 771 and Example 3 on page 775

CEMPTY=*empty-area-outline-color*

outlines empty map areas in the specified color. This option affects only map areas that are empty. Empty map areas are generated in block maps only when a map area is omitted from the response data set and the ALL option is included in the PROC GMAP statement.

The default outline color is the same as the default COUTLINE= color.

See also: ALL on page 740 and "Displaying Map Areas and Response Data" on page 738

COUTLINE=*nonempty-area-outline-color* **| SAME**

outlines non-empty map areas in the specified color. SAME specifies that the outline color of a map area is the same as the interior pattern color.

The default outline color depends on the PATTERN statement:

☐ If no PATTERN statement is specified, the default outline color is the foreground color (the first color in the colors list).

☐ If a PATTERN statement or the V6COMP graphics option is specified, the default is COUTLINE=SAME.

Note: If you specify empty map patterns, (VALUE=MEMPTY in a PATTERN statement) you should not change the outline color from the default value, SAME, to a single color. Otherwise all the outlines will be one color and you will not be able to distinguish between the empty areas. △

Featured in: Example 3 on page 775

CTEXT=*text-color*

specifies a color for the text in the legend. If you omit the CTEXT= option, a color specification is searched for in this order:

1 the CTEXT= option in a GOPTIONS statement

2 the default, the first color in the colors list.

The CTEXT= color specification is overridden if you also use the COLOR= suboption of a LABEL= or VALUE= option in a LEGEND definition that is assigned to the map legend. The COLOR= suboption determines the color of the legend label or the color of the legend value descriptions, respectively.

DESCRIPTION='*entry-description*'
DES='*entry-description*'

specifies the description of the catalog entry for the map. The maximum length for *entry-description* is 40 characters. The description does not appear on the map. By default, the GMAP procedure assigns a description of the form BLOCK MAP OF *variable*, where *variable* is the name of the map variable.

Featured in: Example 5 on page 779

DISCRETE

treats a numeric response variable as a discrete variable rather than as a continuous variable. When you use DISCRETE, the response variable values are not grouped into ranges; instead, the GMAP procedure uses a separate response level (block height, pattern, and color) for each different value of the formatted response variable. The LEVELS= option is ignored when you use the DISCRETE option.

Use this option if your numeric response variable is assigned a user-written format.

Note: If the data do not contain a value in a particular range of the format, that formatted range is not displayed in the legend. △

Featured in: Example 3 on page 775 and Example 5 on page 779 (with the CHORO statement)

HTML=ized variable*

identifies the variable in the input data set whose values create links in the HTML file created by the ODS HTML statement. These links are associated with an area of the chart and point to the data or graph you wish to display when the user drills down on the area.

HTML_LEGEND=variable*

identifies the variable in the input data set whose values create links in the HTML file created by the ODS HTML statement. These links are associated with a legend value and point to the data or graph you wish to display when the user drills down on the value.

LEGEND=LEGEND<1...99>

assigns the specified LEGEND definition to the map legend. LEGEND= is ignored if the specified LEGEND definition is not currently in effect. In the GMAP procedure, the BLOCK statement produces a legend unless you use the NOLEGEND option. If you use the SHAPE= option in a LEGEND statement, only the value BAR is valid.

See also: "LEGEND Statement" on page 187

Featured in: Example 2 on page 773 and Example 5 on page 779

LEVELS=number-of-response-levels*

specifies the number of response levels that are to be graphed when the response variables are continuous. Each level is assigned a different block height, pattern, and color combination.

If you do not use the LEVELS= option or the DISCRETE option, the GMAP procedure determines the number of response levels that use the formula FLOOR(1+3.3 log(N)), where N is the number of unique map area identification variable values.

The LEVELS= option is ignored when you use the DISCRETE option.

Featured in: Example 2 on page 773

MIDPOINTS=*value-list*

specifies the response levels for the range of response values that are represented by each level (block height, pattern, and color combination).

For numeric response variables, value-list is either an explicit list of values or a starting and an ending value with an interval increment, or a combination of both forms:

n <...n>

n TO *n* <BY *increment*>

n <...n > TO *n* <BY *increment*> <*n<...n* >>

By default the increment value is 1. You can specify discrete numeric values in any order. In all forms, *n* can be separated by blanks or commas. For example,

```
midpoints=(2 4 6)
midpoints=(2,4,6)
midpoints=(2 to 10 by 2)
```

If a numeric variable has an associated format, the specified values must be the *unformatted* values. *For character response variables, value-list* is a list of unique character values enclosed in quotes and separated by blanks:

'value-1' <...'value-n'>

The values are character strings that are enclosed in single quotation marks and separated by blanks. For example,

```
midpoints='Midwest' 'Northeast' 'Northwest'
```

Specify the values in any order. If a character variable has an associated format, the specified values must be the *formatted* values.

You can selectively exclude some response variable values from the map, as shown here:

```
midpoints='Midwest'
```

Only those observations for which the response variable exactly matches one of the values listed in the MIDPOINTS= option are shown on the map. As a result, observations may be excluded inadvertently if values in the list are misspelled or if the case does not match exactly.

Featured in: Example 5 on page 779

MISSING

accepts a missing value as a valid level for the response variable.

See also: "Displaying Map Areas and Response Data" on page 738

NAME=*'entry-name'*

specifies the name of the catalog entry for the map. The maximum length for *entry-name* is 8 characters. The default name is GMAP. If the specified name duplicates the name of an existing entry, SAS/GRAPH software adds a number to the duplicate name to create a unique name, for example, GMAP1.

Featured in: Example 5 on page 779

NOLEGEND

suppresses the legend.

SHAPE=*3D-block-shape*

specifies the shape of the blocks. Use this option to enhance the look of the block shape, or to specify a different shape. *3D-block-shape* can be one of the following:

- □ BLOCK
- □ CYLINDER
- □ HEXAGON
- □ PRISM
- □ STAR

The CBLKOUT= option is not valid when SHAPE=CYLINDER.

Featured in: Example 2 on page 584 Example 3 on page 586 Example 7 on page 596

XSIZE=*map-width <units>*
YSIZE=*map-height <units>*

specify the physical dimensions of the map to be drawn, where *n* is the number of units. By default, the map uses the entire procedure output area.

Valid *units* are CM (centimeters), IN (inches), or PCT (percentage of the graphics output area). By default, the unit is character cells (CELLS).

If you specify values for *n* that are greater than the dimensions of the procedure output area, the map is drawn using the default size.

XVIEW=*x*
YVIEW=*y*
ZVIEW=*z*

specify coordinates of the viewing position in the reference coordinate system. In this system, the four corners of the map lie on the X-Y plane at coordinates (0,0,0), (0,1,0), (1,1,0), and (1,0,0). No axes are actually drawn on the maps that are produced by PROC GMAP, but imagine that the maps are drawn in an X-Y plane.

Your viewing position cannot coincide with the viewing reference point at coordinates (0.5,0.5,0), the center of the map. The value for *z* cannot be negative.

If you omit the XVIEW=, YVIEW=, and ZVIEW= options, the default coordinates are (0.5,–2,3). This viewing position is well above and to the south of the center of the map. Specify one, two, or all three of the view coordinates; any that you do not explicitly specify are assigned the default values.

Featured in: Example 2 on page 773

Figure 19.5 on page 747 shows the position of the viewing reference point, as well as the default viewing position.

Figure 19.5 Viewing Position and Viewing Reference Point

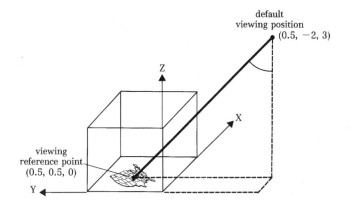

About Block Maps and Patterns

Block maps are different from other maps in that they display two different types of areas that use patterns:

- □ the blocks themselves, which represent the response levels
- □ the map areas from which the blocks rise.

By default, the blocks use solid pattern fills and the map areas use a hatch pattern of slanting lines. The map areas in block maps are the *only* map areas that by default do not use solid fills. The map areas and their outlines use the first color in the colors list regardless of whether the list is the device's default colors list or one specified with the COLORS= option in a GOPTIONS statement.

The BLOCK statement has the following options that explicitly control the outline colors used by the blocks and the map areas.

- □ CBLKOUT=
- □ CEMPTY=
- □ COUTLINE=

In addition the AREA= option controls how the map areas are patterned.

When you use PATTERN statements to define the patterns for the map, you must be sure to specify the correct type of pattern for the area. The blocks use bar/block patterns and the map areas use map/plot patterns. See "PATTERN Statement" on page 211 for more information on specifying patterns.

Note: If you specify only one PATTERN statement and include only the COLOR= option, that color will be used for both the blocks and the map areas. For example, this statement makes the blocks solid blue and the map areas blue hatch. △

```
pattern1 color=blue;
```

CHORO Statement

Creates two-dimensional maps in which values of the specified response variables are represented by varying patterns and colors.

Requirements: At least one response variable is required. You must use the ID statement in conjunction with the CHORO statement.

Global statements: FOOTNOTE, LEGEND, PATTERN, TITLE

Description

The CHORO statement specifies the variable or variables that contain the data represented on the map by patterns that fill the map areas. This statement automatically

- □ determines the midpoints
- □ assigns patterns to the map areas.

You can use statement options to enhance the appearance of the map, for example, by selecting the colors and patterns that fill the map areas. Other statement options control the selection of ranges for the response variable.

In addition, you can use global statements to modify the map area patterns and legend, as well as add titles and footnotes to the map. You can also use an Annotate data set to enhance the map.

CHORO*response-variable(s) </ option(s)>;*

option(s) can be one or more options from any or all of the following categories:

□ appearance options:

ANNOTATE=*Annotate-data-set*

CEMPTY=*empty-area-outline-color*

COUTLINE=*nonempty-area-outline-color* | SAME

XSIZE=*map-width <units>*

YSIZE=*map-height <units>*

□ mapping options:

DISCRETE

LEVELS=*number-of-response-levels*

MIDPOINTS=*value-list*

MISSING

□ legend options:

CTEXT=*text-color*

LEGEND=LEGEND<1...99>

NOLEGEND

□ description options:

DESCRIPTION='*entry-description*'

NAME='*entry-name*'

□ ODS options

HTML=*variable*

HTML_LEGEND=*variable*

Required Arguments

response-variable(s)

specifies one or more variables in the response data set that contains response values that are represented on the map. Each response variable produces a separate map. All variables must be in the input data set. Separate multiple response variables with blanks.

Missing values for the response variable are not considered valid response values unless you use the MISSING option.

Response variables can be either numeric or character. Numeric response variables with continuous values are grouped into ranges, or response levels. Each response level is assigned a different combination of pattern and color. Character variables and numeric variables (when you use the DISCRETE option) have a different response level for each unique response variable value. Numeric variables are treated as continuous unless you use DISCRETE.

For numeric response variables with continuous values, the MIDPOINTS= or LEVELS= option controls the selection of response level ranges.

See also: "About Response Variables" on page 737

Options

Options in a CHORO statement affect all graphs that are produced by that statement. You can specify as many options as you want and list them in any order.

ANNOTATE=*Annotate-data-set*
ANNO=*Annotate-data-set*
specifies a data set to annotate maps that are produced by the CHORO statement.

See also: Chapter 10, "The Annotate Data Set," on page 403

Featured in: Example 6 on page 786

CEMPTY=*empty-area-outline-color*
outlines empty map areas in the specified color. This option affects the map areas that are empty. Empty map areas are generated in choro maps either

- □ when there is no response value for a map area and the MISSING option is not used, or

- □ when a map area is omitted from the response data set and the ALL option is included in the PROC GMAP statement.

The default outline color is the same as the default COUTLINE= color.

See also: ALL on page 740 and "Displaying Map Areas and Response Data" on page 738

COUTLINE=*nonempty-area-outline-color* **|** **SAME**
outlines non-empty map areas in the specified color. SAME specifies that the outline color of a map area is the same as the interior pattern color.

The default outline color depends on the PATTERN statement:

- □ If no PATTERN statement is specified, the default outline color is the foreground color (the first color in the colors list).

- □ If a PATTERN statement or the V6COMP graphics option is specified, the default is COUTLINE=SAME.

Note: If you specify empty map patterns, (VALUE=MEMPTY in a PATTERN statement) you should not change the outline color from the default value, SAME, to a single color. Otherwise all the outlines will be one color and you will not be able to distinguish between the empty areas. △

Featured in: Example 4 on page 778

CTEXT=*text-color*
specifies a color for the text in the legend. If you omit the CTEXT= option, a color specification is searched for in this order:

1 the CTEXT= option in a GOPTIONS statement

2 the default, the first color in the colors list.

The CTEXT= color specification is overridden if you also use the COLOR= suboption of a LABEL= or VALUE= option in a LEGEND definition that is assigned to the map legend. The COLOR= suboption determines the color of the legend label or the color of the legend value descriptions, respectively.

DESCRIPTION=*'entry-description'*
DES=*'entry-description'*
specifies a description of the catalog entry for the map. The maximum length for *entry-description* is 40 characters. The description does not appear on the map. By default, the GMAP procedure assigns a description of the form CHOROPLETH MAP OF *variable*, where *variable* is the name of the map variable.

Featured in: Example 5 on page 779

DISCRETE

treats a numeric response variable as a discrete variable rather than as a continuous variable. When you use the DISCRETE option, the response variables are not grouped into ranges; instead, the GMAP procedure uses a separate response level (pattern and color combination) for each different value of the formatted response variable. The LEVELS= option is ignored when you use the DISCRETE option.

Use this option if your numeric response variable is assigned a user-written format.

Note: If the data do not contain a value in a particular range of the format, that formatted range is not displayed in the legend. △

Featured in: Example 5 on page 779

HTML=*variable*

identifies the variable in the input data set whose values create links in the HTML file created by the ODS HTML statement. These links are associated with an area of the chart and point to the data or graph you wish to display when the user drills down on the area.

Featured in: Example 5 on page 779

HTML_LEGEND=*variable*

identifies the variable in the input data set whose values create links in the HTML file created by the ODS HTML statement. These links are associated with a legend value and point to the data or graph you wish to display when the user drills down on the value.

Featured in: Example 5 on page 779

LEGEND=LEGEND<1...99>

assigns the specified LEGEND definition to the map legend. LEGEND= is ignored if the specified LEGEND definition is not currently in effect. In the GMAP procedure, the CHORO statement produces a legend unless you use the NOLEGEND option. If you use the SHAPE= option in a LEGEND statement, only the value BAR is valid.

See also: "LEGEND Statement" on page 187

Featured in: Example 2 on page 773

LEVELS=*number-of-response-levels*

specifies the number of response levels to be graphed when the response variables are continuous. Each level is assigned a different combination of color and fill pattern.

If you do not use the LEVELS= option or the DISCRETE option, the GMAP procedure determines the number of response levels that use the formula $FLOOR(1+3.3 \log(N))$, where N is the number of unique map area identification variable values.

The LEVELS= option is ignored when you use the DISCRETE or MIDPOINTS= option.

Featured in: Example 2 on page 773

MIDPOINTS=*value-list*

specifies the response levels for the range of response values that are represented by each level (pattern and color combination).

For numeric response variables, value-list is either an explicit list of values, or a starting and an ending value with an interval increment, or a combination of both forms:

$n <...n>$

n TO n <BY *increment* >

$n <...n>$ TO n <BY *increment* > <$n <...n>$ >

By default the increment value is 1. You can specify discrete numeric values in any order. In all forms, n can be separated by blanks or commas. For example,

```
midpoints=(2 4 6)
midpoints=(2,4,6)
midpoints=(2 to 10 by 2)
```

If a numeric variable has an associated format, the specified values must be the *unformatted* values.

For character response variables, value-list is a list of unique character values enclosed in quotation marks and separated by blanks:

'value-1' <...'value-n'>

The values are character strings enclosed in single quotation marks and separated by blanks. For example,

```
midpoints='Midwest' 'Northeast' 'Northwest'
```

Specify the values in any order. If a character variable has an associated format, the specified values must be the *formatted* values.

You can selectively exclude some response variable values from the map, as shown here:

```
midpoints='Midwest'
```

Only those observations for which the response variable exactly matches one of the values that are listed in the MIDPOINTS= option are shown on the map. As a result, observations may be excluded inadvertently if values in the list are misspelled or if the case does not match exactly.

Featured in: Example 8 on page 790

MISSING

accepts a missing value as a valid level for the response variable.

See also: "Displaying Map Areas and Response Data" on page 738

NAME=*'entry-name'*

specifies the name of the catalog entry for the map. The maximum length for *entry-name* is eight characters. The default name is GMAP. If the specified name duplicates the name of an existing entry, SAS/GRAPH software adds a number to the duplicate name to create a unique entry, for example, GMAP1.

Featured in: Example 5 on page 779

NOLEGEND

suppresses the legend.

Featured in: Example 6 on page 786

XSIZE=*map-width <units>*
YSIZE=*map-height <units>*

specify the physical dimensions of the map that is to be drawn, where *n* is the number of units. By default, the map uses the entire procedure output area.

Valid *units* are CM (centimeters), IN (inches), or PCT (percentage of the graphics output area). By default, the unit is character cells (CELLS).

If you specify values for *n* that are greater than the dimensions of the procedure output area, the map is drawn using the default size.

If you specify either the XSIZE= or YSIZE= option without specifying the other option, the GMAP procedure rescales the dimension for the option that was not specified to retain the original shape of the map.

PRISM Statement

Creates three-dimensional prism maps in which levels of magnitude of the specified response variables are represented by polyhedrons (raised polygons) of varying height, pattern, and color.

Requirements: At least one response variable is required. You must use the ID statement in conjunction with the PRISM statement.

Global statements: FOOTNOTE, LEGEND, PATTERN, TITLE

Description

The PRISM statement specifies the variable or variables that contain the data that are represented on the map by raised map areas. This statement automatically

□ determines the midpoints

□ assigns patterns to the map areas.

You can use statement options to control the ranges of the response values, specify the angle of view, and enhance the appearance of the map.

In addition, you can use global statements to modify the map area patterns and the legend, as well as add titles and footnotes to the map. You can also use an Annotate data set to enhance the map.

For maps that contain intersecting polygons or polygons within polygons, extremely complicated maps, or maps that contain line segments that cross, use the GREDUCE procedure to reduce and simplify the map if necessary.

PRISM *response-variable(s) </ option(s)>*;

option(s) can be one or more options from any or all of the following categories:

□ appearance options:

    ANNOTATE=*Annotate-data-set*

    CEMPTY=*empty-area-outline-color*

    COUTLINE=*nonempty-area-outline-color* | SAME

    XLIGHT=*x*

    YLIGHT=*y*

    XSIZE=*map-width <units>*

    YSIZE=*map-height <units>*

    XVIEW=*x*

    YVIEW=*y*

    ZVIEW=*z*

□ mapping options:

    DISCRETE

    LEVELS=*number-of-response-levels*

    MIDPOINTS=*value-list*

    MISSING

□ legend options:

    CTEXT=*text-color*

    LEGEND=LEGEND<1...99>

    NOLEGEND

□ description options:

DESCRIPTION=*'entry-description'*

NAME=*'entry-name'*

□ ODS options

HTML=*variable*

HTML_LEGEND=*variable*

Required Arguments

response-variable(s)

specifies one or more variables in the response data set that contains response values represented on the map. Each response variable produces a separate map. All variables must be in the input data set. Separate multiple response variables with blanks.

Missing values for the response variable are not considered valid unless you use the MISSING option in the PRISM statement.

Response variables can be either numeric or character. Numeric response variables with continuous values are grouped into ranges, or response levels. Each response level is assigned a different prism height and a different pattern and color combination. Character variables and numeric variables (when you use the DISCRETE option) have a different response level for each unique response variable value. This means that the prism height can be used to identify discrete values, but prism height does not reflect the specific value. Use the legend to determine the exact value of a discrete variable. Numeric variables are treated as continuous unless you use DISCRETE.

For numeric response variables with continuous values, you can control the selection of response level ranges using the MIDPOINTS= or LEVELS= option. By default, the GMAP procedure determines the number of levels for the map using the formula FLOOR(1+3.3 log(N)), where N is the number of unique map area identification variable values.

See also: "About Response Variables" on page 737

Options

Options in a PRISM statement affect all graphs that are produced by that statement. You can specify as many options as you want and list them in any order.

ANNOTATE=*Annotate-data-set*
ANNO=*Annotate-data-set*
specifies a data set to annotate maps that are produced by the PRISM statement.

Note: Annotate coordinate systems 1, 2, 7, and 8 are not valid with prism maps. △

See also: Chapter 10, "The Annotate Data Set," on page 403

CEMPTY=*empty-area-outline-color*
outlines empty map areas in the specified color. This option affects the map areas that are empty. Empty map areas are generated in prism maps either

□ when there is no response value for a map area and the MISSING option is not used, or

□ when a map area is omitted from the response data set and the ALL option is included in the PROC GMAP statement.

The default outline color is the same as the default COUTLINE= color.

See also: ALL on page 740 and "Displaying Map Areas and Response Data" on page 738

COUTLINE=*nonempty-area-outline-color* | SAME
outlines non-empty map areas in the specified color. SAME specifies that the outline color of a map area is the same as the interior pattern color.
The default outline color depends on the PATTERN statement:

☐ If no PATTERN statement is specified, the default outline color is the foreground color (the first color in the colors list).

☐ If a PATTERN statement or the V6COMP graphics option is specified, the default is COUTLINE=SAME.

Note: If you specify empty map patterns, (VALUE=MEMPTY in a PATTERN statement) you should not change the outline color from the default value, SAME, to a single color. Otherwise all the outlines will be one color and you will not be able to distinguish between the empty areas. △

Featured in: Example 7 on page 788

CTEXT=*text-color*
specifies a color for the text in the legend. If you omit the CTEXT= option, a color specification is searched for in this order:

1 the CTEXT= option in a GOPTIONS statement

2 the default, the first color in the colors list.

The CTEXT= color specification is overridden if you also use the COLOR= suboption of a LABEL= or VALUE= option in a LEGEND definition assigned to the map legend. The COLOR= suboption determines the color of the legend label or the color of the legend value descriptions, respectively.

DESCRIPTION='*entry-description*'
DES='*entry-description*'
specifies the description of the catalog entry for the chart. The maximum length for *entry-description* is 40 characters. The description does not appear on the chart. By default, the GMAP procedure assigns a description of the form PRISM MAP OF *variable*, where *variable* is the name of the map variable.

DISCRETE
treats a numeric response variable as a discrete variable rather than as a continuous variable. The DISCRETE option does not group the response values into ranges; instead, the GMAP procedure uses a separate response level (prism height, color, and surface pattern) for each different value of the formatted response variable. The LEVELS= option is ignored when you use the DISCRETE option.
Use this option if your numeric response variable is assigned a user-written format.

Note: If the data do not contain a value in a particular range of the format, that formatted range is not displayed in the legend. △

Featured in: Example 5 on page 779 (with CHORO statement)

HTML=*variable*
identifies the variable in the input data set whose values create links in the HTML file created by the ODS HTML statement. These links are associated with an area of the chart and point to the data or graph you wish to display when the user drills down on the area.

HTML_LEGEND=*variable*
identifies the variable in the input data set whose values create links in the HTML file created by the ODS HTML statement. These links are associated with a legend

value and point to the data or graph you wish to display when the user drills down on the value.

LEGEND=LEGEND<1...99>

assigns the specified LEGEND definition to the map legend. LEGEND= is ignored if the specified LEGEND definition is not currently in effect. In the GMAP procedure, the PRISM statement produces a legend unless you use the NOLEGEND option. If you use the SHAPE= option in a LEGEND statement, only the value BAR is valid.

See also: "LEGEND Statement" on page 187

Featured in: Example 8 on page 790

LEVELS=*number-of-response-levels*

specifies the number of response levels to be graphed when the response variables are continuous. Each level is assigned a different prism height, surface pattern, and color combination.

If neither the LEVELS= option nor the DISCRETE option is used, the GMAP procedure determines the number of response levels that use the formula FLOOR(1+3.3 log(N)), where N is the number of unique map area identification variable values.

The LEVELS= option is ignored when you use the DISCRETE or MIDPOINTS= option.

Featured in: Example 2 on page 773

MIDPOINTS=*value-list*

specifies the response levels for the range of response values that are represented by each level (prism height, pattern, and color combination).

For numeric response variables, *value-list* is either an explicit list of values, or a starting and an ending value with an interval increment, or an combination of both forms:

n <...n>

n TO n <BY *increment*>

n <...n> TO n <BY *increment* > <n <...n> >

By default the increment value is 1. You can specify discrete numeric values in any order. In all forms, n can be separated by blanks or commas. For example,

```
midpoints=(2 4 6)
midpoints=(2,4,6)
midpoints=(2 to 10 by 2)
```

If a numeric variable has an associated format, the specified values must be the *unformatted* values.

For character response variables, *value-list* has this form:

'value-1' <...'value-n'>

The values are character strings enclosed in single quotation marks and separated by blanks. For example,

```
midpoints='Midwest' 'Northeast' 'Northwest'
```

Specify the values in any order. If a character variable has an associated format, the specified values must be the *formatted* values.

You can selectively exclude some response variable values from the map, as shown here:

```
midpoints='Midwest'
```

Only those observations for which the response variable exactly matches one of the values listed in the MIDPOINTS= option are shown on the map. As a result, observations may be inadvertently excluded if values in the list are misspelled or if the case does not match exactly.

Featured in: Example 8 on page 790

MISSING

accepts a missing value as a valid level for the response variable.

See also: "Displaying Map Areas and Response Data" on page 738

NAME=*'entry-name'*

specifies the name of the catalog entry for the map. The maximum length for *entry-name* is eight characters. The default name is GMAP. If that name that you specify duplicates the name of an existing entry, SAS/GRAPH software adds a number to the duplicate name to create a unique entry, for example, GMAP1.

NOLEGEND

suppresses the legend.

XLIGHT=*x*
YLIGHT=*y*

specify the coordinates of the imagined light source in the map coordinate system. The position of the light source affects the way the sides of the map polygons are shaded. Although you can specify any point for the light source using the XLIGHT= and YLIGHT= options, the light source is actually placed in one of only four positions.
Table 19.1 on page 757 shows how the point you specify is positioned.

Table 19.1 Light Source Coordinates

Specified Light Source	Light Source Position
in quadrants I or II, or on the X or +Y axis	behind the map (point A), and all side polygons are shadowed
on or within approximately 10 degrees of the Y axis	the viewing position (point D), and none of the side polygons are shadowed
in quadrant III (except within 10 degrees of the Y axis)	to the left of the map (point B), and the right-facing sides of polygons are shadowed
in quadrant IV (except within 10 degrees of the Y axis)	to the right of the map (point C), and the left-facing side polygons are shadowed

Figure 19.6 on page 758 illustrates the light source positions. Assume that your viewing position, selected by the XVIEW=, YVIEW=, and ZVIEW= options, is point D.

Figure 19.6   Coordinates of Imagined Light Source in a Map Coordinate System

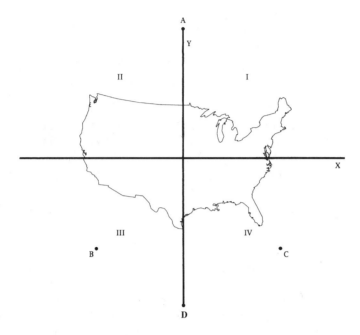

By default, the light source position is the same as the viewing position specified by the XVIEW=, YVIEW=, and ZVIEW= options. The light source position cannot coincide with the viewing reference point (0.5,0.5), which corresponds with the position directly above the center of the map.

See also: XVIEW= on page 758

Featured in: Example 8 on page 790

XSIZE=*map-width <units>*
YSIZE=*map-height <units>*
>   specify the physical dimensions of the map that is to be drawn, where *n* is the number of units. By default, the map uses the entire procedure output area.
>
>   Valid *units* are CM (centimeters), IN (inches), or PCT (percentage of the graphics output area). By default, the unit is character cells (CELLS).
>
>   If you specify values for *map-width* and *map height* that are greater than the dimensions of the procedure output area, the map is drawn using the default size. And if you specify one value and not the other, the dimension is adjusted to maintain the correct aspect ratio.

XVIEW=*x*
YVIEW=*y*
ZVIEW=*z*
>   specify the viewing position coordinates for the map. In this system, the four corners of the map lie on the X-Y plane at coordinates (0,0,0), (0,1,0), (1,1,0), and (1,0,0). No axes are actually drawn on the maps that are produced by PROC GMAP, but imagine that the maps are drawn in an X-Y plane.
>
>   Your viewing position cannot coincide with the viewing reference point at coordinates (0.5,0.5,0), the center of the map. The value for *z* cannot be negative.
>
>   If you omit the XVIEW=, YVIEW=, and ZVIEW= options, the default coordinates are (0.5,–2,3). This viewing position is well above and to the south of the center of

the map. Specify one, two, or all three of the view coordinates; any that you do not explicitly specify are assigned the default values.

Figure 19.5 on page 747 shows the position of the viewing reference point, as well as the default viewing position.

To ensure that the polygon edges are distinguishable, the angle from vertical must be less than or equal to 45 degrees. If you specify a ZVIEW= value such that this condition cannot be satisfied (that is, a very small value), PROC GMAP increases the ZVIEW= value automatically so that the angle is 45 degrees or less.

Featured in: Example 8 on page 790

SURFACE Statement

Creates three-dimensional surface maps in which levels of magnitude of the specified response variables are represented by spikes of varying height.

Requirements: At least one response variable is required and must be numeric. The ID statement must be used in conjunction with the SURFACE statement.

Global statements: FOOTNOTE, TITLE

Description   The SURFACE statement specifies the variable or variables that contain the data that are represented on the map by raised map areas. This statement automatically determines the midpoints. You can use statement options to control spike proportions, specify the angle of view, and modify the general appearance of the map. For example, you can select the color and number of lines for the representation of the surface area. You can control the selection of spike heights and base widths.

In addition, you can use global statements to add titles and footnotes to the map. You can also use an Annotate data set to enhance the map.

SURFACE*response-variable(s)* < */ option(s)*>;

option(s) can be one or more options from any or all of the following categories:

□ appearance options:

ANNOTATE=*Annotate-data-set*
CBODY=*surface-map-color*
CONSTANT=*n*
NLINES=*number-of-lines*
ROTATE=*degrees*
TILT=*degrees*
XSIZE=*map-width* <*units*>
YSIZE=*map-height* <*units*>

□ description options:

DESCRIPTION='*entry-description*'
NAME='*entry-name*'

Required Arguments

response-variable(s)

specifies one or more variables in the response data set that contains response values for map areas in the map data set. *Response-variable* must be numeric and must contain only positive values. Each response variable produces a separate map. All variables must be in the input data set. Separate multiple response variables with blanks.

The GMAP procedure scales response variables for presentation on the map. The height of the spikes on the map correspond to the relative value of the response variable, not to the actual value of the response variable. However, when the viewing angle is changed, the spikes may not appear this way. The spikes in the front may appear to be higher than the spikes in the back, which represent greater values.

See also: "About Response Variables" on page 737

Options

SURFACE statement options affect all maps that are produced by that statement.

ANNOTATE=*Annotate-data-set*
ANNO=*Annotate-data-set*

specifies a data set to annotate maps that are produced by the SURFACE statement.

Note: Annotate coordinate systems 1, 2, 7, and 8 are not valid with surface maps. △

See also: Chapter 10, "The Annotate Data Set," on page 403

CBODY=*surface-map-color*

specifies the color that is used to draw the surface map. By default, the first color in the current colors list is used.

CONSTANT=*n*

specifies a denominator to use in the distance decay function. This function determines the base width of the spike that is drawn at each map area center.

By default, CONSTANT=10. Values greater than 10 yield spikes that are wider at the base. Values less than 10 yield spikes that are narrower at the base.

Let x_k and y_k represent the coordinates, and z_k represent the function value at the center of each map area. The z_k values are scaled from 1 to 11. A square grid of x by y points (where the size of the grid is the NLINES= option value) and the associated function value *f(x,y)* are generated from the map area center value using this formula:

$$f(x,y) = \sum^{k} \left(1 - 1.5^k + .5D^{3k} \right) \triangle^{kzk}$$

where

$$D^k = \left(x - x^k \right)^2 + \left(y - y^k \right)^k$$

and

$$\triangle^k = \left[\mathrm{martix\,cdelim} = \mathrm{XXXXXXXXXXXXXX}\, 1 \,\mathrm{if}\, D^k < 1,\, 0\,\mathrm{otherwise.} \right]$$

Featured in: Example 10 on page 792

DESCRIPTION='*entry-description*'
DES='*entry-description*'

specifies the description of the catalog entry for the map. The maximum length for *entry-description* is 40 characters. The description does not appear on the map. By default, the GMAP procedure assigns a description of the form SURFACE MAP OF *variable*, where *variable* is the name of the map variable.

NAME='*entry-name*'

specifies the name of the catalog entry for the map. The maximum length for *entry-name* is eight characters. The default name is GMAP. If the specified name duplicates the name of an existing entry, SAS/GRAPH software adds a number to the duplicate name to create a unique entry, for example, GMAP1.

NLINES=*number-of-lines*
N=*number-of-lines*

specifies the number of lines, *n*, used to draw the surface map. Values for *n* are 50 to 100; the higher the value, the more solid the map appears and the more resources used. By default, NLINES=50.

Featured in: Example 10 on page 792

ROTATE=*degrees*

specifies the degrees of the angle at which to rotate the map about the Z axis in the map coordinate system. *Degrees* can be any angle. Positive values indicate rotation in the counterclockwise direction. By default, ROTATE=70. The ROTATE= option also affects the direction of the lines that are used to draw the surface map.

Featured in: Example 10 on page 792

TILT=*degrees*

specifies the degrees of the angle at which to tilt the map about the X axis in the map coordinate system. *Degrees* can be 0 to 90. Increasing values cause the map to tilt backward and makes the spikes more prominent. Decreasing values make the map shape more distinguishable and the spikes less prominent. TILT=90 corresponds to viewing the map edge-on, while TILT=0 corresponds to viewing the map from directly overhead. By default, TILT=70.

Featured in: Example 10 on page 792

XSIZE=*map-width* *<units>*
YSIZE=*map-height* *<units>*

specify the physical dimensions of the map to be drawn, where *n* is the number of units. By default, the map uses the entire procedure output area.

Valid *units* are CM (centimeters), IN (inches), or PCT (percentage of the graphics output area). By default, the unit is character cells (CELLS).

If you specify values for *map-width* and *map-height* that are greater than the dimensions of the procedure output area, the map is drawn using the default size. And if you specify only one dimension, the other is scaled to maintain the aspect ratio.

SAS/GRAPH Map Data Sets

Many map data sets are provided with SAS/GRAPH software. Some of the more commonly used map data sets are listed in the following table (see the MAPS.METAMAPS data set for details on all the Institute-supplied map data sets). The items listed under each of the variable names describes the value type. For example, *proj* means that the value for the specified variable is a projected value and *long* or *lat* means that the value is unprojected longitude or latitude. If a variable does not exist in the map data set, *n/a* is used in the table.

Note: The last two items in the table (Continents and International) are categories of map data sets. The map data sets in these categories contain individual countries, continents, or subdivisions. To see the complete list of map data sets that are provided in each of these categories, see the MAPS.METAMAPS data set. △

Table 19.2   SAS/GRAPH Map Data Sets

Version 6 Variables				Current Variables				Compatible with V6?
Map Data Sets	X	Y	LONG	LAT	X	Y	LONG	LAT	
US	proj	proj	n/a	n/a	proj	proj	n/a	n/a	yes
USCITY1	proj	proj	long	lat	proj	proj	long	lat	yes2
USCENTER	proj	proj	long	lat	proj	proj	long	lat	yes
STATES	long	lat	n/a	n/a	long	lat	n/a	n/a	yes
COUNTIES	long	lat	n/a	n/a	long	lat	n/a	n/a	yes
COUNTY	long	lat	n/a	n/a	long	lat	n/a	n/a	yes
USCOUNTY	proj	proj	n/a	n/a	proj	proj	n/a	n/a	yes
CANADA	proj	proj	n/a	n/a	proj	proj	n/a	n/a	yes
CANADA2	proj	proj	n/a	n/a	proj	proj	n/a	n/a	yes
CANADA3	long	lat	n/a	n/a	long	lat	n/a	n/a	yes
CANADA4	long		n/a	n/a	long	lat	n/a	n/a	yes
WORLDPRJ	proj	proj	n/a	n/a	not available in current version	not available in current version	not available in current version	not available in current version	no
WORLDMAP	long	lat	n/a	n/a	not available in current version	not available in current version	not available in current version	not available in current version	no
WORLD	not available in Version 6	not available in Version 6	not available in Version 6	not available in Version 6	proj	proj	long	lat	no
Continents	proj	proj	n/a	n/a	proj	proj	long	lat	yes
International	proj	proj	n/a	n/a	proj	proj	long	lat	yes3

1   The USCITY and USCENTER map data sets contain coordinates for labeling (see "Specialty Map Data Sets" on page 736 for details)

2   Contact Technical Support for a program that can be used to create the data sets from MAPS.WORLD.

3   The Version 6 data sets that contained multiple countries have been divided into individual data sets, beginning in Version 7.

Locating Map Data Sets

A collection of map data sets is supplied with SAS/GRAPH. Contact your SAS Support Consultant to verify the name and location of the SAS data library that contains the map data sets at your site before you use the map data sets. Many sites automatically assign a libref of MAPS to the SAS data library that contains the Institute-supplied map data sets. However, if you use the map data sets regularly and your site does not automatically assign a libref to the data library that contains the map data sets, you can add a LIBNAME statement to your AUTOEXEC file that defines the location of the map data set library. If you do this, the libref for the maps is established automatically whenever you begin a SAS session.

Accessing Descriptions of Map Data Sets

You may need detailed information on the map data sets in order to determine their size, the variables they contain, or whether they are projected or unprojected. You can get this information by using the CONTENTS or DATASETS procedure, or browsing the METAMAPS data set in the MAPS library (or the library where your Institute-supplied map data sets reside). For example, these statements list the map data sets in the SAS data library that is assigned to the libref MAPS:

```
libname maps 'SAS-data-library';

proc datasets lib=maps;
run;
```

Note: Be sure to replace *SAS-data-library* with the location of the SAS data library that contains map data sets at your site. △

The following statements provide detailed information on the map data sets, including the number of observations, the variables in each data set, and a description of each variable:

```
libname maps 'SAS-data-library';

proc contents data=maps.canada3;
run;
```

To see the contents and descriptions of all of the Institute-supplied map data sets you can specify DATA=MAPS._ALL_ in the CONTENTS procedure. See the *SAS Procedures Guide* for more information on the CONTENTS and DATASETS procedures.

Using FIPS Codes and Province Codes

The map area identification variable in some map data sets that are included with SAS/GRAPH contain standardized numeric codes. The data sets for the United States contain a variable whose values are FIPS (Federal Information Processing System) codes. The data sets for Canada contain standard province codes or census division codes. When you use the GMAP procedure, the variables that identify map areas in your response data set must have the same values as the map area identification variables in the map data set that you are using. If the map area identification variables in your response data set are state or province names or abbreviations, convert them to FIPS codes or province codes before using the response data set with one of the Institute-supplied map data sets. Table 19.3 on page 764 lists the FIPS codes for the United States and Table 19.4 on page 764 lists the standard codes for Canadian provinces.

Table 19.3 U.S. FIPS Codes

FIPS Code	State	FIPS Code	State
01	Alabama	30	Montana
02	Alaska	31	Nebraska
04	Arizona	32	Nevada
05	Arkansas	33	New Hampshire
06	California	34	New Jersey
08	Colorado	35	New Mexico
09	Connecticut	36	New York
10	Delaware	37	North Carolina
11	District of Columbia	38	North Dakota
12	Florida	39	Ohio
13	Georgia	40	Oklahoma
15	Hawaii	41	Oregon
16	Idaho	42	Pennsylvania
17	Illinois	44	Rhode Island
18	Indiana	45	South Carolina
19	Iowa	46	South Dakota
20	Kansas	47	Tennessee
21	Kentucky	48	Texas
22	Louisiana	49	Utah
23	Maine	50	Vermont
24	Maryland	51	Virginia
25	Massachusetts	53	Washington
26	Michigan	54	West Virginia
27	Minnesota	55	Wisconsin
28	Mississippi	56	Wyoming
29	Missouri	72	Puerto Rico

Table 19.4 Canadian Province Codes

Province Code	Province
10	Newfoundland
11	Prince Edward Island
12	Nova Scotia
13	New Brunswick

Province Code	Province
24	Quebec
35	Ontario
46	Manitoba
47	Saskatchewan
48	Alberta
59	British Columbia
60	Yukon
61	Northwest Territories

Note: The ID variables in Canadian maps are character. △

The CNTYNAME data set contains a cross-reference of names and FIPS codes for all counties in the United States. The CANCENS data set contains a cross-reference of census district names and codes for Canadian provinces.

Base SAS software provides several functions that convert state names to FIPS codes and vice versa. The following table lists these functions and a brief description of each. See *SAS Language Reference: Dictionary* for more information.

Table 19.5 FIPS and Postal Code Functions

Function	Description
STFIPS	converts state postal code to FIPS state code
STNAME	converts state postal code to state name in upper case
STNAMEL	converts state postal code to state name in mixed case
FIPNAME	converts FIPS code to state name in upper case
FIPNAMEL	converts FIPS code to state name in mixed case
FIPSTATE	converts FIPS code to state postal code

Using SAS/GRAPH Map Data Sets

You can customize the area that is displayed on your map by using only part of a particular map data set. There are several ways to accomplish this. You can use WHERE processing or a DATA step to subset the map data to be used by the GMAP procedure. You can also use the GPROJECT procedure to create a rectangular subset of a map data set by using minimum and maximum longitude and latitude values.

You can combine map data sets in either of these situations:

□ The map data sets to be combined were originally projected together.

□ The map data sets all contain the same type of coordinates. That is, all are in radians or all are in degrees.

Institute-supplied map data sets that have coordinates expressed only as longitude and latitude, with variable names LONG and LAT, must be renamed X and Y and should be projected before displaying.

Subsetting Map Data Sets

Some of the map data sets that are included with SAS/GRAPH contain a large number of observations. Programs that use only a few states or provinces will run faster if you exclude the unused portion of the map data set or use an already reduced map data set. The SAS System provides several ways to accomplish this. One is to use the WHERE statement or WHERE= data set option within the GMAP procedure to select only the states or provinces you want.

For example, to use only the observations for Quebec in the CANADA data set, begin the GMAP procedure with this statement:

```
proc gmap map=maps.canada(where=(province='24'));
```

If you use the WHERE statement, the WHERE condition applies to both the map data set and the response data sets. The WHERE= data set option applies only to the data set that you specify in the argument in which the WHERE= option appears.

The WHERE statement and WHERE= data set option are most useful when you produce a simple map and do not need to make any other changes to the data set.

Another approach is to use a DATA step to create a subset of the larger data set. This code illustrates another way to extract the observations for Quebec from the CANADA data set:

```
data quebec;
   set maps.canada(where=(province='24'));
```

This approach is most useful when you want to create a permanent subset of a map data set or when you need to make additional changes to the map data set.

Also see Chapter 25, "The GREMOVE Procedure," on page 905 for an example how to use GREMOVE to create a regional map from one of the data sets that are supplied with SAS/GRAPH.

Reducing Map Data Sets

You can reduce map data sets. A *reduced map data set* is one that can be used to draw a map that retains the overall appearance of the original map but that contains fewer points, requires considerably less storage space, and can be drawn much more quickly. You can improve performance by plotting fewer observations for each map area. You reduce a map data set when you subset it on the variable DENSITY. You can add the variable DENSITY to a map data set by using the GREDUCE procedure. For more information, see Chapter 24, "The GREDUCE Procedure," on page 895.

An *unreduced map data set* contains all of the coordinates that were produced when the map was digitized. This type of map data set has more observations than most graphics output devices can accurately plot. Some unreduced map data sets already contain a DENSITY variable like the one calculated by the GREDUCE procedure, so it is not necessary to use the GREDUCE procedure to process these data sets. Values for DENSITY range from 0 through 6 (the lower the density, the coarser the boundary line).

A statement of this form excludes all points with a density level of 2 or greater:

```
proc gmap map=maps.states(where=(density<2));
```

The resulting map is much coarser than one drawn by using all of the observations in the data set, but it is drawn much faster.

Another way to create a reduced map data set is to use a DATA step to exclude observations with larger density values:

```
data states;
   set maps.states(where=(density<2));
```

Projecting Map Data Sets

Map data can be stored as unprojected or projected coordinates. Unprojected map data contains spherical coordinates, that is, longitude and latitude values usually expressed in radians. * A few map data sets that are provided with SAS/GRAPH contain only unprojected coordinates and should be projected before you use them. They are

CANADA3

CANADA4

COUNTIES

COUNTY

STATES

Projected map data contains Cartesian coordinates. The GMAP procedure is designed to plot maps by using projected map data sets. Most SAS/GRAPH map data sets contain projected coordinates that are stored as X and Y. If the projection supplied with the map data set does not meet your needs, you can use the GPROJECT procedure to create a different projection. You should select a projection method that least distorts the regions that you are mapping. (All projection methods inherently distort map regions.) See Chapter 23, "The GPROJECT Procedure," on page 873 for more information.

Note: Using an unprojected map data set with the GMAP procedure can cause your map to be reversed and distorted. △

Controlling the Display of Lakes

Some countries contain a lake that is located completely within a single unit area. Occasionally these lakes can be a problem. For example, displaying lakes in prism maps may cause undesirable results. In addition, displaying lakes may not be appropriate for some applications. In these cases, you may want to remove the lakes from the map data set before you proceed.

Map data sets that contain coordinates for a lake that is located within a single internal division are identified by the presence of the character variable LAKE. The value of LAKE is 1 for points that correspond to lakes and 0 otherwise. The following statements illustrate how to delete the lakes from your map data sets using WHERE processing:

```
proc gmap map=maps.chile(where=(lake='0'))
          data=maps.chile;
   id id;
   choro id / levels=1 nolegend;
   title box=1 f=none h=4
         'Chile with Lakes Removed';
run;
```

You can also create a new map data set that is a subset of the map data set:

```
data nolake;
   set maps.chile;
   if lake='0';
run;
```

---

* If your data is in degrees, it can be converted to radians by multiplying by the degree-to-radian constant [atan(1)/45].

Creating Map Data Sets

In addition to using map data sets that are supplied with SAS/GRAPH software, you may want to create your own map data sets. Map data sets are not limited to geographic data; you use them to define other spaces such as floor plans or street diagrams. This section explains more about the structure of map data sets.

A unit area is defined by observations in the map data set that have the same identification (ID) variable value. A unit area may be composed of a single polygon or a collection of polygons. A polygon is defined by all of the observations that have the same SEGMENT variable value.

□ If the unit area is a single polygon, all values of SEGMENT are the same.

□ If the unit area contains multiple polygons, such as islands, the SEGMENT variable has multiple values. For example, in the MAPS.US data set, the state of Hawaii (a unit area) contains six different values in the SEGMENT variable, one for each island in the state.

□ If the unit area contains enclosed polygons, such as lakes, the SEGMENT variable has one value but the interior polygon is defined by separate boundaries. For example, in the CANADA2 data set supplied with SAS/GRAPH, the map data for the Northwest Territories (a unit area) use enclosed polygons for two lakes.

Creating a unit area that is a single polygon.

This DATA step creates a SAS data set that contains coordinates for a unit area with a single polygon, a square:

```
data square;
   input id x y;
   datalines;
1 0 0
1 0 40
1 40 40
1 40 0
;
```

This data set does not have a SEGMENT variable.

Creating a unit area that contains multiple polygons.

Use different values of the SEGMENT variable to create separate polygons within a single unit area. For example, this DATA step assigns two values to the SEGMENT variable. The resulting data set produces a single unit area that contains two polygons, as shown in Figure 19.7 on page 769:

```
data map;
   input id $ 1-8 segment x y;
   datalines;
square    1 0 0
square    1 0 4
square    1 4 4
square    1 4 0
square    2 5 5
square    2 5 7
square    2 7 7
```

```
square    2 7 5
;
```

Figure 19.7   Single Unit Area with Two Segments (Polygons)

Creating a unit area that contains enclosed polygons as holes.

Use separate boundaries to create an enclosed polygon (that is, a polygon that falls within the primary polygon for a single segment). The separate boundaries are separated from the primary polygon boundary by missing values for X and Y. For example, the data set that is created by this DATA step produces the map shown in Figure 19.8 on page 770:

```
data map;
   input id $ 1-8 segment x y;
   datalines;
square    1 0 0
square    1 0 4
square    1 4 4
square    1 4 0
square    1 . .
square    1 1 1
square    1 2 2
square    1 3 1
;
```

Figure 19.8   Single Unit Area with Hole

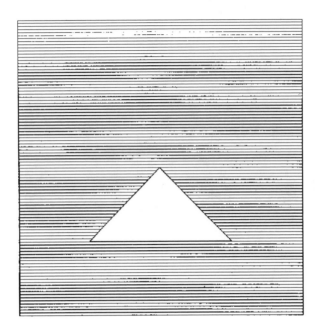

Creating a unit area that contains enclosed polygons as cities.

Ordinarily, if one unit area is surrounded by another, the pattern of the external unit area is drawn over the pattern for the internal one, instead of around it. Avoid this problem by adding an observation to the map data for the external unit area with missing values for X and Y, followed by the coordinates of the internal unit area, but using the ID values for the external unit area. For example, this DATA step creates a data set that produces the map shown in Figure 19.9 on page 771:

```
data map;
   input id $ 1-8 segment x y;
   datalines;
square   1 0 0
square   1 0 4
square   1 4 4
square   1 4 0
square   1 . .
square   1 1 1
square   1 2 2
square   1 3 1
triangle 1 1 1
triangle 1 2 2
triangle 1 3 1
;
```

Figure 19.9 Unit Area within a Unit Area

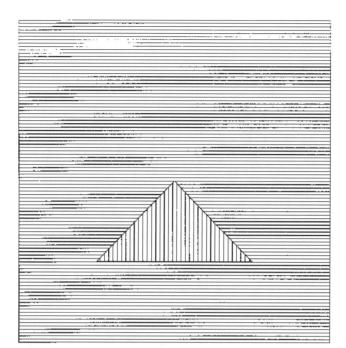

Note: A single map segment (a section of a unit area with a single value of the SEGMENT variable) cannot contain multiple polygons without at least one observation with missing values for X and Y. All segments within the map data sets that are supplied by SAS/GRAPH contain a single polygon that can have one or more separate boundaries, each separated by an observation with missing values for X and Y. △

Examples

The following examples include features from one or more of the GMAP statements.

Example 1: Producing a Simple Block Map

Procedure features:
   ID statement
   BLOCK statement option:
      CBLKOUT=
Sample library member: GR19N01

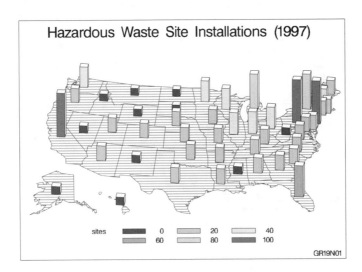

This example produces a block map that shows the total number of hazardous waste sites in each state in 1997. Since the DISCRETE option is not used, the response variable is assumed to have a continuous range of values. Because neither the LEVELS= nor MIDPOINTS= option is used, the GMAP procedure selects a number of levels based on the number of map areas and then calculates the appropriate response levels. The legend shows the midpoint value of each level.

The blocks use the default pattern, which is a solid fill that rotates through the colors list. Because the colors list is specified in the GOPTIONS statement, all colors are used in the rotation. CBLKOUT= outlines the blocks in black, instead of using the default outline color, which is the first color in the list– in this case, BLUE.

The map areas use the default pattern for map areas in a block map. This is the first hatch pattern for maps, M2N0. By default, both the fill and the outline use the first color in the colors list.

Assign the librefs and set the graphics environment. COLORS= specifies the colors list, which is used by the default patterns and outlines. CTEXT= specifies the color for all text on the output.

```
libname reflib 'SAS-data-library';
libname maps 'SAS-data-library';
goptions reset=global gunit=pct border cback=white
         colors=(blue green lime lipk cyan red)
         ctext=black ftext=swiss htitle=6 htext=3;
```

Create response data set REFLIB.SITES. This data set contains a map area identification variable, STATE, and a response variable, SITES. STATE contains the FIPS codes for each state and matches the values of STATE in the MAPS.US data set. SITES contains the total number of waste sites installed in the state.

```
data reflib.sites;
   length stcode $ 2;
   input region stcode $ sites;
   state=stfips(stcode);
   datalines;
6   AR  12
10  AK  7...moredata lines...
3   WV  6
```

```
8   WY   3
;
```

Define title and footnote for map.

```
title1 'Hazardous Waste Site Installations (1997)';
footnote1 j=r 'GR19N01 ';
```

Produce the block map. The ID statement specifies the variable that is in both the map data set and the response data set and defines map areas. The BLOCK statement specifies the variable in the response data set that contains the response values for each of the map areas. CBLKOUT= specifies the color for the block outlines.

```
proc gmap map=maps.us data=reflib.sites;
   id state;
   block sites / cblkout=black;
run;
quit;
```

Example 2: Specifying Response Levels in a Block Map

Procedure features:
    BLOCK statement options:
        LEGEND=
        LEVELS=
        SHAPE=
        XVIEW=
        ZVIEW=

Other features:
    LEGEND statement
    PATTERN statement

Data set: REFLIB.SITES

Sample library member: GR19N02

This example uses LEVELS= to specify the number of response levels for the blocks. LEVELS= tells GMAP how many response levels and GMAP calculates the midpoints. Eight PATTERN statements explicitly define a color for each of these response levels.

A single PATTERN statement uses the REPEAT= option to define an empty map/plot pattern outlined in black for all the map areas.

The example also changes the viewpoint by rotating the map to provide a better view of the northeast states. As a result, the blocks appear shorter.

Assign the librefs and set the graphics environment.

```
libname reflib 'SAS-data-library';
libname maps 'SAS-data-library';
goptions reset=global gunit=pct border cback=white
        colors=(black blue green red)
        ctext=black ftext=swiss htitle=6 htext=3;
```

Define title and footnote for map.

```
title1 'Hazardous Waste Site Installations (1997)';
footnote1 j=r 'GR19N02 ';
```

Define the patterns for the blocks. PATTERN statements 1-8 specify bar/block patterns and cannot be used by the map areas. They are applied to the blocks in order of the response level.

```
pattern1 value=solid color=lime;
pattern2 value=solid color=cyan;
pattern3 value=solid color=green;
pattern4 value=solid color=blue;
pattern5 value=solid color=lipk;
pattern6 value=solid color=red;
pattern7 value=solid color=gray;
pattern8 value=solid color=black;
```

Define a pattern for the map areas. PATTERN9 defines a single map pattern that is repeated for each of the 50 map areas (states). The pattern is an empty fill with a black border. VALUE= defines a map/plot pattern, which cannot be used by the blocks. Specifying a color causes PATTERN9 to generate only one pattern definition. REPEAT= specifies the number of times to repeat the pattern definition.

```
pattern9 value=mempty color=black repeat=50;
```

Define legend characteristics. LABEL= produces a two line label and places it to the left of the legend values. FRAME draws a border around the legend using the first color in the colors list.

```
legend1 value=(justify=left)
        label=('Number' justify=left 'of Sites:'
               position=(middle left))
        frame;
```

Produce the block map. LEVELS= specifies the number of response levels for the graph. SHAPE= draws the blocks as 3D cylinders. XVIEW= changes the viewpoint for the map so that the map appears to be slightly rotated. ZVIEW= raises the height of the viewpoint. LEGEND= assigns the LEGEND1 statement to the map legend.

```
proc gmap map=maps.us data=reflib.sites;
   id state;
   block sites / levels=8
                 shape=cylinder
                 xview=0.75
                 zview=5
                 legend=legend1;
run;
quit;
```

Example 3: Assigning a Format to the Response Variable

Procedure features:
    BLOCK statement options:
        AREA=
        CBLKOUT=
        COUTLINE=
        DISCRETE
Other features:
    FORMAT statement
    LEGEND statement
    PATTERN statement
Data set: REFLIB.SITES
Sample library member: GR19N03

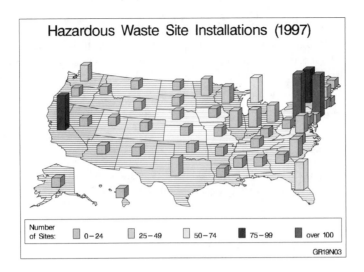

This example creates a format that defines the ranges of values for the response values and assigns this format to the response variable. These ranges appear in the legend and make the map easier to understand. When a format is assigned to a numeric response variable, the DISCRETE option must be used so that each formatted value is treated as a separate response level.

The example also patterns the map areas by region. To do this, both data sets must contain the ID variable, REGION. The response data set, REFLIB.SITES, already contains REGION, so the program only needs to add it to the map data set. Then the map data set is sorted by both the ID variables, REGION and STATE. Finally, the AREA= option specifies that the ID variable REGION is the one by which the map areas are patterned.

Assign the librefs and set the graphics environment.

```
libname reflib 'SAS-data-library';
libname maps 'SAS-data-library';
goptions reset=global gunit=pct border cback=white
        colors=(black blue green red)
        ftext=swiss htitle=6 htext=3;
```

Create map data set REFLIB.STATES1 by adding REGION to the MAPS.US map data set.

```
data reflib.states1;
   set maps.us;
   select;
      when (state in (9,23,25,33,44,50))      region=1;
      when (state in (34,36))                 region=2;
      when (state in (10,11,24,42,51,54))     region=3;
      when (state in (1,12,13,21,28,37,45,47)) region=4;
      when (state in (17,18,26,27,39,55))     region=5;
      when (state in (5,22,35,40,48))         region=6;
      when (state in (19,20,29,31))           region=7;
      when (state in (8,30,38,46,49,56))      region=8;
      when (state in (4,6,15,32))             region=9;
      otherwise                               region=10;
   end;
```

```
run;
```

Sort the new map data set. The map data must be sorted in the order of the ID variables.

```
proc sort data=reflib.states1 out=reflib.states2;
   by region state;
run;
```

Create a format for SITES. SITESFMT. defines and labels the ranges of values for SITES.

```
proc format;
   value sitesfmt low-24='0-24'
                  25-49='25-49'
                  50-74='50-74'
                  75-99='75-99'
                  100-high='over 100';
run;
```

Define title and footnote for map.

```
title1 'Hazardous Waste Site Installations (1997)';
footnote j=r 'GR19N03 ';
```

Define a hatch pattern for the map areas. PATTERN1 defines a dense hatch pattern for the map areas. Because there are four colors in the colors list, the pattern rotation must be repeated three times to create enough patterns for the ten regions.

```
pattern1 value=m3n0 r=3;
```

Define a solid pattern for the blocks. PATTERN2 through PATTERN6 define the patterns for the block surfaces.

```
pattern2 value=solid color=green;
pattern3 value=solid color=cyan;
pattern4 value=solid color=lime;
pattern5 value=solid color=blue;
pattern6 value=solid color=red;
```

Define legend characteristics. ACROSS= places all the legend values on one line.

```
legend1 shape=bar(2,4) across=5
        value=(j=l)
        label=('Number' j=l 'of Sites:')
        frame;
```

Produce the block maps. The FORMAT statement assigns SITESFMT. to the response variable. DISCRETE specifies that each formatted value is a separate response level. AREA= specifies that the map surface should be patterned by the first variable in the ID statement, REGION. CBLKOUT= and COUTLINE= specify the color that outlines the blocks and the regions, respectively.

```
proc gmap map=reflib.states2 data=reflib.sites;
   format sites sitesfmt.;
   id region state;
   block sites / discrete
                 area=1
                 legend=legend1
                 shape=block
                 cblkout=black
                 coutline=black;
run;
quit;
```

Example 4: Producing a Simple Choropleth Map

Procedure features:
   ID statement
   CHORO statement option:
       COUTLINE=
Data set: REFLIB.SITES
Sample library member: GR19N04

This example produces a choropleth (2D) map that shows the total number of hazardous waste sites in each state in 1997. Since the DISCRETE option is not used, the response variable is assumed to have a continuous range of values. Because neither the LEVELS= nor MIDPOINTS= option is used, the GMAP procedure selects a number of levels based on the number of map areas and then calculates the appropriate response levels. The legend shows the midpoint value of each level.

The map areas use the default pattern, which is a solid fill that rotates through the colors list. Because the colors list is specified in the GOPTIONS statement, all colors are used in the rotation. COUTLINE= outlines the map areas in gray, instead of the default outline color, which is the first color in the list, in this case, BLUE.

Assign the librefs and set the graphics environment. COLORS= specifies the colors list, which is used by the default patterns and outlines. CTEXT= specifies the color for all text on the output.

```
libname reflib 'SAS-data-library';
libname maps 'SAS-data-library';
goptions reset=global gunit=pct border cback=white
        colors=(blue green lime lipk cyan red)
        ctext=black ftext=swiss htitle=6 htext=3;
```

Define title and footnote for map.

```
title1 'Hazardous Waste Site Installations (1997)';
footnote1 j=r 'GR19N04 ';
```

Produce the choropleth map. The ID statement specifies the variable that is in both the map data set and the response data set that defines map areas. COUTLINE= specifies the color for the map area outlines.

```
proc gmap map=maps.us data=reflib.sites;
   id state;
   choro sites / coutline=gray;
run;
quit;
```

Example 5: Creating Maps with Drill-down for the Web

Procedure Features:
   CHORO statement options:

   > DES=
   > DISCRETE
   > HTML=
   > NAME=

   BLOCK statement options:

   > BLOCKSIZE=
   > DES=
   > MIDPOINTS=
   > NAME=

ODS Features:
   ODS HTML statement :

   > BODY=

CONTENTS=
FRAME=
NOGTITLE
PATH=

Other Features:
  BY statement
  GOPTIONS statement
  LEGEND statement
  PATTERN statement
  TITLE statement
Sample library member: GR19N05

This example shows how to create a 2D choropleth map with simple drill-down functionality for the Web. When this map is displayed in a browser, you can select an area of the map and display additional information about the data.

The example explains how to use the ODS HTML statement and the HTML procedure options to create the drill-down. It shows how to

☐ explicitly name the HTML files and open and close them throughout the program

☐ use BY-group processing with ODS HTML, including storing multiple graphs in one file and incrementing anchor names, catalog entry names, and graphics file names

☐ use the PATH= option to specify the destination for the HTML and GIF files created by the ODS HTML statement

☐ use the NAME= option to name the graphics catalog entries

☐ assign anchor names to the graphics output with the ANCHOR= option in the ODS HTML statement

☐ add an HTML HREF string to a data set to define a link target

☐ assign link targets with the HTML= procedure option

☐ use DES= to control the text of the table of contents entry

☐ suppress the titles in the GIF files and display them in the HTML file.

For more information, see "ODS HTML Statement" on page 200.

The example also illustrates other CHORO and BLOCK statement options.

The program produces one choro map that shows Environmental Protection Agency (EPA) regions and block maps of the states in each region. Each block map shows the number of hazardous waste sites for each state in the selected region. Figure 19.10 on page 781 shows the map of the EPA regions.

Figure 19.10 Browser View of Regional Map

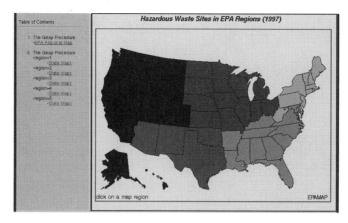

Figure 19.11 on page 781 shows the block map that appears when you select Region 5 in the map.

Figure 19.11 Browser View of Region 5 Block Map

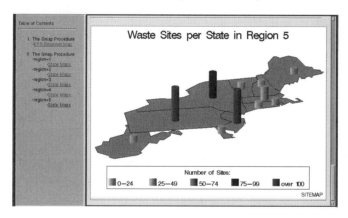

Assign the libref and the Web-server path. FILENAME assigns the fileref ODSOUT, which specifies a destination for the HTML and GIF files produced by the example program. To assign that location as the HTML destination for program output, ODSOUT is specified later in the program on the ODS HTML statement's PATH= option. ODSOUT must point to a Web-server location if procedure output is to be viewed on the Web.

```
libname maps 'SAS-MAPS-library';
filename odsout 'path-to-Web-server-space';
```

Close the ODS Listing destination for procedure output, and set the graphics environment. To conserve system resources, ODS LISTING closes the Listing destination for procedure output. Thus, the graphics output is not displayed in the GRAPH window, although it is written to the catalog.

```
ods listing close;
goptions reset=global gunit=pct cback=white
```

```
            colors=(black blue green red)
            ftext=swiss htitle=6 htext=3.5;
```

Create the data set STATES. STATES contains the FIPS codes for each state and the total number of hazardous waste sites installed in each state.

```
data sites;
    length stcode $ 2;
    input region stcode $ sites;
    state=stfips(stcode);
    datalines;
1    AK    12
4    AL    7
4    AR    12
2    AZ    10
1    CA    90
1    CO    15
5    CT    15
5    DE    18
4    FL    52
4    GA    15
1    HI    4
3    IA    16
1    ID    8
3    IL    38
3    IN    30
3    KS    10
4    KY    16
4    LA    15
5    MA    30
4    MD    13
5    ME    12
3    MI    72
3    MN    30
3    MO    22
4    MS    1
1    MT    8
4    NC    22
3    ND    0
3    NE    10
5    NH    18
5    NJ    105
2    NM    9
1    NV    1
5    NY    78
3    OH    34
2    OK    10
1    OR    10
5    PA    100
5    RI    12
4    SC    26
3    SD    2
4    TN    14
```

```
2    TX   26
1    UT   12
4    VA   25
5    VT   8
1    WA   49
3    WI   40
5    WV   6
1    WY   3
;
```

Add the HTML variable to SITES and create the NEWSITES data set. The HTML
variable REGIONDRILL contains the targets for the values of the variable REGION.

```
data newsites;
   length regiondrill $40;
   set sites;
   if region=1 then
      regiondrill='HREF="hazsite_statebody.html#Region1"';
   if region=2 then
      regiondrill='HREF="hazsite_statebody.html#Region2"';
   if region=3 then
      regiondrill='HREF="hazsite_statebody.html#Region3"';
   if region=4 then
      regiondrill='HREF="hazsite_statebody.html#Region4"';
   if region=5 then
      regiondrill='HREF="hazsite_statebody.html#Region5"';
run;
```

Assign graphics options for producing the ODS HTML output. DEVICE=GIF causes the
ODS HTML statement to generate the graphics output as GIF files. TRANSPARENCY causes
the graphics output to use the Web-page background as the background of the graph.

```
goptions device=gif transparency;
```

Open the ODS HTML destination. BODY= names the file for storing HTML output.
CONTENTS= names the HTML file that contains the table of contents to the HTML procedure
output. The contents file links to each of the body files written to the HTML destination.
FRAME= names the HTML file that integrates the contents and body files. NOGTITLE suppress
the graph titles from the SAS/GRAPH output and displays them through the HTML page.
PATH= specifies the ODSOUT fileref as the HTML destination for all the HTML and GIF files.

```
ods html body='hazsite_mapbody.html'
         contents='hazsite_contents.html'
         frame='hazsite_frame.html'
         nogtitle
         path=odsout;
```

Define the title and footnote for the map of the EPA regions.

```
title1 'Hazardous Waste Sites in EPA Regions (1997)';
footnote1 h=3 j=l 'click on a map region' j=r 'EPAMAP ';
```

Define a map pattern for each region. Each PATTERN statement defines one map/plot pattern. The patterns are assigned to the map areas that represent the EPA regions

```
pattern1 value=msolid color=blue;
pattern2 value=msolid color=green;
pattern3 value=msolid color=red;
pattern4 value=msolid color=lime;
pattern5 value=msolid color=cyan;
```

Generate the regional map. The ID statement specifies the variable that defines the map areas and is in both the map data set and the response data set. DISCRETE specifies that each value of the numeric response variable, STATE, be treated as a separate response level. HTML= specifies REGIONDRILL as the variable that contains the targets for the map regions. Specifying HTML variables causes SAS/GRAPH to add an image map to the HTML body file. DES= specifies the description that is stored in the catalog and used in the Table of Contents. NAME= specifies the name of the graphics catalog entry. Because the PATH= destination is a file storage location and not a specific file name, the catalog entry name EPAMAP is automatically assigned to the GIF file.

```
proc gmap map=maps.us data=newsites;
   id state;
   choro region / discrete
                  html=regiondrill
                  coutline=black
                  nolegend
                  des='EPA Regional Map'
                  name='epamap';
run;
quit;
```

Open a new body file for the state maps. Assigning a new body file closes HAZSITE_MAPBODY.HTML. The contents and frame files, which remain open, will provide links to all body files. ANCHOR= specifies the name of the anchor that identifies the link target. This name is automatically incremented when the graphics output is generated. GTITLE uses titles in the GIF files.

```
ods html body='hazsite_statebody.html'
         anchor='Region1'
         gtitle
         path=odsout;
```

Assign new graphics options for ODS HTML output.

```
goptions notransparency
         border;
```

Sort the response data set NEWSITES in order of the BY variable. The data must be in sorted order before running the GMAP procedure with BY-group processing.

```
proc sort data=newsites;
   by region;
run;
```

Define legend characteristics for the state maps. VALUE= specifies text for the legend values that describes the ranges specified by MIDPOINTS= in the BLOCK statement.

```
legend1 shape=bar(3,4)
        label=('Number of Sites'
               position=(top center))
        value=(j=l '0-24' '25-49' '50-74' '75-99' 'over 100')
        frame;
```

Define a pattern for the map areas. Because the procedure uses BY-group processing to generate the maps, all map areas use the same map pattern.

```
pattern1 value=ms color=gray;
```

Define the patterns for the blocks.

```
pattern2 value=solid color=lipk;
pattern3 value=solid color=cyan;
pattern4 value=solid color=green;
pattern5 value=solid color=blue;
pattern6 value=solid color=red;
```

Suppress the default BY-line and define a title that includes the BY-values. #BYVAL inserts the value of the BY variable into the title of each block map.

```
options nobyline;
title1 'Wastes Sites per State in Region #byval(region)';
footnote1 h=3 j=r 'SITEMAP ';
```

Generate the block maps for each region. MIDPOINTS= defines the midpoints of the ranges described in the legend. NAME= is a full 8 characters ending in **1** so the incremented names match the regions. NAME= specifies the name of the first catalog entry. Because BY-group processing generates multiple graphs from one BLOCK statement, the name assigned by NAME= is incremented to provide a unique name for each piece of output. These names are automatically assigned to the GIF files. DES= specifies the description that is stored in the catalog and used in the Table of Contents. Because BY-group processing is used, the same description is assigned to all the output.

```
proc gmap map=maps.us data=newsites;
   by region;
   id state;
   block sites / midpoints=(12 37 62 87 112)
```

```
                              legend=legend1
                              shape=cylinder
                              blocksize=4
                              coutline=black
                              des='State Maps'
                              name='states01';
    run;
    quit;
```

Close the ODS HTML destination, and open the ODS Listing destination. You must close the HTML destination before you can view the output with a browser.

```
    ods html close;
    ods listing;
```

Example 6: Labeling the States on a U.S. Map

Procedure features:
    CHORO statement options:
            ANNOTATE=
            NOLEGEND
Other features:
    Annotate Facility
Sample library member: GR19N06

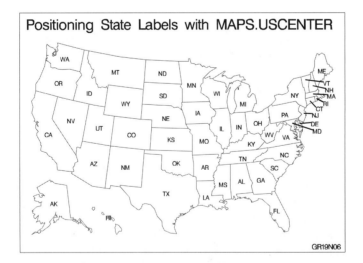

This example uses the MAPS.USCENTER data set and the Annotate facility to add postal code labels to each state. The program first builds an Annotate data set that contains the instructions for drawing the labels. Some of the labels are in the center of the state and others use external labeling with leader lines. The CHORO statement assigns the Annotate data set to the map.

Note: The coordinates in MAPS.USCENTER have been projected to match coordinates in the MAPS.US data set. △

Assign the librefs and set the graphics environment.

```
libname reflib 'SAS-data-library';
libname maps 'SAS-data-library';
goptions reset=global gunit=pct border cback=white
        colors=(black blue green red)
        ftext=swiss htitle=6 htext=3;
```

Create annotate data set, REFLIB.CENTER, from MAPS.USCENTER. The annotate data set labels each state with a two-letter abbreviation. MAPS.USCENTER provides the x and y coordinates for the labels. FLAG, which is initially turned off, signals when external labeling is in effect. The labels are drawn after the map because the value of WHEN is **a** (after).

```
data reflib.center;
   length function $ 8;
   retain flag 0 xsys ysys '2' hsys '3' when 'a'
          style 'swiss';
   set maps.uscenter
       (where=(fipstate(state) ne 'DC')
       drop=long lat);
```

The FIPSTATE function creates the label text by converting the FIPS codes from MAPS.USCENTER to two-letter postal codes.

```
function='label';
text=fipstate(state);
size=2.5;
position='5';
```

If the labeling coordinates are outside the state (**OCEAN='Y'**), Annotate adds the label and prepares to draw the leader line. **Note:** OCEAN is a character variable and is, therefore, case sensitive. **OCEAN='Y'** must specify an uppercase Y.

```
if ocean='Y' then
   do;
      position='6';
      output;
      function='move';
      flag=1;
   end;
```

When external labeling is in effect, Annotate draws the leader line and resets the flag.

```
else if flag=1 then
   do;
```

```
                    function='draw';
                    size=.25;
                    flag=0;
                end;
            output;
    run;
```

Define title and footnote for map.

```
title 'Positioning State Labels with MAPS.USCENTER';
footnote j=r 'GR19N06 ';
```

Define pattern characteristics. PATTERN1 defines a single map pattern that is repeated for each of the 50 map areas (states). The pattern is an empty fill with a blue border. VALUE= defines a map/plot pattern, which cannot be used by the blocks. Specifying a color causes PATTERN1 to generate only one pattern definition. REPEAT= specifies the number of times to repeat the pattern definition.

```
pattern1 value=mempty color=blue repeat=50;
```

Produce the choropleth map. NOLEGEND suppresses the legend. ANNOTATE= specifies the data set to annotate the map.

```
proc gmap data=maps.us map=maps.us;
    id state;
    choro state / nolegend
                  annotate=reflib.center;
    run;
    quit;
```

Example 7: Producing a Simple Prism Map

Procedure features:
  ID statement
  PRISM statement option:
       COUTLINE=
Data set: REFLIB.SITES
Sample library member: GR19N07

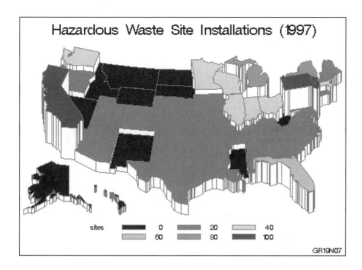

This example produces a prism map of the hazardous waste sites. Since the DISCRETE option is not used, the response variable is assumed to have a continuous range of values. Because neither the LEVELS= nor MIDPOINTS= option is used, the GMAP procedure selects a number of levels based on the number of map areas and then calculates the appropriate response levels. The legend shows the midpoint value of each level.

The map areas use the default pattern, which is a solid fill that rotates through the colors list. Because the colors list is specified in the GOPTIONS statement, all colors are used in the rotation. COUTLINE= outlines the map areas in gray, instead of the default outline color, which is the first color in the list, in this case, BLUE.

Since the XVIEW=, YVIEW=, and ZVIEW= options are not used, the default viewing position, above and to the east and south of the center of the map, is used. Since the XLIGHT= and YLIGHT= options are not used, none of the side polygons of the prisms are shadowed. The light source is the same as the viewing position.

Assign the librefs and set the graphics environment. COLORS= specifies the colors list, which is used by the default patterns and outlines. CTEXT= specifies the color for all text.

```
libname reflib 'SAS-data-library';
libname maps 'SAS-data-library';
goptions reset=global gunit=pct border cback=white
        colors=(blue green lime lipk cyan red)
        ctext=black ftext=swiss htitle=6 htext=3;
```

Define title and footnote for the map.

```
title1 'Hazardous Waste Site Installations (1997)';
footnote1 j=r 'GR19N07 ';
```

Produce the prism map. The ID statement specifies the variable in the map data set and the response data set that defines map areas. COUTLINE= specifies the map area outline color.

```
proc gmap map=maps.us data=reflib.sites;
   id state;
   prism sites / coutline=gray;
run;
```

```
quit;
```

Example 8: Specifying Midpoints in a Prism Map

Procedure features:
    PRISM statement options:

        LEGEND=
        MIDPOINTS=
        XLIGHT=
        XVIEW=
        ZVIEW=

Other features:
    LEGEND statement

Data set: REFLIB.SITES

Sample library member: GR19N08

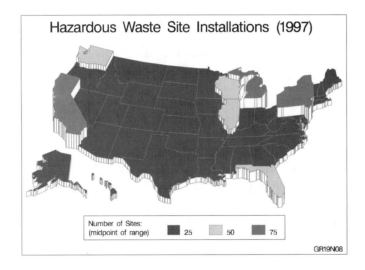

This example explicitly specifies the midpoints for three response levels. Each response level uses the default solid pattern and a color from the colors list.

The example also changes the map viewpoint and light source.

Assign the librefs and set the graphics environment. COLORS= specifies the colors list, which is used by the default patterns and outlines. CTEXT= specifies the color for all text.

```
libname reflib 'SAS-data-library';
libname maps 'SAS-data-library';
goptions reset=global gunit=pct border cback=white
        colors=(blue green red) ctext=black
        ftext=swiss htitle=6 htext=3;
```

Define title and footnote for map.

```
title1 'Hazardous Waste Site Installations (1997)';
footnote1 j=r 'GR19N08 ';
```

Define legend characteristics. CBORDER= draws a black frame around the legend. If FRAME were specified, it would be BLUE, the first color in the colors list.

```
legend shape=bar(4,4)
       value=(j=l)
       label=('Number of Sites:'
              j=l '(midpoint of range)')
       cborder=black;
```

Produce the prism map. MIDPOINTS= specifies three response levels for the map. XLIGHT= moves the light source to the right and adds shadows to the left-side polygons of the prisms. XVIEW= and ZVIEW= shift the viewing point to the right and upward, respectively. This reduces the number of prisms that are partially hidden by taller neighbors.

```
proc gmap map=maps.us data=reflib.sites;
   id state;
   prism sites / midpoints=25 50 75
                 xlight=5
                 xview=.75
                 zview=5
                 legend=legend
                 coutline=gray;
run;
quit;
```

Example 9: Producing a Simple Surface Map

Procedure features:
   SURFACE statement
Data set: REFLIB.SITES
Sample library member: GR19N09

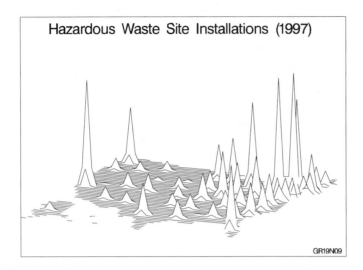

This example produces a surface map that shows the total number of hazardous waste sites in each state in 1997. Because the CONSTANT= and NLINES= options are not used, the GMAP procedure draws a surface that consists of 50 lines and uses the default decay function to calculate spike height and base width. And because the ROTATE= and TILT= options are not used, the map is rotated 70 degrees around the Z axis and tilted 70 degrees with respect to the X axis.

Assign the librefs and set the graphics environment. COLORS= specifies the colors list. By default the map uses the first color in the list.

```
libname reflib 'SAS-data-library';
libname maps 'SAS-data-library';
goptions reset=global gunit=pct border cback=white
         colors=(black blue green red)
         ftext=swiss htitle=6 htext=3;
```

Define title and footnote for the map.

```
title1 'Hazardous Waste Site Installations (1997)';
footnote1 j=r 'GR19N09 ';
```

Produce the surface map. The ID statement specifies the variable in the map data set and the response data set that defines the map areas.

```
proc gmap map=maps.us data=reflib.sites;
   id state;
   surface sites;
run;
quit;
```

Example 10: Rotating and Tilting a Surface Map

Procedure features:

SURFACE statement options:
    CONSTANT=
    NLINES=
    ROTATE=
    TILT=

Data set: REFLIB.SITES

Sample library member: GR19N10

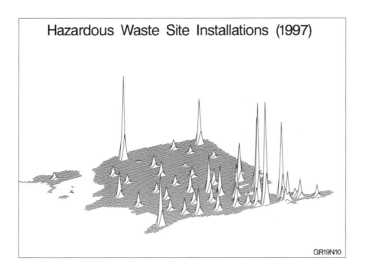

This example tilts and rotates the surface map and uses more lines to draw the surface.

Assign the librefs and set the graphics environment.

```
libname reflib 'SAS-data-library';
libname maps 'SAS-data-library';
goptions reset=global gunit=pct border cback=white
         colors=(black blue green red)
         ftext=swiss htitle=6 htext=3;
```

Define title and footnote for the map.

```
title1 'Hazardous Waste Site Installations (1997)';
footnote1 j=r 'GR19N10 ';
```

Produce the surface map. CONSTANT= specifies a value that is less than the default value so the spikes are narrower at the base. NLINES= specifies the maximum number of map lines, which gives the best map shape resolution. ROTATE= and TILT= adjust the map orientation to make the crowded spikes in the northeast portion of the map easier to distinguish.

```
proc gmap map=maps.us data=reflib.sites;
   id state;
   surface sites / constant=4
```

```
                              nlines=100
                              rotate=40
                              tilt=60;
          run;
          quit;
```

CHAPTER

20

The GOPTIONS Procedure

Overview

The GOPTIONS procedure provides information about the values of graphics options and the global statement definitions that are currently in effect in your session. The values displayed are either the defaults of the current device driver or user-defined values that have been assigned in your SAS session. You can use the GOPTIONS procedure to

□ list the current values of all of the graphics options, or of one specified option

□ display the values of all of the AXIS, FOOTNOTE, LEGEND, PATTERN, SYMBOL, and TITLE definitions that are currently in effect.

Note: Do not confuse the GOPTIONS procedure with the GOPTIONS statement. The GOPTIONS procedure lists the values that are defined in a GOPTIONS statement as well as in any other global statement definitions. See "GOPTIONS Statement" on page 182 for a list of the graphics options that you can set with the GOPTIONS statement. See Chapter 9, "Graphics Options and Device Parameters Dictionary," on page 301 for a complete description of each graphics option. △

The list of graphics options displays in the SAS LOG window and includes the names of the options, the current values, and a brief description of each one. You can use PROC GOPTIONS statement options to control what information is listed and where it appears in the LOG window. Output 20.1 on page 795 contains part of a sample LOG listing.

Output 20.1   Parital Output from the GOPTIONS Procedure

```
                      SAS/GRAPH software options and parameters
                   (executing in DMS Programming Environment environment)
     NOADMGDF                       GDDM driver output an ADMGDF file
     ASPECT=                        Aspect ratio (width/height) for software characters
     NOAUTOCOPY                     Automatic hardcopy after display
     NOAUTOFEED                     Automatic paper feed after plot
     NOAUTOSIZE                     Change character cell size to preserve device
                                    catalog rows and columns
     BAUD=                          Communications line speed
     BINDING=NOBINDING              Binding edge
     NOBORDER                       Draw a border around display or plot
     CBACK=                         Background color
     CBY=                           BY line color
     CELL                           Hardware characters must be on cell boundaries
     CHARACTERS                     Use hardware characters
     CHARTYPE=                      Select hardware font
     CIRCLEARC                      Use hardware circle/arc generator
     NOCOLLATE                      Collate output
     COLORS=( )                     Default color list
     CPATTERN=                      Default pattern color
     CSYMBOL=                       Default symbol color
     CTEXT=                         Default text color
     CTITLE=                        Default title, footnote and note color
     DASH                           Use hardware dashed line generator
     DASHSCALE=                     Dash pattern scale factor
     DELAY=                         Animation delay time in milliseconds
     DEVADDR=                       IBM Device address, qname, or node name
     DEVICE=                        Default device driver
     DEVMAP=DEFAULT                 Output character map for hardware text
     DISPLAY                        Display graph on device
     DISPOSAL=NONE                  Image animation disposal method
     DRVINIT=                       Host command executed before driver initialization
     DRVTERM=                       Host command executed after driver termination
     NODUPLEX                       Duplex printing
     NOERASE                        Erase graph upon completion
     FASTTEXT                       Use quicker, less precise, integer font rendering
                                    routines; generally unsuitable for multiple device
                                    or templated replay situations.
```

Note: All of the graphics options that are displayed by the GOPTIONS procedure are described in Chapter 9, "Graphics Options and Device Parameters Dictionary," on page 301. △

Procedure Syntax

PROC GOPTIONS *<option(s)>*;

PROC GOPTIONS Statement

Lists the graphics options, and their values and descriptions in the LOG window. Optionally, it lists the currently defined global statements. By default, each listed item is displayed on a separate line.

Syntax

PROC GOPTIONS <*option(s)*>;

option(s) can be one or more options from the following categories:

□ item request options

    AXIS

    FOOTNOTE

    LEGEND

    OPTION=*graphics-option*

    PATTERN

    SYMBOL

    TITLE

□ listing format options

    CENTIMETERS

    NOLIST

    NOLOG

    SHORT

Options

You can specify as many options as you want and list them in any order.

AXIS
A

requests a list of all current AXIS definitions. AXIS also lists the current values for all graphics options, unless you use the NOLIST option. If you have not defined any AXIS statements, the GOPTIONS procedure issues a message.

CENTIMETERS
CM

displays the values of the HORIGIN=, HSIZE=, PAPERFEED=, PAPERLIMIT=, VORIGIN=, and VSIZE= graphics options in units of centimeters (CM). These graphics options use units of IN or CM only, and their values are always stored as inches even if you specify CM. Therefore, the GOPTIONS procedure displays these values in inches, unless you specify the CENTIMETERS option.

Note: The CENTIMETERS option does not affect the graphics options that can use unit specifications of CELLS, CM, IN, PCT, and PT. △

FOOTNOTE
F

requests a list of all of the current FOOTNOTE and TITLE definitions. FOOTNOTE also lists the current values for all of the graphics options, unless you use the NOLIST option. If you have not defined any FOOTNOTE or TITLE statements, the GOPTIONS procedure issues a message.

Featured in: Example 1 on page 798

LEGEND

L

> requests a list of all of the current LEGEND definitions. LEGEND lists the current values for all of the graphics options, unless you use the NOLIST option. If you have not defined any LEGEND statements, the GOPTIONS procedure issues a message.

NOLIST

N

> suppresses the display of graphics options. Use the NOLIST option in conjunction with the appropriate statement request option when you want to list only the current AXIS, FOOTNOTE, LEGEND, PATTERN, SYMBOL, or TITLE definitions.
>
> **Featured in:**   Example 1 on page 798

NOLOG

> displays the output in the OUTPUT window instead of the LOG window.

OPTION=*graphics-option*

> requests information on the specified graphics option. For these options, requesting one displays the value of both:
> - □   HSIZE= and VSIZE=
> - □   HPOS= and VPOS=
> - □   XMAX= and YMAX=
> - □   XPIXELS= and YPIXELS=

PATTERN

P

> requests a list of all of the current PATTERN definitions. PATTERN lists the current values for all of the graphics options, unless you use the NOLIST. If you have not defined any PATTERN statements, the GOPTIONS procedure issues a message.

SHORT

> suppresses the descriptions of the graphics options and displays the graphics options values in an alphabetical list in paragraph form.
>
> **Featured in:**   Example 2 on page 799

SYMBOL

S

> requests a list of all of the current SYMBOL definitions. SYMBOL lists the current values for all of the graphics options, unless you use the NOLIST. If you have not defined any SYMBOL statements, the GOPTIONS procedure issues a message.

TITLE

T

> requests a list of all of the current TITLE and FOOTNOTE definitions. TITLE lists the current values for all of the graphics options, unless you use the NOLIST option. If you have not defined any FOOTNOTE or TITLE statements, the GOPTIONS procedure issues messages.

Examples

Example 1: Displaying TITLE and FOOTNOTE Statements

Procedure features:

PROC GOPTIONS statement:
    FOOTNOTE
    NOLIST
Sample library member: GR20N01

This example uses the FOOTNOTE option to display the current definitions of both the FOOTNOTE and TITLE statements. It also uses the NOLIST option to suppress the list of graphics options. Output 20.2 on page 799 shows the listing that appears in the LOG.

Output 20.2 Using the NOLIST Option (GR20N01)

```
TITLE1 HEIGHT=6 COLOR=BLUE FONT=SWISSB 'Production Quality' ;
TITLE2 HEIGHT=4 COLOR=BLUE FONT=SWISSB 'January through June';

FOOTNOTE1 HEIGHT=3 COLOR=GREEN FONT=SWISS 'Data from SASDATA.QUALITY' ;

FOOTNOTE2 HEIGHT=3 COLOR=GREEN FONT=SWISS '* denotes approximations' ;
```

Clear all global statements.

```
goptions reset=global;
```

Define titles and footnotes.

```
title1 h=6 c=blue f=swissb 'Production Quality';
title2 h=4 c=blue f=swissb 'January through June';
footnote1 h=3 c=green f=swiss 'Data from SASDATA.QUALITY';
footnote2 h=3 c=green f=swiss '* denotes approximations';
```

Produce the listing. The NOLIST and FOOTNOTE options control the information that appears in the LOG window.

```
proc goptions nolist footnote;
run;
```

Example 2: Displaying Graphics Options without the Description

Procedure features:
    PROC GOPTIONS statement:
        SHORT
Sample library member: GR20N02

This example uses the SHORT option to display only the values of graphics options without the description of each graphics option. Output 20.3 on page 800 shows the listing that appears in the LOG window.

Output 20.3   Using the SHORT Option (GR20N02)

```
              SAS/GRAPH software options and parameters
            (executing in DMS Programming Environment environment)
NOADMGDF ASPECT= NOAUTOCOPY NOAUTOFEED NOAUTOSIZE BAUD= BINDING=NOBINDING
BORDER CBACK= CBY= CELL CHARACTERS CHARTYPE= CIRCLEARC NOCOLLATE COLORS=( BLUE
GREEN RED ) CPATTERN=BLUE CSYMBOL= CTEXT=RED CTITLE=GREEN DASH DASHSCALE=
DELAY= DEVADDR= DEVICE= DEVMAP=DEFAULT DISPLAY DISPOSAL=NONE DRVINIT= DRVTERM=
NODUPLEX NOERASE FASTTEXT FBY= FCACHE=3 FILECLOSE= FILL FILLINC= FONTRES=NORMAL
FTEXT=SWISSB FTITLE= FTRACK=TIGHT GACCESS= GCLASS=G GCOPIES=(0, 20)
GDDMCOPY=FSCOPY GDDMNICKNAME= GDDMTOKEN= GDEST=LOCAL GEND= GEPILOG= GFORMS=
NOGOPT10 NOGOPT11 NOGOPT12 NOGOPT13 NOGOPT14 NOGOPT15 GOPTINT1=0 GOPTINT2=0
GOPTDBL1= GOPTDBL2= GOPTSTR1= GOPTSTR2= GOUTMODE=APPEND GOUTTYPE=INDEPENDENT
GPROLOG= GPROTOCOL= GRAPHRC GSFLEN= GSFMODE=PORT GSFNAME= NOGSFPROMPT GSIZE=
GSTART= GUNIT=PERCENT GWAIT= GWRITER=SASWTR HANDSHAKE= HBY=4   HORIGIN= HPOS=
HSIZE= HTEXT=3  HTITLE=6  INBIN= INTERPOL= ITERATION= NONINTERLACED
KEYMAP=DEFAULT LFACTOR= OFFSET= OFFSHADOW=(0.0625 in., -0.0625 in.) OUTBIN=
PAPERFEED= PAPERLIMIT= PAPERSIZE= PAPERTYPE= PENMOUNTS= PENSORT PIEFILL NOPCLIP
POLYGONCLIP POLYGONFILL POSTGEPILOG= POSTGRAPH= POSTGPROLOG= PPDFILE=
PREGEPILOG= PREGRAPH= PREGPROLOG= PROMPT PROMPTCHARS='000A010D05000000'X
RENDER=MEMORY RENDERLIB=WORK REPAINT= NOREVERSE NOROTATE SIMFONT= SPEED= NOSWAP
SYMBOL TARGETDEVICE= NOTRANSPARENCY TRANTAB= UCC= NOUSERINPUT NOV5COMP NOV6COMP
VORIGIN= VPOS= VSIZE= XMAX= XPIXELS= YMAX= YPIXELS=
```

Set the graphics environment. The values of the graphics options specified in this statement appear in the LOG listing.

```
goptions reset=global gunit=pct border
         ftext=swissb htitle=6 htext=3
         ctext=red cpattern=blue ctitle=green
         colors=(blue green red) hby=4;
```

Produce the listing. The SHORT option suppresses the display of the description of each graphics option.

```
proc goptions short;
run;
```

CHAPTER
21

The GPLOT Procedure

Overview

The GPLOT procedure plots the values of two or more variables on a set of coordinate axes (X and Y). The coordinates of each point on the plot correspond to two variable values in an observation of the input data set. The procedure can also generate a separate plot for each value of a third (classification) variable. It can also generate bubble plots in which circles of varying proportions representing the values of a third variable are drawn at the data points.

The procedure produces a variety of two-dimensional graphs including

□ simple scatter plots

□ overlay plots in which multiple sets of data points display on one set of axes

□ plots against a second vertical axis

□ bubble plots

□ logarithmic plots (controlled by the AXIS statement).

In conjunction with the SYMBOL statement the GPLOT procedure can produce join plots, high-low plots, needle plots, and plots with simple or spline-interpolated lines. The SYMBOL statement can also display regression lines on scatter plots.

The GPLOT procedure is useful for

□ displaying long series of data, showing trends and patterns

□ interpolating between data points

□ extrapolating beyond existing data with the display of regression lines and confidence limits.

About Plots of Two Variables

Plots of two variables display the values of two variables as data points on one horizontal axis (X) and one vertical axis (Y). Each pair of X and Y values forms a data point.

Figure 21.1 on page 802 shows a simple scatter plot that plots the values of the variable HEIGHT on the vertical axis and the variable WEIGHT on the horizontal axis. By default, the PLOT statement scales the axes to include the maximum and minimum data values and displays a plus sign (+) at each data point. It labels each axis with the name of its variable or an associated label and displays the value of each major tick mark.

Figure 21.1   Scatter Plot of Two Variables (GR21N04(a))

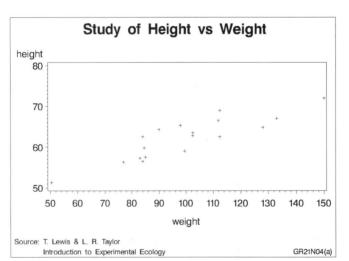

The program for this plot is in Example 4 on page 839. For more information on producing scatter plots, see "PLOT Statement" on page 818.

You can also overlay two or more plots (multiple sets of data points) on a single set of axes and you can apply a variety of interpolation techniques to these plots. See "About Interpolation Methods" on page 805.

About Plots with a Classification Variable

Plots that use a classification variable produce a separate set of data points for each unique value of the classification variable and display all sets of data points on one set of axes.

Figure 21.2 on page 803 shows multiple line plots that compare yearly temperature trends for three cities. The legend explains the values of the classification variable, CITY.

Figure 21.2 Plot of Three Variables with Legend (GR21N08(a))

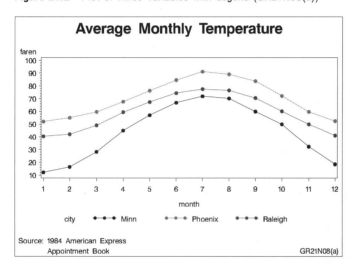

By default, plots with a classification variable generate a legend. In the code that generates the plot for Figure 21.2 on page 803, a SYMBOL statement connects the data points and specifies the plot symbol that is used for each value of the classification variable (CITY). The program for this plot is in Example 8 on page 847. For more information on how to produce plots with a classification variable, see "PLOT Statement" on page 818.

About Bubble Plots

Bubble plots represent the values of three variables by drawing circles of varying sizes at points that are plotted on the vertical and horizontal axes. Two of the variables determine the location of the data points, while the values of the third variable control the size of the circles.

Figure 21.3 on page 804 shows a bubble plot in which each bubble represents a category of engineer that is shown on the horizontal axis. The location of each bubble in relation to the vertical axis is determined by the average salary for the category. The size of each bubble represents the number of engineers in the category relative to the total number of engineers in the data.

By default, the BUBBLE statement scales the axes to include the maximum and minimum data values and draws an unlabeled circle at each data point. It labels each axis with the name of its variable or an associated label and displays the value of each major tick mark.

Figure 21.3   Bubble Plot (GR21N01)

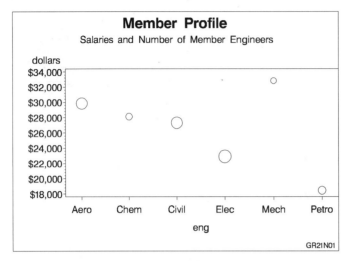

The program for this plot is in Example 1 on page 834. For more information on producing bubble plots, see "BUBBLE Statement" on page 809.

About Plots with Two Vertical Axes

Plots with two vertical axes have a right vertical axis that can

□ display the same variable values as the left axis

□ display left axis values in a different scale

□ plot a second dependent (Y) variable, thereby producing one or more overlay plots.

In Figure 21.4 on page 805 the right axis displays the values of the vertical coordinates in a different scale from the scale that is used for the left axis.

Figure 21.4 Plot with a Right Vertical Axis (GR21N09)

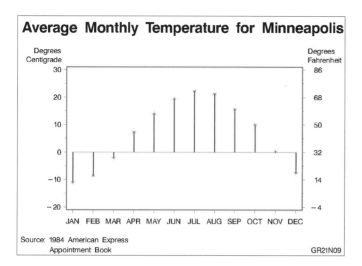

The program for this plot is in Example 9 on page 851. For more information on how to produce plots with a right vertical axis, see "PLOT2 Statement" on page 828 and "BUBBLE2 Statement" on page 815.

About Interpolation Methods

In addition to these graphs, you can produce other types of plots such as box plots or high-low-close plots by specifying various interpolation methods with the SYMBOL statement. Use the SYMBOL statement to

☐ connect the data points with straight lines

☐ specify regression analysis to fit a line to the points and, optionally, display lines for confidence limits

☐ connect the data points to the zero line on the vertical axis

☐ display the minimum and maximum values of Y at each X value and mark the mean value, display standard deviations that connect the data points with lines or bars, generate box plots, or plot high-low-close stock market data

☐ specify that a pattern fill the polygon that is defined by data points

☐ smooth plot lines with spline interpolation

☐ use a step function to connect the data points

"SYMBOL Statement" on page 226 describes all interpolation methods.

Concepts

Parts of a Plot

Some terms used with GPLOT procedure are illustrated in Figure 21.5 on page 806 and Figure 21.6 on page 806.

Figure 21.5   GPLOT Procedure Terms

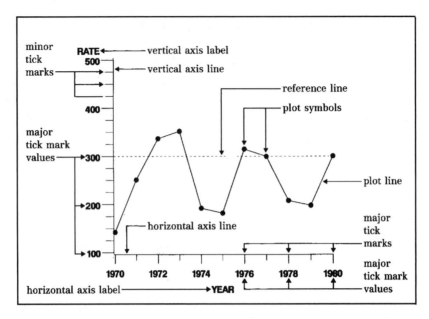

Figure 21.6   Additional GPLOT Procedure Terms

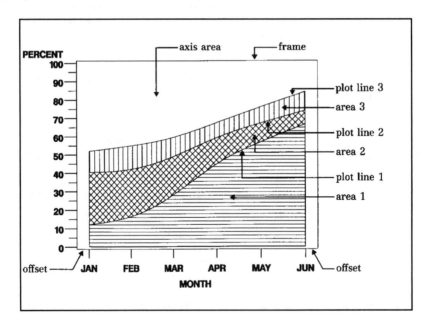

About the Input Data Set

The input data set that is used by the GPLOT procedure must contain at least one variable to plot on the horizontal axis and one variable to plot on the vertical axis. Typically, the horizontal axis shows an independent variable (time, for example), and the vertical axis shows a dependent variable (temperature, for example). Variables can be character or numeric. Graphs are automatically scaled to the values of the character data or to include the values of numeric data, but you can control scaling with procedure options or with associated AXIS statements.

Missing Values

If the value of either of the plot variables is missing, the GPLOT procedure does not include the observation in the plot. If you specify interpolation with a SYMBOL definition, the plot is not broken at the missing value. To break the plot line or area fill at the missing value, use the PLOT statement's SKIPMISS option. SKIPMISS is available only with join or spline interpolations.

Values Out of Range

Exclude data values from a graph by restricting the range of axis values with the VAXIS= or HAXIS= options or with the ORDER= option in an AXIS statement. When an observation contains a value outside of the specified axis range, the GPLOT procedure excludes the observation from the plot and issues a message to the log.

If you specify interpolation with a SYMBOL definition, by default values outside of the axis range are excluded from interpolation calculations and as a result may change interpolated values for the plot. Values that are omitted from interpolation calculations have a particularly noticeable effect on the high-low interpolation methods: HILO, STD, and BOX. In addition, regression lines and confidence limits will represent only part of the original data.

To specify that values out of range are included in the interpolation calculations, use the MODE= option in a SYMBOL statement. When MODE=INCLUDE, values that fall outside of the axis range are included in interpolation calculations but excluded from the plot. The default (MODE=EXCLUDE) omits observations that are outside of the axis range from interpolation calculations. See the MODE= option of the SYMBOL statement in "SYMBOL Statement" on page 226 for details.

Sorted Data

Data points are plotted in the order in which the observations are read from the data set. Therefore, if you use any type of interpolation that generates a line, sort your data by the horizontal axis variable.

Logarithmic Axes

If your data contain logarithmic values or if the data values vary over a wide range or contain large values, you may want to specify a logarithmic axis for the horizontal or vertical axis. Logarithmic axes can be specified with the AXIS statement options LOGBASE= and LOGSTYLE=. See "AXIS Statement" on page 162 for a complete discussion.

Procedure Syntax

Requirements: At least one PLOT or BUBBLE statement is required. A PLOT2 or BUBBLE2 statement can be used in conjunction with a PLOT or BUBBLE statement.

Global statements: AXIS, FOOTNOTE, LEGEND, PATTERN, SYMBOL, TITLE

Reminder: The procedure can include BY, FORMAT, LABEL, WHERE, and NOTE statements.

Supports: RUN-group processing Output Delivery System (ODS)

> **PROC GPLOT** <DATA=*input-data-set*>
>   <ANNOTATE=*Annotate-data-set*>
>   <GOUT=<*libref.*>*output-catalog*>
>   <IMAGEMAP=*output-data-set*>
>   <UNIFORM>;
> **BUBBLE** *plot-request(s)* </option(s)>;
>   **BUBBLE2** *plot-request(s)* </option(s)>;
> **PLOT** *plot-request(s)* </option(s)>;
>   **PLOT2** *plot-request(s)* </option(s)>;

PROC GPLOT Statement

Identifies the data set that contains the plot variables. Optionally specifies uniform axis scaling for all graphs as well as annotation and an output catalog.

Requirements: An input data set is required.

Syntax

> **PROC GPLOT** <DATA=*input-data-set*>
>   <ANNOTATE=*Annotate-data-set*>
>   <GOUT=<*libref.*>*output-catalog*>
>   <IMAGEMAP=*output-data-set*>
>   <UNIFORM>;

Options

ANNOTATE=*Annotate-data-set*
ANNO=*Annotate-data-set*
    specifies a data set to annotate all graphs that are produced by the GPLOT procedure. To annotate individual graphs, use ANNOTATE= in the action statement.
    See also: Chapter 10, "The Annotate Data Set," on page 403

DATA=*input-data-set*
    specifies the SAS data set that contains the variables to plot. By default, the procedure uses the most recently created SAS data set.
    See also: "SAS Data Sets" on page 25 and "About the Input Data Set" on page 806

GOUT=< *libref.* >*output-catalog*
    specifies the SAS catalog in which to save the graphics output that is produced by the GPLOT procedure. If you omit the libref, SAS/GRAPH looks for the catalog in the temporary library called WORK and creates the catalog if it does not exist.
    See also: "Storing Graphics Output in SAS Catalogs" on page 49

IMAGEMAP=*output-data-set*
    creates a SAS data set that contains information that can be used to implement a drill-down plot. IMAGEMAP= can be used only if the PLOT or PLOT2 statements are used, and the PLOT or PLOT2 statement must use the HTML= option or the HTML_LEGEND= option or both.
    The Imagemap information is used in the HTML file that references the graph. It determines where the drill-down hot zones are, and it links those hot zones to other

files or images. If HTML= is used on the PLOT or PLOT2 statement, th
are defined as hot zones, unless AREA= is also used, in which case ther·
points and the areas between plot lines are defined as hot zones. If HTM
is used, the legend symbols are defined as hot zones. Information for th
stored in the variables referenced by the HTML= and HTML_LEGEND= options.

See also: "Customizing Web Pages for Drill-down Graphs" on page 100

UNIFORM

specifies that the same axis scaling is used for all graphs that are produced by the
procedure. By default, the range of axis values for each axis is based on the minimum
and maximum values in the data and, therefore, may vary from graph to graph and
among BY groups. Using the UNIFORM option forces the value range for each axis to
be the same for all graphs. Thus, if the procedure produces multiple graphs with both
left and right vertical axes, the UNIFORM option scales all of the left axes the same
and all of the right axes the same, based on the minimum and maximum data values.

In addition, UNIFORM forces the assignment of SYMBOL statements for the
category variable without regard to the BY-group variable, and, if a legend is
generated, makes the legend the same across graphs.

BUBBLE Statement

**Creates bubble plots in which a third variable is plotted against two variables represented by the
horizontal and vertical axes; the value of the third variable controls the size of the bubble.**

Requirements: At least one plot request is required.

Global statements: AXIS, FOOTNOTE, TITLE

Description

The BUBBLE statement specifies one or more plot requests that name
the horizontal and left vertical axis variables and the variable that controls the size of
the bubbles. This statement automatically

- □ centers each circle at a data point that is determined by the values of the vertical
  and horizontal axes variables
- □ scales the axes to include the maximum and minimum data values
- □ labels each axis with the name of its variable or associated label
- □ displays each major tick mark value
- □ draws circles for values that are located within the axes.

You can use statement options to control axis scaling, draw reference lines, modify
the appearance of axes, control the display of the bubbles, and specify annotation.

In addition, you can use global statements to modify axes (AXIS statement), and add
text to the graph (TITLE, NOTE, and FOOTNOTE statements). You can also use the
Annotate data set to enhance the plot.

Syntax

BUBBLE *plot-request(s)* *</option(s)>*;

option(s) can be one or more options from any or all of the following categories:

- □ bubble appearance options:

    BCOLOR=*bubble-color*

           BFONT=*font*

           BLABEL

           BSCALE=AREA | RADIUS

           BSIZE=*multiplier*

☐ plot appearance options:

           ANNOTATE=*Annotate-data-set*

           CAXIS=*axis-color*

           CFRAME=*background-color*

           CTEXT=*text-color*

           FRAME | NOFRAME

           GRID

           NOAXIS

☐ horizontal axis options:

           AUTOHREF

           CHREF=*reference-line-color*

           HAXIS=*value-list* | AXIS<1...99>

           HMINOR=*number-of-minor-ticks*

           HREF=*value-list*

           HZERO

           LHREF=*line-type*

☐ vertical axis options:

           AUTOVREF

           CVREF=*reference-line-color*

           LVREF=*line-type*

           VAXIS=*value-list* | AXIS<1...99>

           VMINOR=*number-of-minor-ticks*

           VREF=*value-list*

           VREVERSE

           VZERO

☐ catalog entry description options:

           DESCRIPTION='*entry-description*'

           NAME='*entry-name*'

Required Arguments

plot-request(s)

    each specifies the variables to plot and produces a separate graph. All variables must be in the input data set. Multiple plot requests are separated with blanks. A plot request must have this form:

y-variable*x-variable=bubble-size

    plots the values of two variables and draws a circle (bubble) at each data point. The value of the third variable determines the size of the bubble.

    y-variable

        variable plotted on the left vertical axis.

x-variable
  variable plotted on the horizontal axis.

bubble-size
  variable that dictates the size of the bubbles. *Bubble-size* must be numeric. If the value of *bubble-size* is positive, bubbles are drawn with a solid line; if it is negative, bubbles are drawn with a dashed line.

Options

  Options in a BUBBLE statement affect all graphs that are produced by that statement. You can specify as many options as you want and list them in any order.

ANNOTATE=*Annotate-data-set*
ANNO=*Annotate-data-set*
  specifies a data set to annotate plots that are produced by the BUBBLE statement.

  See also: Chapter 10, "The Annotate Data Set," on page 403

AUTOHREF
  draws reference lines at all major tick marks on the horizontal axis.

AUTOVREF
  draws reference lines at all major tick marks on the vertical axis.

BCOLOR=*bubble-color*
  specifies the color for the bubbles. If you omit the BCOLOR= option, the first color in the colors list is used for the bubble color.

  Featured in: Example 2 on page 835 and Example 3 on page 837

BFONT=*font*
  specifies the font to use for bubble labels. See Chapter 6, "SAS/GRAPH Fonts," on page 125 for details on how to specify *font*. If you omit the BFONT= option, a font specification is searched for in this order:

  1 the FTEXT= option in a GOPTIONS statement
  2 the default hardware font.

  See also: The BLABEL option for information on the location and color of labels.

  Featured in: Example 2 on page 835

BLABEL
  labels the bubbles with the values of the third variable. If the variable has a format, the formatted value is used. By default, bubbles are not labeled.

  The procedure normally places labels directly outside of the circle at 315 degrees rotation. If a label in this position does not fit in the axis area, other 45-degree placements (that is, 45, 135, and 225 degrees) are attempted. If the label cannot be placed at any of the positions (45, 135, 225, or 315 degrees) without being clipped, the label is omitted. However, labels may collide with other bubbles or previously placed labels.

  Labels display in the color specified by the CTEXT= option. If you omit CTEXT=, the default is the first color in the colors list.

  Featured in: Example 2 on page 835

BSCALE=AREA | RADIUS
  specifies whether the bubble-scaling proportion is based on the area of the circles or the radius measure. By default, BSCALE=AREA.

  The value that is assigned to the BSCALE= option affects how large the bubbles appear in relation to each other. For example, suppose the third variable value is twice as big for one bubble as it is for another. If BSCALE=AREA, the area of the larger bubble will be twice the area of the smaller bubble. If BSCALE=RADIUS, the radius of the larger bubble will be twice the radius of the smaller bubble and the larger bubble will have more than twice the area of the smaller bubble.

BSIZE=*multiplier*

specifies an overall scaling factor for the bubbles so that you can increase or decrease the size of all bubbles by this factor. By default, BSIZE=5.

Featured in: Example 2 on page 835 and Example 3 on page 837

CAXIS=*axis-color*

CA=*axis-color*

specifies the color for the axis line and all major and minor tick marks. By default, the procedure uses the first color in the colors list.

If you use the CAXIS= option, it may be overridden by

1 the COLOR= option in an AXIS definition, which in turn is overridden by

2 the COLOR= suboption of the MAJOR= or MINOR= option in an AXIS definition.

Featured in: Example 2 on page 835 and Example 3 on page 837

CFRAME=*background-color*

CFR=*background-color*

fills the axis area with the specified color. If the FRAME option is also in effect, the procedure determines the color of the frame according to the precedence list given for the FRAME option description.

CHREF=*reference-line-color*

CH=*reference-line-color*

specifies the color for reference lines that are requested by the HREF= and AUTOHREF= options. By default, these reference lines display in the color of the horizontal axis.

CTEXT=*text-color*

C=*text-color*

specifies the color for all text on the axes, including tick mark values, axis labels, and bubble labels.

If you omit the CTEXT= option, a color specification is searched for in this order:

1 the CTEXT= option in a GOPTIONS statement

2 the default, the first color in the colors list.

If you use the CTEXT= option, it overrides the color specification for the axis label and the tick mark values in the COLOR= option in an AXIS definition that is assigned to the axis.

If you use CTEXT=, the color specification is overridden in this situation: if you also use the COLOR= suboption of a LABEL= or VALUE= option in an AXIS definition that is assigned to the axis, that suboption determines the color of the axis label or the color of the tick mark values, respectively.

CVREF=*reference-line-color*

CV=*reference-line-color*

specifies the color for reference lines that are requested by the VREF= and AUTOVREF= options. By default, these reference lines display in the color of the vertical axis.

DESCRIPTION='*entry-description*'

DES='*entry-description*'

specifies the description of the catalog entry for the plot. The maximum length for *entry-description* is 40 characters. The description does not appear on the plot. By default, the procedure assigns a description of the form BUBBLE OF *variable*variable=variable*.

The *entry-description* can include the #BYLINE, #BYVAL, and #BYVAR substitution options, which work as they do when used on TITLE, FOOTNOTE, and NOTE statements. For more information, refer to the description of the options on page 262, and "Substituting BY Line Values in a Text String" on page 266. The 40-character limit applies before the substitution takes place for these options; thus, if in the SAS program the entry-description text exceeds 40 characters, it is truncated to 40 characters, and then the substitution is performed.

The descriptive text is shown in the "description" portion of each of the following:

☐ in the Results window

☐ among the catalog-entry properties that you can view from the Explorer window

☐ in the Table of Contents that is generated when you use CONTENTS= on an ODS HTML statement (see "Linking to Output through a Table of Contents" on page 86), assuming the GPLOT output is generated while the contents page is open

☐ in the Description field of the PROC GREPLAY window

FRAME | NOFRAME
FR | NOFR

specifies whether a frame is drawn around the axis area. The default is FRAME; however, if the V6COMP option is in effect on the GOPTIONS statement, the default is NOFRAME. If you also use a BUBBLE2 or PLOT2 statement and your plotting statements have conflicting frame specifications, FRAME is used.

For the frame color, a specification is searched for in this order:

1 the CAXIS= option

2 the COLOR= option in the AXIS definition assigned to the vertical axis

3 the COLOR= option in the AXIS definition assigned to the horizontal axis

4 the default, the first color in the colors list.

To fill the axis area with a background color, use the CFRAME= option.

GRID

draws reference lines at all major tick marks on both axes. You get the same result when you use all of these options in a BUBBLE statement: AUTOHREF, AUTOVREF, FRAME, LVREF=34, and LHREF=34. The line type for GRID is 34.

The line color is the color of the axis.

HAXIS=*value-list* | AXIS<1 . . . 99>

specifies major tick mark values for the horizontal axis or assigns an AXIS definition. See the HAXIS on page 824 option for a description of *value-list*. If you assign an AXIS definition that does not currently exist, the option is ignored. By default, the procedure scales the axis and provides an appropriate number of tick marks.

Note: If data values fall outside of the range that is specified by the HAXIS= option, then by default the outlying data values are not used in interpolation calculations. △

See also: "About the Input Data Set" on page 806 for more information on values out of range.

Featured in: Example 2 on page 835

HMINOR=*number-of-minor-ticks*
HM=*number-of-minor-ticks*

specifies the number of minor tick marks that are drawn between each major tick mark on the horizontal axis. Minor tick marks are not labeled. The HMINOR=

option overrides the NUMBER= suboption of the MINOR= option in an AXIS definition. You must specify a positive number.

Featured in: Example 1 on page 834

HREF=*value-list*

draws one or more reference lines perpendicular to the horizontal axis at points that are specified by *value-list*. See the HAXIS on page 824 option for a description of *value-list*.

See also: CHREF= on page 812 for a description of color specifications for reference lines.

HZERO

specifies that tick marks on the horizontal axis begin in the first position with a value of zero. The HZERO request is ignored if negative values are present for the horizontal variable or if the horizontal axis has been specified with the HAXIS= option.

LHREF=*line-type*
LH=*line-type*

specifies the line type for drawing reference lines that are requested by the AUTOHREF or HREF= option. *Line-type* can be 1 through 46. By default, LHREF=1, a solid line. See Figure 8.22 on page 249 for examples of available line types.

LVREF=*line-type*
LV=*line-type*

specifies the line type for drawing reference lines that are requested by the AUTOVREF or VREF= option. *Line-type* can be 1 through 46. By default, LVREF=1, a solid line. See Figure 8.22 on page 249 for examples of available line types.

NAME='*entry-name*'

specifies the name of the catalog entry for the graph. The maximum length for *entry-name* is eight characters. The default name is GPLOT. If the specified name duplicates the name of an existing entry, SAS/GRAPH software adds a number to the duplicate name to create a unique entry, for example, GPLOT1.

NOAXIS
NOAXES

suppresses the axes, including axis lines, axis labels, all major and minor tick marks, and tick mark values.

VAXIS=*value-list* | AXIS<1...99>

specifies the major tick mark values for the vertical axis or assigns an AXIS definition. See the HAXIS on page 824 option for a description of *value-list*.

Featured in: Example 2 on page 835 and Example 3 on page 837

VMINOR=*number-of-minor-ticks*
VM=*number-of-minor-ticks*

specifies the number of minor tick marks that are drawn between each major tick mark on the vertical axis. Minor tick marks are not labeled. VMINOR= overrides the NUMBER= suboption of the MINOR= option in an AXIS definition. You must specify a positive number.

Featured in: Example 2 on page 835

VREF=*value-list*

draws one or more reference lines perpendicular to the vertical axis at points that are specified by *value-list*. See the HAXIS on page 824 option for a description of *value-list*.

See also: CVREF= on page 812 for a description of color specifications for reference lines.

VREVERSE
specifies that the order of the values on the vertical axis should be reversed.

VZERO
specifies that tick marks on the vertical axis begin in the first position with a zero. The VZERO request is ignored if the vertical variable either contains negative values or has been ordered with the VAXIS= option or the ORDER= option in an AXIS statement.

Controlling the Display of Bubbles

The BUBBLE statement draws circles only for values that are located within the axes. Observations with values that lie outside of the axis area are not plotted. If a bubble size value causes a bubble to overlap the axis, the bubble is clipped against the axis line. The bubbles for the highest axis value and lowest axis value may be clipped unless you modify the axes in either of the following ways:

 □ by offsetting the first and last values

 □ by adding values to the range that is represented by the axis.

Specify the range of values on an axis with the HAXIS= or VAXIS= option, or with AXIS definitions.

To add a right vertical axis, use a BUBBLE2 statement.

BUBBLE2 Statement

Creates a second vertical axis on the right side of a graph produced by an accompanying BUBBLE or PLOT statement. A second dependent variable can be plotted against this axis.

Requirements: You cannot use the BUBBLE2 statement alone. You can use it only with a BUBBLE or PLOT statement. At least one plot request is required.

Global statements: AXIS, FOOTNOTE, TITLE

Description The BUBBLE2 statement specifies one or more plot requests that name the horizontal and right vertical axis variables and the variable that controls the size of the bubbles. This statement automatically

 □ scales the axes to include the maximum and minimum data values

 □ labels each axis with the name of its variable or an associated label

 □ displays each major tick mark value

 □ draws circles for values that are located within the axes.

You can use statement options to control right vertical axis scaling, draw reference lines on the right vertical axis, control the display of the bubbles, and specify annotation.

In addition, you can use global statements to modify the axes (AXIS statement), and add text to the graph (TITLE, NOTE, and FOOTNOTE statements). You can also use the Annotate data set to enhance the plot.

Syntax

BUBBLE2 *plot-request(s)* <*/option(s)*>;

option(s) can be one or more options from any or all of the following categories:

□ bubble appearance options:

BCOLOR=*bubble-color*

BFONT=*font*

BLABEL

BSCALE=AREA | RADIUS

BSIZE=*multiplier*

□ plot appearance options:

ANNOTATE=*Annotate-data-set*

CAXIS=*axis-color*

CFRAME=*background-color*

CTEXT=*text-color*

FRAME | NOFRAME

GRID

NOAXIS

□ vertical axis options:

AUTOVREF

CVREF=*reference-line-color*

LVREF=*line-type*

VAXIS=*value-list* | AXIS<1...99>

VMINOR=*number-of-minor ticks*

VREF=*value-list*

VREVERSE

VZERO

Required Arguments

plot-request(s)
each specifies the variables to plot and produces a separate graph. All variables must be in the input data set. Multiple plot requests are separated with blanks. A plot request must have this form:

y-variable*x-variable=bubble-size
plots the values of two variables and draws a circle (bubble) at each data point. The value of the third variable determines the size of the bubble. All variables must be in the input data set.

y-variable
variable plotted on the *right* vertical axis; typically it is different from *y-variable* in the accompanying BUBBLE or PLOT statement.

x-variable
variable plotted on the horizontal axis; it is the same as *x-variable* in the accompanying BUBBLE or PLOT statement.

bubble-size
variable that dictates the size of the bubbles. *Bubble-size* must be numeric. If the value of *bubble-size* is positive, bubbles are drawn with a solid line; if it is negative, bubbles are drawn with a dashed line.

Options

Options for the BUBBLE2 statement are identical to those for the BUBBLE statement except for these options, which are ignored if specified:

AUTOHREF

CHREF=

DESCRIPTION=

HAXIS=

HMINOR=

HREF=

HZERO=

LHREF=

NAME=

See "BUBBLE Statement" on page 809 for complete descriptions of options used with the BUBBLE2 statement.

Coordinating BUBBLE and BUBBLE2 Plot Requests

The BUBBLE2 statement draws circles only for values that are located within the axes. Bubbles are not drawn for values that lie outside of the axis range. If a bubble size value causes a bubble to overlap the axis, the bubble is clipped against the axis line.

In the BUBBLE2 statement, either *y-variable* or *bubble-size* may differ from the variables in the BUBBLE statement. Here are some possible combinations of plot requests for BUBBLE and BUBBLE2 statement pairs and how they affect the plot:

☐ The vertical axis variables Y and Y2 are different, but the bubble size variable, S, is the same in both:

```
bubble y*x=s;
   bubble2 y2*x=s;
```

These plot requests generate a plot in which both sets of bubbles have the same value (size) but different locations on the graph.

☐ The vertical axis variables are the same, Y, but the bubble size variables, S and S2, are different:

```
bubble y*x=s;
   bubble2 y*x=s2;
```

The resulting plot has two identical vertical axes and two sets of concentric bubbles of different sizes.

☐ Both the vertical axis variables, Y and Y2, and the bubble size variables, S and S2, are different:

```
bubble y*x=s;
   bubble2 y2*x=s2;
```

These plot requests produce the equivalent of an overlay plot in which two different sets of bubbles plotted against different vertical axes are displayed on the same graph.

The plot requests on the BUBBLE and BUBBLE2 statements must be evenly matched, for example:

```
bubble  y*x=s  b*a=c;
     bubble2 y2*x=s b2*a=c2;
```

These statements produce two graphs each with two vertical axes. The first pair of plot requests (Y*X=S and Y2*X=S) produce one graph in which the variable X is plotted on the horizontal axis, the variable Y is plotted on the left axis, and the variable Y2 is plotted on the right axis. In this pair, the value of S is the same for both requests. The second pair of plot requests (B*A=C and B2*A=C2) produce another graph in which the variable A is plotted on the horizontal axis, the variable B is plotted on the left axis, and the variable B2 is plotted on the right axis.

Any modifications to horizontal axes specifications must be identical for both statements; if they are different, the BUBBLE2 axis specification is ignored.

If the scale of values for the left and right vertical axes is the same and you want both axes to represent the same range of values, specify the range with a VAXIS= option in both the BUBBLE and BUBBLE2 statements.

PLOT Statement

Creates plots in which an independent variable is plotted on the horizontal axis and a dependent variable is plotted on the left vertical axis.

Requirements: At least one plot request is required.

Global statements: AXIS, FOOTNOTE, LEGEND, PATTERN, SYMBOL, TITLE

Supports: Drill-down functionality

Description   The PLOT statement specifies one or more plot requests that name the horizontal and left vertical axis variables, and optionally a third classification variable. This statement automatically

- □ scales the axes to include the maximum and minimum data values
- □ plots data points within the axes
- □ labels each axis with the name of its variable and displays each major tick mark value.

You can use statement options to manipulate the axes, modify the appearance of your graph, and describe catalog entries. You can use SYMBOL definitions to modify plot symbols for the data points, join data points, draw regression lines, plot confidence limits, or specify other types of interpolations. For more information on the SYMBOL statement, see "About SYMBOL Definitions" on page 828.

In addition, you can use global statements to modify the axes; add titles, footnotes, and notes to the plot; or modify the legend if one is generated by the plot. You can also use an Annotate data set to enhance the plot.

Syntax

PLOT *plot-request(s)* *</option(s)>*;

option(s) can be one or more options from any or all of the following categories:

- □ plot options:

    AREAS=*n*

    GRID

    LEGEND | LEGEND=LEGEND<1...99>

    NOLEGEND

OVERLAY

REGEQN

SKIPMISS

☐ appearance options:

ANNOTATE=*Annotate-data-set*

CAXIS=*axis-color*

CFRAME=*background-color*

CTEXT=*text-color*

FRAME | NOFRAME

NOAXIS | NOAXES

☐ horizontal axis options:

AUTOHREF

CHREF=*reference-line-color*

HAXIS=*value-list* | AXIS<1...99>

HMINOR=*number-of-minor-ticks*

HREF=*value-list*

HZERO

LHREF=*line-type*

☐ vertical axis options:

AUTOVREF

CVREF=*reference-line-color*

LVREF=*line-type*

VAXIS=*value-list* | AXIS<1...99>

VMINOR=*number-of-minor-ticks*

VREF=*value-list*

VREVERSE

VZERO

☐ catalog entry description options:

DESCRIPTION='*entry-description*'

NAME='*entry-name*'

☐ ODS options:

HTML=*variable*

HTML_LEGEND=*variable*

Required Arguments

plot-request(s)

each specifies the variables to plot and produces a separate graph, unless you specify OVERLAY. All variables must be in the input data set. Multiple plot requests are separated with blanks. You can plot character or numeric variables. A plot request can be any of these:

y-variable*x-variable<=n>

plots the values of two variables and, optionally, assigns a SYMBOL definition to the plot.

y-variable
>   variable plotted on the left vertical axis.

x-variable
>   variable plotted on the horizontal axis.

n
>   number of the *n*th generated SYMBOL definition.

>   *Note:* The *n*th generated SYMBOL definition is not necessarily the same as the *n*th SYMBOL statement. Plot requests of the form *y-variable*x-variable=n* assign the SYMBOL definition that is designated by *n* to the plot that is produced by *y-variable*x-variable*. See "About Plot Requests that Assign a SYMBOL Definition" on page 828 for more information. △

(y-variable(s))(x-variable(s))*
>   plots the values of two or more variables and produces a separate graph for each combination of Y and X variables. That is, each Y*X pair is plotted on a separate set of axes, unless you specify OVERLAY.

y-variable(s)
>   variables plotted on the left vertical axes.

x-variable(s)
>   variables plotted on the horizontal axes.
>   If you use only one *y-variable* or only one *x-variable*, omit the parentheses for that variable, for example,

```
plot (temp rain)*month;
```

>   This plot request produces two plots, one of TEMP and MONTH and one of RAIN and MONTH.

*y-variable*x-variable=third-variable*
>   plots the values of two variables against a third classification variable

y-variable
>   variable plotted on the left vertical axis.

x-variable
>   variable plotted on the horizontal axis.

third-variable
>   classification variable against which *y-variable* and *x-variable* are plotted. *Third-variable* can be character or numeric, but numeric variables should contain discrete rather than continuous values, or should be formatted to provide discrete values.
>   A separate plot (set of data points) is produced for each unique value of *third-variable*; all plots are drawn on the same set of axes, and a legend is automatically generated to show the plot symbol and color for each value of the classification variable.

>   *Note:* If a BY statement is used to produce multiple plots, you can make the legend the same across graphs by specifying the UNIFORM option in the PROC GPLOT statement. △
>   The following plot request produces a graph with a plot line for each department and a legend that shows the plot symbol for each department:

```
plot sales*weekday=dept;
```

>   For an example of a plot that specifies a *third-variable*, see Example 8 on page 847.

You can use more than one type of plot request in a single PLOT statement (provided that you do not specify OVERLAY), for example

```
plot temp*month rain*month=2;
```

Options

Options in a PLOT statement affect all graphs that are produced by that statement. You can specify as many options as you want and list them in any order.

ANNOTATE=*Annotate-data-set*
ANNO=*Annotate-data-set*
 specifies a data set to annotate plots that are produced by the PLOT statement.

 See also: Chapter 10, "The Annotate Data Set," on page 403

AREAS=*n*
 fills all the areas below plot line *n* with a pattern. The value of *n* specifies which areas to fill:

 □ AREAS=1 fills the first area.

 □ AREAS=2 fills both the first and second areas, and so forth.

 If you specify a value for AREAS= that is greater than the number of bounded areas in the plot, the area between the top plot line and the axis frame is filled.

 Before an area can be filled, the data points that border the area must be joined by a line. Use a SYMBOL statement with one of these interpolation methods to join the data points:

 INTERPOL=JOIN

 INTERPOL=STEP

 INTERPOL=R*series*

 INTERPOL=SPLINE | SM | L
 See "SYMBOL Statement" on page 226 for details on interpolation methods.

 By default, the AREAS= option fills areas by rotating a solid pattern through the colors list, starting with the first color in the list. If it needs more patterns, it rotates hatch patterns, beginning with the M2N0 pattern (see "PATTERN Statement" on page 211 for more information on map/plot patterns). However, if the V6COMP graphics option is in effect, or if color is limited to a single color with the CPATTERN= or COLORS= graphic options, the solid pattern is skipped and the first default pattern is M2N0. If the COLORS= graphic option specifies a single color, use as many SYMBOL statements as you have areas to fill in the plot because the INTERPOL= setting does not automatically apply to multiple symbol definitions.

 Note: If your device's default colors list is in effect and the first color in the list is black, color rotation begins with the second color in the list (no solid black patterns), unless the V6COMP graphics option is in effect. See "How Default Patterns and Outlines Are Generated" on page 220 for more information. △

 You can alter the default pattern behavior by specifying patterns and colors on PATTERN statements that specify map and plot patterns. A separate PATTERN definition is needed for each specified area.

 If you specify PATTERN statements, AREAS= uses the lowest numbered PATTERN statement first. If it runs out of patterns, it uses the default behavior for map and plot patterns (see "PATTERN Statement" on page 211 for details).

 Pattern definitions are assigned to the areas below the plot lines in the order the plots are drawn. The first area is that between the horizontal axis and the plot line that is drawn first. The second area is that above the first plot line and below the plot line that is drawn second, and so forth. If the line that is drawn second lies below the line that is drawn first, the second area is hidden when the first is filled.

The plots with the lower line values must be drawn first to prevent one area fill from overlaying another. If the lines cross, only the part of an area that is above the previous line is visible.

Therefore, if you produce multiple plots by submitting multiple plot requests and using the OVERLAY option, the plot requests must be ordered in the PLOT statement so that the plot request that produces the lowest line values is the first (leftmost) plot request, the plot request that produces the next lowest line values is the second plot request, and so on.

If you produce multiple plots with a *y-variable*x-variable=third-variable* plot request, the lines are plotted in order of increasing third variable values. Therefore, the data must be recoded so that the lowest value of the third variable produces the lowest plot line, the next lowest value produces the next lowest plot line, and so on.

AREAS= works only if all plot lines are generated by the same PLOT or PLOT2 statement.

If you use the VALUE= option in the SYMBOL statement, some symbols may be hidden. If reference lines are also specified with AREAS=, they are drawn behind the pattern fill.

Featured in: Example 7 on page 846

AUTOHREF

draws reference lines at all major tick marks on the horizontal axis. If the AREAS= option is also used, the filled areas cover the reference lines. To draw lines on top of the filled areas, use the ANNOTATE= option in either the PROC GPLOT statement or the PLOT statement.

AUTOVREF

draws reference lines at all of the major tick marks on the vertical axis. If you also use the AREAS= option, the filled areas cover the reference lines. To draw lines on top of the filled areas, use the ANNOTATE= option in either the PROC GPLOT statement or the PLOT statement.

CAXIS=*axis-color*
CA=*axis-color*

specifies the color for the axis line and all major and minor tick marks. By default, the procedure uses the first color in the colors list.

If you use the CAXIS= option, it may be overridden by

□ the COLOR= option in an AXIS definition, which in turn is overridden by

□ the COLOR= suboption of the MAJOR= or MINOR= option in an AXIS definition for major and minor tick marks.

Featured in: Example 5 on page 842

CFRAME=*background-color*
CFR=*background-color*

fills the axis area with the specified color. If the FRAME option is also in effect, the procedure determines the color of the frame according to the precedence list given later in the FRAME option description.

CHREF=*reference-line-color*
CH=*reference-line-color*

specifies the color for reference lines that are requested by the HREF= and AUTOHREF options. By default, these reference lines display in the color of the horizontal axis.

CTEXT=*text-color*
C=*text-color*

specifies the color for all text on the axes, including tick mark values and axis labels. If the PLOT request generates a legend, the CTEXT= option also colors the legend label and the value descriptions.

If you omit the CTEXT= option, a color specification is searched for in this order:

1 the CTEXT= option in a GOPTIONS statement

2 the default, the first color in the colors list.

If you use the CTEXT= option, it overrides the color specification for the axis label and the tick mark values in the COLOR= option in an AXIS definition that is assigned to the axis.

If you use the CTEXT= option, the color specification is overridden in one or more of these situations:

□ If you also use the COLOR= suboption of a LABEL= or VALUE= option in a AXIS definition that is assigned to the axis, that suboption determines the color of the axis label or the color of the tick mark values, respectively.

□ If you also use the COLOR= suboption of a LABEL= or VALUE= option in a LEGEND definition that is assigned to the legend, it determines the color of the legend label or the color of the legend value descriptions, respectively.

Featured in: Example 5 on page 842

CVREF=*reference-line-color*
CV=*reference-line-color*

specifies the color for reference lines that are requested by the VREF= and AUTOVREF= options. By default, these reference lines display in the color of the vertical axis.

Featured in: Example 5 on page 842

DESCRIPTION='*entry-description*'
DES='*entry-description*'

specifies the description of the catalog entry for the plot. The maximum length for *entry-description* is 40 characters. The description does not appear on the plot. By default, the procedure assigns a description of the form PLOT OF *y-variable**x-variable, where *y-variable* and *x-variable* are the names of the plot variables.

The *entry-description* can include the #BYLINE, #BYVAL, and #BYVAR substitution options, which work as they do when used on TITLE, FOOTNOTE, and NOTE statements. For more information, refer to the description of the options on page 262, and "Substituting BY Line Values in a Text String" on page 266. The 40-character limit applies before the substitution takes place for these options; thus, if in the SAS program the entry-description text exceeds 40 characters, it is truncated to 40 characters, and then the substitution is performed.

The descriptive text is shown in the "description" portion of each of the following:

□ in the Results window

□ among the catalog-entry properties that you can view from the Explorer window

□ in the Table of Contents that is generated when you use CONTENTS= on an ODS HTML statement (see "Linking to Output through a Table of Contents" on page 86), assuming the GPLOT output is generated while the contents page is open

□ in the Description field of the PROC GREPLAY window

FRAME | NOFRAME
FR | NOFR

specifies whether a frame is drawn around the axis area. The default is FRAME; however, if the V6COMP option is in effect on the GOPTIONS statement, the default is NOFRAME. If you also use a BUBBLE2 or PLOT2 statement and your plotting statements have conflicting frame specifications, FRAME is used.

For the frame color, a specification is searched for in this order:

1 the CAXIS= option

2 the COLOR= option in the AXIS definition assigned to the vertical axis

3 the COLOR= option in the AXIS definition assigned to the horizontal axis

4 the default, the first color in the colors list.

To fill the axis area with a background color, use the CFRAME= option.

GRID

draws reference lines at all major tick marks on both axes. You get the same result when you use all of these options in a PLOT statement: AUTOHREF, AUTOVREF, FRAME, LVREF=34, and LHREF=34. The line type for GRID is 34. The line color is the color of the axis.

HAXIS=*value-list* | AXIS<1 . . . 99>

specifies major tick mark values for the horizontal axis or assigns an axis definition. By default, the procedure scales the axis and provides an appropriate number of tick marks.

The way you specify *value-list* depends on the type of variable:

□ *For numeric variables, value-list* is either an explicit list of values, or a starting and an ending value with an interval increment, or a combination of both forms:

> *n* <...*n*>
>
> *n* TO *n* <BY *increment*>
>
> *n* <...*n*> TO *n* <BY *increment* > <*n* <...*n*> >

If a numeric variable has an associated format, the specified values must be the *unformatted* values.

□ *For date-time values, value-list* includes any SAS date, time, or datetime value described for the SAS functions INTCK and INTNX, shown here as *SAS-value*:

> '*SAS-value*'i < ...'*SAS-value*'i>
>
> '*SAS-value*'i TO '*SAS-value*' i<BY *interval*>

□ *For character variables, value-list* is a list of unique character values enclosed in quotation marks and separated by blanks:

> '*value-1*' < ...'*value-n*'>

If a character variable has an associated format, the specified values must be the *formatted* values.

For a complete description of *value-list*, see the ORDER= on page 168 option in the AXIS statement.

Note: If data values fall outside of the range that is specified by the HAXIS= option, then by default the outlying data values are not used in interpolation calculations. See "About the Input Data Set" on page 806 for more information on values out of range. △

Featured in: Example 4 on page 839, Example 5 on page 842, and Example 9 on page 851

HMINOR=*number-of-minor-ticks*
HM=*number-of-minor-ticks*

specifies the number of minor tick marks drawn between each major tick mark on the horizontal axis. Minor tick marks are not labeled. The HMINOR= option overrides the NUMBER= suboption of the MINOR= option in an AXIS definition. You must specify a positive number.

Featured in: Example 4 on page 839, Example 5 on page 842, and Example 9 on page 851

HREF=*value-list*

draws one or more reference lines perpendicular to the horizontal axis at points specified by *value-list*. See the HAXIS on page 824 option for a description of *value-list*. If the AREAS= option is also used, the filled areas cover the reference lines. To draw lines on top of the filled areas, use the ANNOTATE= option on either the PROC GPLOT or the PLOT statement.

See also: CHREF= on page 822 for a description of color specifications for reference lines

HTML=*variable*

identifies the variable in the input data set whose values create links in the HTML file created by the ODS HTML statement. These links are associated with the plot points, or if AREA= is used, with the areas between plot lines. The links point to the data or graph that you wish to display when the user drills down on the plot point or area.

HTML_LEGEND=*variable*

identifies the variable in the input data set whose values create links in the HTML file that is created by the ODS HTML statement. These links are associated with a legend value, and they point to the data or graph that you wish to display when the user drills down on the value. For information on creating graphs for the Output Delivery System, see Chapter 5, "Bringing SAS/GRAPH Output to the Web," on page 71.

HZERO

specifies that tick marks on the horizontal axis begin in the first position with a value of zero. The HZERO request is ignored if negative values are present for the horizontal variable or if the horizontal axis has been specified with the HAXIS= option.

LEGEND | LEGEND=LEGEND<1...99>

generates a legend or specifies the legend to use for the plot.

□ a PLOT statement that includes the OVERLAY option does not automatically generate a legend. In these plot types, use LEGEND to produce a default legend, or LEGEND=LEGEND*n* to assign a defined LEGEND statement to the plot. The default legend is centered below the axis frame and identifies which colors and plot symbols represent the *y-variables* that you specify for the plots.

□ a plot request of the form *y-variable*x-variable=third-variable* automatically generates a default legend that identifies which colors and plot symbols represent each value of the classification variable. In these plot types, override the default by using LEGEND=LEGEND*n* to assign a defined LEGEND statement to the plot.

If you use the SHAPE= option in a LEGEND statement, the value SYMBOL is valid. If you use the PLOT statement's AREAS= option, SHAPE=BAR is also valid.

See also: "LEGEND Statement" on page 187

Featured in: Example 6 on page 844

LHREF=*line-type*
LH=*line-type*

specifies the line type for drawing reference lines requested by the AUTOHREF or HREF= option. *Line-type* can be 1 through 46. By default, LHREF=1, a solid line. See Figure 8.22 on page 249 for examples of available line types.

LVREF=*line-type*
LV=*line-type*
> specifies the line type for drawing reference lines requested by the AUTOVREF or VREF= option. *Line-type* can be 1 through 46. By default, LVREF=1, a solid line. See Figure 8.22 on page 249 for examples of available line types.
>
> **Featured in:**   Example 5 on page 842

NAME= '*entry-name***'**
> specifies the name of the catalog entry for the graph. The maximum length for *entry-name* is eight characters. The default name is GPLOT. If the name that you specify duplicates the name of an existing entry, SAS/GRAPH software adds a number to the duplicate name to create a unique entry, for example, GPLOT1.

NOAXIS
NOAXES
> suppresses the axes, including axis lines, axis labels, all major and minor tick marks, and tick mark values.

NOLEGEND
> suppresses the legend that is generated by a plot request of the type *y-variable*x-variable=third-variable*.

OVERLAY
> places all the plots that are generated by the PLOT statement on one set of axes. The axes are scaled to include the minimum and maximum values of all of the variables, and the variable names or labels associated with the first pair of variables label the axes.
>
> The OVERLAY option produces a legend if you include the LEGEND or the LEGEND=*n* option in the PLOT statement.
>
> You cannot use OVERLAY with plot requests of the form *y-variable*x-variable=third-variable*. However, you can achieve an overlay effect by using a PLOT and PLOT2 statement.
>
> **Featured in:**   Example 6 on page 844 and Example 7 on page 846

REGEQN
> displays the regression equation that is specified in the INTERPOL= option of the SYMBOL statement in the lower left hand corner of the plot. You cannot modify the format that is used for the equation.
>
> **Featured in:**   Example 4 on page 839

SKIPMISS
> breaks a plot line or an area fill at occurrences of missing values of the Y variable. By default, plot lines and area fills are not broken at missing values. SKIPMISS is available only with join or spline interpolations. If SKIPMISS is used, observations should be sorted by the independent (horizontal axis) variable. If the plot request is *y-variable*x-variable=third-variable*, observations should also be sorted by the values of the third variable.
>
> **See also:**   "About the Input Data Set" on page 806 for more information about values

VAXIS=*value-list* **| AXIS<1...99>**
> specifies the major tick mark values for the vertical axis or assigns an AXIS definition. See the HAXIS on page 824 option for a description of *value-list*.
>
> **Featured in:**   Example 4 on page 839 and Example 5 on page 842

VMINOR=*number-of-minor-ticks*
VM=*number-of-minor-ticks*
> specifies the number of minor tick marks that are drawn between each major tick mark on the vertical axis. Minor tick marks are not labeled. The VMINOR= option

overrides the NUMBER= suboption of the MINOR= option in an AXIS definition. You must specify a positive number.

Featured in: Example 5 on page 842

VREF=*value-list*

draws one or more reference lines perpendicular to the vertical axis at points that are specified by *value-list* . See the HAXIS on page 824 option for a description of *value-list*. If the AREAS= option is also used, the filled areas cover the reference lines. To draw lines on top of the filled areas, use the ANNOTATE= option in either the PROC GPLOT statement or the PLOT statement.

See also: CVREF= on page 823 for a description of color specifications for reference lines

Featured in: Example 5 on page 842

VREVERSE

specifies that the order of the values on the vertical axis be reversed.

VZERO

specifies that tick marks on the vertical axis begin in the first position with a zero. The VZERO request is ignored if the vertical variable either contains negative values or has been ordered with the VAXIS= option or the ORDER= option in an AXIS statement.

Plot Requests with Multiple Variables

Plot requests with multiple variables produce a separate plot for every Y*X pair, unless you specify OVERLAY. For example, this statement produces four plots like those in Figure 21.7 on page 827 (the actual plots are produced on separate pages):

```
plot (y b)*(x a);
```

Figure 21.7 Graphs Generated by Multiple Plot Requests

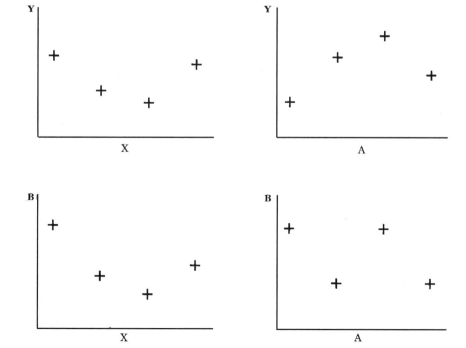

About SYMBOL Definitions

SYMBOL statements control the appearance of plot symbols and lines, and define interpolation methods. They can specify

☐ the shape, size, and color of the plot symbols that mark the data points

☐ plot line style, color, and width

☐ an interpolation method for plotting data

☐ how missing values are treated in interpolation calculations.

SYMBOL definitions are assigned either by default by the GPLOT procedure or explicitly with a plot request.

If no SYMBOL definition is currently in effect, the GPLOT procedure produces a scatter plot of the data points using the default plot symbol, the plus sign (+). If you need more than one SYMBOL definition, the procedure rotates through the current colors list to produce symbols of different colors. If the current colors list contains only one color, or if all the colors are used, additional plot symbols are used.

If SYMBOL definitions have been defined but not explicitly assigned by a plot request of the form *y-variable**x-variable=*n*, the procedure assigns them in the order in which they are generated. For example, this statement creates three plots:

```
plot y*x b*a s*r;
```

The procedure assigns the first generated SYMBOL definition to Y*X, the second generated SYMBOL definition to B*A, and the third to S*R.

If more SYMBOL definitions are needed than have been defined, the procedure uses the default definitions for the plots that remain.

See "SYMBOL Statement" on page 226 for a complete discussion of the features of the SYMBOL statement.

About Plot Requests that Assign a SYMBOL Definition

Plot requests of the form *y-variable**x-variable=*n* are useful when you use the OVERLAY option to produce multiple plots on one graph and you want to assign a particular SYMBOL definition to each plot.

With plot requests of this type it is important to remember that a single SYMBOL statement can generate multiple SYMBOL definitions, so that the SYMBOL definition that is designated by *n* may not be the same as the SYMBOL statement of the same number. That is, the third SYMBOL definition is not necessarily the same as the SYMBOL3 statement. See "SYMBOL Statement" on page 226 for more information.

PLOT2 Statement

Produces one or more plots with the vertical axis on the right side of the graph against which a second dependent variable can be plotted.

Requirements: You cannot use the PLOT2 statement alone. It can be used only with a PLOT or BUBBLE statement. At least one plot request is required.

Global statements: AXIS, FOOTNOTE, LEGEND, PATTERN, SYMBOL, TITLE

Description   The PLOT2 statement specifies one or more plot requests that name the horizontal and right vertical axis variables. This statement automatically

- □ plots data points within the axes
- □ scales the axes to include the maximum and minimum data values
- □ labels each axis with the name of its variable and displays each major tick mark value.

You can use statement options to manipulate the axes and modify the appearance of your graph. You can use SYMBOL definitions to modify plot symbols for the data points, join data points, draw regression lines, plot confidence limits, or specify other types of interpolation. For more information on the SYMBOL statement, see "About SYMBOL Definitions" on page 828.

In addition, you can use global statements to modify the axes; add titles, footnotes, and notes to the plot; or modify the legend if one is generated by the plot. You can also use an Annotate data set to enhance the plot.

Syntax

PLOT2 *plot-request(s)* *</option(s)>*;

option(s) can be one or more options from any or all of the following categories:
- □ plot options:

    AREAS=*n*
    GRID
    LEGEND | LEGEND=LEGEND<1...99>
    NOLEGEND
    OVERLAY
    REGEQN
    SKIPMISS

- □ appearance options:

    ANNOTATE=*Annotate-data-set*
    CAXIS=*axis-color*
    CFRAME=*background-color*
    CTEXT=*text-color*
    FRAME | NOFRAME
    NOAXIS | NOAXES

- □ vertical axis options:

    AUTOVREF
    CVREF=*reference-line-color*
    LVREF=*line-type*
    VAXIS=*value-list* | AXIS<1...99>
    VMINOR=*n*
    VREF=*value-list*
    VREVERSE
    VZERO

Required Arguments

plot-request(s)
    each specifies the variables to plot and produces a separate graph, unless you specify OVERLAY. All variables must be in the input data set. Multiple plot requests are separated with blanks. A plot request can be any of these:

*y-variable*x-variable<=n>*
  plots the values of two variables and, optionally, assigns a SYMBOL definition to the plot.

  y-variable
    variable plotted on the *right* vertical axis.

  x-variable
    variable plotted on the horizontal axis.

  n
    number of the *n*th generated SYMBOL definition.

(y-variable(s))(x-variable(s)))*
  plots the values of two or more variable and produces a separate graph for each combination of Y and X variables.

  y-variable(s)
    variables plotted on the *right* vertical axes.

  x-variable(s)
    variables plotted on the horizontal axes.

*y-variable*x-variable=third-variable*
  plots the values of two variables against a third classification variable

  y-variable
    variable plotted on the *right* vertical axis.

  x-variable
    variable plotted on the horizontal axis.

  third-variable
    classification variable against which *y-variable* and *x-variable* are plotted. *Third-variable* can be character or numeric, but numeric variables should contain discrete rather than continuous values, or should be formatted to provide discrete values.

    For more information about plot requests, see "PLOT Statement" on page 818.

    In a PLOT2 plot request, the independent (X) variable for the horizontal axis must be the same as in the accompanying PLOT or BUBBLE statement. Typically, the dependent (Y) variable for the right vertical axis is different.

    Use the same types of plot requests with a PLOT2 statement that you use with a PLOT statement, but a PLOT2 statement always plots the values of *y-variable* on the right vertical axis.

Options

  Options for the PLOT2 statement are identical to those for the PLOT statement except for these options, which are ignored if you specify them:

  AUTOHREF
  CHREF=
  DESCRIPTION=
  HAXIS=
  HMINOR=
  HREF=
  HTML=
  HTML_LEGEND=
  HZERO=

LHREF=

NAME=

See "PLOT Statement" on page 818 for complete descriptions of options that you can use with the PLOT2 statement.

Matching Plot Requests

The plot requests in both the PLOT and PLOT2 statements must be evenly matched as in this example:

```
plot  y*x  b*a;
    plot2 y2*x b2*a;
```

These statements produce two graphs, each with two vertical axes. The first pair of plot requests (Y*X and Y2*X) produce one graph in which X is plotted on the horizontal axis, Y is plotted on the left axis, and Y2 is plotted on the right axis. The second pair of plot requests (B*A and B2*A) produce another graph in which A is plotted on the horizontal axis, B is plotted on the left axis, and B2 is plotted on the right axis.

Using Multiple Plot Requests   Plot requests of the form *(y-variable(s))*(x-variable(s))* in both the PLOT and PLOT2 statements generate multiple graphs. These statements produce graphs like the ones diagrammed in Figure 21.8 on page 831 (the actual plots are produced on separate pages):

```
plot (y b)*(x a);
    plot2 (y2 b2)*(x a);
```

Figure 21.8   Diagram of Graphs Produced by Multiple Plot Requests in PLOT and PLOT2 Statements

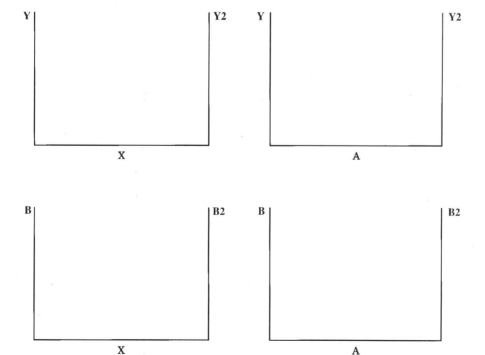

Requesting Plots of Three Variables with a Legend   When both the PLOT and PLOT2 statements use plot requests of the form *y-variable*x-variable=third-variable*, each statement generates a separate legend. If the third variable has two values, these statements produce one graph with four sets of data points, as shown in Figure 21.9 on page 832 (the figure assumes SYMBOL statements are used to specify the plot symbols that are shown and to connect the data points with straight lines):

```
plot y*x=z;
    plot2 y2*x=z;
```

Figure 21.9 Diagram of Multiple Plots on One Graph

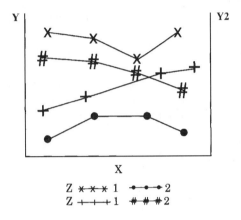

Using a Second Vertical Axis

Displaying the Same Values in a Different Scale   If your data contain the same variable values in two different scales, such as height in inches and height in centimeters, you can display one scale of values on the left axis and the other scale of values on the right axis. If both vertical axes are calibrated so that they represent the same range of values, then for each observation of X the data points for Y and Y2 are the same.

For example, if Y is height in inches and Y2 is height in centimeters and if the Y axis values range from 0 to 84 inches and the Y2 axis values range from 0 to 213.36 centimeters, the plot will be like the diagram shown in Figure 21.10 on page 832.

Figure 21.10 Right Axis with Different Scale of Values

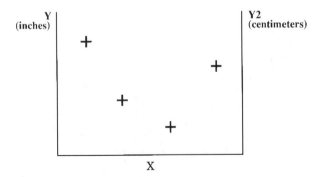

For plots such as these, the PLOT2 statement should use a SYMBOL statement that specifies INTERPOL=NONE and VALUE=NONE.

Displaying Different Values   If your data contain variables with different data values (such as height and weight), you can display one type of data on the left axis and another type of data on the right axis. Because the Y variable and the Y2 variable contain different data, two sets of data points are displayed on the graph. For example, if Y is height and Y2 is weight, the plot will be like the diagram in Figure 21.11 on page 833.

Figure 21.11   Right Axis with Different Values and Different Scale

Displaying the Same Scale on Both Axes   If your data contain two sets of values for the same type of data, you can use the PLOT2 statement to generate a right axis that is calibrated the same as the left axis so that the data points on the right of the graph are easier to read. For example, if Y is high temperatures and Y2 is low temperatures, you can create a graph like the diagram in Figure 21.12 on page 833.

Figure 21.12   Right Axis with Same Scale of Values

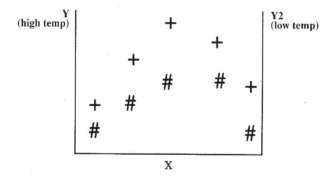

To scale both axes the same, specify the same range of values either with the VAXIS= option in both the PLOT and PLOT2 statements, or with AXIS statements.

Using PATTERN and SYMBOL Definitions

The PLOT2 statement uses PATTERN and SYMBOL definitions in the same way the PLOT statement does. These definitions are assigned in order first to the PLOT statement and then to the PLOT2 statement.

For more information, see "About SYMBOL Definitions" on page 828.

Examples

Example 1: Generating a Simple Bubble Plot

Procedure features:
   BUBBLE statement option:

      HAXIS=

Other features:
   AXIS statement

   FORMAT statement

Sample library member: GR21N01

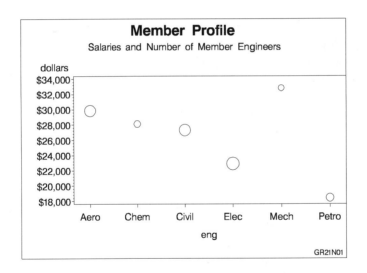

This example shows a bubble plot in which each bubble represents a category of engineer. The plot shows engineers on the horizontal axis and average salaries on the vertical axis. Each bubble's vertical location is determined by the average salary for the category. Each bubble's size is determined by the number of engineers in the category: the more engineers, the larger the bubble.

Assign the libref and set the graphics environment.

```
libname reflib 'SAS-data-library';
goptions reset=global gunit=pct border cback=white
        colors=(black blue green red)
        ftitle=swissb ftext=swiss htitle=6 htext=4;
```

Create the data set. REFLIB.JOBS contains average salary data for several categories of engineer. It also indicates the number of engineers in each category.

```
data reflib.jobs;
   length eng $5;
   input eng dollars num;
   datalines;
Civil 27308 73273
Aero  29844 70192
Elec  22920 89382
Mech  32816 19601
Chem  28116 25541
Petro 18444 34833
;
```

Define titles and footnote.

```
title1 'Member Profile';
title2 'Salaries and Number of Member Engineers';
footnote h=3 j=r 'GR21N01 ';
```

Define axis characteristics. OFFSET= specifies an offset for the tick marks so that bubbles near an axis are not clipped.

```
axis1 offset=(5,5);
```

Generate bubble plot. HAXIS= assigns the AXIS1 statement to the horizontal axis. The salary averages are assigned a dollar format.

```
proc gplot data=reflib.jobs;
   format dollars dollar9.;
   bubble dollars*eng=num / haxis=axis1;
run;
quit;
```

Example 2: Labeling and Sizing Plot Bubbles

Procedure features:
  BUBBLE statement options:
    BCOLOR=
    BFONT=
    BLABEL=
    BSIZE=
    CAXIS=
    HAXIS=
    VAXIS=
    VMINOR
Other features:

AXIS statement

Data set: REFLIB.JOBS on page 835

Sample library member: GR21N02

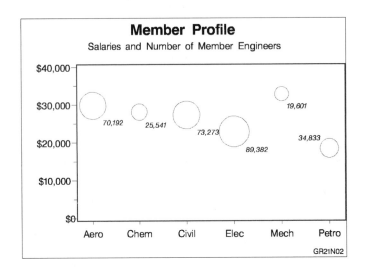

This example modifies the code in Example 1. It shows how BUBBLE statement options control the appearance of bubbles and their labels. It also shows how AXIS statements can modify the plot axes.

Assign the libref and set the graphics environment.

```
libname reflib 'SAS-data-library';
goptions reset=global gunit=pct border cback=white
         colors=(black blue green red)
         ftitle=swissb ftext=swiss htitle=6 htext=4;
```

Define titles and footnote.

```
title1 'Member Profile';
title2 h=4 'Salaries and Number of Member Engineers';
footnote1 h=3 j=r 'GR21N02 ';
```

Define axis characteristics. AXIS1 suppresses the horizontal axis label and uses OFFSET= to move the first and last major tick mark values away from the vertical axes so bubbles are not clipped. AXIS2 uses ORDER= to set major tick mark intervals. This could be done with VAXIS= on the BUBBLE statement, but then you could not suppress the axis label and alter other axis characteristics.

```
axis1 label=none
      offset=(5,5)
      width=3
      value=(height=4);
axis2 order=(0 to 40000 by 10000)
```

```
label=none
major=(height=1.5)
minor=(height=1)
width=3
value=(height=4);
```

Generate bubble plot. VMINOR= specifies one minor tick mark for the vertical axis. BCOLOR= colors the bubbles. BLABEL labels each bubble with the value of variable NUM, and BFONT= specifies the font for labeling text. BSIZE= increases the bubble sizes by increasing the scaling factor size to 12. CAXIS= colors the axis lines and all major and minor tick marks.

```
proc gplot data=reflib.jobs;
   format dollars dollar9. num comma7.0;
   bubble dollars*eng=num / haxis=axis1
                           vaxis=axis2
                           vminor=1
                           bcolor=red
                           blabel
                           bfont=swissi
                           bsize=12
                           caxis=blue;
run;
quit;
```

Example 3: Adding a Right Vertical Axis

Procedure features:
   BUBBLE2 statement options:

   BCOLOR=
   BSIZE=
   CAXIS=
   VAXIS=

Data set: REFLIB.JOBS on page 835

Sample library member: GR21N03

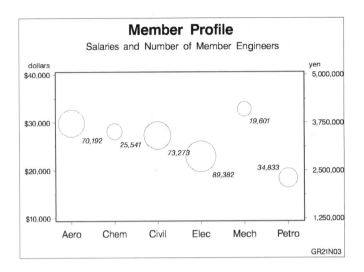

This example modifies Example 2 on page 835 to show how a BUBBLE2 statement generates a right vertical axis that displays the values of the vertical coordinates in a different scale from the scale that is used for the left vertical axis. Salary values are scaled by dollars on the left vertical axis and by yen on the right vertical axis.

BUBBLE and BUBBLE2 statement options control the size and appearance of the bubbles and their labels. In particular, the VAXIS options calibrate the axes so that the data points are identical and only one set of bubbles appears.

Note: If the data points are not identical, two sets of bubbles are displayed. △

Assign the libref and set the graphics environment.

```
libname reflib 'SAS-data-library';
goptions reset=global gunit=pct border cback=white
        colors=(black blue green red)
        ftitle=swissb ftext=swiss htitle=6 htext=3;
```

Create the data set REFLIB.JOBS2 and calculate variable YEN. The DATA step uses a SET statement to read the REFLIB.JOBS data set.

```
data reflib.jobs2;
   set reflib.jobs;
   yen=dollars*125;
run;
```

Define titles and footnote.

```
title1 'Member Profile';
title2 h=4 'Salaries and Number of Member Engineers';
footnote j=r 'GR21N03 ';
```

Define horizontal-axis characteristics.

```
axis1 offset=(5,5)
      label=none
      width=3
      value=(h=4);
```

Generate bubble plot with second vertical axis. In the BUBBLE statement, HAXIS= specifies the AXIS1 definition and VAXIS= scales the left axis. In the BUBBLE2 statement, VAXIS= scales the right axis. Both axes represent the same range of monetary values. The BUBBLE and BUBBLE2 statements ensure that the bubbles generated by each statement are identical by coordinating specifications on BCOLOR=, which colors the bubbles; BSIZE=, which increases the size of the scaling factor to 12; and CAXIS=, which colors the axis lines and all major and minor tick marks. Axis labels and major tick mark values use the default color, which is the first color in the colors list.

```
proc gplot data=reflib.jobs2;
   format dollars dollar7. num yen comma9.0;
   bubble dollars*eng=num / haxis=axis1
                            vaxis=10000 to 40000 by 10000
                            hminor=0
                            vminor=1
                            blabel
                            bfont=swissi
                            bcolor=red
                            bsize=12
                            caxis=blue;

   bubble2 yen*eng=num / vaxis=1250000 to 5000000 by 1250000
                         vminor=1
                         bcolor=red
                         bsize=12
                         caxis=blue;
run;
quit;
```

Example 4: Plotting Two Variables

Procedure features:
    PLOT statement options:
        HAXIS=
        HMINOR=
        REGEQN
        VAXIS=
Other features:
    RUN-group processing
    SYMBOL statement
Sample library member: GR21N04

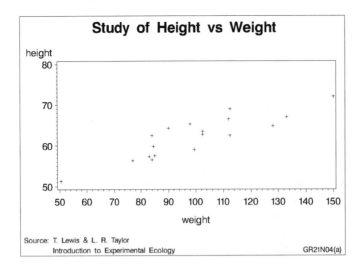

In this example, the PLOT statement uses a plot request of the type *y-variable*x-variable* to plot the variable HEIGHT against the variable WEIGHT. The plot shows that weight generally increases with size.

This example then requests the same plot with some modifications. As shown by the following output, the second plot request specifies a regression analysis with confidence limits, and scales the range of values along the vertical and horizontal axes. It also displays the regression equation specified for the SYMBOL statement. Because the procedure supports RUN-group processing, you do not have to repeat the PROC GPLOT statement to generate the second plot.

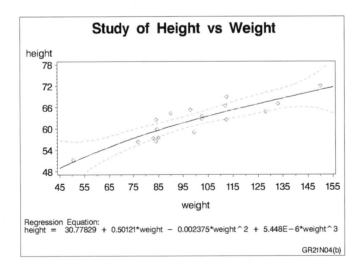

Assign the libref and set the graphics environment.

```
libname reflib 'SAS-data-library';
goptions reset=global gunit=pct border cback=white
         colors=(black blue green red)
         ftitle=swissb ftext=swiss htitle=6 htext=4;
```

Create the data set. REFLIB.STATS contains the heights and weights of numerous individuals.

```
data reflib.stats;
   input height weight;
   datalines;
69.0  112.5
56.5   84.0
...more data lines...
67.0  133.0
57.5   85.0
;
```

Define title and footnotes.

```
title 'Study of Height vs Weight';
footnote1 h=3 j=l ' Source: T. Lewis & L. R. Taylor';
footnote2
   h=3 j=l '          Introduction to Experimental Ecology'
   j=r 'GR21N04(a) ';
```

Generate a default scatter plot.

```
proc gplot data=reflib.stats;
   plot height*weight;
run;
```

Redefine footnotes to make room for the regression equation.

```
footnote1; /* this clears footnote1 */
footnote2 h=3 j=r 'GR21N04(b) ';
```

Define symbol characteristics. INTERPOL= specifies a cubic regression analysis with confidence limits for mean predicted values. VALUE=, HEIGHT=, and CV= specify a plot symbol, size, and color. CI=, CO=, and WIDTH= specify colors and a thickness for the interpolation and confidence-limits lines.

```
symbol1 interpol=rcclm95
        value=diamond
        height=3
        cv=red
        ci=blue
        co=green
        width=2;
```

Generate scatter plot with regression line. HAXIS= and VAXIS= define the range of axes values. HMINOR= specifies one minor tick mark between major tick marks. REGEQN displays the regression equation specified on the SYMBOL1 statement.

```
     plot height*weight / haxis=45 to 155 by 10
                          vaxis=48 to 78 by 6
                          hminor=1
                          regeqn;

run;
quit;
```

Example 5: Connecting Plot Data Points

Procedure features:
  PLOT statement option:

    CAXIS=
    CTEXT
    CVREF
    HAXIS
    HMINOR=
    LVREF=
    VAXIS=
    VMINOR=
    VREF

Other features:
  SYMBOL statement

Sample library member: GR21N05

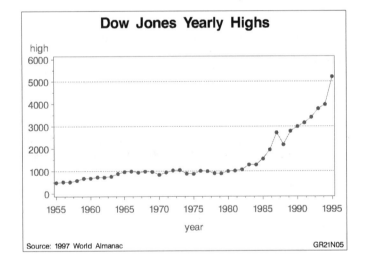

In this example, the PLOT statement uses a plot request of the type *y-variable*x-variable* to plot the variable HIGH against the variable YEAR to show the annual highs of the Dow Jones Industrial Average over several decades.

This example uses a SYMBOL statement to specify a plot symbol and connect data points with a straight line. In addition, the example shows how PLOT statement options can add reference lines and modify the axes (AXIS statements are not used).

Assign the libref and set the graphics environment.

```
libname reflib 'SAS-data-library';
goptions reset=global gunit=pct border cback=white
         colors=(black blue green red)
         ftitle=swissb ftext=swiss htitle=6 htext=4;
```

Create the data set. REFLIB.STOCKS contains yearly highs and lows for the Dow Jones Industrial Average, and the dates of the high and low values each year.

```
data reflib.stocks;
   input year @7  hdate date9. @15 high
               @24 ldate date9. @32 low;
   format hdate ldate date9.;
   datalines;
1955   30DEC55  488.40   17JAN55  388.20
1956   06APR56  521.05   23JAN56  462.35
...more data lines...
1994   31JAN94 3978.36   04APR94 3593.35
1995   13DEC95 5216.47   30JAN95 3832.08
;
```

Define title and footnote.

```
title1 'Dow Jones Yearly Highs';
footnote1 h=3 j=l ' Source: 1997 World Almanac'
          j=r 'GR21N05 ';
```

Define symbol characteristics. SYMBOL1 defines the symbol that marks the data points and specifies its height and color. INTERPOL=JOIN joins the data points with straight lines.

```
symbol1 color=red
        interpol=join
        value=dot
        height=3;
```

Generate the plot and modify the axis values. HAXIS= sets major tick marks for the horizontal axis. VAXIS= sets major tick marks for the vertical axis. HMINOR= and VMINOR= specify the number of tick marks between major tick marks.

```
proc gplot data=reflib.stocks;
   plot high*year / haxis=1955 to 1995 by 5
                    vaxis=0 to 6000 by 1000
                    hminor=3
                    vminor=1
```

Add reference lines and specify colors. VREF= draws reference lines on the vertical axis at three marks. LVREF= specifies the line style (dashed) for the lines; CVREF= specifies blue as the line color. CAXIS= colors the axis lines and all major and minor tick marks. CTEXT= specifies red for all plot text, including axis labels and major tick mark values.

```
                              vref=1000 3000 5000
                              lvref=2
                              cvref=blue
                              caxis=blue
                              ctext=red;
        run;
        quit;
```

Example 6: Generating an Overlay Plot

Procedure features:
    PLOT statement options:

        LEGEND=
        OVERLAY

Other features:
    LEGEND statement

    SYMBOL statement

Data set: REFLIB.STOCKS on page 843

Sample library member: GR21N06

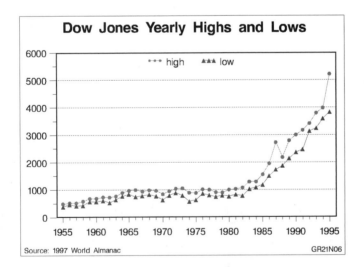

In this example, one PLOT statement plots both the HIGH and LOW variables against the variable YEAR using two plot requests. The OVERLAY option on the PLOT statement determines that both plot lines appear on the same graph. The other PLOT options scale the vertical axis, add a reference line to the plot, and specify the number of minor tick marks on the axes. The SYMBOL, AXIS,and LEGEND statements modify the plot symbols, axes, and legend.

Note: If the OVERLAY option were not specified, each plot request would generate a separate graph. △

Assign the libref and set the graphics environment.

```
libname reflib 'SAS-data-library';
goptions reset=global gunit=pct border cback=white
         colors=(black blue green red)
         ftitle=swissb ftext=swiss htitle=6 htext=4;
```

Define title and footnote.

```
title1 'Dow Jones Yearly Highs and Lows';
footnote1 h=3 j=l ' Source: 1997 World Almanac'
          j=r 'GR21N06 ';
```

Define symbol characteristics. Each SYMBOL statement specifies a color, symbol type, and size for the plot symbols, and connects the data points with a straight line. SYMBOL2 specifies a solid triangle as the plot symbol by combining FONT=MARKER with VALUE=C.

```
symbol1 color=red
        interpol=join
        value=dot
        height=3;
symbol2 font=marker value=C
        color=blue
        interpol=join
        height=2;
```

Define axis characteristics.

```
axis1 order=(1955 to 1995 by 5) offset=(2,2)
      label=none
      major=(height=2) minor=(height=1)
      width=3;

axis2 order=(0 to 6000 by 1000) offset=(0,0)
      label=none
      major=(height=2) minor=(height=1)
      width=3;
```

Define legend characteristics. LABEL= suppresses the legend label. SHAPE= specifies a width and height for legend values. POSITION= centers the legend inside the top of the axis frame. MODE= shares the legend area with other graphics elements.

```
legend1 label=none
        shape=symbol(4,2)
        position=(top center inside)
        mode=share;
```

Generate two plots and display them on the same set of axes. OVERLAY specifies that both plot lines appear on the same graph. LEGEND= assigns the LEGEND1 definition to the graph.

```
proc gplot data=reflib.stocks;
    plot high*year low*year / overlay legend=legend1
                              vref=1000 to 5000 by 1000 lvref=2
                              haxis=axis1 hminor=4
                              vaxis=axis2 vminor=1;
run;
quit;
```

Example 7: Filling Areas in an Overlay Plot

Procedure features:
  PLOT statement options:

  AREAS=
  OVERLAY

Other features:
  GOPTIONS statement
  SYMBOL statement

Data set: REFLIB.STOCKS on page 843

Sample library member: GR21N07

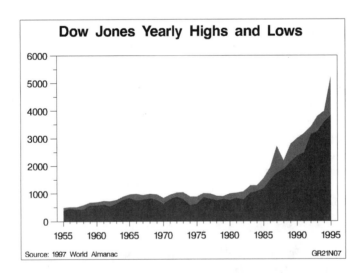

This example uses the AREAS= option in the PLOT statement to fill the areas that are under the plot lines. As in the previous example, two plots are overlaid on the same graph.

Assign the libref and set the graphics environment. COLORS= sets the area colors. CTEXT= sets the color for all text.

```
libname reflib 'SAS-data-library';
goptions reset=global gunit=pct border cback=white
         colors=(blue red) ctext=black
         ftitle=swissb ftext=swiss htitle=6 htext=4;
```

Define title and footnote.

```
title1 'Dow Jones Yearly Highs and Lows';
footnote1 h=3 j=l ' Source: 1997 World Almanac'
          j=r 'GR21N07 ';
```

Define symbol characteristics. INTERPOL= specifies a line to connect data points. The line creates the fill boundary.

```
symbol1 interpol=join;
```

Define axis characteristics.

```
axis1 order=(1955 to 1995 by 5) offset=(2,2)
      label=none
      major=(height=2)
      minor=(height=1);
axis2 order=(0 to 6000 by 1000) offset=(0,0)
      label=none
      major=(height=2)
      minor=(height=1);
```

Generate a plot with filled areas. The plot requests are ordered to draw the lowest plot first. Area 1 occupies the space between the lowest (first) plot line and the horizontal axis, and area 2 is below the highest (second) plot line. This arrangement prevents the pattern for area 1 from overlaying the pattern for area 2. AREAS=2 fills all the areas below the second plot line.

```
proc gplot data=reflib.stocks;
   plot low*year high*year / overlay
                             haxis=axis1
                             hminor=4
                             vaxis=axis2
                             vminor=1
                             caxis=black
                             areas=2;
run;
quit;
```

Example 8: Plotting Three Variables

Procedure features:

PLOT classification variable

Other features:
AXIS statement
SYMBOL statement
RUN-group processing

Sample library member: GR21N08

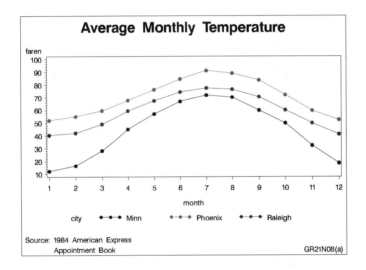

This example shows that when your data contain a classification variable that groups the data, you can use a plot request of the form *y-variable*x-variable=third-variable* to generate a separate plot for every formatted value of the classification variable, which in this case is CITY. With this type of request, all plots are drawn on the same graph and a legend is automatically produced and explains the values of *third-variable*. The default legend uses the variable name CITY for the legend label and the variable values for the legend value descriptions. Because no LEGEND definition is used in this example, the font and height of the legend label and the legend value descriptions are set by the graphics options FTEXT= and HTEXT=. Height specifications in the SYMBOL statement do not affect the size of the symbols in the legend values.

This example then modifies the plot request. As shown in the following output, the plot is enhanced by using different symbol definitions for each plot line, changing axes labels, and scaling the vertical axes differently.

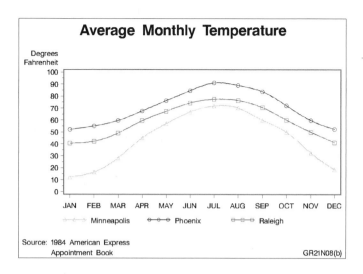

Assign the libref and set the graphics environment.

```
libname reflib 'SAS-data-library';
goptions reset=global gunit=pct border cback=white
        colors=(black blue green red)
        ftitle=swissb ftext=swiss htitle=6 htext=3;
```

Create the data set. REFLIB.CITYTEMP contains the average monthly temperatures of three cities: Raleigh, Minneapolis, and Phoenix.

```
data reflib.citytemp;
   input  month faren city $;
   datalines;
   1      40.5     Raleigh
   1      12.2     Minn
   1      52.1     Phoenix
   ...more data lines...
   12     41.2     Raleigh
   12     18.6     Minn
   12     52.5     Phoenix
;
```

Define title and footnote.

```
title1 'Average Monthly Temperature';
footnote1 j=l ' Source: 1984 American Express';
footnote2 j=l '            Appointment Book'
          j=r 'GR21N08(a) ';
```

Define symbol characteristics. This statement specifies that a straight line connect data points, and that the data points be represented by a 3-unit-high dot. Because no color is specified, the default color behavior is used and each line is a different color.

```
symbol1 interpol=join
        value=dot
        height=3;
```

Generate a plot of three variables. The plot request draws one plot on the graph for each value of CITY and produces a legend that defines CITY values.

```
proc gplot data=reflib.citytemp;
   plot faren*month=city / hminor=0;
run;
```

Modify FOOTNOTE2 to reference new output.

```
footnote2 j=l '         Appointment Book'
           j=r 'GR21N08(b) ';
```

Define new symbol characteristics. SYMBOL statements are assigned to the values of CITY in alphabetical order. For example, the value **Minn** is assigned SYMBOL1.

```
symbol1 color=green interpol=spline
        width=2 value=triangle
        height=3;
symbol2 color=blue interpol=spline
        width=2 value=circle
        height=3;
symbol3 color=red interpol=spline
        width=2 value=square
        height=3;
```

Define new axis characteristics. AXIS1 suppresses the axis label and specifies month abbreviations for the major tick mark labels. AXIS2 specifies a two-line axis label and scales the axis to show major tick marks at every 10 degrees from 0 to 100 degrees.

```
axis1 label=none
      value=('JAN' 'FEB' 'MAR' 'APR' 'MAY' 'JUN'
             'JUL' 'AUG' 'SEP' 'OCT' 'NOV' 'DEC')
      offset=(2)
      width=3;
axis2 label=('Degrees' justify=right 'Fahrenheit')
      order=(0 to 100 by 10)
      width=3;
```

Enhance the legend.

```
legend1 label=none value=(tick=1 'Minneapolis');
```

Generate the enhanced plot. Because the procedure supports RUN-group processing, you do not have to repeat the PROC GPLOT statement to generate the second plot.

```
        plot faren*month=city / haxis=axis1 hminor=0
                                vaxis=axis2 vminor=1
                                caxis=red legend=legend1;
run;
quit;
```

Example 9: Plotting with Different Scales of Values

Procedure features:
  PLOT statement options:

  HAXIS=
  HMINOR=

  PLOT and PLOT2 statement options:

  CAXIS=
  VAXIS=
  VMINOR=

Other features:
  AXIS statement

  SYMBOL statement

Sample library member: GR21N09

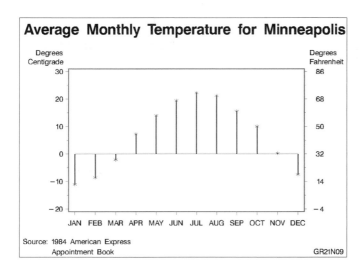

This example shows how a PLOT2 statement generates a right axis that displays the values of the vertical coordinates in a different scale from the scale that is used for the left axis.

In this plot of the average monthly temperature for Minneapolis, temperature variables that represent degrees centigrade (displayed on the left axis) and degrees Fahrenheit (displayed on the right axis) are plotted against the variable MONTH. Although the procedure produces two sets of data points, it calibrates the axes so that the data points are identical and it displays only one plot.

This example uses SYMBOL statements to define symbol definitions. By default, the SYMBOL1 statement is assigned to the plot that is generated by the PLOT statement, and SYMBOL2 is assigned to the plot generated by the PLOT2 statement.

Assign the libref and set the graphics environment.

```
libname reflib 'SAS-data-library';
goptions reset=global gunit=pct border cback=white
        colors=(black blue green red)
        ftitle=swissb ftext=swiss htitle=6 htext=3;
```

Create the data set and calculate centigrade temperatures. REFLIB.MINNTEMP contains average monthly temperatures for Minneapolis.

```
data reflib.minntemp;
   input @10 month
         @23 f2;
   c2=(f2-32)/1.8;
   output;
   datalines;
01JAN83  1   1    40.5  12.2  52.1
01FEB83  2   1    42.2  16.5  55.1
   ...more data lines...
01NOV83  11  4    50.0  32.4  59.8
01DEC83  12  1    41.2  18.6  52.5
;
```

Define title and footnote.

```
title1 'Average Monthly Temperature for Minneapolis';
footnote1 j=l ' Source: 1984 American Express';
footnote2 j=l '            Appointment Book'
          j=r 'GR21N09 ';
```

Define symbol characteristics. INTERPOL=NEEDLE generates a horizontal reference line at zero on the left axis and draws vertical lines from the data points to the reference line. CI= specifies the color of the interpolation line and CV= specifies the color of the plot symbol.

```
symbol1 interpol=needle
        ci=blue
        cv=red
        width=3
        value=star
        height=3;
```

Define symbol characteristics for PLOT2. SYMBOL2 suppresses interpolation lines and plotting symbols; otherwise, they would overlay the lines or symbols displayed by SYMBOL1.

```
symbol2 interpol=none
        value=none;
```

Define axis characteristics. In the AXIS2 and AXIS3 statements, ORDER= controls the scaling of the axes. Both axes represent exactly the same range of temperature, and the distance between the major tick marks on both axes represent an equivalent quantity of degrees (10 for centigrade and 18 for Fahrenheit).

```
axis1 label=none
      value=('JAN' 'FEB' 'MAR' 'APR' 'MAY' 'JUN'
             'JUL' 'AUG' 'SEP' 'OCT' 'NOV' 'DEC')
      offset=(2)
      width=3;
axis2 label=('Degrees' justify=right ' Centigrade')
      order=(-20 to 30 by 10)
      width=3;
axis3 label=(h=3 'Degrees' justify=left 'Fahrenheit')
      order=(-4 to 86 by 18)
      width=3;
```

Generate a plot with a second vertical axis. HAXIS= specifies the AXIS1 definition. VAXIS= specifies AXIS2 and AXIS3 definitions in the PLOT and PLOT2 statements. CAXIS= colors the axis lines and all major and minor tick marks. Axis labels and major tick mark values use the default color. VMINOR= specifies the number of minor tick marks for each axis.

```
proc gplot data=reflib.minntemp;
   plot c2*month  / caxis=red
                    haxis=axis1 hminor=0
                    vaxis=axis2 vminor=1
   plot2 f2*month / caxis=red
                    vaxis=axis3
                    vminor=1;
run;
quit;
```

Example 10: Creating Plots with Drill-down for the Web

Procedure features:
   PLOT statement options:
      HTML=
      HTML_LEGEND=
ODS features:
   ODS HTML statement:
      BODY=
      NOGTITLE
      PATH=
Other features:
   BY statement
   GOPTIONS statement
Sample library member: GR21N10

This example shows how to create a plot with simple drill-down functionality for the Web. If you display the plot in a Web browser, you can select any plot point or legend symbol to display a report on monthly temperatures for the selected city.

The example explains how to use the ODS HTML statement and the HTML procedure options to create the drill-down. It shows how to

□ explicitly name the HTML files and direct the different types of output to different files

□ use BY-group processing with ODS HTML, and determine the anchor names for the different pieces of output

□ use the PATH= option to specify the destination for the HTML and GIF files created by the ODS HTML statement

□ add an HTML HREF string to a data set to define a link target

□ assign link targets with the HTML= and HTML_LEGEND= procedure options

□ suppress the titles in the GIF files and display them in the HTML file.

For more information on drill-down graphs, see "About Drill-down Graphs" on page 90.

This program modifies the code from sample GR21N08, which shows how to generate separate plots for the formatted values of a classification variable. In this example, the code implements drill-down capability for the plot, enabling you to select any plot point or legend symbol to drill down to a report on the yearly temperatures for the corresponding city. Display 21.1 on page 854 shows the drill-down plot as it is viewed in a Browser.

Display 21.1   Browser View of Drill-down Plot

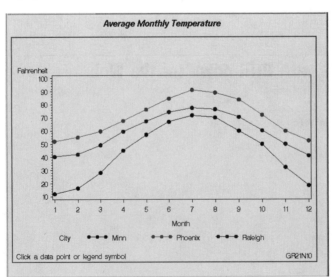

Display 21.2 on page 855 shows the report that appears when you select any plot point or legend symbol that corresponds to the data for Raleigh.

Display 21.2 Browser View of Report on Raleigh Temperatures

Assign the fileref to the Web-server path. FILENAME assigns the fileref ODSOUT, which specifies a destination for the HTML and GIF files produced by the example program. ODSOUT must point to a Web-server location if procedure output is to be viewed on the Web. Later in the program, PATH=ODSOUT is specified on the ODS HTML statement, which directs program output to that location.

```
filename odsout 'path-to-Web-server-space';
```

Close the ODS Listing destination for output. To conserve system resources, use ODS LISTING to close the Listing destination for procedure output. Thus, the graphics output is not displayed in the GRAPH window, although it is written to the catalog.

```
ods listing close;
```

Assign graphics options for producing the ODS HTML output. DEVICE=GIF causes the ODS HTML statement to generate the graphics output as GIF files. TRANSPARENCY causes the graphics output to use the Web-page background as the background of the graph. NOBORDER suppresses the border around the graphics output area, which makes the border treatment the same as that for the non-graphics output that is generated by the example.

```
goptions reset=global gunit=pct
         colors=(black red blue green)
         ftext=swiss ftitle=swissb htitle=6 htext=3
         device=gif transparency noborder;
```

Create the data set CITYTEMP. CITYTEMP contains the average monthly temperatures for three cities.

```
data citytemp;
   input  Month Fahrenheit City $;
   datalines;
   1      40.5    Raleigh
   1      12.2    Minn
```

```
    1        52.1      Phoenix
    2        42.2      Raleigh
    2        16.5      Minn
    2        55.1      Phoenix
    3        49.2      Raleigh
    3        28.3      Minn
    3        59.7      Phoenix
    4        59.5      Raleigh
    4        45.1      Minn
    4        67.7      Phoenix
    5        67.4      Raleigh
    5        57.1      Minn
    5        76.3      Phoenix
    6        74.4      Raleigh
    6        66.9      Minn
    6        84.6      Phoenix
    7        77.5      Raleigh
    7        71.9      Minn
    7        91.2      Phoenix
    8        76.5      Raleigh
    8        70.2      Minn
    8        89.1      Phoenix
    9        70.6      Raleigh
    9        60.0      Minn
    9        83.8      Phoenix
   10        60.2      Raleigh
   10        50.0      Minn
   10        72.2      Phoenix
   11        50.0      Raleigh
   11        32.4      Minn
   11        59.8      Phoenix
   12        41.2      Raleigh
   12        18.6      Minn
   12        52.5      Phoenix
;
```

Add the HTML variable to CITYTEMP and create the NEWTEMP data set. The HTML variable CITYDRILL contains the target locations to associate with the different values of the variable CITY. Each location for CITYDRILL references the file city_reports.html, wh ich will be created by this program. Each location ends with the default anchor name (IDX1, IDX2, and IDX3) that ODS will assign to the target output when it creates that output in file city_reports.html.

```
data newtemp;
   set citytemp;
   length citydrill $ 40;
   if city='Minn' then
      citydrill='HREF="city_reports.html#IDX1"';
   else if city='Phoenix' then
      citydrill='HREF="city_reports.html#IDX2"';
   else if city='Raleigh' then
      citydrill='HREF="city_reports.html#IDX3"';
```

Define titles and footnotes and a symbol definition for the plots.

```
title1 'Average Monthly Temperature';
footnote1 j=l h=3 ' Click a data point or legend symbol'
          j=r 'GR21N10 ';

symbol1 interpol=join
        value=dot
        height=3;
```

Open the HTML destination. PATH= specifies the ODSOUT fileref as the HTML destination for all the HTML and GIF files produced by the program. BODY= names the HTML file for storing the drill-down plot. NOGTITLE suppresses the graph title from the SAS/GRAPH output and displays it through the HTML page. ODS will automatically assign anchor names to each piece of output that is generated while the HTML destination is open.

```
ods html path=odsout
         body='city_plots.html'
         nogtitle;
```

Generate the plot. Both HTML= and HTML_LEGEND= specify CITYDRILL as the variable that contains the targets for the drill-down links. HTML= determines that each plot point will be a hot zone that links to target output, and HTML_LEGEND= determines that the legend symbols will be hot zones that link to target output. This GPLOT procedure generates the first piece of output in this program; thus, the plot receives the first default anchor name, which is IDX.

```
proc gplot data=newtemp;
   plot fahrenheit*month=city / hminor=0
        html=citydrill
        html_legend=citydrill;
run;
quit;
```

Change the HTML file. BODY= opens a new HTML file for storing the reports for city temperatures. The new file is assigned the name city_reports.html, which is the file name assigned above to variable CITYDRILL as part of its target-link locations. The reports that are generated later in this program will all be written to this one HTML file.

```
ods html path=odsout
         body='city_reports.html';
```

Sort data set NEWTEMP in order by city.

```
proc sort data=newtemp;
   by city month;
run;
```

Clear the footnotes, and suppress the default BY-line.

```
goptions reset=footnote;
option nobyline;
```

Print a report of monthly temperatures for each city. The BY statement determines that a separate report is generated for each city. Thus, the REPORT procedure generates three pieces of output. To assign anchor locations to this new output, ODS increments the last anchor name that was used (IDX), and therefore assigns the anchor names IDX1, IDX2, and IDX3 to the output. These are the anchor locations that were specified above as the anchor locations for variable CITYDRILL.

```
title1 'Monthly Temperatures in #byval(city)';
proc report data=newtemp nowindows;
  by city;
  column city month fahrenheit;
  define city       / noprint group;
  define month      / display group;
  define Fahrenheit / display group;
run;
```

Close the HTML destination, and open the LISTING destination.

```
ods html close;
ods listing;
```

CHAPTER

22

The GPRINT Procedure

Overview

The GPRINT procedure converts a text file into graphics output that can be displayed or printed on a graphics output device. You can enhance the output with TITLE, NOTE, and FOOTNOTE statements, or include Annotate graphics, or both. Like output from any other SAS/GRAPH procedure, output from the GPRINT procedure can be stored in catalogs and replayed with the GREPLAY procedure.

You can use the GPRINT procedure when you want to create graphics output from tabular material, reports, or any external text file produced by the SAS System or other software application. To display text and graphics generated by SAS/GRAPH software, use the GSLIDE procedure.

Figure 22.1 on page 859 shows a graphics output generated by the GPRINT procedure from SAS output generated by the MEANS procedure. Titles and footnotes have been added, and the Swiss font has been assigned to the procedure output text.

Figure 22.1   Graph Generated with the GPRINT Procedure

```
┌─────────────────────────────────────┐
│        Regional Sales Report         │
│                                      │
│                                      │
│    R e g i o n      S t a f f        │
│   ─ ─ ─ ─ ─ ─ ─ ─ ─ ─ ─ ─ ─          │
│                                      │
│                                      │
│          N E           4             │
│          N W           3             │
│          S E           2             │
│          S W           4             │
│                                      │
│                                      │
└─────────────────────────────────────┘
```

Concepts

About External Text Files

External text files are files that you have stored outside of SAS. They can be created in several different ways. Four common methods are as follows:

- □ save the contents of the OUTPUT or LOG window to an external file with the FILE command
- □ direct the output from SAS procedures to an external file using the PRINTTO procedure and a FILENAME statement
- □ direct the output from a SAS data step to an external file using the FILE and PUT statements
- □ create a text file from another software application such as a text editor or a spreadsheet program.

Note: Depending on the operating environment and the method used to generate the file, external text files may contain carriage-control characters. For more information on carriage-control characters, see the NOCC option on page 862. △

You can use a FILENAME statement or host command to specify a fileref that points to the location of the external text file that you want to print. This external file serves as the input file for the GPRINT procedure.

Procedure Syntax

Global statements: FOOTNOTE, TITLE

Reminder: The procedure can include the NOTE statement.

Supports: Output Delivery System (ODS)

PROC GPRINT FILEREF=*fileref*
  <*option(s)*>;

PROC GPRINT Statement

The PROC GPRINT statement identifies the external file to be converted to graphics output. Optionally, specifies the text color, a destination catalog for graphics output, and an Annotate data set.

Syntax

PROC GPRINT FILEREF=*fileref*
  <*option(s)*>;

option(s) can be one or more of the following:

ANNOTATE=*Annotate-data-set*
CTEXT=*text-color*
DESCRIPTION='*entry-description*'
GOUT=<*libref.*>*output-catalog*
NAME='*entry-name*'
NOCC
O

Required Arguments

FILEREF=*fileref*

specifies the fileref that is associated with the external file that will be used as input to the GPRINT procedure. *Fileref* must have been previously defined in a FILENAME statement or host command.

See also: "FILENAME Statement" on page 24

Featured in: Example 2 on page 868

Options

Options in the PROC GPRINT statement affect all graphs that the statement produces. You can specify as many options as you want and list them in any order.

ANNOTATE=*Annotate-data-set*
ANNO=*Annotate-data-set*

specifies a data set to annotate the output that the GPRINT procedure produces.

See also: Chapter 10, "The Annotate Data Set," on page 403

CTEXT=*text-color*

specifies the color in which the procedure displays the text from the input file.

If you do not use the CTEXT= option, a color specification is searched for in the following order:

1 the CTEXT= option in a GOPTIONS statement

2 the default, the first color in the colors list.

The CTEXT= option in the PROC GPRINT statement does not affect titles and footnotes generated by TITLE and FOOTNOTE definitions.

Featured in: Example 1 on page 865

DESCRIPTION='*entry-description*'
DES='*entry-description*'

specifies the description of the catalog entry for the chart. The maximum length for *entry-description* is 40 characters. The description does not appear on the chart. By default, the GPRINT procedure assigns the description OUTPUT FROM PROC GPRINT.

GOUT=<*libref.*>*output-catalog*

specifies the SAS catalog in which to save the graphics output produced by the GPRINT procedure. If you omit the libref, SAS/GRAPH looks for the catalog in the temporary library called WORK and creates the catalog if it does not exist.

See also: "Storing Graphics Output in SAS Catalogs" on page 49

NAME='*entry-name*'

specifies the name of the catalog entry for the graph. The maximum length for *entry-name* is 8 characters. The default name is GPRINT. If the specified name duplicates the name of an existing entry, SAS/GRAPH software adds a number to the duplicate name to create a unique entry, for example, GPRINT1.

NOCC

tells the procedure that the external text file does not contain carriage-control characters. If you include the NOCC option, the procedure assumes that the first character on each line of the input file is a text character and not a carriage-control character. If you omit the NOCC option, the characters in column one are read as carriage-control characters. If they are valid carriage-control characters, the GPRINT procedure recognizes and executes them. If they are not valid carriage-control characters, the GPRINT procedure issues an error message.

O

causes a 0 (numeric zero) to be converted to the letter O in the output. This option circumvents the use of a numeric zero with an interior slash that is present on some devices.

Adjusting SAS Output and Graphics Output

The size of SAS output (or other text) in columns and rows and the size of graphics output are independently controlled. Depending on the result you want, you can do either of the following:

□ Adjust the size of your SAS output (or other text) to fit the available space on your graph.

□ Adjust the dimensions of the graphics output area and the size of the cells within the graphics output area to control the size of the characters that are displayed as graphics output by the GPRINT procedure.

You can adjust the size (columns and rows) of any other external text file that you use as input to the GPRINT procedure. Although the following sections explain how to adjust the size of SAS output, the general process can be applied to any text file.

SAS Output Size   SAS output prints in pages. The length (in number of rows) and the width (in number of columns) of the page are determined by the PAGESIZE= and LINESIZE= options, respectively. Each character of SAS output occupies one column of space in a row (one cell), as shown in Figure 22.2 on page 862.

Figure 22.2 SAS Output Size

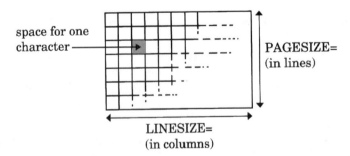

Graphics Output Size   Graphics output is drawn in the graphics output area, which is also divided into cells. The overall dimensions of the graphics output area (width and height) are determined by the values of the device parameters XMAX and YMAX. These values, which determine the aspect ratio of the graphics output area, can be temporarily reduced with the HSIZE= and VSIZE= graphics options.

The number of columns and rows that fill the area is determined by the values of the LCOLS or PCOLS and LROWS or PROWS device parameters. These values, which determine the size and aspect ratio of a cell, can be temporarily altered with the HPOS= and VPOS= graphics options. The more columns and rows there are in a given area, the smaller the cells are. Therefore, using HPOS= and VPOS= to change the number of columns and rows also changes the size of the cells and may change the size of the characters. However, it does not affect the overall dimensions of the graph. For details, see "Maintaining the aspect ratio of cells" on page 864.

See "Procedure Output and the Graphics Output Area" on page 29 for a complete description of the graphics output area. See Chapter 2, "SAS/GRAPH Programs," on page 21 for more information on device parameters and graphics options.

Matching Sizes   When you use the GPRINT procedure to convert SAS output to graphics output, you may need to manipulate the dimensions of either or both to get the proper size characters in the graphics output and to avoid truncating lines. Adjustment may be necessary in the following situations:

☐ If the number of rows per page in the SAS output (PAGESIZE=) exceeds the number of rows in the graphics output area (LROWS or PROWS), then the GPRINT procedure produces additional pages of graphics output.

☐ If the number of rows per page in the SAS output (PAGESIZE=) is much less than the number of rows in the graphics output area (LROWS or PROWS), then the output does not fill the graphics output area.

☐ If the width of a line of SAS output (LINESIZE=) exceeds the number of columns in the graphics output area (LCOLS or PCOLS), then the GPRINT procedure truncates the line.

☐ If the width of SAS output (LINESIZE=) is much less than the number of columns in the graphics output area (LCOLS or PCOLS), then the output does not fill the graphics output area.

You can adjust the size of the SAS output or the size of the graphics output, or both.

Adjusting the size of the SAS output   The following steps show you how to use the PAGESIZE= and LINESIZE= options to adjust the page size of the SAS output to fit the size of the graphics output area.

1 Use the GDEVICE procedure to determine the number of rows (LROWS or PROWS) and the number of columns (LCOLS or PCOLS) on the graphics device that you intend to use. See Chapter 15, "The GDEVICE Procedure," on page 651 for details.

2 Determine the number of columns and rows that you are going to use for SAS/GRAPH titles and footnotes. (If you specify height in units of CELLS, each unit of height equals one row.)

3 Use the OPTIONS statement to set the PAGESIZE= option equal to the number of rows on the device minus the number of positions to be used by TITLE and FOOTNOTE definitions. Set the LINESIZE= option equal to the number of columns on the device minus the number of positions used by titles and footnotes if the titles and footnotes are positioned vertically.

4 Produce the SAS output.

Adjusting the size of the graphics output   The following steps show you how to use the HPOS= and VPOS= graphics options to adjust the number of columns and rows in the graphics output area on the output device so that it can accommodate the page size of your SAS output.

1 Determine the number of columns (LINESIZE=) and rows (PAGESIZE=) in the SAS output.

2 Use the GOPTIONS statement to set the VPOS= graphics option equal to the number of rows in the SAS output plus the number of rows to be used by TITLE

and FOOTNOTE definitions. Set the HPOS= graphics option equal to the number of columns in the SAS output plus the number of columns to be used by titles and footnotes if the titles and footnotes are positioned vertically.

3 Produce the GPRINT output.

Similarly, adjusting the overall dimensions of the graphics output area with the HSIZE= and VSIZE= graphics options may affect the size and possibly the aspect ratio of the cells.

Note: Changing the values of the HPOS= and VPOS= graphics options changes the size of the cells and consequently of characters in the output. On devices with nonscalable hardware fonts, changing the aspect ratio with HPOS= and VPOS= causes the Simulate font to be used instead of hardware characters. However, if you specify software fonts, the change in aspect ratio may be ignored. See "Using Fonts" on page 864 and "Using Hardware Fonts" on page 128 for more information. △

Maintaining the aspect ratio of cells   If you change the values of the HPOS= and VPOS= graphics options to control the size of characters or to match the rows and columns of the external text file, you should try to maintain the same ratio of columns to rows as the original values of the device parameters. For example, suppose you have SAS output with 50 columns and 10 rows, and a graphics device that has 80 columns and 32 rows. The aspect ratio of the device is 5:2. If you print 10 rows of output on a device with 32 rows, you will have 22 blank lines. You can reduce the number of blank lines and increase the size of the characters by reducing the number of rows in the graphics output area with VPOS=. If, in addition to the 10 rows of output, you allow four lines of space for titles and two lines of space for a footnote, you need a total of 16 rows. Therefore, assigning a value of 20 to VPOS= should produce readable text and plenty of space. If VPOS=20, setting HPOS= to 50 retains the original aspect ratio of the device (80:32 or 5:2).

Note that this method allows space for titles and footnotes in terms of rows; the actual size of the titles and footnotes depends on the height specification you use. Using the unit CELLS to define the height of titles and footnotes makes it easier to calculate precisely how much space is available.

Using Fonts

By default, the GPRINT procedure uses the default hardware font with a height of 1 cell to display the text from the external file. However, if you specify a nonscalable hardware font, SAS/GRAPH may use the Simulate font instead. See Chapter 6, "SAS/GRAPH Fonts," on page 125 for details.

Font and height specifications for titles and footnotes are determined by the TITLE and FOOTNOTE definitions. See "TITLE, FOOTNOTE, and NOTE Statements" on page 251 for details.

To specify a font and height for the text, use the FTEXT= and HTEXT= graphics options. If you specify a software font, it is best to use a uniform font such as Swiss Uniform so that your text will be evenly spaced.

CAUTION:
  Changes in the aspect ratio of cells made with the HPOS= and VPOS= graphics options are ignored if you specify software fonts. Change the aspect ratio in the device entry if you want the software characters proportioned to fit the new aspect ratio.   △

If you specify a software font and change the aspect ratio of the cells with the HPOS= and VPOS= graphics options, the change in aspect ratio is ignored and the procedure continues to draw the font in the original proportions. As a result, your text may not fit the graphics output area.

However, if you want the software characters to reflect a change in aspect ratio or if you want the characters to fit the new aspect ratio even if they are distorted, use the LCOLS or PCOLS and LROWS or PROWS device parameters in the device entry to change the aspect ratio of the cells. Using the device entry to specify a change in the aspect ratio enables you to distort the characters. See Chapter 15, "The GDEVICE Procedure," on page 651 for more information on changing device parameters.

Examples

Example 1: Specifying Color Text

Procedure features:
GPRINT procedure options:
CTEXT=
Other features:
GOPTIONS statement
TIMEPLOT procedure
Sample library member: GR22N01

This example creates the REFLIB.DOWHLC data set and generates a graph with color text from output that is produced by the TIMEPLOT procedure. The TIMEPLOT procedure is not a graphics procedure and produces text output only. (See *SAS Procedures Guide* for details on the TIMEPLOT procedure.)

The first part of this example uses the TIMEPLOT procedure with the newly created REFLIB.DOWHLC data set as input to produce Output 22.1 on page 865:

Output 22.1 SAS Output from the TIMEPLOT Procedure

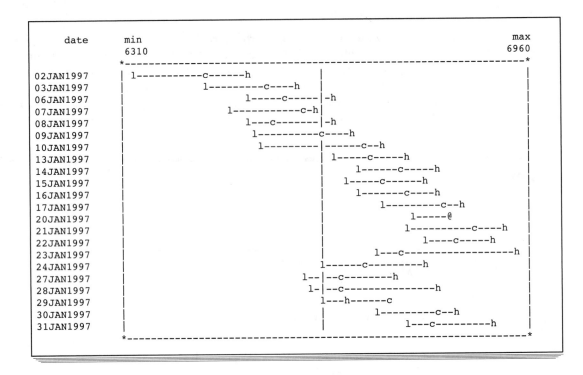

The second part of this example takes the output generated by the TIMEPLOT procedure and converts it to a graph by using the GPRINT procedure. Figure 22.3 on page 866 shows the graph with color text, a title, and a footnote:

Figure 22.3 GPRINT Procedure Output with Enhanced Text (GR22N01)

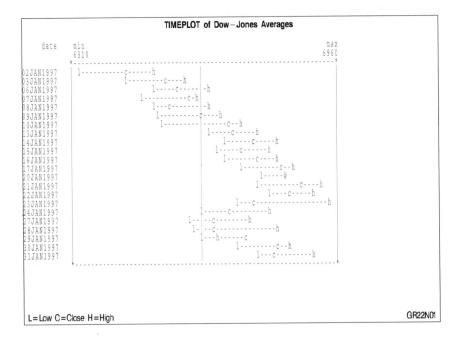

Assign the libref and set the graphics environment. HTEXT= assigns the height for the text in the default unit, cells.

```
libname reflib 'SAS-data-library';
goptions reset=global border cback=white
         colors=(black blue green red)
         ftitle=swissb htitle=3pct
         htext=.8 ftext=none
         hsize=7in vsize=5in;
```

Assign the fileref OUT to the external file.

```
filename out 'external-file';
```

Create the data set REFLIB.DOWHLC.

```
data reflib.dowhlc;
   input date date9. high low close;
   format date date9.;
   datalines;
02JAN1997   6511.38   6318.96   6442.49
03JAN1997   6586.42   6437.10   6544.09
...more data lines...
30JAN1997   6845.03   6719.96   6823.86
31JAN1997   6912.37   6769.99   6813.09
;
```

Suppress the date line and page numbers and set the linesize and pagesize.

```
options nodate nonumber linesize=80 pagesize=60;
```

Specify the destination for all subsequent procedure output.

```
proc printto print=out new;
run;
```

Generate TIMEPLOT graph output. It is sent to external file.

```
proc timeplot data=reflib.dowhlc;
   plot low close high / overlay hiloc ref=mean(low)
                         npp axis=6310 to 6960 by 10;
   id date;
run;
```

Reset destination for printed output to default.

```
proc printto;
run;
```

Define title and footnote.

```
title 'TIMEPLOT of Dow-Jones Averages';
footnote h=3 pct f=swiss
        j=l ' L=Low' ' C=Close' ' H=High'
        j=r 'GR22N01 ';
```

Generate graph from the external file and specify text color. CTEXT= assigns a color to the text produced by the GPRINT procedure.

```
proc gprint fileref=out ctext=red;
run;
```

Example 2: Adjusting the Size of Characters

Procedure features:
　　GPRINT statement options:
　　　　FILEREF=
Other features:
　　FILENAME statement
　　GOPTIONS statement
　　PRINT procedure
　　PRINTTO procedure
Data set: REFLIB.DOWHLC on page 867
Sample library member: GR22N02

This example creates a graph from a text file and increases the size of the text. The first part of this example uses the PRINT procedure to create an external file that contains SAS output. The GPRINT procedure is used to import the text file into a graph. Because the LINESIZE= option (columns) is set to 76 and the PAGESIZE= option (rows) is set to 24, the output is small and occupies only a portion of the page, as shown in Figure 22.4 on page 869:

Figure 22.4 GPRINT Procedure Output with No Adjustments (GR22N02(a))

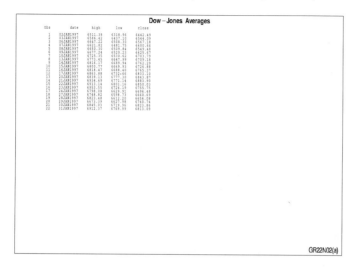

In the second part of this example, the number of columns and rows in the graphics output area is reduced with the HPOS= and VPOS= graphic options. Thus, the size of the characters in the graph increase, as shown in Figure 22.5 on page 869:

Figure 22.5 GPRINT Procedure Output with Adjusted Sizing (GR22N02(b))

Dow–Jones Averages

Obs	date	high	low	close
1	02JAN1997	6511.38	6318.96	6442.49
2	03JAN1997	6586.42	6437.10	6544.09
3	06JAN1997	6647.22	6508.30	6567.18
4	07JAN1997	6621.82	6481.75	6600.66
5	08JAN1997	6650.30	6509.84	6549.48
6	09JAN1997	6677.24	6520.23	6625.67
7	10JAN1997	6725.35	6530.62	6703.79
8	13JAN1997	6773.45	6647.99	6709.18
9	14JAN1997	6816.17	6689.94	6762.29
10	15JAN1997	6800.77	6669.93	6726.88
11	16JAN1997	6818.47	6688.40	6765.37
12	17JAN1997	6863.88	6732.66	6833.10
13	20JAN1997	6839.13	6777.30	6843.87
14	21JAN1997	6934.69	6771.14	6883.90
15	22JAN1997	6913.14	6801.16	6850.03
16	23JAN1997	6953.55	6724.19	6755.75
17	24JAN1997	6798.08	6629.91	6696.48
18	27JAN1997	6748.82	6598.73	6660.69
19	28JAN1997	6823.48	6612.20	6656.08
20	29JAN1997	6673.39	6627.98	6740.74
21	30JAN1997	6845.03	6719.96	6823.86
22	31JAN1997	6912.37	6769.99	6813.09

GR22N02(b)

Assign the libref and set the graphics environment. FTEXT= in the GOPTIONS statement specifies the default hardware font. (This is the default setting.)

```
libname reflib 'SAS-data-library';
goptions reset=global border cback=white
         colors=(black blue green red)
         ftitle=swissb ftext=none
         hsize=7in vsize=5in
```

```
                    hpos=142 vpos=68;
```

Assign the fileref DOW to the external file. The fileref DOW is associated with the external file where the output from PROC PRINT is stored.

```
filename dow 'external-file';
```

Suppress the date line and page numbers. Set the line and page size.

```
options nodate nonumber linesize=76 pagesize=24;
```

Specify the destination for all subsequent procedure output. The PRINTTO procedure directs the SAS output to the external file that the GPRINT procedure subsequently uses as input. PRINT= directs all printed procedure output to the file referenced by the fileref DOW. NEW causes the output file to be replaced each time the program is run.

```
proc printto print=dow new;
run;
```

Send the output to the destination file. The PRINT procedure generates the text and sends it to the external file specified by PROC PRINTTO.

```
proc print data=reflib.dowhlc;
run;
```

Reset destination for printed output to the default. The destination for printed output is reset to the default by resubmitting PROC PRINTTO with no options.

```
proc printto;
run;
```

Define title and footnote.

```
title 'Dow-Jones Averages';
footnote h=3 pct f=swiss j=r 'GR22N02(a) ';
```

Generate graph from the external file. FILEREF= specifies the external file that is used as input. NOCC is omitted because the input text file contains carriage-control characters.

```
proc gprint fileref=dow;
run;
```

Reduce HPOS= and VPOS= to increase cell size.

```
goptions hpos=75 vpos=30;
```

Define the footnote.

```
footnote h=3 pct f=swiss j=r 'GR22N02(b) ';
```

Generate adjusted graph.

```
proc gprint fileref=dow;
run;
```

CHAPTER

23

The GPROJECT Procedure

Overview

The GPROJECT procedure processes map data sets by converting spherical coordinates (longitude and latitude) into Cartesian coordinates for use by the GMAP procedure. This process of converting coordinates from spherical to Cartesian is called *projecting*. In many of the geographic map data sets that are available with SAS/GRAPH software, the observation values are stored as longitude and latitude coordinates on a sphere (which means the map is unprojected). When these observations are plotted by the GMAP procedure, which is designed to plot points on a two-dimensional plane, the resulting map is often reversed and elongated as a result of forcing the curved map surface onto a flat plane.

The GPROJECT procedure enables you to use one of several map projection techniques to project the coordinates onto a two-dimensional plane while attempting to minimize the distortion of area, distance, direction, and shape properties of the original sphere. (The earth is not precisely spherical and the GPROJECT procedure does not attempt to correct this small distortion.) The output map data set that is produced by the procedure contains coordinate values expressed in Cartesian coordinates that can be displayed correctly using the GMAP procedure.

The GPROJECT procedure also can create a rectangular subset of the input map data set by excluding all points with longitude and latitude values that fall outside of a specified range. This provides a handy way to reduce the size of the map data set if you need only a portion of a larger map.

The GPROJECT procedure does not produce any graphics output. Instead, it produces an output map data set, which typically becomes the input map data set for the GMAP procedure (see Chapter 19, "The GMAP Procedure," on page 731).

Figure 23.1 on page 874 and Figure 23.2 on page 874 illustrate the effect of using GPROJECT defaults (Albers projection with standard parallels that are calculated by the procedure) to project a typical map data set with coordinates that are stored as longitude and latitude.

The program for the following maps can be seen in Example 1 on page 885.

Figure 23.1   Map before Projection (GR23N01(a))

Figure 23.2   Map after Projection (GR23N01(b))

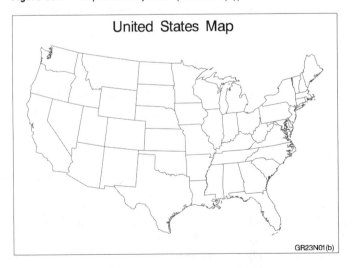

Concepts

About the Input Map Data Set

The input map data set must be in map data set format (see "SAS/GRAPH Map Data Sets" on page 761), and it must contain these variables:

- □ a numeric variable named X that contains the longitude coordinates of the map boundary points.
- □ a numeric variable named Y that contains the latitude coordinates of the map boundary points.
- □ one or more *identification variables* that uniquely identify the unit areas in the map. These variables are listed in the ID statement.

The X and Y variables contain the values that are to be projected.
In addition, the input map data set also can contain

- □ a numeric variable named SEGMENT that distinguishes nonconterminous segments of the unit areas.
- □ a numeric variable named DENSITY that can be used to affect the output from PROC GPROJECT. See "Clipping Map Data Sets" on page 884 for more information.

Other variables in the input map data set do not affect the GPROJECT procedure.

Input Map Data Sets that Contain Only Unprojected Values

Note: Projection is appropriate for map data sets in which the X and Y variable values represent longitude and latitude. Some of the map data sets that are supplied with SAS/GRAPH have already been projected; such data set should not be projected again. △

The following is a list of all of the Institute-supplied data sets that contain X and Y variables whose values are unprojected:

CANADA3
CANADA4
COUNTIES
COUNTY
STATES

See Example 1 on page 885 for an illustration of this type of input map data set and the variables it contains.

Input Map Data Sets that Contain Both Projected and Unprojected Values

Most map data sets contain both sets of variables (X, Y and LONG, LAT) for projected and unprojected maps. In these cases, the X and Y variables will produce a projected map so you don't need to use the GPROJECT procedure. However, you may want to use the LONG and LAT variables to reproject the map using a different projection type. To do this you must first rename the LONG and LAT variables. It is necessary to rename the LONG and LAT variables because the GPROJECT procedure looks for variables that are named X and Y by default. You can create a new map data set using the OUT= option, drop the current X and Y variables, and rename the LONG and LAT variables. Your new data set will then contain unprojected values in X and Y. The following statements illustrate how to do this:

```
proc gproject data=map.austral
               (drop=x y rename=(long=x lat=y))
               out=reflib.newaust;
    id id;
run;
```

For additional information on the supplied SAS/GRAPH map data sets, see "SAS/GRAPH Map Data Sets" on page 761 and the METAMAPS data set in your maps data set directory.

About Coordinate Values

Figure 23.3 on page 876 shows the standard coordinate system for map data sets with coordinates in longitude and latitude. For the longitude and latitude values (below and to the right of the figure, respectively) the upper value is expressed in degrees and the lower value is expressed in radians. A radian is approximately 57.3 degrees.

Figure 23.3 Longitude and Latitude Coordinates

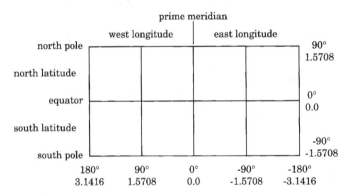

By default, the GPROJECT procedure assumes that the units for the input coordinate values are radians and that values for the horizontal coordinate increase from east to west across the map. If your map coordinates are stored as degrees of arc, use the DEGREE option in the PROC GPROJECT statement. If the horizontal coordinate values in the map increase west-to-east rather than east-to-west, use the EASTLONG option in the PROC GPROJECT statement. See "Options" on page 880 for details of DEGREE and EASTLONG.

The unprojected map data sets that are provided with SAS/GRAPH can be projected if you use the default procedure characteristics: coordinate units in the data sets are radians, and horizontal values increase east-to-west.

About Types of Map Projections

The GPROJECT procedure performs three different types of projection: Albers' equal-area projection with two standard parallels (the default method), Lambert's conformal projection with two standard parallels, or the gnomonic projection (an azimuthal equidistant projection).

These sections describe the basic theory of each projection method. For comparison, Figure 23.4 on page 877 shows an unprojected map of the northern hemisphere.

Figure 23.4 Unprojected Map

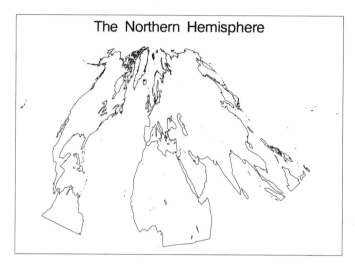

The Northern Hemisphere

Albers' Equal-Area Projection

The *Albers' projection* is a conic projection from the surface of the sphere to a cone secant to the sphere, cutting it at two standard parallels of latitude. The axis of the cone coincides with an extension of the polar axis of the sphere. Each section of the resulting map bears a constant ratio to the area of the sphere. In general, distortion in shape tends to increase toward the poles in latitudes outside of the two standard parallels.

The Albers' projection is well suited to portray areas of large and small east-to-west extent and produces satisfactory results in most cases. However, both standard parallels must lie on the same side of the equator, so this method may not be suitable for map data sets of large north-to-south extent that span the equator. For those map data sets, use the gnomonic projection method.

Figure 23.5 on page 878 illustrates an Albers' equal-area projection of the northern hemisphere.

Figure 23.5 Albers' Projection

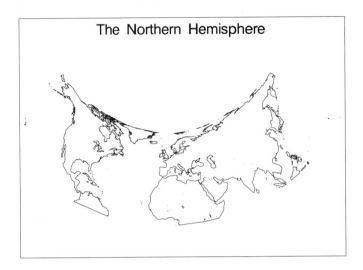

Lambert's Conformal Projection

The *Lambert's projection* is obtained from a secant cone in the same manner as Albers' projection. In the Lambert's projection, meridians of longitude are straight lines that radiate from the apex of the cone, while parallels of latitude are concentric circles. The Lambert's projection is somewhat better than the Albers' projection at representing the original shape of projected unit areas, while the Albers' projection is somewhat better at representing relative sizes of projected unit areas.

The Lambert's projection is ideal for navigational charts and maps of relatively small east-to-west extent. However, as in the Albers' projection, both standard parallels must lie on the same side of the equator, so this method may not be suitable for map data sets that span the equator. For those map data sets, use the gnomonic projection method.

Figure 23.6 on page 878 illustrates a Lambert's conformal projection of the northern hemisphere.

Figure 23.6 Lambert's Projection

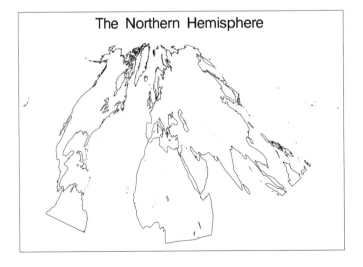

Gnomonic Projection

The *gnomonic projection* is a planar projection from the surface of the sphere directly onto an imaginary plane tangent to the sphere at the map projection pole. By default, the projection pole is placed at the center of the map data set that is to be projected, but you can specify the projection pole to be anywhere on the surface of the sphere. (See POLELONG= and POLELAT= options on page 882.)

In the gnomonic projection, distortion increases as the distance from the map pole increases. Because of this distortion, the PROC GPROJECT procedure deletes all of the observations that lie more than 85 degrees from the map pole. The gnomonic projection is best suited for mapping areas of small east-to-west extent.

Figure 23.7 on page 879 illustrates a gnomonic projection of the northern hemisphere.

Figure 23.7   Gnomonic Projection

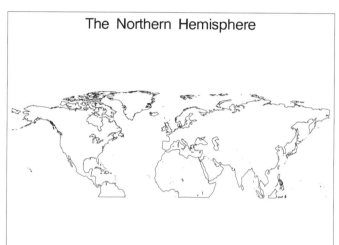

The Northern Hemisphere

Procedure Syntax

Requirements: Exactly one ID statement is required.

PROC GPROJECT *<option(s)>*;
   ID *id-variable(s)*;

PROC GPROJECT Statement

Identifies the input and output map data sets. Optionally specifies the type of projection, and criteria for clipping and projection.

Requirements: An input map data set is required.

Syntax

PROC GPROJECT *<option(s)>*;

option(s) can be one or more options from any or all of the following categories:

☐ data set options:

DATA=*input-map-data-set*

OUT=*output-map-data-set*

☐ projection options:

PARADIV=*n*

PARALEL1=*latitude*

PARALEL2=*latitude*

POLELAT=*latitude*

POLELONG=*longitude*

PROJECT=ALBERS | GNOMON | LAMBERT | NONE

☐ coordinate options:

ASIS | DUPOK

DEGREE

EASTLONG

☐ clipping options:

LATMIN=*min-latitude*

LATMAX=*max-latitude*

LONGMIN=*min-longitude*

LONGMAX=*max-longitude*

Options

ASIS
DUPOK

specify that observations for which the projected values for the X and Y variables are identical to those in the previous observation should be retained. By default, successive identical observations are deleted.

DATA=*input-map-data-set*

identifies the map data set to be processed. By default, the procedure uses the most recently created SAS data set.

See also: "About the Input Map Data Set" on page 875 "SAS Data Sets" on page 25

Featured in: Example 4 on page 891

DEGREE
DEG

specifies that the units for the longitude (X variable) and latitude (Y variable) coordinates are degrees of arc. By default, coordinate units are considered to be radians.

EASTLONG
EAST

specifies that the longitude (X variable) values in the input map data set increase to the east. By default, longitude values increase to the west.

LATMAX=*max-latitude*

specify the maximum latitude that will be included in the projection. Any unit areas that cross the selected latitude are clipped and closed along the specified parallels.

The LATMAX= and LATMIN= options do not have to be paired; you can specify a maximum latitude without specifying a minimum.

When PROJECT=ALBERS, LAMBERT, or GNOMON, PROC GPROJECT treats the value of *max-latitude* as degrees. When PROJECT=NONE, the procedure treats the value as a Cartesian coordinate.

Featured in: Example 3 on page 890

LATMIN=*min-latitude*

specify the minimum latitude that will be included in the projection. Any unit areas that cross the selected latitude are clipped and closed along the specified parallels. The LATMAX= and LATMIN= options do not have to be paired; you can specify a minimum latitude without specifying a maximum.

When PROJECT=ALBERS, LAMBERT, or GNOMON, PROC GPROJECT treats the value of *min-latitude* as degrees. When PROJECT=NONE, the procedure treats the value as a Cartesian coordinate.

Featured in: Example 3 on page 890

LONGMAX=*max-longitude*

specify the maximum longitude to be included in the projection. Any unit areas that cross the selected longitude are clipped and closed along the specified meridians. The LATMAX= and LATMIN= options do not have to be paired; you can specify a maximum longitude without specifying a minimum.

When PROJECT=ALBERS, LAMBERT, or GNOMON, PROC GPROJECT treats the value of *max-longitude* as degrees. When PROJECT=NONE, the procedure treats the value as a Cartesian coordinate.

Featured in: Example 3 on page 890

LONGMIN=*min-longitude*

specify the minimum longitude to be included in the projection. Any unit areas that cross the selected longitude are clipped and closed along the specified meridians. The LATMAX= and LATMIN= options do not have to be paired; you can specify a minimum longitude without specifying a maximum.

When PROJECT=ALBERS, LAMBERT, or GNOMON, the GPROJECT procedure treats the value of *min-longitude* as degrees. When PROJECT=NONE, the procedure treats the value as a Cartesian coordinate.

Featured in: Example 3 on page 890

OUT=*output-map-data-set*

names the new map data set, which contains the coordinates of the new unit areas that are created by the GPROJECT procedure.

By default, the GPROJECT procedure names the new data set that uses the DATA*n* naming convention. That is, the procedure uses the name WORK.DATA*n*, where *n* is the next unused number in sequence. Thus, the first automatically named data set is DATA1, the second is DATA2, and so on.

Featured in: Example 4 on page 891

PARADIV=*n*

specifies the divisor that computes the values used for standard parallels for the Albers' or Lambert's projections when explicit values are not provided. By default PARADIV=4, which causes standard parallels to be set at 1/4 and 3/4 of the range of latitude values in the input map data set.

See also: the PARALEL1= and PARALEL2= on page 882 options

PARALEL1=*latitude*

PARALEL2=*latitude*

specify values for the standard parallels that are used in the Albers' or Lambert's projection. *Latitude* must be in degrees. Positive values indicate north of the equator, and negative values indicate south of the equator. These options are ignored for the gnomonic projection.

By default, the GPROJECT procedure calculates values for the standard parallels. The defaults are chosen to minimize the distortion inherent in the projection process. The algorithm used is

$$\text{PARALEL1} = \text{minlat} + R / P_D$$
$$\text{PARALEL2} = \text{maxlat} - R / P_D$$
where:

R
   is the range of latitude values in the input map data set.

P_D
   is the PARADIV= value (see the discussion of the PARADIV= on page 881option).

minlat
   is the minimum latitude value in the input map data set.

maxlat
   is the maximum latitude value in the input map data set.
   If you do not use PARALEL1= or PARALEL2=, or you omit either option, the GPROJECT procedure uses the calculated value for the missing parameter.

The standard parallels, whether explicitly specified or supplied by the procedure, must lie on the same side of the equator. If they do not, PROC GPROJECT prints an error message and stops (the procedure may calculate standard parallels that lie on opposite sides of the equator). When projecting a map data set that contains unit areas that cross the equator, you may have to explicitly specify standard parallels that both lie on the same side of the equatMor. If this causes excessive distortion of the map, you may be able to use the gnomonic projection instead of the Albers' or Lambert's projection because the gnomonic technique has no such limitations at the equator.

POLELAT=*latitude*

POLELONG=*longitude*

specify a projection pole to use for the gnomonic projection. The projection pole is the point at which the surface of the sphere touches the surface of the imaginary plane onto which the map is projected. POLELAT= specifies the latitude of the projection point.

Units for *latitude* are degrees; positive values indicate north of the equator, and negative values indicate south of the equator. POLELONG= gives the longitude for the projection point. Units for *longitude* are degrees; positive values indicate west of the prime meridian, and negative values indicate east of the prime meridian (unless EASTLONG also has been used in the PROC GPROJECT statement).

If you do not use POLELAT= or POLELONG=, or you omit either option, PROC GPROJECT uses values for the position of the center of the unit areas that are defined by the DATA= data set for the missing parameter.

Note: The map that is defined by the input map data set should not contain points more than 85 degrees (1.48353 radians) from the projection pole; all points that exceed this value are deleted from the output map data set. △

Featured in: Example 2 on page 888

PROJECT=ALBERS | LAMBERT | GNOMON | NONE
specifies the projection method to apply to the map data set. Values for PROJECT= are as follows:

ALBERS
specifies Albers' equal-area projection with two standard parallels.

LAMBERT
specifies Lambert's conformal projection with two standard parallels.

GNOMON
specifies the gnomonic projection, which is an azimuthal projection.

NONE
specifies that no projection should be performed. Use this option in conjunction with the LATMIN=, LATMAX=, LONGMIN=, and LONGMAX= options to perform clipping without projection (for example, on map data sets that have already been projected).

By default, PROJECT=ALBERS.

See also: "About Types of Map Projections" on page 876

Featured in: Example 2 on page 888

ID Statement

Identifies the variable or variables that define the hierarchy of the current unit areas in the input map data set.

Requirements: At least one *id-variable* is required.

Featured in: Example 1 on page 885

Syntax

ID *id-variable(s)*;

Required Arguments

id-variable(s)
specifies one or more variables in the input map data set that identify unit areas. *Id-variable* can be either numeric or character.

Each group of observations with a different ID variable value is evaluated as a separate unit area.

Using the GPROJECT Procedure

The GPROJECT procedure uses a default projection method and default projection criteria to project your map data set. If you do not want to use these defaults, you can use PROC GPROJECT statement options to

☐ select the map projection method

☐ specify the map projection criteria

□ create a rectangular subset of the input map data set.

The following sections describe how you can use PROC GPROJECT statement options to select your own projection method and projection criteria.

Selecting Projections

Except when projecting map data sets that cover large areas, all three types of projections (Albers', Lambert's, and gnomonic) produce relatively similar results when you use default projection criteria, so you usually do not need to be concerned about which projection method to use when you produce maps solely for graphics output.

However, the default projection criteria may be unsuitable in some circumstances. In particular, the default specifications fail when the map that is being projected extends on both sides of the equator. On other occasions, you may want to select a projection method to achieve a particular effect.

For the Albers' and Lambert's projections, the two standard parallels must both lie on the same side of the equator. PROC GPROJECT stops with an error message if this condition is not met, regardless of whether you explicitly specify parallel values or let the procedure calculate default values. See the descriptions of PARALEL1= and PARALEL2= on page 882 for more information on how to specify the two standard parallels.

Controlling Projection Criteria

For both the Albers' and Lambert's projections, PROC GPROJECT calculates appropriate standard parallels. You can override either or both of these selections if you explicitly specify values for the PARALEL1= or PARALEL2= option. You can influence the selection of default parallels if you use the PARADIV= option. See "Options" on page 880 for more information on these options.

For the gnomonic projection, PROC GPROJECT determines the longitude and latitude of the approximate center of the input map data set area. You can override either or both of these selections if you explicitly specify values for the POLELAT= or POLELONG= option. See "Options" on page 880 for more information.

The clipping options, discussed in "Clipping Map Data Sets" on page 884, can also influence the calculations of the default standard parallels by changing the minimum and maximum coordinate values.

Clipping Map Data Sets

The GPROJECT procedure can create rectangular subsets of the input map data set. This capability provides a way to extract a portion of a larger map if you do not need all the original unit areas for your graph. The procedure enables you to clip unit area boundaries at specified parallels of latitude or meridians of longitude or both. Unit areas that fall completely outside of the specified clipping limits are excluded from the output map data set. Unit areas bisected by the clipping limits are closed along the clipping parallels and meridians, and all points outside of the clipping limits are excluded.

If the input map data set contains the DENSITY variable, any new vertex points and corners that are created by PROC GPROJECT are assigned a DENSITY value of 0 in the output map data set. This enables you to use a subset of the clipped map without using PROC GREDUCE to assign new DENSITY values. (See Chapter 24, "The GREDUCE Procedure," on page 895 for information on how to reduce the number of points that you need to draw a map.)

You can specify the minimum latitude to be retained in the output map data set with LATMIN= and the maximum latitude with LATMAX= . Minimum and maximum longitude values are specified with LONGMIN= and LONGMAX=, respectively. See "Options" on page 880 for more details on these options.

This is how the PROC GPROJECT interprets the clipping longitude and latitude values:

□ If you specify PROJECT=NONE in the PROC GPROJECT statement, the procedure assumes that the input map data set is already projected and the clipping longitude and latitude values are Cartesian coordinates. In this case, LATMAX= and LATMIN= specify the top and bottom edges, respectively, of the area that you want to extract, and LONGMAX= and LONGMIN= specify right and left edges, respectively.

You must be familiar with the range of values in the X and Y variables in order to select appropriate clipping limits. Use the MEANS or SUMMARY procedure in base SAS to determine the range of values in X and Y. See the *SAS Procedures Guide* for more information.

□ If PROJECT=ALBERS, LAMBERT, or GNOMON, the clipping values are treated as degrees.

Depending on the size and position of the clipped area and the type of projection that is performed, the resulting map may not be exactly rectangular. PROC GPROJECT performs clipping before projection, so the clipped area may be distorted by the projection process.

To produce a clipped area with a rectangular shape, use PROC GPROJECT in two steps:

1 Project the map using the appropriate projection method and projection criteria.

2 Project the map using PROJECT=NONE, and use LATMIN=, LATMAX=, LONGMIN=, and LONGMAX= to clip the map.

See Example 3 on page 890, for an example of clipping an area from an unprojected map data set.

Examples

The following examples illustrate major features of the GPROJECT procedure. Because these examples use map data sets that are supplied with SAS/GRAPH , you may need to replace *SAS-data-library* in the LIBNAME statement with the actual location of the SAS data library that contains the Institute-supplied map data sets on your system. Contact your SAS Software Consultant for the location of the map data sets at your site. If your site automatically assigns the libref MAPS to the SAS data library that contains the Institute-supplied map data sets, delete the LIBNAME statement in these examples.

Example 1: Using Default Projection Specifications

Procedure features:
  ID statement
Other features:
  LIBNAME statement

Sample library member: GR23N01

This example demonstrates the effect of using PROC GPROJECT on an unprojected map data set without specifying any options. Because PROJECT= is not used in the PROC GPROJECT statement, the Albers' equal-area projection method is used by default. PROC GPROJECT supplies defaults for the standard parallels that minimize distortion of the projected map areas.

Figure 23.8 Map before Projection (GR23N01(a))

Figure 23.8 on page 886 illustrates the output produced the REFLIB.US48 map data set, which contains only unprojected values, X and Y. Output 23.1 on page 886 shows the variables in the data set.

Output 23.1 The REFLIB.US48 Data Set

```
                    US48 Data Set

    OBS     STATE     SEGMENT     DENSITY      X          Y

      1       1          1           3      1.48221    0.56286
      2       1          1           3      1.48226    0.56234
      3       1          1           3      1.48304    0.56231
    .
    .
    .
```

The GPROJECT procedure is used with the REFLIB.US48 map data set as input to create the projected map data set, REFLIB.US48PROJ. The values for X and Y in this new data set are projected (cartesian). Output 23.2 on page 887 shows the variables in the data set.

Output 23.2 The REFLIB.US48PROJ Data Set

```
                        US48PROJ Data Set

        OBS      X          Y        DENSITY    STATE    SEGMENT

          1    0.16068   -0.073470      3         1         1
          2    0.16069   -0.073993      3         1         1
          3    0.16004   -0.074097      3         1         1
          .
          .
          .
```

The new projected map data set, REFLIB.US48PROJ, is used to create the projected map, Figure 23.9 on page 887.

Figure 23.9 Map after Projection (GR23N01(b))

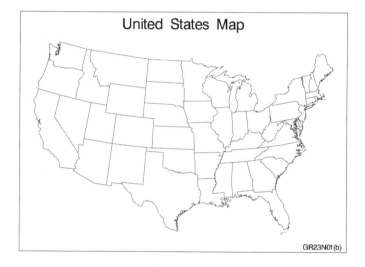

Assign the librefs and set the graphics environment.

```
libname reflib 'SAS-data-library';
libname maps 'SAS-data-library';
goptions reset=global gunit=pct border cback=white
        colors=(black blue green red)
        ftext=swiss htitle=6 htext=3;
```

Create reduced continental U.S. map data set and remove Alaska, Hawaii, and Puerto Rico.

```
data reflib.us48;
   set maps.states;
```

```
      if state ne 2 and state ne 15 and state ne 72;
      if density<4;
   run;
```

Define title and footnote for unprojected map.

```
title 'United States Map';
footnote j=r 'GR23N01(a) ';
```

Define pattern characteristics.

```
pattern value=mempty repeat=50 color=blue;
```

Show unprojected map.

```
proc gmap map=reflib.us48 data=reflib.us48 all;
   id state;
   choro state / nolegend;
run;
```

Project map data set using all default criteria. The ID statement identifies the variable in the input map data set that defines unit areas.

```
proc gproject data=reflib.us48
              out=reflib.us48proj;
   id state;
run;
```

Define footnote for projected map.

```
footnote j=r 'GR23N01(b) ';
```

Show projected map.

```
proc gmap map=reflib.us48proj
          data=reflib.us48proj all;
   id state;
   choro state / nolegend;
run;
quit;
```

Example 2: Emphasizing Map Areas

Procedure features:

PROC GPROJECT options:

> POLELAT=
> POLELONG=
> PROJECT=

Data set: REFLIB.US48 on page 887

Sample library member: GR23N02

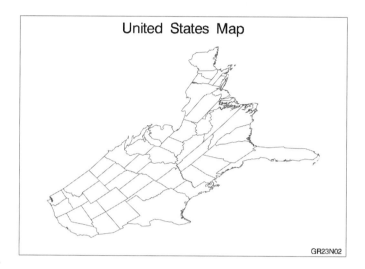

This example uses the gnomonic projection method to create a map in which the east coast of the United States appears disproportionately large compared to the west coast.

Assign the librefs and set the graphics environment.

```
libname reflib 'SAS-data-library';
libname maps 'SAS-data-library';
goptions reset=global gunit=pct border cback=white
        colors=(black blue green red)
        ftext=swiss htitle=6 htext=3;
```

Project map onto a plane centered in the Pacific. PROJECT= specifies the projection method for the map data set. POLELONG= and POLELAT= specify a projection pole for the gnomonic projection. In this example, the pole is positioned in the Pacific Ocean.

```
proc gproject data=reflib.us48
             out=reflib.skew
             project=gnomon
             polelong=160
             polelat=45;
    id state;
run;
```

Define title and footnote for the map.

```
title 'United States Map';
footnote j=r 'GR23N02 ';
```

Define pattern characteristics.

```
pattern value=mempty repeat=49 color=blue;
```

Show the projected map.

```
proc gmap map=reflib.skew data=reflib.skew all;
   id state;
   choro state / nolegend;
run;
quit;
```

Example 3: Clipping an Area from the Map

Procedure features:
    PROC GPROJECT options:
        LONGMAX=
        LONGMIN=
        LATMAX=
        LATMIN=

Sample library member: GR23N03

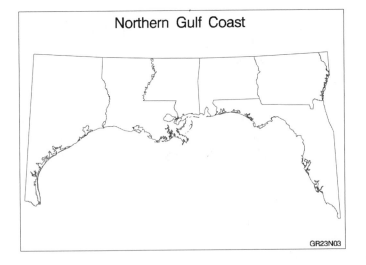

Northern Gulf Coast

GR23N03

This example uses the clipping capabilities of PROC GPROJECT to create a map of the states in the United States that border the Gulf of Mexico. Because the PROJECT= option is not used in the GPROJECT procedure, the Albers' equal-area projection method is used by default.

Assign the librefs and set the graphics environment.

```
libname reflib 'SAS-data-library';
libname maps 'SAS-data-library';
goptions reset=global gunit=pct border cback=white
         colors=(black blue green red)
         ftext=swiss htitle=6 htext=3;
```

Clip and project rectangular subset of the map. LONGMIN= and LONGMAX= specify the minimum and maximum longitudes to be included in the map projection. LATMIN= and LATMAX= specify the minimum and maximum latitudes to be included in the map projection.

```
proc gproject data=maps.states
              out=reflib.gulf
              longmin=81
              longmax=98
              latmin=25
              latmax=33;
   where density<5;
   id state;
run;
```

Define title and footnote for the map.

```
title 'Northern Gulf Coast';
footnote j=r 'GR23N03 ';
```

Define pattern characteristics.

```
pattern value=mempty repeat=7 color=blue;
```

Show the clipped map.

```
proc gmap map=reflib.gulf data=reflib.gulf all;
   id state;
   choro state / nolegend;
run;
quit;
```

Example 4: Projecting an Annotate Data Set

Procedure features:
   PROC GPROJECT options:
      DATA=
      OUT=
   ID statement

Other features:
  CHORO statement

  Annotate data set

Data set: REFLIB.US48 on page 887

Sample library member: GR23N04

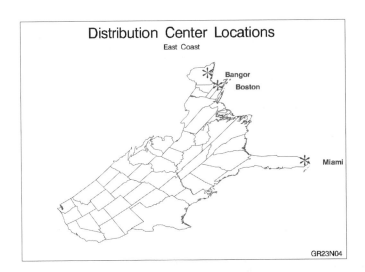

   This example illustrates how to project an Annotate data set for use with a map data set. It labels the locations of Miami, Boston, and Bangor on the map shown in the second example. Because the X and Y variables in the USCITY data set already have been projected to match the US data set, they cannot be used with the map that is produced by the second example. To properly label the projected map, the example uses the same projection method for the city coordinates as the method that is used for the map coordinates. This example illustrates how to use the same projection method for both data sets.

Assign the librefs and set the graphics environment.

```
libname reflib 'SAS-data-library';
libname maps 'SAS-data-library';
goptions reset=global gunit=pct border cback=white
         colors=(black blue green red)
         ftext=swiss htitle=6 htext=3;
```

Create Annotate data set CITIES from the MAPS.USCITY data set. The unprojected LONG and LAT variable values are converted to radians and substituted for the projected X and Y variable values. LONG and LAT are converted by multiplying them by the arccosine of –1 and dividing that amount by 180. The cities are each assigned a value for the NEWST variable, sequentially beginning at 100.

```
data cities(drop=state rename=(newst=state));
   set maps.uscity(keep=lat long city state);
   length function style color $ 8
          position $ 1 text $ 20;
   retain function 'label' xsys ysys '2'
```

```
         hsys '1' when 'b' newst 100;
   if state=12 and city='Miami' or
      state=25 and city='Boston' or
      state=23 and city='Bangor';
   newst+1; color='blue'; size=10; text='T';
      position='5';
      style='marker'; x=long*arcos(-1)/180;
      y=lat*arcos(-1)/180; output;
   newst+1; color='blue'; size=4;
      text='    '||city;
      position='6'; style='swissb'; output;
run;
```

Create data set ALL by combining data set REFLIB.US48 and data set REFLIB.CITIES.

```
data all;
   set reflib.us48 cities;
run;
```

Project the ALL data set. DATA= specifies the data set to be projected. OUT= specifies the name of the new projected data set that is created. The ID statement identifies the variable in the input map data set that defines map areas.

```
proc gproject data=all
              out=allp
              project=gnomon
              polelong=160
              polelat=45;
   id state;
run;
```

Separate the projected data set into the CITIESP Annotate data set and the US48P map data set.

```
data citiesp us48p;
   set allp;
   if state>100 then output citiesp;
   else output us48p;
run;
```

Define title and footnote for the map.

```
title1 'Distribution Center Locations';
title2 'East Coast';
footnote j=r 'GR23N04 ';
```

Define pattern characteristics.

```
pattern value=mempty repeat=49 color=blue;
```

Show the annotated map. The CHORO statement displays the projected map and annotates it using the projected Annotate data set.

```
proc gmap data=us48p map=us48p all;
   id state;
   choro state
         / nolegend
            annotate=citiesp;
run;
quit;
```

References

Pearson, F., II (1977), "Map Projection Equations," Report Number TR-3624, Naval Surface Weapons Center, Dahlgren Laboratory, March, 1977.

Richardus, P. and Adler, R.K. (1972), *Map Projections*, Amsterdam: North-Holland Publishing Company; New York: American Elsevier Publishing Company.

Robinson, A.H. (1978), *Elements of Cartography*, New York: John Wiley & Sons, Inc.

CHAPTER
24

The GREDUCE Procedure

Overview

The GREDUCE procedure processes map data sets so that they can draw simpler maps with fewer boundary points. It creates an output map data set that contains all of the variables in the input map data set plus a new variable named DENSITY. For each observation in the input map data set, the procedure determines the significance of that point for maintaining a semblance of the original shape and gives the observation a corresponding DENSITY value.

You can then use the value of the DENSITY variable to create a subset of the original map data set. The observations in the subset can draw a map that retains the overall appearance of the original map but contains fewer points, requires considerably less storage space, and can be drawn much more quickly.

GREDUCE does not produce any graphics output. Instead, it produces an output map data set that can become either

- □ the input map data set for the GMAP procedure
- □ the input map data set for a DATA step that removes points from the map.

Figure 24.1 on page 896 and Figure 24.2 on page 896 illustrate the effect of reduction on a typical map data set. Figure 24.1 on page 896 uses observations with all DENSITY values as input to the GMAP procedure.

Figure 24.1 CANADA2 Map before Reduction (GR24N01(a))

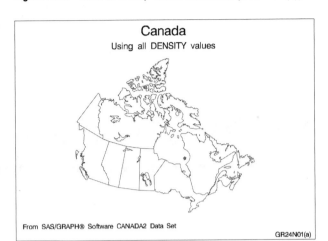

Figure 24.2 on page 896 uses only those observations with a DENSITY value of 0 or 2 as input to the GMAP procedure.

Figure 24.2 CANADA2 Map after Reduction (GR24N01(b))

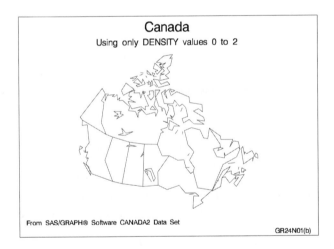

The program for these maps is in Example 1 on page 902.

The reduced map shown in Figure 24.2 on page 896 retains the overall shape of the original but requires only 463 observations compared to the 4302 observations that are needed to produce the map in Figure 24.1 on page 896.

Note: Many of the map data sets that are supplied by SAS Institute already have been processed by GREDUCE. If the map data set contains a DENSITY variable, you do not need to process the data set using GREDUCE. △

See also Chapter 25, "The GREMOVE Procedure," on page 905 for more information on how to

☐ combine groups of unit areas into larger unit areas to create regional maps

☐ remove some of the boundaries in a map and create a subset of a map that combines the original areas.

Concepts

About the Input Map Data Set

The input map data set must be a map data set and contain these variables:

☐ a numeric variable named X that contains the horizontal coordinates of the map boundary points.

☐ a numeric variable named Y that contains the vertical coordinates of the map boundary points.

☐ one or more *identification variables* that uniquely identify the unit areas in the map. These variables are listed in the ID statement.

It also can contain

☐ one or more variables that identify groups of unit areas (for BY-group processing)

☐ the variable SEGMENT, which distinguishes nonconterminous segments of the unit areas.

Any other variables in the input map data set do not affect the GREDUCE procedure.

About Unmatched Area Boundaries

If you are using map data sets in which area boundaries do not match precisely (for example, if the boundaries were digitized with a different set of points), PROC GREDUCE will not be able to identify common boundaries properly, and this results in abnormalities in your maps. These abnormalities include mismatched borders, missing vertex points, stray lines, gaps, and distorted polygons.

If the points in the area boundaries match up except for precision differences, round each X and Y value in your map data set accordingly, using the DATA step function ROUND before using PROC GREDUCE. (See *SAS Language Reference: Dictionary* for information on the ROUND function.)

For example, if the map data set APPROX has horizontal and vertical coordinate values for interior boundaries of unit areas that are exactly equal only to three decimal places, then this DATA step creates a new map data set, EXACT, that will be better suited for use with PROC GREDUCE:

```
data exact;
    set approx;
    if x ne . then x=round(x,.001);
    if y ne . then y=round(y,.001);
  run;
```

See "About Map Data Sets" on page 735 for additional information on map data sets.

Procedure Syntax

Requirements: Exactly one ID statement is required.

Reminder: The procedure can include the BY statement.

PROC GREDUCE *<option(s)>*;

ID *id-variable(s)*;

PROC GREDUCE Statement

Identifies the input and output map data sets. Optionally specifies the reduction criteria.

Requirements: An input map data set is required.

Syntax

PROC GREDUCE *<option(s)>*;

option(s) can be one or more options from any or all of the following categories:

☐ data set options:

DATA=*input-map-data-set*

OUT=*output-map-data-set*

☐ level options:

E1=*min-distance*

E2=*min-distance*

E3=*min-distance*

E4=*min-distance*

E5=*min-distance*

N1=*max-points*

N2=*max-points*

N3=*max-points*

N4=*max-points*

N5=*max-points*

Options

DATA=*input-map-data-set*
    identifies the map data set that you want to process. By default, the procedure uses the most recently created SAS data set.

    See also: "About the Input Map Data Set" on page 897 and "SAS Data Sets" on page 25

E1=*min-distance*
E2=*min-distance*
E3=*min-distance*
E4=*min-distance*
E5=*min-distance*
    specify the minimum distance that a point must lie from a straight line segment to be included at density level 1, 2, 3, 4, or 5, respectively. That is, in a reduced curve of

three points, the middle point is at least a distance that is *min-distance* from a straight line between the two outside points.

Express *min-distance* values in the units for the coordinate system of the input map data set. For example, if the input map data set contains coordinates that are expressed in radians, express the *min-distance* values in radians.

Specify the E*n*= values in decreasing order. For example, the E2= value should be less than the E1= value and so on.

N1=*max-points*
N2=*max-points*
N3=*max-points*
N4=*max-points*
N5=*max-points*

specify that for density level 1, 2, 3, 4, or 5, the boundary of a unit area should contain no more than *max-points* points.

Specify the N*n*= values in increasing order. For example, the N2= value should be greater than or equal to the N1= value and so on.

By default, if you omit N*n*= and E*n* = , the GREDUCE procedure calculates values for the five N*n* = parameters using this formula:

$$ \mathrm{N}n = n^2 \times \mathrm{N_{max}}/36 $$

Here $\mathrm{N_{max}}$ is the maximum number of points in any unit area in the input map data set. However, the restriction that the number of points for any level cannot be less than the number of points in level 0 still applies.

OUT=*output-data-set*

names the new map data set, which contains all of the observations and variables in the original map data set plus the new DENSITY variable. If the input map data set contains a variable named DENSITY, the GREDUCE procedure replaces the values of the variable in the output map data set. The original values of the DENSITY variable from the input map data set are not included in the output map data set.

By default, the GREDUCE procedure names the new data set that uses the DATA*n* naming convention. That is, the procedure uses the name WORK.DATA*n*, where *n* is the next unused number in sequence. Thus, the first automatically named data set is DATA1, the second is DATA2, and so on.

ID Statement

Identifies the variable or variables that define the hierarchy of the current unit areas in the input map data set.

Requirements: At least one *id-variable* is required.
Featured in: Example 1 on page 902

Syntax

ID *id-variable(s)*;

Required Arguments

id-variable(s)

specifies one or more variables in the input map data set that identify unit areas. *Id-variable(s)* can be either numeric or character.

Each group of observations with a different ID variable value is evaluated as a separate unit area.

Using the GREDUCE Procedure

Specifying Density Levels

GREDUCE uses default criteria for determining the appropriate DENSITY variable value for each observation in the input map data set. If you do not want to use the default criteria, use PROC GREDUCE options to select

☐ the maximum number of observations for each DENSITY level

☐ the minimum distance that an intermediate point must lie from a line between two end points to be included in the level.

If you do not explicitly specify criteria, the procedure computes and uses default values.

GREDUCE creates seven density levels, numbered 0 through 6. Specify criteria for density levels 1 through 5. You cannot define criteria for level 0, which is reserved for map vertex points, such as common corners of unit areas. You also cannot define criteria for level 6, which is assigned to those points that do not meet the criteria for any lower level.

Specify the maximum number of observations per density level using Nn= in the PROC GREDUCE statement, and specify the minimum point distance using En= . You must have knowledge of the X and Y variable values in the particular input map data set to determine appropriate values for En=. See En= and Nn= on page 898 for details.

Figure 24.3 on page 900 illustrates how to use the minimum distance parameter to determine which points belong in a particular density level. At density level n, only point C lies at a distance greater than the En= value (70) from a line between points A and B. Thus, after reduction only point C remains between points A and B at density level n, and the resulting reduced boundary is shown in Figure 24.4 on page 901. See Douglas and Peucker (1973) for details of the algorithm used.

Figure 24.3   Points in Data Set before Reduction

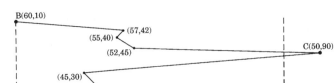

Figure 24.4 Points in Data Set at Density n after Reduction

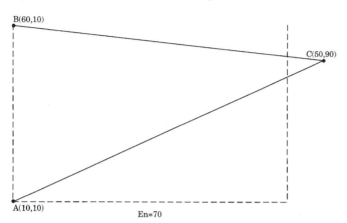

GREDUCE uses the usual Euclidean distance formula to determine the distance between points. For example, the distance d between the points (x_0, y_0) and (x_1, y_1) is GREDUCE uses the usual Euclidean distance formula to determine the distance between points. For example, the distance d between the points (x_0, y_0) and (x_1, y_1) is

$$d = \sqrt{(x_1 - x_0)^2 + (y_1 - y_0)^2}$$

If this distance function is not suitable for the coordinate system in your input map data set, transform the X and Y values to an appropriate coordinate system before using GREDUCE. An example of inappropriate coordinates is latitude and longitude values around one of the poles. In this case, the data values should be projected before they are reduced. See Chapter 23, "The GPROJECT Procedure," on page 873 for more information on map projection.

If you specify both N*n*= and E*n*= values for a density level, GREDUCE attempts to satisfy both criteria. However, the number of points for any level is never reduced below the number of points in density level 0. If you specify a combination of N*n*= or E*n*= values such that the resulting DENSITY values are not in order of increasing density, a note is printed in the SAS log, and the DENSITY values are calculated in increasing order of density.

Subsetting a Map Data Set

A map data set that is processed by GREDUCE does not automatically result in a map that uses fewer points. By default, the GMAP procedure produces a map that uses all of the points in the map data set, even if the data set has been processed by the GREDUCE procedure. To decrease the number of points that produce the map, you must create a subset of the original data set using a DATA step or the WHERE= data set option. For example, to create a subset of a map that uses only the DENSITY values 0, 1, and 2, use this DATA step:

```
data smallmap;
   set map;
   if density <= 2;
```

```
run;
```

Alternatively, you can use WHERE= in the PROC GMAP statement:

```
proc gmap map=map(where=(density<=2))
          data=response;
```

Note: GREDUCE does not reduce the size of the output map data set compared to the input map data set. By default, the output map data set from PROC GREDUCE will be larger than the input map data set because it contains all of the variables and observations from the original data set, with the addition of the DENSITY variable if it was not present in the original data set. If the input map data set already had a DENSITY variable, the output map data set will be the same size as the input map data set. △

Examples

The following example illustrates major features of the GREDUCE procedure. Because the example uses one of the map data sets that are supplied with SAS/GRAPH , you may need to replace *SAS-data-library* in the LIBNAME statement with the actual location of the SAS data library that contains the Institute-supplied map data sets on your system. Contact your SAS Software Consultant for the location of the map data sets at your site. If your site automatically assigns the libref MAPS to the SAS data library that contains the Institute-supplied map data sets, delete the LIBNAME statement in this example.

Example 1: Reducing the Map of Canada

Procedure features:
   ID statement
Other features:
   PROC GMAP option:
      WHERE=
Sample library member: GR24N01

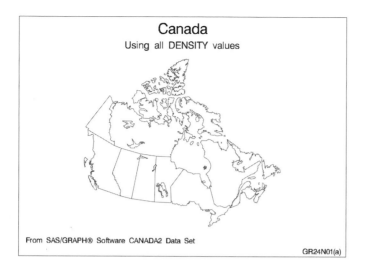

In this example, the GREDUCE procedure creates the DENSITY variable for the CANADA2 map data set that is provided with SAS/GRAPH . First, the map is displayed at its original density by using the GMAP procedure. Second, the map is displayed by using density values of 0 to 2.

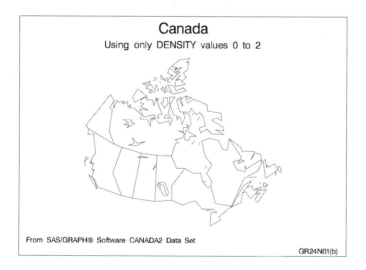

Assign the librefs and set the graphics environment.

```
libname reflib 'SAS-data-library';
libname maps 'SAS-data-library';
goptions reset=global gunit=pct border cback=white
         colors=(black blue green red)
         ftext=swiss htitle=6 htext=3;
```

Define titles and footnotes for the first map.

```
title1 'Canada';
title2 h=4 'Using all DENSITY values';
```

```
footnote1 j=l '  From  SAS/GRAPH
' '02'x
          ' Software CANADA2 Data Set';
footnote2 j=r 'GR24N01(a) ';
```

Define pattern characteristics.

```
pattern value=mempty repeat=12 color=blue;
```

Show the unreduced map. The ID statement specifies the variable in the map data set that defines unit areas.

```
proc gmap map=maps.canada2 data=maps.canada2 all;
  id province;
  choro province / nolegend;
run;
```

The GREDUCE procedure creates a new map data set, REFLIB.CAN2, containing a DENSITY variable. The ID statement specifies the variable in the map data set that defines unit areas.

```
proc greduce data=maps.canada2 out=reflib.can2;
   id province;
run;
```

Define title and footnote for the second map.

```
title2 h=4 'Using only DENSITY values 0 to 2';
footnote2 j=r 'GR24N01(b) ';
```

Show reduced map with density levels 0-2. WHERE= selects map coordinates with the appropriate DENSITY values.

```
proc gmap map=reflib.can2(where=(density<3))
          data=reflib.can2 all;
  id province;
  choro province / nolegend;
run;
quit;
```

References

Douglas, D.H. and Peucker, T.K. (1973), "Algorithms for the Reduction of the Number of Points Required to Represent a Digitized Line or Its Caricature," *The Canadian Cartographer*, 10, 112–122.

CHAPTER

25

The GREMOVE Procedure

Overview

The GREMOVE procedure processes a map data set that is used as input. It does not produce any graphics output. Instead, it produces an output data set that typically becomes the input map data set for the GMAP procedure (see Chapter 19, "The GMAP Procedure," on page 731).

The GREMOVE procedure combines unit areas defined in a map data set into larger unit areas by removing shared borders between the original unit areas. For example, Figure 25.1 on page 906 and Figure 25.2 on page 906 show combined unit areas in a typical map data set by removing state boundaries to create regional census divisions.

Figure 25.1   Map before Removing Borders (GR25N01(a))

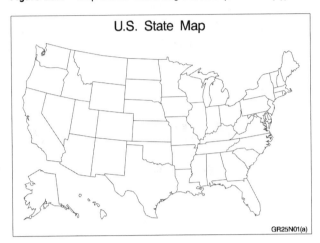

Figure 25.2   Map after Removing Borders (GR25N01(b))

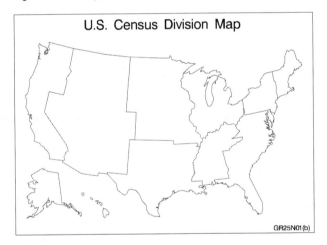

The program for these maps is shown in Example 1 on page 910.

Concepts

The GREMOVE procedure processes the input map data set to remove internal boundaries and creates a new map data set. The PROC GREMOVE statement identifies the input and output map data sets. The ID statement identifies the variable or variables in the input map data set that define the current unit areas. The BY statement identifies the variable or variables in the input map data set that define the new unit areas.

About the Input Map Data Set

The input map data set must be in map data set format (see "About Map Data Sets" on page 735) and it must contain these variables:

□ a numeric variable named X that contains the horizontal coordinates of the map boundary points.

□ a numeric variable named Y that contains the vertical coordinates of the map boundary points.

□ one or more variables that uniquely identify the current unit areas in the map. These variables are listed in the ID statement. Each group of observations with a different ID variable value is evaluated as a separate unit area.

□ one or more variables that identify the new unit areas to be created in the output map data set. These variables are listed in the BY statement.

It may also contain the variable SEGMENT, which is used to distinguish non-conterminous segments of the same unit areas. Other variables may exist in the input map data set, but they do not affect the GREMOVE procedure and they will not be carried into the output map data set.

About the Output Map Data Set

The output map data set contains the newly defined unit areas. These new unit areas are created by removing all interior line segments from the original unit areas. All variables in the input map data set except X, Y, SEGMENT, and the variables listed in the BY statement are omitted from the output map data set.

The output map data set may contain missing X, Y coordinates to construct any polygons that have enclosed boundaries (like lakes or combined regions that have one or more hollow interior regions).

The SEGMENT variable in the output map data set is ordered according to the size of the bounding box around the polygon that it describes. A SEGMENT value of 1 describes the polygon whose bounding box is the largest in the unit area and so on. This information is useful for removing small polygons that clutter up maps.

All current unit areas with common BY-variable value(s) are combined into a single unit area in the output map data set. The new unit area contains

□ all boundaries that are not shared, such as islands and lakes

□ all boundaries that are shared by two different BY groups.

About Unmatched Area Boundaries

If you are using map data sets in which area boundaries do not match precisely (for example, if the boundaries were digitized with a different set of points), PROC GREMOVE will not be able to identify common boundaries properly, resulting in abnormalities in your output data set.

If the points in the area boundaries match up except for precision differences, before using PROC GREMOVE round each X and Y value in your map data set accordingly, using the DATA step function ROUND. See *SAS Language Reference: Dictionary* for information on the ROUND function.

For example, if you have a map data set named APPROX in which the horizontal and vertical coordinate values for interior boundaries of unit areas are exactly equal only to three decimal places, this DATA step creates a new map data set, EXACT, that is better suited for use with the GREMOVE procedure:

```
data exact;
   set approx;
   if x ne . then x=round(x,.001);
   if y ne . then y=round(y,.001);
run;
```

Procedure Syntax

Requirements: The BY and ID statements are required.

PROC GREMOVE <DATA=*input-map-data-set*>
  <OUT=*output-map-data-set*>;
BY <DESCENDING>*variable-l*
    <...<DESCENDING>*variable-n*>
    <NOTSORTED>;
ID *variable(s)*;

PROC GREMOVE Statement

Identifies the input and output map data sets.

Requirements: An input map data set is required.

Syntax

PROC GREMOVE <DATA=*input-map-data-set*>
  <OUT=*output-map-data-set*>;

Options

DATA=*input-map-data-set*
  specifies the map data set that is to be processed. By default, the procedure uses the most recently created SAS data set. The GREMOVE procedure expects the observations in the input map data set to be sorted in ascending order of the BY-variable values.
  See also: "About the Input Map Data Set" on page 906 and "SAS Data Sets" on page 25
  Featured in: Example 2 on page 915

OUT=*output-data-set*
  names the new map data set, which contains the coordinates of the new unit areas created by the GREMOVE procedure. By default, the GREMOVE procedure names the new data set using the DATA*n* naming convention. That is, the procedure uses the name WORK.DATA*n*, where *n* is the next unused number in sequence. Thus, the first automatically named data set is DATA1, the second is DATA2, and so on.
  See also: "About the Output Map Data Set" on page 907
  Featured in: Example 2 on page 915

BY Statement

Lists the variable or variables that identify the new unit areas.

Requirements: At least one variable is required.

See also: "BY Statement" on page 177

Featured in: Example 1 on page 910

Syntax

BY <DESCENDING>*variable-l*
    <...<DESCENDING>*variable-n*>
    <NOTSORTED>;

Required Arguments

variable(s)
    identifies one or more variables in the input map data set that define the new unit areas. *Variable(s)* can be either numeric or character.
    The BY variables in the input map data set become the ID variables for the output map data set.

Options

DESCENDING
    indicates that the input map data set is sorted in descending order. By default, the GREMOVE procedure expects all BY-variable values to appear in ascending order.
    This option affects only the variable that immediately follows the option.

NOTSORTED
    indicates that observations with the same BY-variable values are to be grouped as they are encountered without regard for whether the values are in alphabetical or numerical order. NOTSORTED can appear anywhere in the BY statement. It affects all of the variables that are specified in the statement. NOTSORTED overrides DESCENDING if both appear in the same BY statement.

Ordering Observations

To sort the input map data set, use the SORT procedure in base SAS, for example

```
/* arrange the observations in desired order */
proc sort data=mapdata out=mapsort;
   by state;
run;
   /* remove the county boundaries              */
proc gremove data=mapsort out=newmap;
   by state;
   id county;
run;
```

Notice that the GREMOVE procedure uses the same BY statement as the SORT procedure.

See the *SAS Procedures Guide* for further information on the SORT procedure.

Note: If an observation is encountered for which the BY-variable value is out of the proper order, the GREMOVE procedure stops and issues an error message. △

ID Statement

Identifies the variable or variables that define the hierarchy of the current unit areas in the input map data set.

Requirements: At least one *id-variable* is required.

Featured in: Example 1 on page 910

Syntax

ID *id-variable(s)*;

Required Arguments

id-variable(s)
specifies one or more variables in the input map data set that identify the unit areas to be combined. These variables are not included in the output map data set. *Id-variable(s)* can be either numeric or character.

See also: "About the Input Map Data Set" on page 906

Examples

The following examples illustrate major features of the GREMOVE procedure.

Example 1: Removing State Boundaries from U.S. Map

Procedure features:
   BY statement
   ID statement
Other features:
   SORT procedure
   MERGE procedure
   LIBNAME statement
Sample library member: GR25N01

This example processes the MAPS.US map data set, supplied with SAS/GRAPH, to produce a new map data set containing boundaries for the U.S. Bureau of the Census divisions. Because the MAPS.US map data set does not contain a variable to identify any unit area other than states, this example creates a map data set that contains the census divisions and that can be processed with the GREMOVE procedure.

The STATE variable in the MAPS.US data set, containing numeric FIPS codes for each state, is used as the BY-variable to merge the REFLIB.CBSTATES and MAPS.US data sets. Output 25.1 on page 911 shows the variables that are present in the data set before using the GREMOVE procedure:

Output 25.1 The MAPS.US Data Set

OBS	STATE	MAPS.US Data Set SEGMENT	X	Y
1	1	1	0.16175	-0.10044
2	1	1	0.12305	-0.10415
3	1	1	0.12296	-0.10678
.				
.				
.				
1524	56	1	-0.18757	0.15035
1525	56	1	-0.10158	0.13997
1526	56	1	-0.10398	0.11343

And Figure 25.3 on page 912 shows the map before processing:

Figure 25.3 Map before Removing Borders (GR25N01(a))

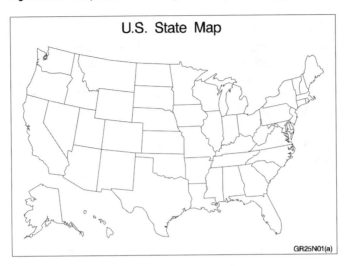

Output 25.2 on page 912 shows the variables that are present in the data set after you use the GREMOVE procedure. Notice that the new map data set contains a new variable called DIVISION:

Output 25.2 The REMSTATE Data Set

```
                    REMSTATE Data Set
        OBS       X          Y        SEGMENT    DIVISION

         1      0.29825    0.17418       1          1
         2      0.29814    0.17820       1          1
         3      0.30206    0.18045       1          1
         .
         .
         .
      1082     -0.18715   -0.16010       8          9
      1083     -0.18747   -0.15971       8          9
      1084     -0.18747   -0.15951       8          9
```

Figure 25.4 on page 913 shows the new map after PROC GREMOVE has removed interior state boundaries.

Figure 25.4 Map after Removing Borders (GR25N01(a))

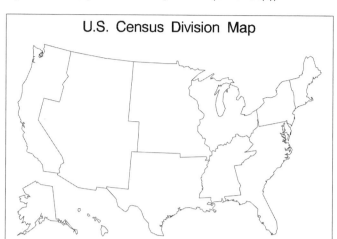

Assign the librefs and set the graphics environment. If the libref MAPS is already assigned, omit the LIBNAME statement.

```
libname reflib 'SAS-data-library';
libname maps 'SAS-maps-library';
goptions reset=global gunit=pct border cback=white
         colors=(black blue green red)
         ftext=swiss htitle=6 htext=3;
```

Create data set REFLIB.CBSTATES. This data set includes a variable, DIVISION, that contains the number of the U.S. Bureau of the Census division for the state. This data step converts letter codes to numeric FIPS codes that match those in the STATE variable of MAPS.US.

```
data reflib.cbstates;
   length state 8 stcode $ 2 division 4;
   input stcode division;
   state=stfips(stcode);
   drop stcode;
   datalines;
CT 1
MA 1
...more data lines...
OR 9
WA 9
;
```

Sort data set in FIPS-code order. Create a sorted data set, CBSORT. It can be properly match-merged with the MAPS.US map data set, which is already sorted in FIPS-code order.

```
proc sort data=reflib.cbstates out=cbsort;
   by state;
```

```
   run;
```

Add DIVISION variable to map data set by merging the CBSORT data set with MAPS.US. Create a new map data set, USCB, that contains all of the state boundary coordinates from the MAPS.US data set plus the added variable DIVISION.

```
data uscb;
   merge cbsort maps.us;
   by state;
run;
```

Sort data set in DIVISION order. Sort USCB by the DIVISION variable to create the DIVSTATE data set.

```
proc sort data=uscb out=divstate;
   by division;
run;
```

Remove interior boundaries within divisions. BY specifies the variable, DIVISION, in the input map data set that identifies the new unit areas. ID specifies the variable, STATE, in the input map data set that identifies the current unit areas.

```
proc gremove data=divstate out=remstate;
   by division;
   id state;
run;
```

Define title and footnote for map.

```
title 'U.S. State Map';
footnote j=r 'GR25N01(a) ';
```

Define pattern characteristics.

```
pattern value=mempty repeat=48 color=blue;
```

Show the original map.

```
proc gmap map=maps.us data=maps.us all;
   id state;
   choro state / nolegend;
run;
```

Define new title and footnote for map.

```
title 'U.S. Census Division Map';
footnote j=r 'GR25N01(b) ';
```

Show the regional map. ID specifies the variable, DIVISION, that identifies the unit areas in the processed data set. CHORO specifies DIVISION as the response variable.

```
proc gmap map=remstate data=remstate all;
   id division;
   choro division / nolegend;
run;
quit;
```

Example 2: Creating an Outline Map of Africa

Procedure features:
   PROC GREMOVE options:
      DATA=
      OUT=

Other features:
   GMAP procedure

Sample library member: GR25N02

This example processes the MAPS.AFRICA map data set, supplied with SAS/ GRAPH, to produce a new map data set that contains no internal boundaries. This is done by adding a new variable, REGION, to the map data set and setting it equal to 1. Unit areas from the input map data set that have the same BY-variable value are combined into one unit area in the output map data set. Output 25.3 on page 915 shows the variables present in the original map data set:

Output 25.3 The MAPS.AFRICA Data Set

		MAPS.AFRICA Data Set		
OBS	ID	SEGMENT	X	Y
1	125	1	0.57679	1.43730
2	125	1	0.57668	1.43467
3	125	1	0.58515	1.42363
.				
.				
.				
3462	990	1	1.04249	0.50398
3463	990	1	1.04184	0.50713
3464	990	1	1.04286	0.50841

Figure 25.5 on page 916 shows the map before processing:

Figure 25.5   Map before Removing Borders (GR25N02(a))

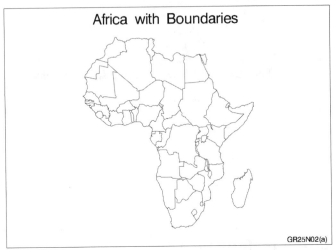

The new REFLIB.AFRICA map data set is created with a new variable, REGION. Output 25.4 on page 916 shows the variables that are present in the new map data set created by the GREMOVE procedure:

Output 25.4   The REFLIB.AFRICA Data Set

```
                     REFLIB.AFRICA Data Set
         OBS        X          Y        SEGMENT      REGION

           1     0.24826    1.02167        1            1
           2     0.25707    1.02714        1            1
           3     0.26553    1.03752        1            1
           .
           .
           .
         982     1.19071    1.30043        3            1
         983     1.18675    1.30842        3            1
         984     1.18518    1.32822        3            1
```

Figure 25.6 on page 917 shows the new map after PROC GREMOVE has removed all of the interior boundaries:

Figure 25.6 Map after Removing Borders (GR25N02(b))

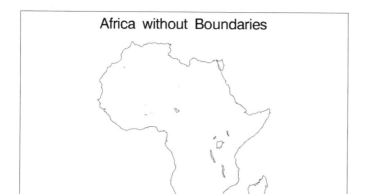

Assign the librefs and set the graphics environment.

```
libname reflib 'SAS-data-library';
libname maps 'SAS-maps-library';
goptions reset=global gunit=pct border cback=white
         colors=(black blue green red)
         ftext=swiss htitle=6 htext=3;
```

Create the NEWAF data set. This new map data set contains all the variables in the SAS/ GRAPH supplied MAPS.AFRICA map data set plus the added variable REGION.

```
data newaf;
   set maps.africa;
   region=1;
run;
```

Remove the unit areas from the AFRICA data set. DATA= specifies the input map data set and OUT= specifies the output map data set. The input map data set has a variable called REGION that is used as the BY-variable to identify the new unit areas. The ID statement specifies the current unit areas from the input map data set.

```
proc gremove data=newaf out=reflib.africa;
   by region;
   id id;
run;
```

Define the title and footnote.

```
title 'Africa with Boundaries';
footnote j=r 'GR25N02(a) ';
```

Define pattern characteristics.

```
pattern value=mempty r=50 color=blue;
```

Display the original map.

```
proc gmap map=maps.africa data=maps.africa all;
   id id;
   choro id / nolegend;
run;
```

Define a new title and footnote for the map.

```
title 'Africa without Boundaries';
footnote j=r 'GR25N02(b) ';
```

Display the map with no boundaries. ID specifies the variable, REGION, that identifies the unit areas in the processed data set.

```
proc gmap data=reflib.africa map=reflib.africa;
   id region;
   choro region / nolegend;
run;
quit;
```

CHAPTER

26

The GREPLAY Procedure

Overview

The GREPLAY procedure displays and manages graphics output that is stored in SAS catalogs. The GREPLAY procedure also creates templates and color maps that you can use when you replay your graphics output. The GREPLAY procedure operates in both windowing and line-mode environments. With the GREPLAY procedure, you can

□ select one or more catalog entries from the same catalog for replay and route them to your display or other devices, such as plotters and printers.

□ use, create, or modify templates. You can use templates to describe positioning on a single display for the graphics output that is stored in one or more catalog entries.

□ use, create, or modify color maps. Color maps enable you to change the colors in graphics output by mapping existing colors to new colors.

□ manage entries in SAS catalogs by

□ creating logical groupings of catalog entries that contain graphics output

□ renaming, deleting, or copying catalog entries that contain graphics output, templates, and color maps

□ rearranging catalog entries that contain graphics output.

□ create new graphics output by replaying one or more catalog entries into panels within a template.

Figure 26.1 on page 921 shows four catalog entries that were replayed into a template and displayed as a single graph.

Figure 26.1 Graphics Output in a Template

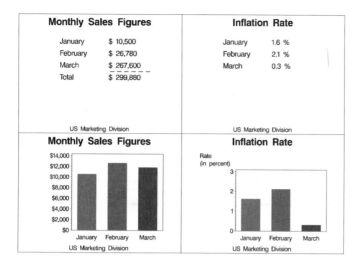

For an example of replaying graphics in a template, see Example 2 on page 954.

Concepts

About Catalog Entries

The GREPLAY procedure uses three kinds of catalog entries:

graphics output
> catalog entries of type GRSEG. The catalog in which these entries are stored is referred to as the input-catalog and output-catalog. The *input-catalog* is the catalog that contains the graphics output, stored in catalog entries, that you want to replay. You can change the input catalog during a catalog management session. The *output-catalog* is the catalog in which graphics output that is produced by the template facility is stored. The output catalog is also the destination of copied catalog entries.

templates
> catalog entries of type TEMPLATE. This catalog is referred to as the template-catalog. The *template-catalog* is the catalog that stores templates that are created by the GREPLAY procedure. The template catalog also may contain previously created templates that you want to modify or templates to use for replaying your graphics output. SASHELP.TEMPLT is the Institute-supplied template catalog.

color maps
> catalog entries of type CMAP. This catalog is referred to as color-map-catalog. The *color-map-catalog* is the catalog that stores color maps that are created by the GREPLAY procedure. The color map catalog also may contain previously created color maps that you want to modify or color maps to use when you replay your graphics output. Note that image entries may exist in this catalog but are not recognized by the GREPLAY procedure.

Note: Image entries may exist in the catalog but are not recognized by PROC GREPLAY. △

You can store all of the previous entry types in a single SAS catalog, or you can store them in separate catalogs and use a different catalog for each type of entry. A single SAS catalog may contain graphics output, color maps, and templates.

Because the GREPLAY procedure operates on catalog entries, you must assign at least one catalog before you can perform any tasks. The GREPLAY procedure has several ways to assign the catalogs, as shown in Table 26.1 on page 922.

Table 26.1   Assigning Catalogs

Catalog	Ways to Assign
input	IGOUT= option in the PROC GREPLAY statement
	IGOUT statement
	IGOUT field in the PROC GREPLAY window
output	GOUT= option in the PROC GREPLAY statement
	GOUT statement
	GOUT field in the PROC GREPLAY window
template	TC= option in the PROC GREPLAY statement
	TC statement
	TC field in the PROC GREPLAY window
color map	CC= option in the PROC GREPLAY statement
	CC statement
	CC field in the PROC GREPLAY window

In addition, you can assign a current template, which you can use when you replay graphics output, and a current color map, which you can use to remap colors when you replay graphics output. To assign the current template, use one of the following:

☐ the TEMPLATE= option in the PROC GREPLAY statement

☐ the TEMPLATE statement

☐ the Template field in the PROC GREPLAY window.

To assign the current color map, use one of the following:

☐ the CMAP= option in the PROC GREPLAY statement

☐ the CMAP statement

☐ the Cmap field in the PROC GREPLAY window.

Duplicate Entry Names

If you try to create a catalog entry with the same name as an existing entry, the GREPLAY procedure uses the following naming conventions to prevent duplication of the name.

☐ For names that are fewer than eight characters, the procedure adds a number to the end of the name. For example, if you copy an entry that is named PLOT to a catalog that already contains an entry with that name, the procedure assigns the name PLOT1 to the new copy.

☐ For names that are eight characters long, the procedure drops the last character from the name before it adds the suffix. For example, if you copy an entry

TITLEONE to a catalog that already contains an entry with that name, the procedure assigns the name TITLEON1 to the copied entry.

☐ Template entries that contain individual entries will reserve the individual entry names as well as the template entry name.

The GREPLAY procedure uses the same technique for the names of entries that contain graphics output that is produced by the template facility.

Ways to Use the GREPLAY Procedure

You can use the GREPLAY procedure to replay or manage catalog entries in two different ways:

☐ by browsing or editing the fields in the GREPLAY procedure windows (see Figure 26.2 on page 946)

☐ by submitting code-based GREPLAY procedure statements (see "Code-based Statements" on page 923).

If you are running SAS software in a nonwindowing environment (such as line mode or batch), you can only submit code-based GREPLAY statements. However, if you are running SAS software in a windowing environment (the SAS Display Manager System, for example), you can use either the GREPLAY windows or the GREPLAY statements.

If your device supports a windowing environment, the GREPLAY procedure automatically opens the GREPLAY procedure windows. Otherwise, the GREPLAY procedure expects you to submit GREPLAY procedure statements.

Windowing Environment

To invoke the GREPLAY windows, submit the PROC GREPLAY statement without the NOFS option, as follows:

```
proc greplay;
run;
```

SAS/GRAPH then opens the PROC GREPLAY window. For more information, see "Using the GREPLAY Procedure" on page 945.

If you are in a windowing environment, you can switch between the windows and code-based statements while you run the procedure. See the "FS Statement" on page 934 and the NOFS window command in the SAS Help facility.

Code-based Statements

If you do not use the GREPLAY windows, you can use code-based statements to replay or manage the catalog entries. The GREPLAY procedure automatically uses code-based statements if you do not have a windowing device or if you are running the GREPLAY procedure in a batch environment. To use the GREPLAY procedure with code-based statements on a windowing device, submit the PROC GREPLAY statement with the NOFS option as follows:

```
proc greplay nofs;
```

Once you submit the PROC GREPLAY statement, you can enter and submit statements and run them without re-entering the PROC GREPLAY statement.

You can exit the GREPLAY procedure with code-based statements in two ways:

☐ submit the END, QUIT, or STOP statement

☐ submit another PROC statement or DATA step.

Procedure Syntax

Requirements: Use statements other than the PROC GREPLAY statement only in a nonwindowing or batch environment, or with the NOFS option. In these environments at least one additional statement is required.

Note: You must have write access to a catalog in order to modify, add, or delete device entries. Only GRSEG entry types may be replayed with the GREPLAY procedure.

Supports: RUN-group processing Output Delivery System (ODS)

PROC GREPLAY <BYLINE>
    <CC=*color-map-catalog*>
    <CMAP=*color-map-entry*>
    <FS>
    <GOUT=<*libref.*>*output-catalog*>
    <IGOUT=<*libref.*>*input-catalog*>
    <IMAGEMAP=*output-data-set*>
    <NOBYLINE>
    <NOFS>
    <PRESENTATION>
    <TC=*template-catalog*>
    <TEMPLATE=*template-entry*>;

? *required –argument*;

BYLINE;

CC *color-map-catalog*;

CCOPY <*color-map-catalog.*>*color-map-entry*<.CMAP>;

CDEF *color-map-entry*
    <*color-definition(s)*>
    <DES='*entry-description*'>;

CDELETE *color-map-entry(s)* | _ALL_;

CMAP *color-map-entry*;

COPY *entry-id(s)* | _ALL_;

DELETE *entry-id(s)* | _ALL_;

DEVICE *device-name*;

FS;

GOUT <*libref.*>*output-catalog*;

GROUP *entry-id(s)*;

IGOUT <*libref.*>*input-catalog* ;

LIST *required-argument*;

MODIFY *modify-pair(s)*;

MOVE *entry-id-1* AFTER | BEFORE *entry-id-2*;

NOBYLINE;

PREVIEW *template-entry(s)* | _ALL_ ;

QUIT | **END** | **STOP**;

REPLAY *entry-id(s)* | _FIRST_ | _LAST_ | _ALL_ ;

TC *template-catalog*;

TCOPY <*template-catalog.*>*template-entry*<.TEMPLATE>;

TDEF *template-entry*

> *<panel definition(s)>*
> *<DES='entry-description'>*;
> **TDELETE** *template-entry(s)* | _ALL_ ;
> **TEMPLATE** *template-entry*;
> **TREPLAY** *select-pair(s)*;

PROC GREPLAY Statement

Determines whether the procedure starts in a windowing or nonwindowing environment, and whether the session is used for catalog management or output presentation.

Syntax

PROC GREPLAY <BYLINE>
    <CC=*color-map-catalog*>
    <CMAP=*color-map-entry*>
    <FS>
    <GOUT=<*libref.*>*output-catalog*>
    <IGOUT=<*libref.*>*input-catalog*>
    <IMAGEMAP=*output-data-set*>
    <NOBYLINE>
    <NOFS>
    <PRESENTATION>
    <TC=*template-catalog*>
    <TEMPLATE=*template-entry*>;

Options

Each PROC GREPLAY statement option has an equivalent statement that you can use instead.

BYLINE

specifies that the BY statement information for the SAS catalog entries should be displayed. The BY statement information appears directly beneath the primary description of the entry. By default, the BY statement information is displayed.

CC=*color-map-catalog*

identifies the color map catalog to be used with the GREPLAY procedure. Use the CMAP= option to assign a current color map that is contained in *color-map-catalog*.

To assign a current color map or create new color maps, you must assign a color map catalog with the CC= option.

To replay graphics output using a color map, you must assign a color map catalog and a current color map with the CC= and CMAP= options.

Featured in: Example 3 on page 956

CMAP=*color-map-entry*

assigns a current color map to use when replaying graphics output, where *color-map-entry* names an existing color map in the catalog specified in the CC= option. If *color-map-entry* is not in the catalog, an error message is written to the SAS log. *Color-map-entry* must have a catalog entry type of CMAP.

If you do not specify a color map catalog using the CC= option when using the CMAP= option, a warning message is written to the SAS log.

To replay graphics output using a color map, you must assign a color map catalog and a current color map with the CC= and CMAP= options.

FS

specifies that the GREPLAY procedure should use windows. By default, if your device supports windows, the GREPLAY procedure uses windows. If your device does not support windows, the procedure begins execution in line-mode and the FS option has no effect.

GOUT=<*libref.*>*output-catalog*

specifies the SAS catalog in which to save the graphics output that is produced by the GREPLAY procedure. In addition, catalog entries that contain graphics output can be copied to *output-catalog*. If you omit the libref, SAS/GRAPH looks for the catalog in the temporary library called WORK and creates the catalog if it does not exist. *Output-catalog* can be the same catalog that is specified in the IGOUT= option.

To copy catalog entries, you must assign an input and, optionally, an output catalog with the IGOUT= and GOUT= options.

See also: "Storing Graphics Output in SAS Catalogs" on page 49

Featured in: Example 2 on page 954

IGOUT=<*libref.*>*input-catalog*

specifies the input catalog to use with the GREPLAY procedure. The input catalog that you specify with the IGOUT= option should be a catalog that contains the graphics output that will be replayed. If you omit the libref, SAS/GRAPH looks for the catalog in the temporary library called WORK. *Input-catalog* can be the same catalog that you specified in the GOUT= option.

To move, group, or delete catalog entries or to replay graphics output, you must assign an input catalog with the IGOUT= option.

To copy catalog entries, you must assign an input and, optionally, an output catalog with the IGOUT= and GOUT= options.

Featured in: Example 2 on page 954

IMAGEMAP=*output-data-set*

must be used in conjunction with the REPLAY statement (see "REPLAY Statement" on page 939). Creates a SAS data set that contains information about the graph that is replayed from the graphics catalog and about areas in that graph. This information includes the shape and coordinates of the areas, and is used to build an HTML file that links the graph areas to other files or images. This linking provides drill-down functionality on the graph. The Imagemap data set also contains the information that is stored in the HTML variable in the data set that generated the original graph. Therefore, in order to use IMAGEMAP= to create an HTML file, the procedure that originally stored the graph in the graphics catalog must have used an HTML variable in the data set that was used to generate the graph, and it must also have specified HTML=, or HTML_LEGEND=, or both.

See also: "Customizing Web Pages for Drill-down Graphs" on page 100

NOBYLINE

suppresses the BY statement information for the SAS catalog entries. The BY statement information appears directly beneath the primary description of the entry. By default, the BY statement information is displayed.

NOFS

specifies that the GREPLAY procedure should use line mode. By default, if your device supports windows, the GREPLAY procedure uses windows. If your device does not support windows, the procedure uses line mode, regardless of whether you used the FS option or the NOFS option.

Featured in: Example 1 on page 952

PRESENTATION

specifies that the GREPLAY procedure should open the PRESENTATION window and use the catalog specified by the IGOUT= option as the input catalog. The

PRESENTATION option is often used in applications to prevent the application users from deleting or reordering the catalog entries. You can only replay graphics output from the PRESENTATION window; you cannot manage catalogs or create templates and color maps from this window.

You must use the IGOUT= option when you use the PRESENTATION option. The PRESENTATION option overrides the NOFS option on full-screen devices.

TC=*template-catalog*

identifies the template catalog to use with the GREPLAY procedure. Use the TEMPLATE= option to assign a current template from *template-catalog*.

To assign a current template or create new templates, you must assign a template catalog with the TC= option.

To replay graphics output in a template, you must assign a template catalog and a current template with the TC= and TEMPLATE= options.

Featured in: Example 1 on page 952

TEMPLATE=*template-entry*

assigns a current template to use when replaying graphics output where *template-entry* names an existing template in the template catalog that is specified in the TC= option. If *template-entry* is not in the catalog, an error message is written to the SAS log. *Template-entry* must have a catalog entry type of TEMPLATE.

When you use the TEMPLATE= option, you must also specify the name of a template catalog with the TC= option. Otherwise, a warning message is written to the SAS log.

Featured in: Example 2 on page 954

Details

When you submit the PROC GREPLAY statement, the mode of operation depends on both the environment in which the statement is submitted and whether the NOFS option is included, as shown in Table 26.2 on page 927.

Table 26.2 Ways of Invoking the GREPLAY Procedure

Environment	Statement	Result
windowing	PROC GREPLAY;	GREPLAY procedure windows
windowing	PROC GREPLAY NOFS;	line mode
nonwindowing	PROC GREPLAY;	line mode

You can switch back and forth between windows and line-mode within a session.

? Statement

Prints the current value of certain PROC GREPLAY options or of the current device driver.

Procedure output: Output is sent to the SAS log.

Syntax

? *required–argument*;

required-argument must be one of the following:

    CC

    CMAP

    DEVICE

    GOUT

    IGOUT

    TC

    TEMPLATE

Required Arguments

CC
> prints the name of the current color map catalog. If no color map catalog has been assigned, the GREPLAY procedure issues a message.

CMAP
> prints the name of the current color map. If no color map has been assigned, the GREPLAY procedure issues a message.

DEVICE
DEV
> prints the name of the current device driver.

GOUT
> prints the name of the current output catalog. If you did not assign an output catalog, the GREPLAY procedure issues a message.

IGOUT
> prints the name of the current input catalog. If you did not assign an input catalog, the GREPLAY procedure issues a message.

TC
> prints the name of the current template catalog. If you did not assign a template catalog, the GREPLAY procedure issues a message.

TEMPLATE
> prints the name of the current template. If you did not assign a template, the GREPLAY procedure issues a message.

BYLINE Statement

Displays BY statement information directly beneath the primary description of the catalog entries when you list the contents of the input catalog.

Note: BY statement information is displayed by default.

See also: NOBYLINE statement

Syntax

BYLINE;

CC Statement

Specifies a color map catalog and allows you to change the color map catalog without exiting the procedure.

Syntax

CC *color-map-catalog*;

Required Arguments

color-map-catalog
identifies the SAS catalog where color maps should be stored or the name of a SAS catalog containing color maps.

CCOPY Statement

Copies a color map from another catalog to the color map catalog or creates a duplicate copy of a color map within the color map catalog.

Requirements: Assign a color map catalog before using the CCOPY statement.

See also: CC statement

Syntax

CCOPY <*color-map-catalog.*>*color-map-entry*<.CMAP>;

Required Arguments

<color-map-catalog.>color-map-entry <.CMAP>
> identifies the color map entry to be copied.

color-map-catalog
> is the SAS catalog that contains the color map to be copied.

color-map-entry
> is the name of the entry color map.

CMAP
> is the catalog entry type.

If a color map of the same name already exists in the color map catalog, the GREPLAY procedure creates a new name.

See also: "Duplicate Entry Names" on page 922

Details

To copy a color map from another catalog to the color map catalog, use the CC statement to specify *color-map-catalog* as the catalog from which the color map should be copied. For example, the following statements copy HP.CMAP from the catalog named ONE.CCAT to the catalog named TARGET.CLRMAP:

```
libname target 'SAS-data-library';
libname one 'SAS-data-library';

proc greplay nofs;
   cc target.clrmap;
   ccopy one.ccat.hp.cmap;
quit;
```

To create a duplicate copy of a color map, simply omit *color-map-catalog* from your CCOPY statement. For example, to create a duplicate copy of the color map named HP.CMAP in the color map catalog, use the following statement:

```
ccopy hp.cmap;
```

CDEF Statement

Defines or modifies a color map in the color map catalog.

Requirements: Assign a color map catalog before using the CDEF statement.

See also: CC statement

Featured in: Example 3 on page 956

Syntax

CDEF *color-map-entry*
> *<color-definition(s)>*
> *<DES='entry-description'>*;

color-definition has the following form:
> *color-number / from-color:to-color*

color-definition has the following form: *color-number / from-color:to-color*

Required Arguments

color-map-entry
  identifies an existing or new color map. *Color-map-entry* is the name of a catalog entry.

  If the color map name is not in the color map catalog, then the procedure creates a new color map. If the color map name is already in the color map catalog, then the procedure modifies or adds to that color map.

Options

color-number / from-color:to-color
  specifies a color pair and how it is defined.

  color-number
    specifies the number of a color pair.

  from-color:to-color
    defines the colors that are being mapped:

    from-color
      is the color to be mapped.

    to-color
      is the new color that replaces *from-color* in the replayed graphics output.

DES='*entry-description*'
  specifies a description of the catalog entry for the color map. The maximum length for the *entry-description* is 40 characters. By default, the GREPLAY procedure assigns a description of **** NEW COLOR MAP **** to the color map.

CDELETE Statement

Deletes one or more color maps from the current color map catalog.

Caution: The GREPLAY procedure does not prompt you to confirm your request to delete color maps.
Alias: CDEL

Syntax

  CDELETE *color-map-entry(s)* | _ALL_ ;

Required Arguments

color-map-entry(s)
  identifies one or more color maps that you want to delete from the color map catalog. You can submit a single entry or a list of entries in one CDELETE statement.

ALL
deletes all of the color maps from the color map catalog.

CMAP Statement

Assigns the current color map to be used when replaying graphics output.

Requirements: Assign a color map catalog before using the CMAP statement.

See also: CC statement

Featured in: Example 3 on page 956

Syntax

CMAP *color-map-entry*;

Required Arguments

color-map-entry
identifies an existing color map, contained in the color map catalog, to use when replaying your graphics output. If the color map is not in the current color map catalog, the GREPLAY procedure issues an error message in the SAS log.

COPY Statement

Copies one or more catalog entries containing graphics output from the input catalog to the output catalog.

Requirements: Assign an input catalog and an output catalog before using the COPY statement.

Note: You cannot use the COPY statement to create a duplicate of an entry containing graphics output in the same catalog. You can have only one copy of an entry containing graphics output in a catalog.

See also: GOUT and IGOUT statements

Syntax

COPY *entry-id(s)* | _ALL_ ;

Required Arguments

One of the following is required:

entry-id(s)
is the number or name of a catalog entry, or the number or name of a group of entries to be copied from the input catalog to the output catalog. Entries must contain graphics output. Multiple *entry-id(s)* can contain both numbers and names.

ALL
    copies all of the graphics output entries in the input catalog to the output catalog.

DELETE Statement

Deletes SAS catalog entries containing graphics output from the current input catalog.

Caution: The GREPLAY procedure does not prompt you to confirm your request to delete an entry containing graphics output.

Alias: DEL

Syntax

DELETE *entry-id(s)* | _ALL_ ;

Required Arguments

One of the following is required:

entry-id(s)
    is the number or name of a catalog entry, or the number or name of a group of entries to be deleted from the input catalog. Entries must contain graphics output. Multiple *entry-id(s)* can contain both numbers and names.

ALL
    deletes all of the graphics output entries in the input catalog.

DEVICE Statement

Specifies the device driver.

Requirements: You must specify a device driver that your graphics device can support and that is available in your SAS session.

Alias: DEV

Syntax

DEVICE *device-name*;

Required Arguments

device-name
    specifies the device driver to use when you replay graphics output. The device driver that you specify becomes the current device and is used for subsequent replays until you submit another DEVICE statement or change the device driver in another way.

FS Statement

Switches from line mode to the **GREPLAY** procedure windows.

Requirements: Your device must support windows.

See also: NOFS on page 926

Syntax

FS;

GOUT Statement

Assigns the current output catalog used by the **GREPLAY** procedure.

Note: You may change the output catalog without exiting the procedure by using the GOUT statement.

Syntax

GOUT <*libref.*>*output-catalog*;

Required Arguments

<*libref.*>*output-catalog*
identifies the SAS catalog that you want to use as an output catalog. By default, the output catalog is WORK.GSEG.

GROUP Statement

Creates groups of entries in the current input catalog.

Syntax

GROUP *entry-id(s)*;

Required Arguments

entry-id(s)
is the number or name of a catalog entry that contains graphics output. All of the entries that are specified in the GROUP statement are included in a single group

with a group header. You can submit a single entry or a list of entries with a single GROUP statement. A list of entries can contain both entry numbers and entry names.

Details

You can manage and display groups of entries with the DELETE, COPY, and REPLAY statements in the same way that you manage single entries.

Only one group can be created per group statement. The default name for a group header is GROUP. The default description for the group header is *** new group ***. The GREPLAY procedure uses a naming convention to avoid duplicate names. See "Duplicate Entry Names" on page 922 for more information on the naming convention.

To change the name (and description) of a group, use the MODIFY statement.

IGOUT Statement

Assigns the current input catalog used by the GREPLAY procedure.

Note: You may change the input catalog without exiting the procedure by using the IGOUT statement.

Syntax

IGOUT *<libref.>input-catalog*;

Required Arguments

<libref.>input-catalog
identifies the SAS catalog with entries that contain graphics output that you want to replay.

LIST Statement

Prints entries in the input, template, and color map catalogs, as well as the contents of templates and color maps.

Procedure output: The output from the LIST statement is sent to the SAS log.

Note: Entries are listed in the order of their creation date.

Featured in: Example 3 on page 956

Syntax

LIST *required-argument*;

required-argument must be one of the following:

CC

CMAP

IGOUT

TC

TEMPLATE

Required Arguments

One of the following is required:

CC

prints the color maps that are in the current color map catalog. If the catalog contains both templates and color maps, only color maps are listed.

CMAP

prints the *From* and *To* color values in the current color map.

IGOUT

prints the number, names, and descriptions of the entries in the input catalog that contains graphics output. In addition, the type of graphics output (dependent or independent) is shown.

TC

prints the templates in the current template catalog. If the catalog contains both templates and color maps, only the templates are listed.

TEMPLATE

prints the panel definition values of the current template.

MODIFY Statement

Changes the name, description, and BY statement information of entries or group headers in the input catalog.

Syntax

MODIFY *modify-pair(s)*;

modify-pair(s) has the following form:
  entry-id / *entry-description(s)*

Required Arguments

entry-id* / *entry-description(s)

specifies the entry to modify.

entry-id

is the number or name of a catalog entry, or the number or name of a group of entries in the input catalog. Entries must contain graphics output. Multiple *entry-id(s)* can contain both numbers and names.

entry-description(s)

must be at least one of the following:

BYLINE='*character-string*'

specifies a character string that can be used for additional information or for BY statement information. *Character-string* can be up to 40 characters long and must be enclosed in quotation marks. BY statement information appears directly beneath the primary description of the catalog entry.

NAME='*entry-name*'
specifies the new name of the catalog entry for the graph. The maximum length for *entry-name* is eight characters. If the specified name duplicates the name of an existing entry, SAS/GRAPH software adds a number to the duplicate name to create a unique entry.

Note: The value for *entry-name* can be either with or without quotation marks. △

DES='*entry-description*'
specifies the description of the catalog entry for the graph. The maximum length for *entry-description* is 40 characters. The description does not appear on the graph.

MOVE Statement

Rearranges entries in the input catalog by moving entries either before or after other entries.

Syntax

MOVE *entry-id-1* AFTER | BEFORE *entry-id-2*;

Required Arguments

entry-id-1
is the name or number of an existing catalog entry or a group header that is to be moved.

entry-id-2
is the name or number of an existing catalog entry or a group header. *Entry-id-1* can be placed before or after *entry-id-2*.

AFTER | BEFORE
specifies whether *entry-id-1* should be moved before or after *entry-id-2*.

Details

To move an entire group, use the name of the group for *entry-id-1*. To move an entry into a group, move the entry after a group header or before or after an entry in the group. For example, this statement moves the entry CHART3 into the group that is named NEW_SALES:

```
move chart3 after new_sales;
```

NOBYLINE Statement

Suppresses BY statement information.

Note: By default, the BY statement information is displayed.

See also: BYLINE statement

Syntax

NOBYLINE;

PREVIEW Statement

Displays the panel outlines for one or more templates using the current device. Use the TC statement to specify the template catalog before using the PREVIEW statement.

Tip: When you preview a list of templates, press END or ENTER to preview the next template in the list.

Note: The graphics output produced when you preview a template is stored in a catalog named WORK.GTEM, which is deleted at the end of your session.

Syntax

PREVIEW *template-entry(s)* | _ALL_ ;

Required Arguments

One of the following is required:

template-entry(s)
identifies one or more template entries that are contained in the current template catalog. You can preview one entry or a list of entries with one PREVIEW statement.

ALL
previews all of the templates in the current template catalog.

QUIT Statement

Exits the GREPLAY procedure.

Aliases: END, STOP

Syntax

QUIT;

REPLAY Statement

Selects one or more entries for replay from the current input catalog.

Note: If any entries specified in a REPLAY statement are not found in the input catalog, PROC GREPLAY issues a message in the SAS log and continues to replay valid entries.

Alias: PLAY

Syntax

REPLAY *entry-id(s)* | _FIRST_ | _LAST_ | _ALL_ ;

Required Arguments

One of the following is required:

entry-id(s)
is the number or name of a catalog entry, or the number or name of a group of entries in the input catalog. Entries must contain graphics output. Multiple *entry-id(s)* can contain both numbers and names. For example, this statement specifies both the entry named GRAPH and the third entry in the catalog:

```
replay graph 3;
```

ALL
replays all of the entries in the input catalog.

FIRST
replays the first entry in the input catalog.

LAST
replays the last entry in the input catalog.

TC Statement

Specifies the template catalog for the GREPLAY procedure.

Note: SASHELP.TEMPLT is the Institute-supplied template catalog.

Tip: Use the TC statement to change the template catalog without exiting the procedure.

Syntax

TC *template-catalog*;

Required Arguments

template-catalog
> identifies the SAS catalog where templates are to be stored or identifies the name of a SAS catalog that contains templates.

TCOPY Statement

Copies templates from another catalog to the template catalog or creates a duplicate copy of a template within the template catalog.

Requirements: Assign a template catalog before using the TCOPY statement.

See also: TC statement

Syntax

TCOPY <*template-catalog.*>*template-entry*<.TEMPLATE>;

Required Arguments

<*template-catalog.*>*template-entry*<.TEMPLATE>
> identifies the template entry that is to be copied.

template-catalog
> is the SAS catalog that contains the template that is to be copied.

template-entry
> is the template entry name.

TEMPLATE
> is the catalog entry type. If a template of the same name already exists in the template catalog, the GREPLAY procedure creates a new name.
>
> See also: "Duplicate Entry Names" on page 922

Details

To copy a template from another catalog to the template catalog, specify *template-catalog* as the catalog from which the template should be copied. For example, if you want to copy NEWTEMP.TEMPLATE from the catalog named ONE.TEMPLT to the catalog named TARGET.TEMPLT, use the following statements:

```
libname target 'SAS-data-library';
libname one 'SAS-data-library';

proc greplay nofs;
   tc target.templt;
   tcopy one.templt.newtemp.template;
quit;
```

To create a duplicate copy of a template, simply omit *template-catalog* from your TCOPY statement. For example, to create a duplicate copy of a template named NEWTEMP within the template catalog, you could use the following statement:

```
tcopy newtemp.template;
```

TDEF Statement

Defines or modifies templates in the current template catalog.

Requirements: Assign a template catalog before using the TDEF statement.

See also: TC statement

Featured in: Example 1 on page 952

Syntax

TDEF*template-entry*
  <panel-definition(s)>
  *<*DES=*'entry-description'>*;

panel-definition has the following form:

  panel-number / <panel-option(s)>

  panel-option(s) can be one or more of the following:
  CLIP
  COLOR=*border-color*
  COPY=*panel-number*
  DEF
  DELETE
  LLX=*x*
  LLY=*y*
  LRX=*x*
  LRY=*y*
  ROTATE=*degrees*
  SCALEX=*factor*
  SCALEY=*factor*
  ULX=*x*
  ULY=*y*
  URX=*x*
  URY=*y*
  XLATEX=*distance*
  XLATEY=*distance*

Required Arguments

template-entry
  identifies an existing or a new template. If the template is not in the template
  catalog, the procedure creates it. If the template is already in the template catalog,
  the procedure modifies or makes additions to that template.

  Only *template-entry* is required, but if you specify only the template name without
  any options, no changes are made to an existing template and no new template is
  created.

Options

CLIP

specifies that any panels behind this panel should be clipped. If clipping is in effect for a panel, only the graphics output that is to be placed in that panel can appear in the space that the panel occupies, unless a previous panel occupies all or part of that space.

COLOR=*border-color*

specifies the color of the panel border. If you omit *border-color*, then no border is displayed around the panel when you replay graphics output in the panel. If you preview a template that contains a panel without a border color, the GREPLAY procedure uses the first color in the colors list as the outline for the border.

COPY=*panel-number*

specifies the number of the panel definition that is to be copied to this panel.

DEF

specifies a default panel. A default panel has the following characteristics:

Panel Corner	Coordinates
lower left	(0,0)
upper left	(0,100)
upper right	(100,100)
lower right	(100,0)

DELETE
DEL

deletes the panel.

DES='*entry-description*'

specifies the description of the catalog entry for the template. The maximum length for *entry-description* is 40 characters. By default, the procedure uses *** new template *** for the description.

LLX=*x*

specifies the X coordinate of the lower-left corner of the panel. Units for *x* are percentage of the graphics output area.

LLY=*y*

specifies the Y coordinate of the lower-left corner of the panel. Units for *y* are percentage of the graphics output area.

LRX=*x*

specifies the X coordinate of the lower-right corner of the panel. Units for *x* are percentage of the graphics output area.

LRY=*y*

specifies the Y coordinate of the lower-right corner of the panel. Units for *y* are percentage of the graphics output area.

panel-number

identifies the number of the panel that is being defined or modified.

ROTATE=*degrees*

specifies the rotation angle for the panel. The coordinates of the panel corners are automatically adjusted.

SCALEX=*factor*

specifies the scale factor for the X coordinates in the panel. You can use this scale factor to increase or decrease the size of the panel in the X direction or to reverse the X coordinates for the panel.

SCALEY=*factor*

specifies the scale factor for Y coordinates in the panel. You can use this scale factor to increase or decrease the size of the panel in the Y direction or to reverse the Y coordinates for the panel.

ULX=*x*

specifies the X coordinate of the upper-left corner of the panel. Units for x are percentage of the graphics output area.

ULY=*y*

specifies the Y coordinate of the upper-left corner of the panel. Units for y are percentage of the graphics output area.

URX=*x*

specifies the X coordinate of the upper-right corner of the panel. Units for x are percentage of the graphics output area.

URY=*y*

specifies the Y coordinate of the upper-right corner of the panel. Units for y are percentage of the graphics output area.

XLATEX=*distance*

specifies the distance to move the X coordinates of the panel. Units for *distance* are percentage of the graphics output area.

XLATEY=*distance*

specifies the distance to move the Y coordinates of the panel. Units for *distance* are percentage of the graphics output area.

Details

Use coordinate values that are less than 0 and greater than 100 in the LLX=, LLY=, LRX=, LRY=, ULX=, ULY=, URX=, and URY= options to zoom in on the graphics output. That is, you can see only that part of the replayed graphics output in the range from 0 to 100 percent of the graphics output area.

The values that you supply for the SCALEX= and SCALEY= options are used to change the size and orientation of the panel. The scale factors are used for the corresponding X and Y coordinates of the panel. For example, if you specify

```
scalex=.5
scaley=2
```

the X coordinates are scaled to half the original size, and the Y coordinates are scaled to twice the original size.

If you supply a scale factor of 0, all of the coordinates are set to the same value. If you use a scale factor of 1, nothing happens. If you use a scale factor greater than 1, the values of the coordinates are increased and hence the size of the panel increases. If you use a scale factor less than 1 but greater than 0, the values of the coordinates are decreased and hence the size of the panel decreases. If you use a negative scale factor, the coordinates are reversed and hence the panel (and any graphics output replayed in the panel) is reversed.

TDELETE Statement

Deletes templates from the template catalog.

Caution: The GREPLAY procedure does not prompt you to confirm your request to delete templates.

Alias: TDEL

Syntax

TDELETE *template-entry(s)* | _ALL_ ;

Required Arguments

One of the following is required:

template-entry(s)
identifies a template that is to be deleted from the template catalog. You can submit a single entry or a list of entries in a single TDELETE statement.

ALL
deletes all of the templates in the template catalog.

TEMPLATE Statement

Assigns a current template to use when replaying graphics output.

Requirements: Assign a template catalog before using the TEMPLATE statement.

Note: If you specify a template that is not in the current template catalog or if you specify a template before you have assigned a template catalog, the GREPLAY procedure issues an error message.

Featured in: Example 1 on page 952

Syntax

TEMPLATE *template-entry*;

Required Arguments

template-entry
identifies an existing template to use when replaying graphics output. Use the TREPLAY statement to replay graphics output in the template.

TREPLAY Statement

Selects one or more catalog entries from the same catalog for replay in template panels.

Requirements: Assign a template catalog and a current template before using the TREPLAY statement.

Alias: TPLAY

See also: TC statement

Featured in: Example 2 on page 954

Syntax

TREPLAY *select-pair(s);*

select-pair has the following form:
   panel-number:entry-id

select-pair has the following form: *panel-number:entry-id*

Required Arguments

panel-number:entry-id
   specifies the panel number and the name of a catalog entry.

   panel-number
      is the number of the panel in the current template in which to replay the graphics output.

   entry-id
      is the name or number of a catalog entry that contains the graphics output to be replayed in *panel-number*.

Details

   When you replay existing GRSEG entries in a template, the GREPLAY procedure creates new graphics output that is stored in the output catalog.

   You can replay as many entries as you want in a single TREPLAY statement as shown here:

```
treplay 1:plot1 2:plot2 3:chart1;
```

   The order in which you list the entries in the TREPLAY statement determines the order in which they are played into the template. PLOT1 will be placed in panel 1 of the current template, PLOT2 will be placed in panel 2, and CHART1 will be placed in panel 3. You can use entry numbers in the place of entry names.

Using the GREPLAY Procedure

Using the GREPLAY Windows

   You can use the GREPLAY windows instead of code-based statements to replay and manage catalog entries. You perform tasks that use the GREPLAY procedure windows by entering values in the fields that are displayed in the windows and by issuing commands from the command line.

There are five GREPLAY windows:

- □ PROC GREPLAY window
- □ PRESENTATION window
- □ DIRECTORY window
- □ TEMPLATE DESIGN window
- □ COLOR MAPPING window.

Figure 26.2 on page 946 shows how these windows relate to each other. Each window can be scrolled forward or backward as needed to display additional fields and information.

Figure 26.2 GREPLAY Procedure Windows

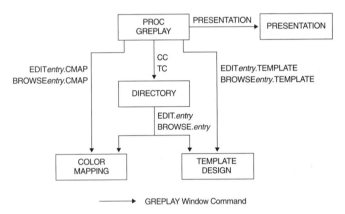

This section briefly describes the GREPLAY windows; for a complete description of each window and its fields, refer to the SAS Help facility.

GREPLAY Window Commands

You can navigate and manipulate the GREPLAY windows by entering commands on the command line or by selecting them from the menus. For a complete description of all the GREPLAY window commands, refer to the SAS Help facility.

PROC GREPLAY Window

This window is the first to appear when you submit the PROC GREPLAY statement on a full-screen device without the PRESENTATION or NOFS option. You can use it to both replay graphics output and to manage catalog entries that contain graphics output.

Display 26.1 The PROC GREPLAY Window

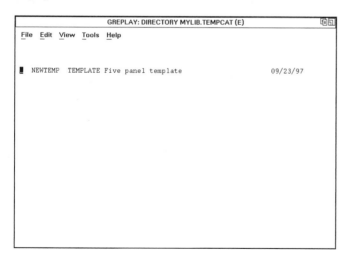

```
                              PROC GREPLAY                        [回][司]

  File  Edit  View  Tools  Help

IGOUT: REFLIB.EXCAT        GOUT: _____     Device: HP7475
TC:   █_____    Template: _____        Scroll: PAGE
CC:   _____     Cmap: _____


Sel  Name      Type   Description                          Created

____ GR23N01B   I     CHOROPLETH MAP OF STATE              03/24/98
____ GR23N02    I     CHOROPLETH MAP OF STATE              03/24/98
____ GR23N03    I     CHOROPLETH MAP OF STATE              03/24/98
____ GR23N04    I     CHOROPLETH MAP OF STATE              03/24/98
____ GR21N01    I     Bubble of dollars * eng = num        03/24/98
____ GR21N02    I     Bubble of dollars * eng = num        03/24/98
____ GR21N03    I     Bubble of dollars * eng = num        03/24/98
____ GR21N04A   I     Plot of height * weight              03/24/98
____ GR21N04B   I     Plot of height * weight              03/24/98
____ GR21N05    I     Plot of high * year                  03/24/98
____ GR21N06    I     Plot of high * year                  03/24/98
____ GR21N07    I     Plot of low * year                   03/24/98
____ GR21N08A   I     Plot of faren * month = city         03/24/98
```

PRESENTATION Window

This window is a modified version of the PROC GREPLAY window that enables you
to replay graphics output while it prevents you from deleting entries or changing
templates and color maps. Once you have created and organized your catalog, you may
want to use the PRESENTATION window in an application for replaying graphics
output.

DIRECTORY Window

This window lists the names of the catalog entries, gives a brief description of each,
and indicates the date on which each entry was created or last changed. Although all
catalog entry types are displayed in the DIRECTORY window, you can manage only
entries of type CMAP or TEMPLATE from this window.

Display 26.2 The DIRECTORY Window

```
                GREPLAY: DIRECTORY MYLIB.TEMPCAT (E)             [回][司]

  File  Edit  View  Tools  Help



█  NEWTEMP   TEMPLATE Five panel template            09/23/97
```

TEMPLATE DESIGN Window

This window lets you design templates that you can use to present graphics output.
You design a template by specifying the coordinates of its panels and determining the
order in which the template panels are filled. Once you enter coordinates for a panel,
you can alter them easily by using the Scale, Xlate (translate), and Rotate utility fields.
These utility fields recalculate coordinate values automatically.

Display 26.3   The TEMPLATE DESIGN Window

```
                                                                    ⌐⌐
  File  Edit  View  Tools  Help

  TEMPLATE: NEWTEMP                              TC: REFLIB.TEMPCATʋʋʋ
  DESC: Five panel template                      Scroll: PAGE
                                                 Device: HP7475
 Panel Clp Color      L-left U-left U-right L-right  Scale  Xlate  Rotate

 ▌ 1   _   BLUE    X:   0.0    0.0   50.0   50.0   X: ____  ____   ___
                   Y:  10.0   50.0   50.0   10.0   Y: ____  ____

   2   _   RED     X:   0.0    0.0   50.0   50.0   X: ____  ____   ___
                   Y:  50.0   90.0   90.0   50.0   Y: ____  ____

   3   _   GREEN   X:  50.0   50.0  100.0  100.0   X: ____  ____   ___
                   Y:  50.0   90.0   90.0   50.0   Y: ____  ____

```

COLOR MAPPING Window

This window allows you to map colors in existing graphics output to new colors
when you replay the graphics output. When you replay graphics output that is
contained in a catalog entry and assign a current color map, any color in the graphics
output that appears in the From column of the color map is mapped to the
corresponding color in the To column of the color map. Using a color map does not
change the contents of the replayed graphics output and does not produce new graphics
output unless a template is also used.

Display 26.4   The COLOR MAPPING Window

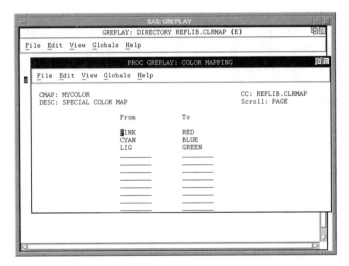

Table 26.3 GREPLAY Procedure Windows

If you are in the...	and you want to open the...	then...
PROC GREPLAY statement	PROC GREPLAY window	Submit the PROC GREPLAY statement without using the PRESENTATION or NOFS options.
	PRESENTATION window	Submit the PROC GREPLAY statement and include the PRESENTATION and IGOUT= options.
PROC GREPLAY window	PRESENTATION window	Specify a catalog and issue the PRES command.
	DIRECTORY window	Specify a template catalog and issue the TC command. OR Specify a color map catalog and issue the CC command.
	TEMPLATE DESIGN window	Specify a template catalog and issue the following command: edit *template-name*.template
	COLOR MAPPING window	Specify a color map catalog and issue the following command: edit *color-map-name*.cmap
DIRECTORY window	TEMPLATE DESIGN window	Place an S beside the name of an existing template. OR Issue the following command: edit *template-name*.template
	COLOR MAPPING window	Place an S beside the name of an existing color map. OR Issue the following command: edit *color-map-name*.cmap

Managing Catalog Entries

You can replay entries or perform a variety of catalog management tasks with GREPLAY code-based statements. Table 26.4 on page 950 lists several common tasks and the statements that you use to perform them.

Table 26.4   Ways of Performing Common GREPLAY Procedure Tasks

Task	Code-based Statement
copy graphics output (GRSEGs) from the input catalog to the output catalog*	COPY statement
arrange GRSEG entries into logical groupings	GROUP statement
reorder the entries	MOVE statement
delete unneeded GRSEG entries	DELETE statement
change entry names and descriptions of entries in the input catalog	MODIFY statement
replay an entry from the input catalog	REPLAY statement
replay an entry in a template panel	TREPLAY statement

*You must assign an output catalog before copying graphics output.

Replaying Catalog Entries

To select catalog entries for replay, first assign an input catalog that contains the graphics output that is to be replayed. Then assign the entry with the REPLAY statement.

For example, the following statements replay the GRSEG entry named GRAPH1 from the catalog MYLIB.GRAPHS, which is assigned with the IGOUT= option:

```
libname mylib 'SAS-data-library';

proc greplay igout=mylib.graphs nofs;
    replay graph1;
run;
quit;
```

If you do not specify an output catalog with the GOUT= option in the PROC statement of the SAS/GRAPH procedure that creates the graphics output, the graphics output is automatically stored in the WORK.GSEG catalog. Replay the graphics output that is stored in this catalog as follows:

```
proc greplay nofs;
    igout work.gseg;
    replay _all_;
run;
quit;
```

Creating Templates and Color Maps

You can use the GREPLAY procedure to create templates and color maps. You can use templates to replay graphics output from several catalog entries on a single display, or to change the shape or size of graphics output. You can use color maps to remap colors when replaying graphics output.

A color map is a list of up to 256 pairs of colors that enables you to change the colors in graphics output by mapping the original colors to a list of new colors. Color maps are useful for controlling how colors that are not available on the current device are remapped.

When you assign a current color map and replay graphics output that is stored in a catalog entry, any color in your graphics output that appears in the From column of the color map is mapped to the corresponding color in the To column of the color map. The new colors are not saved with the graphics output, and you do not create new graphics output when you use a color map to replay graphics output.

Table 26.5 Ways of Performing Common GREPLAY Procedure Tasks

Task	In line mode
assign a color map catalog	CC statement
copy a color map from another catalog	CCOPY statement
define or modify a color map in the current catalog	CDEF statement
assign a color map to use when you replay graphics output	CMAP statement
delete unneeded entries	DELETE statement
assign a template catalog	TC statement
copy a template from another catalog	TCOPY statement
delete a template	TDELETE statement
define a template	TDEF statement
display the panel outlines for a template	PREVIEW statement
assign a template to use when you replay graphics output	TEMPLATE statement
replay an entry in a template panel	TREPLAY statement

Before you create a template, you must assign a template catalog. If you are use the GREPLAY procedure in line mode, use the TDEF statement to define a template and the PREVIEW statement to preview a template. For example, the following statements define and preview a template named TEMPLT:

```
tdef templt 1/def;
preview templt;
```

Before you create a color map, you must assign a color map catalog. If you use the GREPLAY procedure in line mode, use the CDEF statement to define a color map. For example, the following statement defines a color map named CLRMAP:

```
cdef clrmap 1 / cyan : blue;
```

Replaying Graphics Output in a Template

You can use the GREPLAY procedure to create new graphics output by replaying existing graphics output in templates. You can use the templates that are provided with SAS/GRAPH software and stored in the catalog SASHELP.TEMPLT, or you can create your own templates. Before you can replay graphics output in a template, you must assign a template catalog and a current template, as well as an input catalog. Then assign the entries to the template with the TREPLAY statement.

For example, the following statements replay the entries GRAPH1 and GRAPH2 into the V2 template, which is stored in the catalog SASHELP.TEMPLT. The TC statement specifies the catalog that contains the template, and the TEMPLATE statement specifies the template. The TREPLAY statement assigns each entry to a panel. (The V2 template has two panels, so there is an assignment for panel 1 and panel 2.)

```
proc greplay igout=mylib.graphs nofs;
   tc sashelp.templt;
   template v2;
   treplay 1:graph1 2:graph2;
run;
```

When you replay graphics output in a template, the new graphics output that is created by the GREPLAY procedure is automatically provided a default name and is stored in the output catalog, WORK.GSEG.

Templates are often used to describe positioning for replaying graphics output from several catalog entries on a single display.

Examples

The following examples illustrate major features of the GREPLAY procedure.

Example 1: Creating a Template

Procedure features:
   GREPLAY statement options:
      NOFS
      TC=
   TDEF statement
   TEMPLATE statement
Sample library member: GR26N01

This example creates a template with five panels. Four of the panels are small and equal in size. The fifth panel is a large, full-size panel that can be used later to display a common title or footnote for the entire template (see). In this example, the LIST statement displays the template contents in the log. Output 26.1 on page 954 shows the template definition that is written to the log file. The template that is defined here is also used in Example 2 on page 954.

Assign the libref and set the graphics environment.

```
libname reflib 'SAS-data-library';
goptions reset=global gunit=pct border cback=white
        colors=(black blue green red)
        ftext=swissb htitle=6 htext=3
```

Start the GREPLAY procedure. NOFS starts the procedure in line-mode. TC=assigns TEMPCAT as the template catalog.

```
proc greplay tc=reflib.tempcat nofs;
```

Define a template with four panels. The TDEF statement defines a template named NEWTEMP and places it in the previously defined template catalog. Each definition identifies the panel number and specifies the coordinates of the four corners. The panels are arranged within the template as follows: panel 1 is lower left; panel 2 is upper left; panel 3 is upper right; panel 4 is lower right; panel 5 is the full size so that it can contain a common title and footnote for all the template entries. COLOR= draws a border for each panel in the specified color.

```
tdef newtemp des='Five panel template'

     1/llx=0    lly=10
       ulx=0    uly=50
       urx=50   ury=50=
       lrx=50   lry=10
       color=blue

     2/llx=0    lly=50
       ulx=0    uly=90
       urx=50   ury=90=
       lrx=50   lry=50
       color=red

     3/llx=0    lly=50
       ulx=0    uly=90
       urx=100  ury=90=
       lrx=100  lry=50
       color=green

     4/llx=50   lly=10
       ulx=50   uly=50
       urx=100  ury=50=
       lrx=100  lry=10
       color=cyan
```

Assign the current template. The TEMPLATE statement assigns the newly created template NEWTEMP as the current template.

```
template newtemp;
```

Write the contents of the current template to the log.

```
    list template;
quit;
```

Output 26.1   Defining a Template (GR26N01)

```
.
.
.

64         /* list contents of current template */
65      list template;

NEWTEMP        Five panel template

Pan Clp Color       Ll-x  Ll-y  Ul-x  Ul-y  Ur-x  Ur-y  Lr-x  Lr-y

  1       BLUE       0.0  10.0   0.0  50.0  50.0  50.0  50.0  10.0
  2       RED        0.0  50.0   0.0  90.0  50.0  90.0  50.0  50.0
  3       GREEN     50.0  50.0  50.0  90.0 100.0  90.0 100.0  50.0
  4       CYAN      50.0  10.0  50.0  50.0 100.0  50.0 100.0  10.0
  5       LIPK       0.0   0.0   0.0 100.0 100.0 100.0 100.0   0.0

66   quit;
.
.
.
```

Example 2: Replaying Graphics Output in a Template

Procedure features:
   GREPLAY statement options:

   GOUT=
   IGOUT=
   TEMPLATE=
   TREPLAY statement

Other features:
   PROC GSLIDE

Sample library member: GR26N02

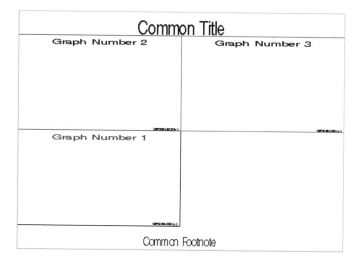

The TREPLAY statement replays into the template NEWTEMP four catalog entries that contain graphics output. The NEWTEMP template is defined in Example 1 on page 952. It contains four equally sized panels and one large, full-size panel. Note that assignments are made to all but one of the panels. Because the fourth panel is not listed in the TREPLAY statement, it does not appear in the graphics output. The HSIZE= and VSIZE= options are adjusted and then reset to default in order to reflect the dimensions of the different-sized template panels.

> ***Assign the libref and set the graphics environment.*** HSIZE= and VSIZE= are set for the dimensions of template panels 1, 2, 3, and 4.

```
libname reflib 'SAS-data-library';
goptions reset=all gunit=pct border
        cback=white colors=(black blue green red)
        ftext=swiss htitle=8 htext=5 nodisplay
        hsize=4in vsize=3.8in;
```

> ***Generate three graphs in the permanent catalog GRAFCAT.*** The GSLIDE procedure creates three text slides and stores them in REFLIB.GRAFCAT as specified by the GOUT= option. By default, these are stored as GSLIDE, GSLIDE1, and GSLIDE2.

```
proc gslide gout=reflib.grafcat;
   title c=red 'Graph Number 1';
   footnote h=3 j=r 'GR26N02(a) ';
run;
   title 'Graph Number 2';
   footnote h=3 j=r 'GR26N02(b) ';
run;
   title 'Graph Number 3';
   footnote h=3 j=r 'GR26N02(c) ';
run;
```

> ***Reset HSIZE= and VSIZE= to the default values and generate a text slide with PROC GSLIDE.*** Resetting the HSIZE and VSIZE values enables you to create a text slide with the proper aspect ratio for use in template panel 5.

```
goptions hsize=0in vsize=0in;
proc gslide gout=reflib.grafcat;
   title 'Common Title';
   footnote 'Common Footnote';
run;
```

Display the graphics output.

```
goptions display;
```

Start the GREPLAY procedure. IGOUT= assigns GRAFCAT as the input catalog. GOUT= assigns EXCAT as the output catalog. TEMPLATE= assigns NEWTEMP as the current template.

```
proc greplay igout=reflib.grafcat gout=reflib.excat
             tc=reflib.tempcat nofs;
   template=newtemp;
```

Replay three graphs into template. The TREPLAY statement assigns three entries to panels in the NEWTEMP template. Each assignment is a panel number and the name of a graphics output entry. Names are the default names assigned by the GSLIDE procedure.

```
treplay 1:gslide
        2:gslide1
        3:gslide2
        5:gslide3;
quit;
```

Example 3: Creating a Color Map

Procedure features:
   GREPLAY statement option:
      CC=
      GOUT=
   CDEF statement
   CMAP statement
   LIST statement
Sample library member: GR26N03

This example uses the CDEF statement to define a color map. The LIST statement is used in this example to display the color map definition in the log. Output 26.2 on page 957 shows a partial listing of the log.

Assign the libref and set the graphics environment.

```
libname reflib 'SAS-data-library';
goptions reset=global gunit=pct border cback=white
```

```
colors=(black blue green red)
ftext=swissb htitle=6 htext=3;
```

Start the GREPLAY procedure. CC= assigns CLRMAP as the color map catalog. GOUT= specifies the permanent catalog in which to place the graphics output.

```
proc greplay cc=reflib.clrmap gout=reflib.excat nofs;
```

Define a color map. The CDEF statement defines a color map named MYCOLOR that contains three color pairs.

```
cdef mycolor des='Special Color Map'
     1 / pink  : red
     2 / cyan  : blue
     3 / lig   : green;
```

Specify current color map and write contents to the log. The CMAP statement assigns MYCOLOR as the current color map. The contents of CMAP are listed in the log.

```
   cmap mycolor;
   list cmap;
quit;
```

Output 26.2   Defining a Color Map (GR26N03)

```
.
.
75        /* list the contents of the color map */
76     list cmap;

MYCOLOR        Special Color Map

       FROM        TO

  1    PINK        RED
  2    CYAN        BLUE
  3    LIG         GREEN

77  quit;
.
```

CHAPTER

27

The GSLIDE Procedure

Overview

The GSLIDE procedure produces graphics output that consists of text and straight lines that are generated by TITLE, FOOTNOTE, and NOTE statements. In addition, the procedure provides an easy way to add titles, notes, and footnotes to output that is produced entirely with an Annotate data set.

The GSLIDE procedure is useful for creating text slides for presentations. You can also overlay text slides on other graphics output with the GREPLAY procedure.

About Text Slides

Text slides contain text and graphics that are generated by SAS/GRAPH statements. To display an external text file as graphics output, use the GPRINT procedure.

Figure 27.1 on page 959 shows a slide containing text that was produced with TITLE, FOOTNOTE, and NOTE statements.

Figure 27.1   Text Slide Produced by the GSLIDE Procedure (GR27N01)

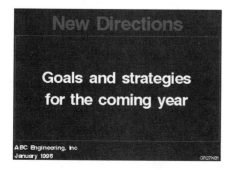

The program for this slide is in Example 1 on page 963.

About Annotate Output

Annotate output is generated by commands that are stored in an Annotate data set. Use the GSLIDE procedure to display Annotate output when you want to include TITLE and FOOTNOTE statements on the output and use certain graphics options such as BORDER. To display Annotate graphics without these, use the GANNO procedure. See Chapter 10, "The Annotate Data Set," on page 403 for more information on creating and displaying Annotate data sets.

Figure 27.2 on page 960 shows output from an Annotate data set that is displayed with titles and footnotes that were generated by TITLE and FOOTNOTE statements.

Figure 27.2 Output from an Annotate Data Set Displayed with the GSLIDE Procedure (GR27N02)

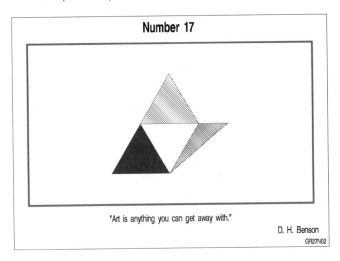

The program for this slide is in Example 2 on page 965.

Procedure Syntax

Requirements: At least one of these is required: a TITLE, FOOTNOTE, or NOTE statement; an appearance option; the BORDER graphics option.

Global statements: FOOTNOTE, TITLE

Reminder: The procedure can include the SAS/GRAPH NOTE statement.

Supports: RUN-group processing Output Delivery System (ODS)

PROC GSLIDE *<option(s)>*;

PROC GSLIDE Statement

Creates a text slide. Optionally, it provides a border, specifies annotation, and assigns an output catalog. This is the only statement in the procedure.

Syntax

PROC GSLIDE <*option(s)*>;

option(s) can be one or more options from any or all of the following categories:

□ appearance options:

ANNOTATE=*Annotate-data-set*

BORDER

CFRAME=*frame-color*

FRAME

LFRAME=*line-type*

WFRAME=*n*

□ description options:

DESCRIPTION='*entry-description*'

GOUT=<*libref.*>*output-catalog*

NAME='*entry-name*'

□ HTML option:

<IMAGEMAP=*output-data-set*>

Options

You can specify as many options as you want and list them in any order.

ANNOTATE=*Annotate-data-set*
ANNO=*Annotate-data-set*

specifies a data set that includes Annotate variables that identify graphics commands and parameters.

See also: Chapter 10, "The Annotate Data Set," on page 403

Featured in: Example 2 on page 965

BORDER

draws a border around the graphics output area, which includes the title area, the footnote area, and the procedure output area. A color specification for the border is searched for in the following order:

1 the CTITLE= option in a GOPTIONS statement

2 the CTEXT= option in a GOPTIONS statement

3 the default, the first color in the colors list.

See also: "Drawing Frames and Borders" on page 962

Featured in: Example 1 on page 963

CFRAME=*frame-color*

draws a frame around the procedure output area in the specified color. If you use both the CFRAME= and FRAME options, FRAME is ignored.

Note: CFRAME= does not color the background of the slide. △

See also: "Drawing Frames and Borders" on page 962

Featured in: Example 1 on page 963

DESCRIPTION='*entry-description*'
DES='*entry-description*'
 specifies the description of the catalog entry for the chart. The maximum length for *entry-description* is 40 characters. The description does not appear on the chart. By default, the GSLIDE procedure assigns the description OUTPUT FROM PROC GSLIDE.

FRAME
 draws a frame around the procedure output area. By default, the frame color is the first color in the colors list. If you want to specify a different color for the frame, use the CFRAME= option instead.

See also: "Drawing Frames and Borders" on page 962

GOUT=<*libref.*>*output-catalog*
 specifies the SAS catalog in which to save the graphics output produced by the GSLIDE procedure. If you omit the libref, SAS/GRAPH looks for the catalog in the temporary library called WORK and creates the catalog if it does not exist.

See also: "Storing Graphics Output in SAS Catalogs" on page 49

IMAGEMAP=*output-data-set*
 creates a SAS data set that contains information about the graph and about areas in the graph. This information includes the shape and coordinates of the areas, and is used to build an HTML file that links the graph areas to other files or images. This linking provides drill-down functionality on the graph. The Imagemap data set also contains the information that is stored in the HTML variable in the Annotate data set. Therefore, in order to use IMAGEMAP= to create an HTML file, you must also use the HTML variable in the Annotate data set.

See also: "Customizing Web Pages for Drill-down Graphs" on page 100 and "HTML Variable" on page 462

LFRAME=*line-type*
 specifies the line type for a frame and draws a frame around the procedure output area. Values for *line-type* are 1 through 46. Line types are shown in Figure 8.22 on page 249. By default, LFRAME=1, which produces a solid line.

NAME='*entry-name*'
 specifies the name of the catalog entry for the graph. The maximum length for *entry-name* is eight characters. The default name is GSLIDE. If the specified name duplicates the name of an existing entry, SAS/GRAPH software adds a number to the duplicate name to create a unique entry, for example, GSLIDE1.

WFRAME=*n*
 specifies the width of the frame where *n* is a number. The thickness of the frame increases directly with *n*, but the thickness of the line may vary from device to device. By default, WFRAME=1, which is the thinnest line. The WFRAME= option also draws the frame.

See also: "Drawing Frames and Borders" on page 962

Featured in: Example 1 on page 963

Drawing Frames and Borders

Like the BORDER option in a GOPTIONS statement, the BORDER option in the PROC GSLIDE statement draws a box around the graphics output area. However, the border generated by the GSLIDE procedure remains in effect only for the duration of the procedure.

Both BORDER options use the color specified by the CTITLE= or CTEXT= graphics option if either of these options is used; otherwise, the border color is the first color in the colors list.

While the BORDER option draws a box around the graphics output area, the FRAME option draws a box or frame around the procedure output area. In this case, titles and footnotes are outside of the frame. (See "Procedure Output and the Graphics Output Area" on page 29 for a description of the procedure output area.) Use FRAME to draw a frame in the default color, line type, and width. Otherwise, use one or more of the CFRAME=, LFRAME=, or WFRAME= options.

You can specify a colored frame with the CFRAME= option. Note that CFRAME= does not fill the procedure output area with color. However, you can use the CBACK= graphics option to provide a background color for the graphics output area. You can specify the type of line for the frame with the LFRAME= option and the width of the frame with the WFRAME= option.

Using Data-dependent Coordinates

If you use the GSLIDE procedure with Annotate data sets that contain data-dependent coordinates, the resulting coordinate values may exceed the range of 0 to 100 used by the graphics output area, and some of the output may not be displayed. In this case, use the GANNO procedure, which can scale the output to fit the available space. See also Chapter 12, "The GANNO Procedure," on page 503 for details.

Using RUN Groups

Although the GSLIDE procedure has no action statements, it can use RUN-group processing to display all currently defined titles, footnotes, and notes, as well as specified annotation, each time you submit a RUN statement. TITLE and FOOTNOTE statements that are defined while the GSLIDE procedure is active remain in effect after the procedure ends. NOTE definitions remain in effect until the GSLIDE procedure ends, at which time they are canceled. To cancel NOTE definitions while the procedure is active, specify RESET=NOTE in a GOPTIONS statement or submit a null NOTE statement. See "RUN-Group Processing" on page 28 for details.

Examples

Example 1: Producing Text Slides

Procedure features:
   PROC GSLIDE options:

      BORDER
      CFRAME=
      WFRAME=

Other features:
   NOTE statement

Sample library member: GR27N01

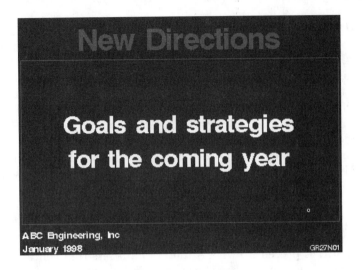

This example uses FOOTNOTE, NOTE, and TITLE statements to produce a text slide. PROC GSLIDE statement options add both a border and a frame.

Set the graphics environment.

```
goptions reset=global gunit=pct cback=blue
         colors=(white) ftext=swissb htitle=12 htext=4;
```

Define titles and footnotes.

```
title color=pink 'New Directions';
footnote1 j=l ' ABC Engineering, Inc';
footnote2 j=l ' January 1998'
          j=r h=3 f=swiss 'GR27N01 ';
```

Generate the slide and define additional text. BORDER draws a box around the entire graphics output area. CFRAME= draws a red box around the procedure output area. WFRAME= specifies the thickness of the frame. The first NOTE statement, which has no text, simply leaves a large blank line above the text specified by the second NOTE statement. The second JUSTIFY= causes a line break.

```
proc gslide border
            cframe=red
            wframe=4;
   note height=20;
   note height=10
        justify=center 'Goals and strategies'
        justify=center 'for the coming year';
run;
quit;
```

Example 2: Displaying Annotate Graphics

Procedure features:
    PROC GSLIDE option:
        ANNOTATE=
Other features:
    Annotate data set
Sample library member: GR27N02

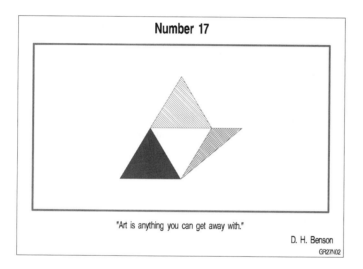

In this example, the GSLIDE procedure displays Annotate graphics along with current TITLE and FOOTNOTE definitions. See Chapter 10, "The Annotate Data Set," on page 403 for information on creating Annotate data sets.

Set the graphics environment.

```
goptions reset=global gunit=pct cback=white
         colors=(black blue green red)
         ftitle=swissb htitle=6 ftext=swiss htext=3;
```

Create the Annotate data set, ART. ART contains the commands that draw the design of triangles.

```
data art;
   length function color style $ 8;
   input function $ x y color $ style $;
   xsys='5'; ysys='5';
   datalines;
poly       30  20  blue     solid
polycont   50  20  .        .
polycont   40  50  .        .
poly       50  20  green    x1
polycont   70  50  .        .
```

```
polycont  60  50   .        .
poly      40  50   red      11
polycont  60  50   .        .
polycont  50  80   .        .
;
```

Define title and footnotes displayed by the procedure. FOOTNOTE statements 4 and 5 have no text and are angled vertically to add space on the left and right sides between the border of the output and the frame that surrounds the procedure output area.

```
title 'Number 17';
footnote1 h=4 '"Art is anything you can get away with."';
footnote2 j=r h=4 'D. H. Benson     ';
footnote3 j=r 'GR27N02 ';
footnote4 h=3 angle=90;
footnote5 h=3 angle=-90;
```

Display the annotate graphics on the slide with the title and footnotes. The GSLIDE procedure displays the graphics elements drawn by the commands in the Annotate data set specified by the ANNOTATE= option.

```
proc gslide annotate=art
            border
            wframe=6
            cframe=red;
run;
quit;
```

CHAPTER

28

The GTESTIT Procedure

Overview

The GTESTIT procedure is a diagnostic tool for testing the installation of SAS/
GRAPH software and the configuration of your device. Use the GTESTIT procedure
when you want to

- test a new device
- test the settings of a device driver that you are developing
- identify the colors and some of the SAS/GRAPH lines and fills for your device
- review some of your current settings of device parameters and graphics options
- test changes in settings of device parameters and graphics options.

The GTESTIT procedure produces three pictures that help you determine the
configuration of your graphics device and graphics options and parameters. Refer to
"About the Pictures" on page 968 for examples of the pictures. Although it does not
show the settings of all device parameters and graphics options, the GTESTIT
procedure does show some of the most commonly used ones.

If you use a GOPTIONS statement to change one or more graphics options for the
current SAS session, or if you run the GDEVICE procedure to change the parameter
settings for your device, you can use the GTESTIT procedure to confirm that those
changes took effect.

For example, if you use the GOPTIONS statement to set HPOS=45 and
COLORS=(RED GREEN), you can display picture 1 in the GTESTIT procedure to
confirm that the graphics output area is divided into 45 columns and that foreground
colors have been limited to red and green.

See Chapter 9, "Graphics Options and Device Parameters Dictionary," on page 301, Chapter 15, "The GDEVICE Procedure," on page 651, and Chapter 3, "Device Drivers," on page 37 for more information on setting graphics options and device parameters.

About the Pictures

Figure 28.1 on page 968 shows a test pattern and gives the values of some of the device settings that are currently in effect. Table 28.1 on page 970 describes the graphics options and device parameters that are displayed in the picture. The values of most of the displayed settings are determined by device parameters that are specified in the catalog entry for the current device or by graphics options that are specified in a GOPTIONS statement.

Note: The following two statements do not return the same parameters when used with PICTURE=1: △

```
goptions dev=xcolor target=ps nodisplay;
goptions dev=ps nodisplay;
```

The LOG window for picture 1, shown in Output 28.1 on page 971, lists some of the same settings that are displayed by picture 1, plus some additional settings.

Figure 28.1   Picture 1 of the GTESTIT Procedure

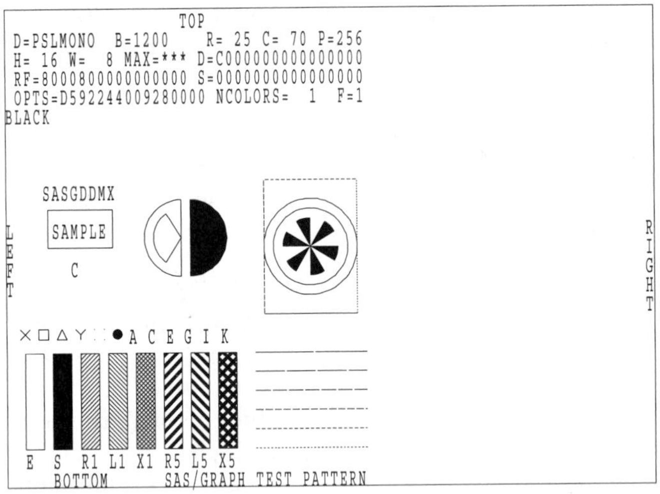

Picture 2 tests your device's ability to draw lines. Picture 2 always displays in the first color of the current colors list. Figure 28.2 on page 969 shows picture 2 of the GTESTIT procedure.

Figure 28.2 Picture 2 of the GTESTIT Procedure

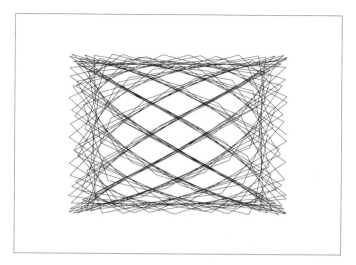

Picture 3 tests your device's ability to draw simple polygons, polygons with multiple boundaries (also known as *holes*), ellipses, and justified text. Figure 28.3 on page 969 shows picture 3 of the GTESTIT procedure.

Figure 28.3 Picture 3 of the GTESTIT Procedure

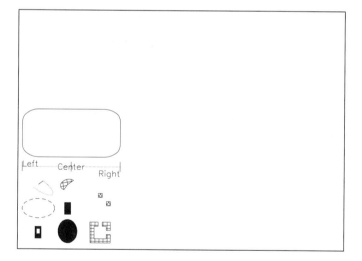

Table 28.1 on page 970 explains the values displayed in picture 1 of the GTESTIT procedure. It also provides the equivalent graphics option or device parameter. Chapter 9, "Graphics Options and Device Parameters Dictionary," on page 301 includes a complete description of the graphics options and device parameters.

Table 28.1 GTESTIT Values Displayed in Picture 1

GTESTIT Value	Equivalent Graphics Option or Device Parameter	Description
D=	DEVICE=	shows the device driver you are using.
R=	VPOS=	shows the number of rows.
C=	HPOS=	shows the number of columns.
P=	MAXCOLORS=	shows the total number of colors (foreground and background) that your device can display. If your device can display more than 15 colors, picture 1 shows only 15 colors, but the LOG window lists all of the available colors.
H=	&#30	shows the height of character cells in pixels.
W=	&#30	shows the width of character cells in pixels.
MAX=	MAXPOLY=	shows the maximum number of vertices that can be processed by a hardware polygon command. If MAX=0, then the number of vertices is unbounded. If MAX=***, then the value is greater than 999.
D= *	DASHLINE=	shows the hardware dashed-line patterns available. The value displayed is a hexadecimal string.
RF= *	RECTFILL=	shows the hardware rectangle-fill patterns available. The value displayed is a hexadecimal string.
S= *	SYMBOLS=	shows the hardware symbols available. The value displayed is a hexadecimal string.
OPTS= *	DEVOPTS=	shows the other hardware options available. The value displayed is a hexadecimal string.
NCOLORS=	COLORS=	shows the number of colors in the colors list or the number of foreground colors.

GTESTIT Value	Equivalent Graphics Option or Device Parameter	Description
F=	FILLINC=	shows the solid fill increment (the number of pixels between strokes when doing a solid fill).

* In the device entry, this field may be blank. If blank, the value displayed by the GTESTIT procedure comes from an internal default in the device driver.

About the LOG

shows a sample of the information that appears in the LOG window after running picture 1 in the GTESTIT procedure. An asterisk (*) after the P=, MAX=, or F= option indicates that the value for that option is greater than 999.

Output 28.1   Sample Log from GTESTIT Procedure

```
1    proc gtestit picture=1;
2    run;
3    quit;
D=PSCOLOR  B=1200    R= 25 C= 70 P=256
H= 16 W=   9 MAX=*** D=C000000000000000
RF=8000800000000000  S=0000000000000000
OPTS=D59A244009280000 NCOLORS=  1
Background color = WHITE
Color 1 = BLACK
Ratio = 0.71429
Hsize = 5.99539
Vsize = 4.28242
F=1
```

Table 28.2 on page 971 lists GTESTIT values that appear only in the LOG window for picture 1: these values do not appear in the picture itself. Table 28.2 on page 971 also provides the equivalent graphics option or device parameter. Chapter 9, "Graphics Options and Device Parameters Dictionary," on page 301 contains complete information about the graphics options and device parameters.

Table 28.2   GTESTIT Values Shown in the LOG Window

GTESTIT Value	Equivalent Graphics Option or Device Parameter	Description
Background color=	CBACK=	tells the background color used.
Color1=...Colorn=	COLORS=	lists the default colors list for the device. N is equal to the NCOLORS= value.

GTESTIT Value	Equivalent Graphics Option or Device Parameter	Description
Ratio=	ASPECT=	shows the aspect ratio of the device, which is the ratio of width to height of character cells.
Hsize=	HSIZE=	shows the horizontal size of the area used on the device for the graphics display. The default unit is inches.
Vsize=	VSIZE=	shows the vertical size of the area used on the device for the graphics display. The default unit is inches.

Procedure Syntax

Supports: Output Delivery System (ODS)

PROC GTESTIT <PICTURE=1 | 2 | 3>
    <GOUT=<*libref.*>*output-catalog*>;

PROC GTESTIT Statement

Syntax

PROC GTESTIT <PICTURE=1 | 2 | 3>
    <GOUT=<*libref.*>*output-catalog*>;

Options

GOUT=< *libref.* **>***output-catalog*
    specifies the SAS catalog in which to save the graphics output produced by the GTESTIT procedure. If you omit the libref, SAS/GRAPH looks for the catalog in the temporary library called WORK and creates the catalog if it does not exist.
    See also: "Storing Graphics Output in SAS Catalogs" on page 49

PICTURE=1 | 2 | 3
PIC=1 | 2 | 3
    indicates the number of the test pattern to display. By default, all three display. If you include more than one PICTURE= option, the GTESTIT procedure displays only the last picture you specify.
    Values for PICTURE= are

1
    shows available colors and patterns, line types, and fills.

2
    shows the test pattern for continuous drawing ability.

3

shows the test pattern for drawing polygons, ellipses, and justified text.

Examples

Example 1: Testing a GOPTIONS Statement

Features:

GOPTIONS statement

GTESTIT procedure

Sample library member: GR28N01

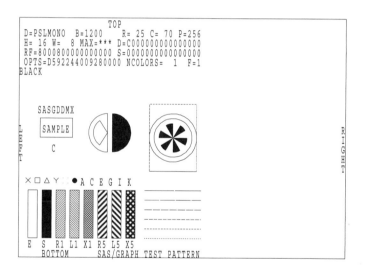

This example illustrates how you can use the GTESTIT procedure to confirm the settings specified on a GOPTIONS statement. In this example, the GOPTIONS statement enlarges the size of the elements in the graphics output by decreasing the number of columns from the default number of columns for the device, resets the font to the default, and specifies a limited colors list.

Set the graphics environment. HPOS= selects 45 columns. VPOS= selects 25 rows. FTEXT= resets the font to the default font. COLORS= can determine the colors displayed in picture 1 and listed in the LOG, and the value of NCOLORS=.

```
goptions hpos=45
         vpos=25
         ftext=
         colors=(blue red green);
```

Display the first picture of the GTESTIT procedure.

```
proc gtestit picture=1;
run;
quit;
```

CHAPTER
29

The G3D Procedure

Overview

The G3D procedure produces three-dimensional graphs that plot one vertical variable (z) for a position on a plane that is specified by two horizontal variables (x and y). The coordinates of each point correspond to the values of three numeric variable values in an observation of the input data set. The observation may contain values in the form $z=f(x,y)$ or independent values such as the altitude at a given longitude and latitude.

You can use the G3D procedure to

☐ produce surface plots or scatter plots

☐ examine the shape of your data

☐ observe data trends in a scatter plot without having a complete grid of x and y variable values

□ produce scatter plots in which size, shape, or color represents a data class or the value of a fourth variable.

About Surface Plots

Surface plots show the three-dimensional shape of your data and are useful for examining data trends. The plots represent the shape of the surface that is described by the values of two horizontal variables, x and y, and a third vertical variable, z. The values of the horizontal variables are plotted on x and y axes, which form a horizontal plane. The values of the vertical variable are plotted on a z axis, rising above that plane to form a three-dimensional surface.

Figure 29.1 on page 976 shows an example of a surface plot that uses all default settings for the plot. The axes are scaled to include the maximum and minimum values for each of the plotted variables x, y, and z. Each variable's value range is divided into three even intervals, which form the major axes tick marks, and the axes are labeled with the names of the plotted variables or associated labels. The horizontal plane formed by the x and y axes is rotated 70° around the z axis and also tilted 70° toward you, and the plot is colored with the colors that are defined in the current colors list.

Figure 29.1   Sample G3D Surface Plot (GR29N01)

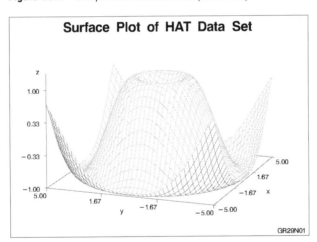

The program for this plot is shown in Example 1 on page 994. For more information on producing surface plots, see "PLOT Statement" on page 981.

About Scatter Plots

Scatter plots are three-dimensional plots that are similar to surface plots, but they represent the data as points instead of surfaces. Scatter plots show trends or concentrations in the data by classifying the data by size, color, shape, or a combination of these features. As with surface plots, the values of the x and y variables in scatter plots form a horizontal plane, and the values of the z variable rise above that plane. Rather than forming a surface, however, the values of the z variable are represented as individual symbols that are connected to the horizontal plane with lines called *needles*. Optionally, you can suppress the needles.

Figure 29.2 on page 977 shows a simple scatter plot. As with surface plots, default settings for scatter plots scale the axes to include the maximum and minimum values for each of the plotted variables x, y, and z, and divide each variable's value range into three even intervals to form the major axes tick marks. Default settings also rotate the horizontal plane 70° around the z axis and tilt it 70° toward you, label each axis with the name of the plotted variable or an associated label, and color the plot with colors that are defined in the current colors list. The default settings also add reference lines to the horizontal plane to mark the major x and y axes tick marks, and represent each data point with a pyramid, which is connected to the horizontal plane with a needle.

Figure 29.2 Sample G3D Scatter Plot (GR29N04)

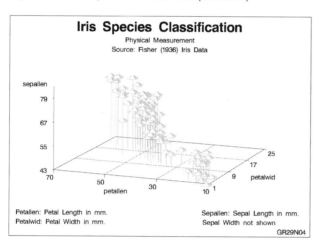

The program for this plot is shown in Example 4 on page 998. For more information on producing scatter plots, see "SCATTER Statement" on page 985.

Concepts

Parts of a Three-dimensional Plot

Figure 29.3   G3D Procedure Terms

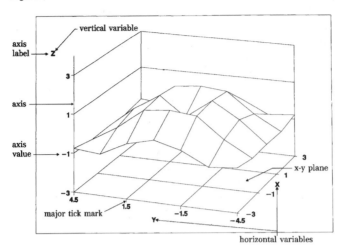

About the Input Data Set

The G3D procedure requires data sets that include three numeric variables: two horizontal variables plotted on the x and y axes that define an x-y plane, and a vertical variable plotted on the z axis rising from the { it x-y} plane.

Data for Surface Plots

For surface plots, the observations in the input data set should form an evenly spaced grid of horizontal (x and y) values and exactly one vertical (z) value for each of these combinations. For example, data that contains 5 distinct values for x and 10 distinct values for y should be part of a data set that contains 50 observations with values for x, y, and z.

Only one z point is plotted for each combination of x and y. For example, you cannot draw a sphere using the PLOT statement. If there is more than one observation for a combination of x and y in the data set, only the last such point is used.

For the G3D procedure to produce a satisfactory surface plot, the data set must contain nonmissing z values for at least 50 percent of the grid cells. When the G3D procedure cannot produce a satisfactory surface plot because of missing z values, SAS/GRAPH issues a warning message and a graph may not be produced. To correct this problem, process the data set with the G3GRID procedure and use the processed data set as the input data set for G3D. The G3GRID procedure interpolates the necessary values to produce a data set with nonmissing z values for every combination of x and y. The G3GRID procedure can also smooth data for use with the G3D procedure. See Chapter 30, "The G3GRID Procedure," on page 1007 for more information on the G3GRID procedure.

Data for Scatter Plots

An input data set for scatter plots must include at least two observations that contain different values for each of the three variables that are specified in the plot request so that the G3D procedure can scale the axes. If the data set does not meet these requirements, SAS/GRAPH software issues an error message and no graph is produced.

For scatter plots, only one z value is plotted for a combination of x and y. For example, you cannot draw a sphere using the SCATTER statement. If there is more than one observation for a combination of x and y in the data set, only the last point is used. See "Simulating an Overlaid Scatter Plot" on page 991 for information on producing scatter plots with more than one vertical value for each *x,y* combination.

Changing Data Ranges

By default for both surface plots and scatter plots, the range of the *z* axis is defined by the minimum and maximum *z* values in the input data set. Restrict or expand the range of the *z* axis by using the ZMIN= and ZMAX= options in the PLOT or SCATTER statement. To restrict the range of an *x* or *y* axis, use a WHERE statement in the PROC step or a WHERE or IF statement in a DATA step to create a subset of the data set.

Note: AXIS and LEGEND definitions are not supported by the G3D procedure. Use the Annotate facility or TITLE, FOOTNOTE, and NOTE statements to produce legends, tick mark values, and axis labels. See "About Controlling the Axes" on page 980 and "SCATTER Statement" on page 985 for information on controlling axis labels and tick mark values with PLOT statement and SCATTER statement options. △

About Rotating and Tilting the Plot

For both surface plots and scatter plots, you can rotate the *x-y* plane about the *z* axis, or tilt the plot toward you. When you rotate a plot, you can view data from any angle around the three-dimensional graph. This is useful for bringing into view data points that were previously hidden by other data points on a plot. Tilting a plot enables you to accentuate the location of data points.

Figure 29.4 on page 979 shows how rotating and tilting can change the viewing angle of a graph.

Note: At certain combinations of tilt and rotation angles, the tick mark values may overlap. △

Figure 29.4 Rotating and Tilting a Graph

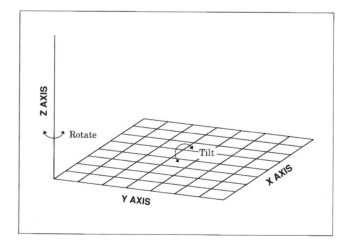

About Controlling the Axes

Because the relationship between a plot's surface and the actual data values can be difficult to interpret, you can improve a graph by changing the number of tick marks on the axes or restricting the range of the vertical (z) variable.

The G3D procedure does not support AXIS definitions; however, you can use PLOT or SCATTER statement options to

□ suppress the axes

□ suppress axis labels

□ suppress tick mark values

□ specify the number of tick marks

□ specify minimum and maximum values for the z axis

□ specify whether grid lines connect axis tick marks.

You can also change the font and height of axis labels and axis values by specifying the desired font and height with the FTEXT= and HTEXT= options on a GOPTIONS statement.

For information on how to reverse the values on an axis, see "Reversing Values on an Axis" on page 992.

Procedure Syntax

Requirements: At least one PLOT or SCATTER statement is required.

Global statements: FOOTNOTE, TITLE

Reminder: The procedure can include the BY, FORMAT, LABEL, NOTE, and WHERE statements.

Supports: Output Delivery System (ODS)

PROC G3D <DATA=*input-data-set*>
  <ANNOTATE=*Annotate-data-set*>
  <GOUT=<*libref.*>*output-catalog*>;
  PLOT *plot-request</options>*;
  SCATTER *plot-request</option(s)>*;

PROC G3D Statement

Identifies the data set that contains the plot variables. Optionally specifies annotation and an output catalog.

Requirements: An input data set is required.

Syntax

PROC G3D <DATA=*input-data-set*>
  <ANNOTATE=*Annotate-data-set*>

<GOUT=<*libref.*>*output-catalog*>;

Options

ANNOTATE=*Annotate-data-set*
ANNO=*Annotate-data-set*
  specifies a data set to annotate all of the graphs that are produced by the G3D
  procedure. To annotate individual graphs, use ANNOTATE= in the action statement.
  See also: Chapter 10, "The Annotate Data Set," on page 403

DATA=*input-data-set*
  specifies the SAS data set that contains the variables to plot. By default, the
  procedure uses the most recently created SAS data set.
  See also: "SAS Data Sets" on page 25 "About the Input Data Set" on page 978

GOUT=< *libref.* **>***output-catalog*
  specifies the SAS catalog in which to save the graphics output that is produced by the
  G3D procedure. If you omit the libref, SAS/GRAPH the catalog if it does not exist.
  See also: "Storing Graphics Output in SAS Catalogs" on page 49

PLOT Statement

**Creates three-dimensional surface plots using values of three numeric variables from the input
data set.**

Requirements: Exactly one plot request is required.
Global statements: FOOTNOTE, TITLE

Description   The PLOT statement specifies one plot request that identifies the three
numeric variables to plot. This statement automatically

  □ scales the axes to include the maximum and minimum values for each of the
    plotted variables *x*, *y*, and *z*

  □ divides the value range for each variable into three even intervals, which are
    represented by four major tick marks on the axis

  □ rotates the *x*-*y* plane 70° around the *z* axis and tilts it 70° toward you, labeling
    each axis with the name of the plotted variable or an associated label

  □ colors the plot with colors that are defined in the current colors list: axis labels
    and tick mark labels display in the first color from the list, axes display in the
    second color, the top of the surface plot displays in the third color, and the bottom
    of the surface plot (if visible) displays in the fourth color.

You can use statement options to modify any of the three plot axes as well as the
general appearance of the graph, control the viewing angle, and specify characteristics
for reference lines.

In addition, you can use global statements to add text to the graph, and an Annotate
data set to enhance the plot.

Syntax

  PLOT *plot-request* <*/option(s)*>;

plot-request must be

y*x=z

option(s) can be one or more options from any or all of the following categories:

□ appearance options:

ANNOTATE=*Annotate-data-set*

CBOTTOM=*bottom-surface-color*

CTOP=*top-surface-color*

ROTATE=*angle-list*

SIDE

TILT=*angle-list*

XYTYPE=1 | 2 | 3

□ axes options:

CAXIS=*axis-color*

CTEXT=*text-color*

GRID

NOAXIS | NOAXES

NOLABEL

XTICKNUM=*number-of-ticks*

YTICKNUM=*number-of-ticks*

ZMAX=*max-value*

ZMIN=*min-value*

ZTICKNUM=*number-of-ticks*

□ catalog entry description options:

DESCRIPTION='*entry-description*'

NAME='*entry-name*'

Required Arguments

y*x=z

specifies three numeric variables from the input data set:

y

is one of the variables that is plotted on the horizontal (*x-y*) plane.

x

is another of the variables that is plotted on the horizontal (*x-y*) plane.

z

is the variable that is plotted on the vertical (*z*) axis.

Options

Options in a PLOT statement affect all graphs that are produced by that statement. You can specify as many options as you want and list them in any order.

ANNOTATE=*Annotate-data-set*
ANNO=*Annotate-data-set*

specifies a data set to annotate plots that are produced by the PLOT statement.

See also: Chapter 10, "The Annotate Data Set," on page 403

CAXIS=*axis-color*
> specifies a color for axis lines and tick marks. By default, axes are displayed in the second color in the current colors list.

CBOTTOM=*bottom-surface-color*
> specifies a color for the bottom of the plot surface. By default, the bottom surface is displayed in the fourth color in the current colors list.
>
> **Featured in:**   Example 2 on page 996

CTEXT=*text-color*
> specifies a color for all text on the axes, including tick mark values and axis labels. If you omit this option, a color specification is searched for in this order:
>
> 1 the CTEXT= option in a GOPTIONS statement
>
> 2 the default, the first color in the colors list.

CTOP=*top-surface-color*
> specifies a color for the top of the plot surface. By default, the top surface is displayed in the third color in the current colors list.
>
> **Featured in:**   Example 2 on page 996

DESCRIPTION=*'entry-description'*
DES=*'entry-description'*
> specifies the description of the catalog entry for the chart. The maximum length for *entry-description* is 240 characters. The description does not appear on the chart. By default, the procedure assigns a description of the form PLOT OF *y*x=z*, where *y*x=z* is the request that is specified in the PLOT statement.

GRID
> draws reference lines at the major tick marks on all axes.
>
> **Featured in:**   Example 2 on page 996

NAME=*'entry-name'*
> specifies the name of the catalog entry for the graph. The maximum length for *entry-name* is 8 characters. The default name is G3D. If the specified name duplicates the name of an existing entry, SAS/GRAPH software adds a number to the duplicate name to create a unique entry, for example, G3D1.

NOAXIS
NOAXES
> specifies that a plot have no axes, axis labels, or tick mark values.

NOLABEL
> specifies that a plot have no axis labels or tick mark values. Use this option if you want to generate axis labels and tick mark values with an Annotate data set.

ROTATE=*angle-list*
> specifies one or more angles at which to rotate the *x-y* plane about the perpendicular *z* axis. The units for *angle-list* are degrees. By default, ROTATE=70. *Angle-list* is either an explicit list of values, or a starting and an ending value with an interval increment, or a combination of both forms:
>
> *n* <...*n*>
>
> *n* TO *n* <BY *increment*>
>
> *n* <...*n*> TO *n* <BY *increment* > <*n* <...*n*> >
>
> The values specified in *angle-list* can be negative or positive and can be larger than 360°. For example, a rotation angle of 45° can also be expressed as

```
rotate=405
rotate=-315
```

You can specify a sequence of angles to produce separate graphs for each angle. The angles that are specified in the ROTATE= option are paired with any angles that are specified with the TILT= option. If one option contains fewer values than the other, the last value in the shorter list is paired with the remaining values in the longer list.

See also: TILT= option on page 984

Featured in: Example 2 on page 996

SIDE

produces a surface graph with a side wall.

Featured in: Example 3 on page 997

TILT=*angle-list*

specifies one or more angles at which to tilt the graph toward you. The units for *angle-list* are degrees. By default, TILT=70. *Angle-list* is either an explicit list of values, or a starting and an ending value with an interval increment, or a combination of both forms:

   n <...*n*>

   n TO *n* <BY *increment*>

   n <...*n*> TO *n* <BY *increment* > <*n* <...*n*> >
   The values that are specified in *angle-list* must be 0 through 90.

You can specify a sequence of angles to produce separate graphs for each angle. The angles that are specified in the TILT= option are paired with any angles that are specified with the ROTATE= option. If one option contains fewer values than the other, the last value in the shorter list is paired with the remaining values in the longer list.

See also: ROTATE= option on page 983

Featured in: Example 3 on page 997

XTICKNUM=*number-of-ticks*
YTICKNUM=*number-of-ticks*
ZTICKNUM=*number-of-ticks*

specify the number of major tick marks that are located on a plot's x, y, or z axis, respectively. The value for n must be 2 or greater. By default, XTICKNUM=4, YTICKNUM=4, and ZTICKNUM=4.

Featured in: Example 2 on page 996

XYTYPE=1 | 2 | 3

specifies the direction of lines that are used to represent the surface. XYTYPE=1 displays the surface by using lines that represent y axis values. That is, it only draws lines that are parallel to the x axis. XYTYPE=2 displays the surface by using lines that represent x axis values, and draws only lines that are parallel to the y axis. XYTYPE=3 displays the surface by using lines that represent values for both the x and y axes, and creates a fishnet-like surface. By default, XYTYPE=3. See Figure 29.5 on page 985 for an example of the effect of XYTYPE= on the appearance of the surface.

ZMAX=*max-value*
ZMIN=*min-value*

specify the maximum and minimum values that are displayed on a plot's z axis. By default, the z axis is defined by the minimum and maximum z values that are in the data set. You can use the ZMIN= and ZMAX= options to extend the z axis beyond this range. The value specified by ZMAX= must be greater than that specified by ZMIN=.

If you specify a ZMAX= or ZMIN= value within the actual range of the z variable values, the plot's data values are clipped at the specified level. For example, if the minimum z value in the data set is 0 and you specify ZMIN=1, the values of z that are less than 1 will be plotted as if they are 1.

Featured in: Example 2 on page 996

Changing the Surface Appearance

Use the XYTYPE= option to change the appearance of the plot surface. This option lets you select the direction of the lines that form the surface plot. Figure 29.5 on page 985 shows examples of each type of plot surface.

Figure 29.5 Surface Appearance for Different XYTYPE= Values

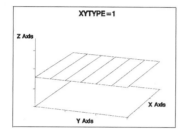
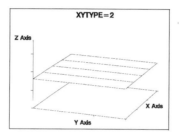
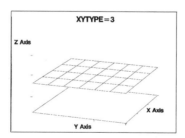

SCATTER Statement

Creates three-dimensional scatter plots using values of three numeric variables from the input data set.

Requirements: Exactly one plot request is required.

Global statements: FOOTNOTE, TITLE

Alias: SCAT

Description   The SCATTER statement specifies one plot request that identifies the three numeric variables to plot. This statement automatically

□ scales the axes to include the maximum and minimum values for each of the plotted variables x, y, and z

□ divides the range for each variable into three even intervals that are represented by four major tick marks on the axis

□ uses reference lines to mark the major tick marks on the *x* and *y* axes

□ rotates the *x-y* plane 70° around the *z* axis and tilts it 70° toward you, labeling each axis with the name of the plotted variable or an associated label

□ colors the plot with colors that are defined in the current colors list: axis labels and tick mark labels display in the first color from the colors list, axes in the second color, and data points in the third color

□ represents each data point with a pyramid that is connected to the horizontal plane with a needle.

You can use statement options to modify any of the three plot axes as well as the general appearance of the graph, control the viewing angle, and specify characteristics for reference lines. In addition, if the needles drawn from the data points to the base plane complicate a graph, you can suppress them.

You can use global statements to add text to the graph, and an Annotate data set to enhance the plot.

Syntax

SCATTER *plot-request* </ *option(s)*>;

plot-request must be

y*x=z

option(s) can be one or more options from any or all of the following categories:

□ appearance options:

ANNOTATE=*Annotate-data-set*

COLOR='*data-point-color*' | *data-point-color-variable*

NONEEDLE

ROTATE=*angle-list*

SHAPE='*symbol-name*' | *shape-variable*

SIZE=*symbol-size* | *size-variable*

TILT=*angle-list*

□ axes options:

CAXIS=*axis-color*

CTEXT=*text-color*

GRID

NOAXIS | NOAXES

NOLABEL

XTICKNUM=*number-of-ticks*

YTICKNUM=*number-of-ticks*

ZMAX=*max-value*

ZMIN=*min-value*

ZTICKNUM=*number-of-ticks*

□ catalog entry description options:

DESCRIPTION='*entry-description*'

NAME='*entry-name*'

Required Arguments

y*x=z
  specifies three numeric variables from the input data set:

  y
    is one of the variables that is plotted on the horizontal (*x-y*) plane.

  x
    is another of the variables that is plotted on the horizontal (*x-y*) plane.

  z
    is the variable that is plotted on the vertical (*z*) axis.

  The SCATTER statement does not require a full grid of observations for the horizontal variable.

Options

  Options in a SCATTER statement affect all graphs that are produced by that statement. You can specify as many options as you want and list them in any order.

ANNOTATE=*Annotate-data-set*
ANNO=*Annotate-data-set*
  specifies a data set to annotate plots that are produced by the SCATTER statement.
  See also: Chapter 10, "The Annotate Data Set," on page 403

CAXIS=*axis-color*
  specifies a color for axis lines and tick marks. By default, axes display in the second color in the colors list.
  Featured in: Example 6 on page 1003

COLOR='*data-point-color*' | *data-point-color-variable*
  specifies a color name or a character variable in the input data set whose values are color names. These color values determine the color or colors of the shapes that represent a plot's data points. Color values must be valid color names for the device that is used. By default, plot shapes display in the third color in the current colors list.

  If you specify COLOR='*data-point-color*', all shapes are drawn in that color. For example, the procedure uses BLUE for all graph shapes when you specify

```
color='blue'
```

  If you specify COLOR=*data-point-color-variable*, the color of the symbol is determined by the value of the color variable for that observation. For example, the procedure uses the value of the variable CLASS as the color for each data point shape when you specify

```
color=class
```

  Using COLOR=*data-point-color-variable* enables you to assign different colors to the shapes to classify data.
  Featured in: Example 5 on page 999

CTEXT=*text-color*
  specifies a color for all text on the axes, including tick mark values and axis labels. If you omit this option, a color specification is searched for in this order:

  1 the CTEXT= option in a GOPTIONS statement
  2 the default, the first color in the colors list.

DESCRIPTION='*entry-description*'
DES='*entry-description*'

specifies the description of the catalog entry for the chart. The maximum length for *entry-description* is 40 characters. The description does not appear on the chart. By default, the procedure assigns a description of the form SCATTER OF $y*x=z$, where $y*x=z$ is the request that is specified in the SCATTER statement.

GRID

draws reference lines at the major tick marks on all axes.

Featured in: Example 5 on page 999

NAME='*entry-name*'

specifies the name of the catalog entry for the graph. The maximum length for *entry-name* is eight characters. The default name is G3D. If the specified name duplicates the name of an existing entry, SAS/GRAPH software adds a number to the duplicate name to create a unique entry, for example, G3D1.

NOAXIS
NOAXES

specifies that a plot have no axes, axis labels, or tick mark values.

NOLABEL

specifies that a plot have no axis labels or tick mark values. Use this option if you want to generate axis labels and tick mark values with an Annotate data set.

NONEEDLE

specifies that a plot have no lines that connect the shapes representing data points to the x-y plane. The NONEEDLE option option has no effect when SHAPE='PILLAR' or SHAPE='PRISM'.

Featured in: Example 5 on page 999

ROTATE=<i>angle-list</i>

specifies one or more angles at which to rotate the x-y plane about the perpendicular z axis. The units for angle-list are degrees. By default, ROTATE=70. *Angle-list* is either an explicit list of values, or a starting and an ending value with an interval increment, or a combination of both forms:

n <...*n*>

n TO *n* <BY *increment*>

n <...*n*> TO *n* <BY *increment* > <*n* <...*n*> >

The values specified in *angle-list* can be negative or positive and can be larger than 360°. For example, a rotation angle of 45° can also be expressed

```
rotate=405
rotate=-315
```

You can specify a sequence of angles to produce separate graphs for each angle. The angles that are specified in the ROTATE= option are paired with any angles that are specified with the TILT= option. If one option contains fewer values than the other, the last value in the shorter list is paired with the remaining values in the longer list.

See also: TILT= option on page 990.

Featured in: Example 6 on page 1003

SHAPE='*symbol-name*' | *shape-variable*

specifies a symbol name or a character variable whose values are symbol names. Symbols represent a scatter plot's data points. By default, SHAPE='PYRAMID'.

Values for *symbol-name* are

BALLOON

CLUB

CROSS

CUBE

CYLINDER

DIAMOND

FLAG

HEART

PILLAR

POINT

PRISM

PYRAMID

SPADE

SQUARE

STAR.

Figure 29.6 on page 989 illustrates these symbol types with needles.

Figure 29.6   Scatter Plot Symbols

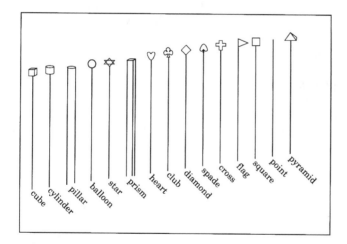

If you specify SHAPE='*symbol-name*', all data points are drawn in that shape. For example, the procedure draws all data points as balloons when you specify

```
shape='balloon'
```

If you specify SHAPE=*shape-variable*, the shape of the data point is determined by the value of the shape variable for that observation. For example, the procedure uses the value of the variable CLASS for a particular observation as the shape for that data point when you specify

```
shape=class
```

Using SHAPE=*shape-variable* enables you to assign different shapes to the data points to classify data.

Featured in: Example 5 on page 999

SIZE=*symbol-size* | *size-variable*

specifies either a constant or a numeric variable, the values of which determine the size of symbol shapes on the scatter plot.

If you specify SIZE=*symbol-size*, all data points are drawn in that size. For example, if you specify SIZE=3, the procedure draws all symbol shapes three times the normal size. By default, SIZE=1.0. The units are in default symbol size.

If you specify SIZE=*size-variable*, the size of the data point is determined by the value of the size variable for that observation. For example, when you specify SIZE=CLASS, the procedure uses the value of the variable CLASS for each observation as the size of that data point. If you use SIZE=*size-variable*, you can assign different sizes to the data points to classify data.

Featured in: Example 6 on page 1003

TILT=*angle-list*

specifies one or more angles at which to tilt the graph toward you. The units for *angle-list* are degrees. By default, TILT=70. *Angle-list* is either an explicit list of values, or a starting and an ending value with an interval increment, or a combination of both forms:

n <...*n*>

n TO *n* <BY *increment*>

n <...*n*> TO *n* <BY *increment* > <*n* <...*n*> >

The values that are specified in *angle-list* must be 0 through 90.

You can specify a sequence of angles to produce separate graphs for each angle. The angles that are specified in the TILT= option are paired with any angles that are specified with the ROTATE= option. If one option contains fewer values than the other, the last value in the shorter list is paired with the remaining values in the longer list.

See also: ROTATE= option on page 988

XTICKNUM=*number-of-ticks*
YTICKNUM=*number-of-ticks*
ZTICKNUM=*number-of-ticks*

specify the number of major tick marks that are located on a plot's x,{ it y}, or z axis, respectively. The value for n must be 2 or greater. By default, XTICKNUM=4, YTICKNUM=4, and ZTICKNUM=4.

Featured in: Example 6 on page 1003

ZMAX=*max-value*
ZMIN=*min-value*

specify the maximum and minimum values that are displayed on a plot's z axis. By default, the z axis is defined by the minimum and maximum z values in the data. You can use the ZMIN= and ZMAX= options to extend the z axis beyond this range. The value that is specified by ZMAX= must be greater than that specified by ZMIN=. If you specify a ZMAX= or ZMIN= value within the actual range of the z variable values, the plot's data values are clipped at the specified level.

Featured in: Example 6 on page 1003

Changing the Appearance of the Points

Use the COLOR=, SHAPE=, and SIZE= options to change the appearance of your scatter plot or to classify data using color, shape, size, or any combination of these features. Figure 29.6 on page 989 illustrates the shape names that you can specify in the SHAPE= option.

For example, to make all of the data points red balloons at twice the normal size, use

```
scatter y*x=z /color='red' shape='balloon' size=2;
```

To size your points according to the values of the variable TYPE in your input data set, use

```
scatter y*x=z / size=type;
```

For an example, see Example 5 on page 999.

Simulating an Overlaid Scatter Plot

You can approximate an overlaid scatter plot by graphing multiple values for the vertical (*z*) variables for a single (*x, y*) position in a single scatter plot. To do this, add a small value to the value of one of the horizontal variables (*x* or *y*) to give the observation a slightly different (*x, y*) position. Thus, you enable the procedure to plot both values of the vertical (*z*) variable. Represent each different vertical (*z*) variable with a different symbol, size, or color. The resulting plot appears to be multiple plots overlaid on the same axes.

For example, suppose you want to graph a data set that contains two values for the vertical variable Z for each combination of variables X and Y. You could produce the original data set with a DATA step like this:

```
data planes;
    input x y z shape $;
    datalines;
1 1 1 PRISM
1 2 1 PRISM
1 3 1 PRISM
2 1 1 PRISM
2 2 1 PRISM
2 3 1 PRISM
3 1 1 PRISM
3 2 1 PRISM
3 3 1 PRISM
1 1 2 BALLOON
1 2 2 BALLOON
1 3 2 BALLOON
2 1 2 BALLOON
2 2 2 BALLOON
2 3 2 BALLOON
3 1 2 BALLOON
3 2 2 BALLOON
3 3 2 BALLOON
;
```

The SHAPE variable is assigned a different value for each different Z value for a single combination of X and Y values.

Ordinarily, the SCATTER statement only plots the Z value for the last observation for a single combination of X and Y. However, you can use a DATA step to assign a slightly different *x, y* position to all observations where Z is greater than 1:

```
data planes2;
    set planes;
    if z > 1 then x = x + .000001;
run;
```

Then you can use a SCATTER statement to produce a plot like the one in Figure 29.7 on page 992:

```
proc g3d data=planes2;
    scatter x*y=z / zmin=0 shape=shape;
run;
quit;
```

Figure 29.7 Simulated Overlaid Scatter Plot

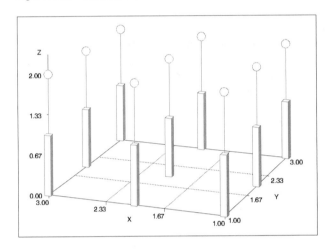

Reversing Values on an Axis

Although you can use the SCATTER statement's ROTATE option to alter the view of a plot and therefore the general orientation to axes values, you cannot use SCATTER statement options to reverse axis values for one of the plot variables. To do this, you can multiply that variable's values by -1 to reverse the values themselves, which has the result of reversing the axis when those values are used to generate a plot. You should then use PROC FORMAT to define a format that displays the variable's values as they exist in the original data.

For example, the following code generates the scatter plot shown in Figure 29.8 on page 993:

```
data original;
    input y x z;
    datalines;
-1.15 1 .01
-1.00 2 .02
 1.20 3 .03
 1.25 4 .04
 1.50 5 .05
 2.10 1 .06
 2.15 2 .07
 2.20 3 .08
 2.25 4 .09
 2.30 5 .10

;
```

```
title1 'Default Y Axis Order';

/* default Y axis order */
proc g3d data=original;
   scatter y * x = z;
run;
```

Figure 29.8 Default Y-axis Order

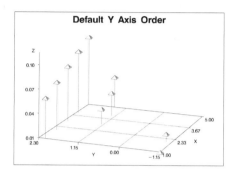

To reverse the Y axis in the plot that is shown in Figure 29.8 on page 993, you can write a DATA step like the following to reverse the Y values and, therefore, reverse the Y axis when the values are plotted:

```
data minus_y;
   set original;
   y=-y;
run;
```

The previous code creates the MINUS_Y data set by reading the ORIGINAL data set, and then multiplying the values of variable Y by -1. Although plotting Y values from the MINUS_Y data set would reverse values on the Y axis, it would misrepresent the original data. Such a plot would label the axis with the negative-Y values. You can correct the problem by using PROC FORMAT to display Y values as they are stored in the ORIGINAL data set:

```
proc format;
  picture reverse
     low - < 0  = '09.00'
     0 < - high = '09.00' (prefix='-')
     0          = '09.00';
run;
```

Here, the PICTURE statement defines a picture format named REVERSE, which you can refer to in DATA and PROC steps by using the name followed by a period. A picture format is a template for printing numbers. The '09.00' specifications are *digit selectors* that indicate which digits or columns in the variable values will display in output; columns that do not have a specified digit selector will not be displayed in output. Thus, a picture format for displaying the values of variable Y needs a column for a minus sign, a column for units, and two columns for decimals. The digit selector 0 specifies that no leading zeros will display in a column, and the digit selector 9 specifies that a leading zero will display in a column.

The PICTURE statement defines this new picture format for three data ranges. The lowest value in the data up to but not including zero will display with no prefix, which means negative values will display without a minus sign. All values above (but not including) zero to the highest value in the data will be displayed with the specified prefix, which in this case is a minus sign. Because zero is excluded from both ranges, it is assigned its own picture with no prefix.

You can now assign the REVERSE format to the Y values from the MINUS_Y data set and use Y to generate a scatter plot. The resulting plot displays Y's negative values without a prefix, and its positive values display with a minus sign prefix. This effectively represents Y values as they are stored internally in the ORIGINAL data set, thus correcting the data misrepresentation that results from multiplying Y by -1.

The following code generates the scatter plot shown in Figure 29.9 on page 994:

```
title1 'Reverse Y Axis Order';

/* reverses order of default Y axis */
proc g3d data=minus_y;
    format y reverse.;
    scatter y * x = z;
run;
quit;
```

Figure 29.9 Reverse Y-axis Order

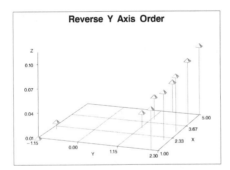

Examples

Example 1: Generating a Default Surface Plot

Procedure features:
   PLOT statement
Sample library member: GR29N01

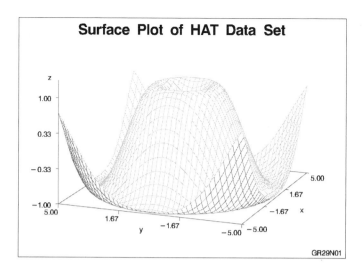

This example shows a surface plot that reveals the shape of a generated data set named HAT. The PLOT statement in this example relies entirely on procedure defaults. The axes are scaled to include all data values and are labeled with the names of the axes variables. The axes major tick marks are divided into three even intervals, and the horizontal plane is rotated 70° around the z axis and tilted 70° toward you. The plot is displayed with the colors that the GOPTIONS statement defines for the colors list.

Assign the libref and set the graphics environment.

```
libname reflib 'SAS-data-library';
goptions reset=global gunit=pct border cback=white
         colors=(black blue green red)
         ftext=swiss ftitle=swissb htitle=6 htext=4;
```

Create the data set. REFLIB.HAT is generated data that produces a symmetric surface pattern, which is useful for illustrating the PLOT statement and its options.

```
data reflib.hat;
   do x=-5 to 5 by 0.25;
      do y=-5 to 5 by 0.25;
         z=sin(sqrt(x*x+y*y));
         output;
      end;
   end;
run;
```

Define title and footnote.

```
title 'Surface Plot of HAT Data Set';
footnote j=r 'GR29N01 ';
```

Generate the surface plot.

```
proc g3d data=reflib.hat;
   plot y*x=z;
```

```
run;
quit;
```

Example 2: Rotating a Surface Plot

Procedure Features
PLOT statement options:

>CBOTTOM=
>CTOP=
>GRID
>ROTATE=
>YTICKNUM=
>ZMAX=
>ZMIN=
>ZTICKNUM=

Data set: REFLIB.HAT on page 995
Sample library member: GR29N02

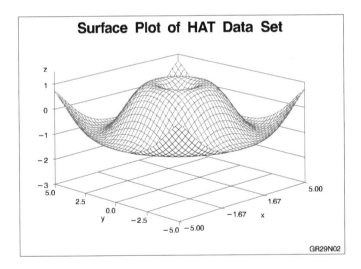

This example rotates the surface plot that is shown in Example 4 on page 998 and enhances its axes by adding reference lines and increasing the number of tick marks on the *y* and *z* axes. It also raises the plot above the horizontal *x-y* plane.

Assign the libref and set the graphics environment.

```
libname reflib 'SAS-data-library';
goptions reset=global gunit=pct border cback=white
         colors=(black blue green red)
         ftext=swiss ftitle=swissb htitle=6 htext=4;
```

Define title and footnote.

```
title 'Surface Plot of HAT Data Set';
footnote j=r 'GR29N02 ';
```

Generate the surface plot. GRID draws reference lines for all x, y, and z axis tick marks. ROTATE= specifies a rotation angle of 45°. CTOP= and CBOTTOM= change the colors of the plot's top and bottom surfaces. YTICKNUM= and ZTICKNUM= specify the number of tick marks for the y and z axes. ZMIN= and ZMAX= specify minimum and maximum values for the z axis. Specifying a minimum value that is below the minimum value in the data effectively raises the plot above the horizontal plane.

```
proc g3d data=reflib.hat;
   plot y*x=z / grid
               rotate=45
               ctop=red
               cbottom=black
               yticknum=5
               zticknum=5
               zmin=-3
               zmax=1;
run;
quit;
```

Example 3: Tilting Surface Plot

Procedure features:
    PLOT statement options:
        SIDE
        TILT=
Data set: REFLIB.HAT on page 995
Sample library member: GR29N03

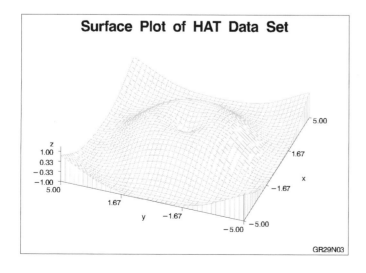

This example modifies that shown in Example 1 on page 994 by tilting the surface plot 15° toward you and adding a side wall.

Assign the libref and set the graphics environment.

```
libname reflib 'SAS-data-library';
goptions reset=global gunit=pct border cback=white
         colors=(black blue green red)
         ftext=swiss ftitle=swissb htitle=6 htext=4;
```

Define title and footnote.

```
title 'Surface Plot of HAT Data Set';
footnote j=r 'GR29N03 ';
```

Generate the surface plot. SIDE draws a side wall for the graph. TILT= specifies a tilt angle of 15° for the plot, which doesn't affect the default rotation of 70°.

```
proc g3d data=reflib.hat;
   plot y*x=z / side
                tilt=15;
run;
quit;
```

Example 4: Generating a Simple Scatter Plot

Procedure features:
SCATTER statement
Sample library member: GR29N04

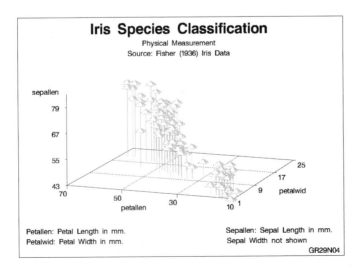

This example shows a scatter plot that examines the results of measuring the petal length, petal width, and sepal length for the flowers of three species of iris. The SCATTER statement in this example relies entirely on procedure defaults, which scale the axes to include all data values, label the axes with the names of the axes variables, divide the axes into three even intervals, rotate the horizontal plane $70°$ around the z axis and tilt it $70°$ toward you, and display the plot with the colors that are defined for the colors list. The data points are represented by pyramids, which are connected to the horizontal plane with needles.

Assign the libref and set the graphics environment.

```
libname reflib 'SAS-data-library';
goptions reset=global gunit=pct border cback=white
         colors=(black blue green red)
         ftext=swiss ftitle=swissb htitle=6 htext=4;
```

Create data set. REFLIB.IRIS contains petal and sepal measurements for the flowers of three iris species, which are identified by species numbers.

```
data reflib.iris;
   input sepallen sepalwid petallen petalwid spec_no;
   datalines;
50 33 14 02 1
64 28 56 22 3
...more data lines...
63 33 60 25 3
53 37 15 02 1
;
```

Define titles and footnotes.

```
title1 'Iris Species Classification';
title2 'Physical Measurement';
title3 'Source: Fisher (1936) Iris Data';
footnote1 j=l '  Petallen: Petal Length in mm.'
          j=r 'Sepallen: Sepal Length in mm.   ';
footnote2 j=l '  Petalwid: Petal Width in mm.'
          j=r 'Sepal Width not shown        ';
footnote3 j=r 'GR29N04 ';
```

Generate a simple scatter plot.

```
proc g3d data=reflib.iris;
   scatter petallen*petalwid=sepallen;
run;
quit;
```

Example 5: Using Shapes in Scatter Plots
Procedure features:

SCATTER statement options:
COLOR=
GRID
NONEEDLE
SHAPE=

Other features:
DATA step
LABEL statement
NOTE statement
Data set: REFLIB.IRIS on page 999
Sample library member: GR29N05

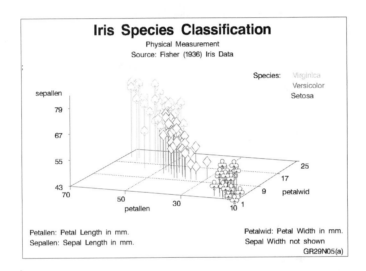

This program modifies that shown in Example 4 on page 998 to use shape symbols and color to distinguish information for various iris species. It also uses NOTE statements to simulate a plot legend.

The program then generates a second plot to modify the first. As shown by the following output, the second plot request suppresses the needles that connect data points to the horizontal plane, and adds reference lines to make it easier to interpret data values. It also labels the plot axes with descriptive text.

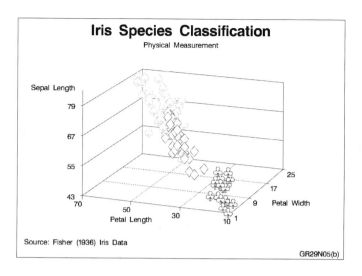

Iris Species Classification
Physical Measurement

Sepal Length

Petal Length

Petal Width

Source: Fisher (1936) Iris Data

GR29N05(b)

Assign the libref and set the graphics environment.

```
libname reflib 'SAS-data-library';
goptions reset=global gunit=pct border cback=white
         colors=(black blue green red)
         ftext=swiss ftitle=swissb htitle=6 htext=4;
```

Create data set. REFLIB.IRIS2 uses a DATA step to read and modify the REFLIB.IRIS data set. The DATA step adds a variable that identifies the iris species. It also adds two additional variables that store shape and color values for each iris species. These shapes and colors will distinguish iris species in the plot.

```
data reflib.iris2;
   set reflib.iris;
   length species $12. colorval $8. shapeval $8.;
   if spec_no=1 then
      do;
         species='setosa';
         shapeval='club';
         colorval='blue';
      end;
   if spec_no=2 then
      do;
         species='versicolor';
         shapeval='diamond';
         colorval='red';
      end;
   if spec_no=3 then
      do;
         species='virginica';
         shapeval='spade';
         colorval='green';
      end;
run;
```

Define titles and footnotes.

```
title1 'Iris Species Classification';
title2 'Physical Measurement';
title3 'Source: Fisher (1936) Iris Data';
footnote1 j=l '  Petallen: Petal Length in mm.'
          j=r 'Petalwid: Petal Width in mm. ';
footnote2 j=l '  Sepallen: Sepal Length in mm.'
          j=r 'Sepal Width not shown       ';
footnote3 j=r 'GR29N05(a) ';
```

Generate the plot. COLOR= specifies the variable that contains color information for the iris species. SHAPE= specifies the variable that contains shape information for the iris species.

```
proc g3d data=reflib.iris2;
   scatter petallen*petalwid=sepallen
        / color=colorval
          shape=shapeval;
```

Create a legend using NOTE statements. The first NOTE statement clears any existing notes. The second NOTE statement identifies the color key used for the different iris species.

```
   note;
   note j=r 'Species:    ' c=green 'Virginica        '
        j=r c=red 'Versicolor      '
        j=r c=blue 'Setosa          ';
run;
```

Define new title and footnotes.

```
title3;
footnote1 j=l '  Source: Fisher (1936) Iris Data';
footnote2 j=r 'GR29N05(b) ';
```

Generate the plot. NONEEDLE suppresses the line drawn from the x-y plane to the plot point. GRID draws reference lines for x, y, and z axis tick marks.

```
proc g3d data=reflib.iris2;
   scatter petallen*petalwid=sepallen
        / noneedle
          grid
          color=colorval
          shape=shapeval;
```

Change the axes labels. To improve axes labels, the LABEL statement associates labels with variable names.

```
   label petallen='Petal Length'
         petalwid='Petal Width'
```

```
              sepallen='Sepal Length';
    run;
    quit;
```

Example 6: Rotating a Scatter Plot

Procedure features:
    SCATTER statement options
        CAXIS=
        ROTATE=
        SIZE=
        XTICKNUM
        YTICKNUM=
        ZMAX=
        ZMIN=
        ZTICKNUM=

Other features: DATA step

Sample library member: GR29N06

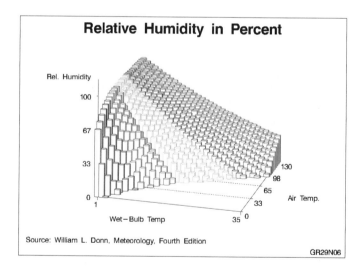

This example produces a scatter plot of humidity data. It uses color to distinguish air temperature ranges. The plot is rotated -15°.

Assign the libref and set the graphics environment.

```
libname reflib 'SAS-data-library';
goptions reset=global gunit=pct border cback=white
        colors=(black blue green red)
        ftext=swiss ftitle=swissb htitle=6 htext=4;
```

Create data set REFLIB.HUMID. The DATA step varies color according to specified air-temperature ranges.

```
data reflib.humid;
   length colorval $ 8.;
   label wtemp='Wet-Bulb Temp';
   label relhum='Rel. Humidity';
   label atemp='   Air Temp.';
   input atemp wtemp relhum;
   if atemp<26 then colorval="blue";
   else if atemp>=26 and atemp<+52 then colorval="red";
   else if atemp>=52 and atemp<+78 then colorval="green";
   else if atemp>=78 and atemp<+104 then colorval="lib";
   else if atemp>104 then colorval="pink   ";
   datalines;
0    1    67
0    2    33
...more data lines...
130  34   29
130  35   28
;
```

Define title and footnotes.

```
title 'Relative Humidity in Percent';
footnote1 j=l '  Source: William L. Donn, Meteorology, Fourth Edition';
footnote2 j=r 'GR29N06 ';
```

Generate the plot. CAXIS= specifies a color for the axis lines and tick marks. ROTATE= specifies a rotation angle for the plot. SIZE= specifies the size of the plot symbols. XTICKNUM=, YTICKNUM=, and ZTICKNUM= specify the number of tick marks for the x, y, and z axes. ZMIN= and ZMAX= specify the minimum and maximum values for the z axis.

```
proc g3d data=reflib.humid;
   scatter atemp*wtemp=relhum
         / shape='pillar'
           color=colorval
           caxis=blue
           rotate=-15
           size=.5
           yticknum=5
           xticknum=2
           zticknum=4
           zmin=0
           zmax=100;
   run;
   quit;
```

References

Fisher, R.A. (1936), "The Use of Multiple Measurements in Taxonomic Problems," *Annals of Eugenics*, 7, 179–188.

Watkins, S.L. (1974), "Algorithm 483, Masked Three-Dimensional Plot Program with Rotations (J6)," in *Collected Algorithms from ACM,* New York: Association for Computing Machinery.

CHAPTER

30

The G3GRID Procedure

Overview

The G3GRID procedure processes an existing SAS data set to create a data set that the G3D or GCONTOUR procedure can use to produce three-dimensional surface or contour plots. The procedure creates a data set whose horizontal (x and y) variable values form a complete grid, and it interpolates the value of the vertical (z) variables for each point on the x-y plane. Using the G3GRID procedure, you can

- create a rectangular grid of interpolated or smoothed values from irregularly spaced observations for use in a three-dimensional surface or contour plot

- complete a rectangular grid of interpolated or smoothed values for an input data set that has an insufficient number of observations to produce a three-dimensional surface or contour plot

- interpolate or smooth noisy data for a three-dimensional graph.

The G3GRID procedure does not produce graphics output. Instead, it produces an output data set that you can use as the input data set for the G3D or GCONTOUR procedure.

Figure 30.1 on page 1008 and Figure 30.2 on page 1008 illustrate the effect of the G3GRID procedure on data.

Figure 30.1 on page 1008 shows a collection of data points, where $z=f(x, y)$. These points are randomly distributed and cannot be displayed with a G3D surface plot, although they can be displayed with a scatter plot.

Figure 30.1   Scatter Plot of Data Set before G3GRID Processing (GR30N01(a))

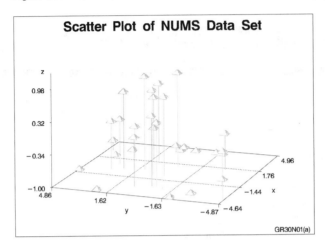

Figure 30.2 on page 1008 shows a surface plot of the data set that is created by a G3GRID interpolation of the original data set shown in Figure 30.1 on page 1008.

Figure 30.2   Surface Plot of Data Set after G3GRID Processing (GR30N01(b))

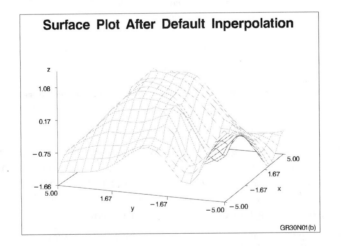

Note: The evenly distributed horizontal (x, y) data points form a grid for the three-dimensional graph. △

Concepts

About the Input Data Set

The input data set must contain at least three numeric variables:

□ two horizontal variables, (x, y)

□ one or more vertical variables, z through z-n, that will be interpolated or smoothed as if it were a function of the two horizontal variables.

The procedure can process multiple vertical variables for each pair of horizontal variables that you specify. If you specify more than one vertical variable, the G3GRID procedure performs a separate analysis and produces interpolated or smoothed values for each vertical variable. If more than one observation in the input data set has the same values for both horizontal variables, x and y, a warning message is printed, and only the first such point is used in the interpolation.

By default, the interpolation is performed after both variables are similarly scaled because the interpolation methods assume that the scales of x and y are comparable.

Multiple Vertical Variables

In the GRID statement, you can name multiple vertical variables (z through z-n) and produce a data set that contains two horizontal variables and multiple vertical variables. You can use the resulting data set to produce plots of the relationships of the two horizontal variables to different vertical variables.

Horizontal Variables Along a Nonlinear Curve

If the points that are generated by the horizontal variables tend to lie along a curve, a poor interpolation or spline may result. In such cases, the vertical variable(s) and one of the horizontal variables should be modeled as a function of the remaining horizontal variable. You can use a scatter plot of the two horizontal variables to help determine the appropriate function.

If the horizontal variable points are collinear, the procedure interpolates the function as constant along lines perpendicular to the line in the plane that is generated by the input data points.

About the Output Data Set

The output data set contains the two horizontal variables, the interpolated or smoothed vertical variables, and the BY variables, if any. If the GRID statement's SMOOTH= option is used, the output data set also contains a variable named _SMTH_, with a value equal to that of the smoothing parameter.

You can control both the number of x and y values in the output data set and the values themselves. In addition, you can specify an interpolation method.

Interpolation Methods

The G3GRID procedure can use one of three interpolation methods: bivariate interpolation (the default), spline interpolation, and smoothed spline interpolation.

Default Bivariate Interpolation

Unless you specify the SPLINE option, the G3GRID procedure is an interpolation procedure. That is, it calculates z values for x, y points that are missing from the input grid. The surface that is formed by the interpolated data passes precisely through the data points in the input data set.

This default method of interpolation works best for fairly smooth functions with values given at uniformly distributed points in the plane. If the data points in the input data set are erratic, the default interpolated surface can be erratic.

This default method is a modification of that described by Akima (1978). This method consists of

1 dividing the plane into nonoverlapping triangles that use the positions of the available points

2 fitting a bivariate fifth degree polynomial within each triangle

3 calculating the interpolated values by evaluating the polynomial at each grid point that falls in the triangle.

The coefficients for the polynomial are computed based on

□ the values of the function at the vertices of the triangle

□ the estimated values for the first and second derivatives of the function at the vertices.

The estimates of the first and second derivatives are computed using the n nearest neighbors of the point, where n is the number specified in the GRID statement's NEAR= option. A Delauney triangulation (Ripley 1981, p. 38) is used for the default method. The coordinates of the triangles are available in an output data set if requested by the OUTTRI= option in the PROC G3GRID statement.

Spline Interpolation

If you specify the SPLINE option, a method is used that produces an interpolation or smoothing that is optimally smooth in a certain sense (Harder and Desmarais 1972, Meinguet 1979). The surface that is generated can be thought of as one that would be formed if a stiff, thin metal plate were forced through or near the given data points. For large data sets, this method is substantially more expensive than the default method.

The function u, formed when you specify the SPLINE option, is determined by letting

$$t_j = (x_j, y_j)$$

$$t = (x, y)$$

and

$$|t - t_j| = \left((x - x_j)^2 + (y - y_j)^2 \right)^{1/2}$$

$$\mathbf{u}(x, y) = \Sigma_{j=1}^{n} c_j \mathrm{E}(t, t_j) + d_0 + d_1 x + d_2 y$$

where

$$E(s,t) = |s-t|\, log\,(|s-t|).$$

The coefficients c_1, c_2,..., c_n and d_1, d_2, d_3 of this polynomial are determined by these equations:

$$(\mathbf{E} + \mathrm{n}\lambda\mathbf{I})\,\mathbf{c} + \mathbf{T}\,\mathbf{d} = \mathbf{z}$$

and

$$\mathbf{T}'\mathbf{c} = \mathbf{0}$$

where

E
  is the $n \times n$ matrix $E(t_i, t_j)$

I
  is the $n \times n$ identity matrix

λ
  is the smoothing parameter that is specified in the SMOOTH= option

c
  is $(c_1,..., c_n)$

z
  is $(z_1,..., z_n)$

d
  is (d_1, d_2, d_3)

T
  is the $n \times 3$ matrix whose ith row is $(1, x_i, y_i)$.

See Wahba (1979) for more detail.

Spline Smoothing

To produce a smoothed spline, you can use the GRID statement's SMOOTH= option with the SPLINE option. The value or values specified in the SMOOTH= option are substituted for λ in the equation that is described in "Spline Interpolation" on page 1010. A smoothed spline trades closeness to the original data points for smoothness. To find a value that produces the best balance between smoothness and fit to the original data, you can try several values for the SMOOTH= option.

Procedure Syntax

Requirements: Exactly one GRID statement is required.

Reminder: The procedure can include the SAS/GRAPH BY statement.

Supports: Output Delivery System (ODS)

> PROC G3GRID <DATA=*input-data-set*>
>   <OUT=*output-data-set*>
>   <OUTTRI=*output-data-set*>;
>   GRID *grid-request* </option(s)>;

PROC G3GRID Statement

Identifies the input data set. Optionally specifies one or two output data sets.

Requirements: An input data set is required.

Syntax

> PROC G3GRID <DATA=*input-data-set*>
>   <OUT=*output-data-set*>
>   <OUTTRI=*output-data-set*>;

Options

DATA=*input-data-set*
    specifies the SAS data set that contains the variables to process. By default, the procedure uses the most recently created SAS data set.
    See also: "SAS Data Sets" on page 25 and "About the Input Data Set" on page 1009

OUT=*output-data-set*
    specifies the output data set. The data set contains any BY variables that you specify, the interpolated or smoothed values of the vertical variables (z through z-n), and the coordinates for all grid positions on the horizontal (x-y) plane. If you specify smoothing, the output data set also contains a variable named _SMTH_, whose value is a smoothing parameter. The observations in this data set are ordered by any variables that you specify with a BY statement. By default, the output of PROC G3GRID creates WORK.DATA1.
        Depending on the shape of the original data and the options you use, the output data set may contain values for the vertical (z through z-n) values that are outside of the range of the original values in the data set.
    Featured in: Example 1 on page 1016

OUTTRI=*output-data-set*
    specifies an additional output data set that contains triangular coordinates. The data set will contain any BY variables that you specify, the two horizontal variables giving the horizontal (x -y) plane coordinates of the input points, and a variable named TRIANGLE that uses integer values to label the triangles. The observations in this data set are ordered by any variables that you specify with a BY.
        The data set contains three observations for each value of the variable TRIANGLE. The three observations give the coordinates of the three vertices of the triangle. Points on the convex hull of the input data set of points are also assumed to lie in degenerate triangles whose other vertices are at infinity. The points in the convex hull can be recovered by keeping only those triangles with exactly two missing vertices.
        By default, no OUTTRI= data set is produced. OUTTRI= is not valid when you specify the SPLINE option in the GRID statement.

GRID Statement

Specifies the three numeric variables for interpolation or smoothing. Optionally specifies the number of observations (*x* and *y* values) in the output data set; output values for the two horizontal variables *x,y*; and the interpolation method for the vertical variables.

Requirements: Exactly one grid request is required.

Syntax

GRID *grid-request </option(s)>*;

*grid-request*must be:

$y*x=z(s)$

grid-request must be

$y*x=z(s)$

option(s) can be one or more options from any or all of the following categories:

☐ grid options:

AXIS1=*ascending-value-list*

AXIS2=*ascending-value-list*

NAXIS1=*n*

NAXIS2=*n*

☐ interpolation options:

JOIN

NEAR=*n*

NOSCALE

PARTIAL

SMOOTH=*ascending-value-list*

SPLINE

Required Arguments

*y*x=z(s)*

specifies three or more numeric variables from the input data set:

y

is one of the variables that forms the horizontal (*x-y*) plane.

x

is another of the variables that forms the horizontal (*x-y*) plane.

z(s)

is one or more vertical variables for the interpolation.

Although the GRID statement can specify only two horizontal variables, it can include multiple vertical variables. Separate vertical variables with blanks:

```
grid x*y=z w u v;
```

Options

AXIS1=*ascending-value-list*

specifies a list of numeric values to assign to the first (*y*) variable in the grid request for the output data set. Numbers that you specify with this option determine the number of values for *y* and override a value that you specify with the NAXIS1= option. *Ascending-value-list* must be in ascending order. It is either an explicit list of values, or a starting and an ending value with an interval increment, or a combination of both forms:

n <...*n*>

n TO *n* <BY *increment*>

n <...*n*> TO *n* <BY *increment* > <*n* <...*n*> >

Featured in:　Example 1 on page 1016 and Example 4 on page 1022

AXIS2=*ascending-value-list*

specifies a list of numeric values to assign to the second (*x*) variable in the grid request for the output data set. Numbers that you specify with this option determine the number of values for *x* and override a value that you specify with the NAXIS2= option. *Ascending-value-list* must be in ascending order. It is either an explicit list of values, or a starting and an ending value with an interval increment, or a combination of both forms:

n <...*n*>

n TO *n* <BY *increment*>

n <...*n*> TO *n* <BY *increment* > <*n* <...*n*> >

Featured in:　Example 1 on page 1016 and Example 4 on page 1022

JOIN

uses a linear interpolation within a set of triangular regions that are formed from the input data set. This interpolation method creates values in the range of the initial values of the vertical variable, but the resulting interpolated surface may not be smooth.

NAXIS1=*n*

specifies the number of values for the first (*y*) variable in the grid request for the output data set. You can determine the actual values used for *y* by taking the minimum and maximum values of *y* and dividing the range into *n*–1 equal sections. By default, NAXIS1=11.

A value specified with NAXIS1= is ignored if values are also specified with AXIS1=.

NAXIS2=*n*

specifies the number of values for the second (*x*) variable in the grid request for the output data set. You can determine the actual values that are used for *x* by taking the minimum and maximum values of *x* and dividing the range into *n*–1 equal sections. By default, NAXIS2=11.

A value specified with NAXIS2= is ignored if values are also specified with AXIS2=.

NEAR=*n*

specifies the number of nearest data points to use for computing the estimates of the first and second derivatives. As NEAR= values become larger, time and computation costs increase significantly. NEAR= is ignored if you specify SPLINE. The value of *n* must be greater than or equal to 3. By default, NEAR=3.

If the number of input data points is insufficient for the number that you specify with NEAR=, a smaller number of data points is used.

Featured in:　Example 3 on page 1021

NOSCALE

specifies that the x and y variables not be scaled to the same range before interpolation. By default, the interpolation is performed after both variables are similarly scaled because the interpolation methods assume that the scales of x and y are comparable.

PARTIAL

specifies that a spline be used to estimate the derivatives for the biquintic polynomial interpolation. A bivariate spline is fit to the nearest neighbors and used to estimate the needed derivatives. This option produces results that are less smooth than those produced by the SPLINE option and uses fewer computer resources. However, the results produced by PARTIAL are smoother than those that are produced by the default. If you use both PARTIAL and the SPLINE option, PARTIAL is ignored.

Featured in: Example 3 on page 1021

SMOOTH=*ascending-value-list*

specifies a list of numbers for smoothing parameters. Use this option only when you also use the SPLINE option. *Ascending-value-list* must be in ascending order. It is either an explicit list of values, or a starting and an ending value with an interval increment, or a combination of both forms:

n <...n>

n TO n <BY *increment*>

n <...n> TO n <BY *increment* > <n <...n> >

For each value λ of the smoothing parameter, a function $u\,(x, y)$ is formed that minimizes

$$\frac{1}{n}\Sigma_{j=1}^{n}\left(\mathbf{u}\left(\mathbf{x_j}, \mathbf{y_j}\right) - \mathbf{z_j}\right)^2 + \lambda\Sigma_{j=0}^{2}\int\limits_{-\infty}^{\infty}\int^{\infty}{}^{2}\,dx dy$$

where n is the number of data points and the pairs (x_j, y_j) are the available points, with corresponding function values z_j (Wahba 1979).

The higher the value of the smoothing parameter, the smoother the resulting interpolation. The lower the smoothing parameter, the closer the resulting surface is to the original data points. A smoothing parameter of 0 produces the same results as the SPLINE option without SMOOTH=.

This procedure repeats for each value of the smoothing parameter. The output data set that you specify in the OUT= option contains the interpolated values, the values of the grid points, and the values of the smoothing parameter in the variable _SMTH_. The output data set contains a separate grid for each value of the smoothing parameter.

Featured in: Example 2 on page 1019

SPLINE

specifies the use of a bivariate spline (Harder and Desmarais 1972, Meinguet 1979) to interpolate or to form a smoothed estimate if you also use the SMOOTH= option. This option results in the use of an order n^3 algorithm, where n is the number of input data points. Consequently, this method can be time-consuming. If you use more than 100 input points, the procedure may use excessive time.

Featured in: Example 2 on page 1019 and Example 4 on page 1022

Controlling Observations in the Output Data Set

By default, the G3GRID procedure produces a data set with 121 observations for combinations of 11 values for each of the horizontal variables, x and y. To create a data set with a different number of observations, use the GRID statement's NAXIS1= or NAXIS2= options to specify the number of the values of y or x, respectively. Or, use the GRID statement's AXIS1= or AXIS2= options to specify the actual values for y or x, respectively.

Table 30.1 on page 1016 shows the number of observations that will be in the output data set if you use any of these options.

Table 30.1   Number of Observations Contained in the Output Data Set

Options Specified	Number of Observations in Output Data Set
None	121
AXIS1=	(number of values for AXIS1=) * 11
AXIS2=	(number of values for AXIS2=) * 11
NAXIS1=	(value of NAXIS1=) * 11
NAXIS2=	(value of NAXIS2=) * 11
AXIS1=, AXIS2=	(number of values for AXIS1=) * (number of values for AXIS2=)
AXIS1=, NAXIS1=	(number of values for AXIS1=) * 11
AXIS1=, NAXIS2=	(number of values for AXIS1=) * (value of NAXIS2=)
AXIS2=, NAXIS1=	(number of values for AXIS2=) * (value of NAXIS1=)
AXIS2=, NAXIS2=	(number of values for AXIS2=) * 11
NAXIS1=, NAXIS2=	(value of NAXIS1=) * (value of NAXIS2=)

If you specify multiple smoothing parameters, the number of observations in the output data set will be the number shown in Table 30.1 on page 1016 multiplied by the number of smoothing values that you specify in the SMOOTH= option. If you use BY-group processing, multiply the number in the table by the number of BY groups.

Depending on the shape of the original data and the options that you specify, the output data set may contain values for the vertical (z) values that are outside of the range of the original values in the data set.

Examples

Example 1: Using the Default Interpolation Method

Procedure features:
   G3GRID statement options:
      OUT=
   GRID statement options:
      AXIS1=
      AXIS2=
Other features:
   DATA step

G3D procedure

Sample library member: GR30N01

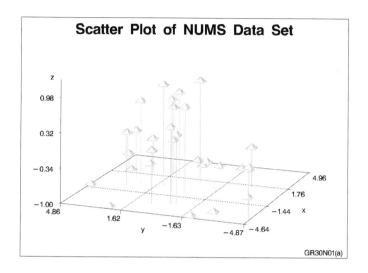

This example demonstrates the default interpolation method that is used by the GRID statement. The example first generates a scatter plot of random data to show the concentration of data values before processing with the G3GRID procedure. The original data do not contain enough combinations of *x*, *y*, and *z* values to generate a surface plot with the G3D procedure, or a contour plot with the GCONTOUR procedure.

The example then runs the G3GRID procedure to interpolate additional *x*, *y*, and *z* values. Because no interpolation method is specified, the default interpolation method is used. The resulting output data set is used as input to the G3D procedure, which generates the surface plot shown in the following output.

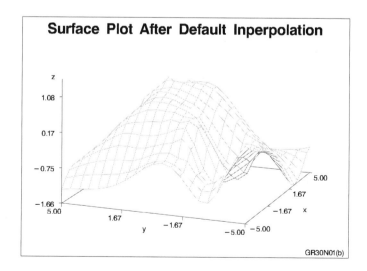

Assign the libref and set the graphics environment.

```
libname reflib 'SAS-data-library';
goptions reset=global gunit=pct border cback=white
         colors=(black blue green red)
         ftext=swiss ftitle=swissb htitle=6 htext=3;
```

Create data set. REFLIB.NUMS uses a set of randomly sampled points to create the data used in this and all remaining examples in this chapter.

```
data reflib.nums;
   keep x y z;
   do i=1 to 30;
      x=10*ranuni(33)-5;
      y=10*ranuni(35)-5;
      z=sin(sqrt(x*x+y*y));
      output;
   end;
run;
```

Define title and footnote.

```
title 'Scatter Plot of NUMS Data Set';
footnote j=r 'GR30N01(a) ';
```

Generate the scatter plot.

```
proc g3d data=reflib.nums;
   scatter y*x=z;
run;
```

Process points with PROC G3GRID. OUT= on G3GRID specifies a name for a temporary output data set. GRID specifies the variables Y*X=Z for the output data set. AXIS@@@ 1

```
proc g3grid data=reflib.nums out=default;
   grid y*x=z / axis1=-5 to 5 by .5
                axis2=-5 to 5 by .5;
run;
```

Define new title and footnote.

```
title 'Surface Plot after Default Interpolation';
footnote j=r 'GR30N01(b) ';
```

Generate a surface plot. The G3D procedure uses as its input data set the G3GRID procedure's output data set.

```
proc g3d data=default;
   plot y*x=z;
```

```
run;
quit;
```

Example 2: Using Spline Interpolation and a Smoothed Spline

Procedure features:

   GRID statement options:

      SMOOTH=
      SPLINE

Data set: REFLIB.NUMS on page 1018

Sample library member: GR30N02

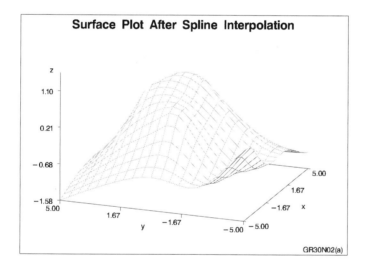

This example extends Example 1 to specify a spline interpolation method on the GRID statement. The output data set, when used in PROC G3D, generates a smoother surface plot than the surface plot that results from the default interpolation shown in Example 1.

This example then specifies a smoothed spline interpolation method on the GRID statement. As shown by the following output, the resulting surface plot is smoother still.

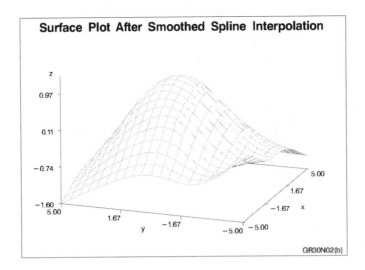

Assign the libref and set the graphics environment.

```
libname reflib 'SAS-data-library';
goptions reset=global gunit=pct border cback=white
         colors=(black blue green red)
         ftext=swiss ftitle=swissb htitle=5 htext=3;
```

Define title and footnote.

```
title 'Surface Plot After Spline Interpolation';
footnote j=r 'GR30N02(a) ';
```

Process points with PROC G3GRID. SPLINE specifies the bivariate spline method for the data set interpolation.

```
proc g3grid data=reflib.nums out=spline;
   grid y*x=z / spline
                axis1=-5 to 5 by .5
                axis2=-5 to 5 by .5;
run;
```

Generate a surface plot.

```
proc g3d data=spline;
   plot y*x=z ;
run;
```

Define title and footnote for second plot.

```
title 'Surface Plot After Smoothed Spline Interpolation';
footnote j=r 'GR30N02(b) ';
```

Process points with PROC G3GRID. SMOOTH= specifies the smoothing parameter to use during spline interpolation.

```
proc g3grid data=reflib.nums out=smoothed;
   grid y*x=z / spline
                smooth=.05
                axis1=-5 to 5 by .5
                axis2=-5 to 5 by .5;
run;
```

Generate a surface plot.

```
proc g3d data=smoothed;
   plot y*x=z;
run;
quit;
```

Example 3: Using Partial Spline Interpolation

Procedure features:
   GRID statement options:
      NEAR
      PARTIAL
Data set: REFLIB.NUMS on page 1018
Sample library member: GR30N03

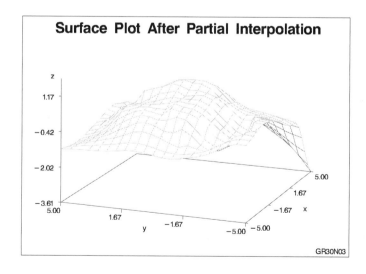

This example specifies a partial spline interpolation method on the GRID statement, using eight nearest neighbors for computing the estimates of the first and second derivatives. The output data set, when used in PROC G3D, generates a smoother surface plot than the surface plot that results from the default interpolation shown in Example 1, but not as smooth as the surface plot that results from the spline interpolation shown in Example 2.

Assign the libref and set the graphics environment.

```
libname reflib 'SAS-data-library';
goptions reset=global gunit=pct border cback=white
        colors=(black blue green red)
        ftext=swiss ftitle=swissb htitle=6 htext=3;
```

Define title and footnote.

```
title 'Surface Plot after Partial Interpolation';
footnote j=r 'GR30N03 ';
```

Process points with PROC G3GRID. PARTIAL specifies that a spline be used to estimate the derivatives for the biquintic polynomial interpolation. NEAR= specifies the number of nearest neighbors to be used for computing the estimates of the first and second derivatives.

```
proc g3grid data=reflib.nums out=partial;
    grid y*x=z / partial
                near=8
                axis1=-5 to 5 by .5
                axis2=-5 to 5 by .5;
run;
```

Generate the surface plot.

```
proc g3d data=partial;
    plot y*x=z;
run;
quit;
```

Example 4: Using Spline Interpolation

Procedure features:
   GRID statement options:

   AXIS1=
   AXIS2=
   SPLINE

Data set: REFLIB.NUMS on page 1018

Sample library member: GR30N04

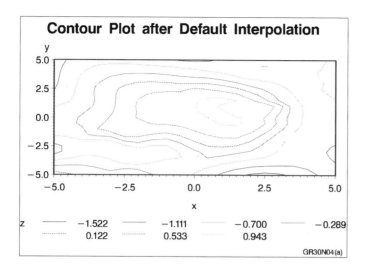

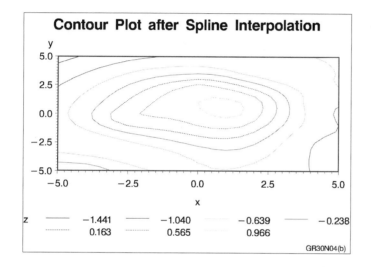

This example demonstrates the default and spline interpolation methods when used by the GCONTOUR procedure to generate contour plots from the resulting output data sets.

Assign the libref and set the graphics environment.

```
libname reflib 'SAS-data-library';
goptions reset=global gunit=pct border cback=white
         colors=(black blue green red)
         ftext=swiss ftitle=swissb htitle=6 htext=3;
```

Define title and footnote.

```
title 'Contour Plot after Default Interpolation';
footnote j=r 'GR30N04(a) ';
```

Define axis characteristics.

```
axis1 width=3;
```

Process points with PROC G3GRID. AXIS@@@ 1

```
proc g3grid data=reflib.nums out=numdef;
   grid y*x=z / axis1=-5 to 5 by .5
               axis2=-5 to 5 by .5;
run;
```

Generate the contour after default interpolation.

```
proc gcontour data=numdef;
   plot y*x=z / haxis=axis1 vaxis=axis1;
run;
```

Define new title and footnote.

```
title 'Contour Plot after Spline Interpolation';
footnote j=r 'GR30N04(b) ';
```

Process points with PROC G3GRID. SPLINE specifies the bivariate spline method for the data set interpolation.

```
proc g3grid data=reflib.nums out=numspl;
   grid y*x=z / spline
               axis1=-5 to 5 by .5
               axis2=-5 to 5 by .5;
run;
```

Show the contour after spline interpolation.

```
proc gcontour data=numspl;
   plot y*x=z / haxis=axis1 vaxiss=axis1;
run;
quit;
```

References

Akima, Hiroshi (1978), "A Method of Bivariate Interpolation and Smooth Surface Fitting for Irregularly Distributed Data Points," *ACM Transaction on Mathematical Software*, 4, 148–159.

Harder, R.L. and Desmarais, R.N. (1972), "Interpolation Using Surface Splines," *Journal of Aircraft*, 9, 189–191.

Meinguet, Jean (1979), "Multivariate Interpolation at Arbitrary Points Made Simple," *Journal of Applied Mathematics and Physics*, 30, 292–304.

Ripley, B.D. (1981), *Spatial Statistics*, New York: John Wiley & Sons, Inc.

Wahba, Grace (1979), "How to Smooth Curves and Surfaces with Splines and Cross-validation," in U.S. Army Research Office Report 79–2, *Proceedings of the 24th Conference on the Design of Experiments*.

The DATA Step Graphics Interface

Overview

The DATA Step Graphics Interface (DSGI) enables you to create graphics output within the DATA step or from within an SCL application. Through DSGI, you can call the graphics routines used by SAS/GRAPH software to generate an entire custom graph or to add features to an existing graph. You can use DSGI to write a custom graphics application in conjunction with all the power of the programming statements accessible by the DATA step.

DSGI provides many of the same features as the Annotate facility, but it also has many advantages over the Annotate facility.

- You can use DSGI functions and routines through SCL.

- You can save disk space. DSGI graphics can be generated through the DATA step without creating an output data set. The graphics output is stored as a catalog entry in the catalog you select and, optionally, is displayed after the DATA step is submitted.

- DSGI generates graphics faster than the Annotate facility. With the Annotate facility, you must first create a data set and then submit a PROC step to display the graphics output. In DSGI, you eliminate the PROC step because the graphics output is generated after the DATA step.

- DSGI supports viewports and windows, which enable you to specify the dimensions, position, and scale of the graphics output. They also allow you to include multiple graphs in the same graphics output.

You should consider using the Annotate facility for enhancing procedure output and using DSGI for creating custom graphics without using a graphics procedure.

DSGI is based upon the Graphics Kernal System (GKS) standard, although it does not follow a strict interpretation, nor is it implemented on a particular level of GKS. GKS was used to provide a recognizable interface to the user. Because of its modularity, the standard allows for enhancements to DSGI without the side effect of converting programs between versions of SAS/GRAPH software.

This chapter explains the concepts used to create graphics output with DSGI. The discussion provides an overview of the functions and routines used in DSGI. For complete details of each function and routine, see Chapter 32, "DATA Step Graphics Interface Dictionary," on page 1075.

Display 31.1 on page 1029 shows a pie chart that was created entirely with DSGI functions. Display 31.2 on page 1029 is an example of a text slide that was created with DSGI statements.

Display 31.1 Exploded Pie Chart Generated with the DSGI

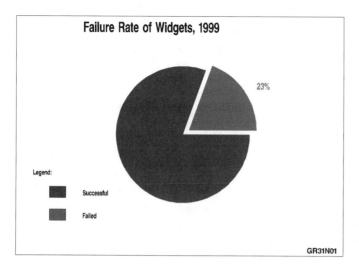

Display 31.2 Text Slide Created Using the DSGI

Production Information for Widgets Assembly

JAN 1999 – JUN 1999

MONTH	TEMP	SPEED	PERCENT FAILED
JAN	100	90	4.950
FEB	110	90	4.792
MAR	120	90	5.042
APR	130	90	5.700
MAY	140	90	6.766
JUN	150	90	8.240

GR31N02

Syntax

DSGI uses GASK routines and functions to draw graphics elements. These statements have the following syntax:

CALL GASK(*operator, arguments*);

return-code-variable=function-name (operator, arguments);

where

arguments   are the additional required variables or values for the routine or function.

return-code-variable   is an arbitrary name and can be any numeric variable name. It will hold the return code upon execution of the function.

function-name   is the DSGI command you want to execute and must be one of the following: GDRAW, GINIT, GPRINT, GRAPH, GSET, or GTERM.

operator   is a character string that names the function you either want to submit or for which you want the current settings. When used with functions, *operator* can take different values depending on *function-name*.

Requirements

When using DSGI statements, the following formats for arguments must be used:

☐ All *x* and *y* coordinates are expressed in units of the current window system. (See "The Current Window System" on page 1033 for details.)

☐ The arguments used with DSGI functions can be expressed as either constants or variables. The arguments used with GASK routines must be variable names since values are returned through them. See Chapter 32, "DATA Step Graphics Interface Dictionary," on page 1075 for a complete explanation of each argument used with DSGI functions and routines.

☐ All arguments that are character constants must be enclosed in either single or double quotation marks.

Applications of the DATA Step Graphics Interface

With the DATA Step Graphics Interface you can

☐ enhance existing graphs

☐ create custom graphs.

Enhancing Existing Graphs

You can use DSGI to enhance graphs that were previously generated by using SAS/GRAPH procedures. You can add text and other graphics elements. You can also alter the appearance of the existing graph by scaling or reducing it. To enhance a graph produced by a SAS/GRAPH graphics procedure, you must insert the existing graph into graphics output being generated with DSGI.

To insert a graph, you must provide DSGI with the following information:

☐ the catalog in which the existing graph is located

☐ the name of the existing graph

☐ the coordinates of the place in the graphics output where you want to insert the existing graph

☐ a square coordinate system ((0,0) to (100,100))

☐ the statements to draw enhancements to the existing graph.

The coordinates that DSGI uses to position existing graphs, enhancements to that graph, or graphics elements are based on units of percent of the window system currently defined. See "Using Viewports and Windows" on page 1050.

Creating Custom Graphs

You can produce custom graphs with DSGI without using a data set to produce the graphics output. DSGI enables you to generate

□ arcs

□ bars

□ ellipses

□ elliptical arcs

□ lines

□ markers

□ pie slices

□ polygons (filled areas)

□ text.

To create custom graphs, you must provide the system with the following information:

□ DSGI statements to draw graphics elements

□ the coordinates of the graphics elements in the output.

In addition, you can specify the color, pattern, size, style, and position of these graphics elements.

Using the DATA Step Graphics Interface

The following sections provide general information about using DSGI, including general steps for using DSGI, how to produce and store graphs, how the data sets used with DSGI are structured, how SAS/GRAPH global statements can be used with DSGI, and how to debug DSGI programs. The sections also explain some of the basic concepts of DSGI, including information about operating states and windowing systems.

Summary of Use

To generate graphics output using DSGI, you generally follow these steps:

1 On a grid that matches the dimensions of the graphics output, sketch the output you want to produce.

2 Determine the coordinates of each graphics element.

3 In the DATA step, write the program to generate the graphics output. The basic steps are to

    a initialize DSGI

    b open a graphics segment

    c generate graphics elements

    d close the graphics segment

    e end DSGI.

4 Submit the DATA step with a final RUN statement to display the output.

Note: The DISPLAY graphics option must be in effect for the graphics output to be displayed. See Chapter 9, "Graphics Options and Device Parameters Dictionary," on page 301 for more information about the DISPLAY graphics option. △

Producing and Storing DSGI Graphs

When you create or enhance graphs with DSGI, the DSGI graphics are displayed and stored as part of the graphics output. When you execute the DATA step, DSGI creates a catalog entry using the name from the GRAPH('CLEAR', . . .)function.

By default, DSGI uses the name DSGI if you have not specified a name with the GRAPH('CLEAR', . . .)function. By default, the catalog entry is stored in WORK.GSEG unless you specify another catalog with the GSET('CATALOG', . . .)function.

If you generate another graph using a name that matches an existing catalog entry in the current catalog, DSGI uses the default naming conventions for the catalog entry. See "Names and Descriptions of Catalog Entries" on page 51 for a description of the conventions used to name catalog entries.

If you want to store your output in a permanent library or in a different temporary catalog, you must use the GSET('CATALOG', . . .)function. This function allows you to specify the libref and catalog name for the output catalog. Before you use the GSET('CATALOG', . . .)function, you must allocate the libref using a LIBNAME statement.

You can redisplay DSGI graphics output stored in catalog entries using the GREPLAY procedure or the GRAPH window.

Structure of DSGI Data Sets

The DSGI DATA step is usually not written to produce an output data set. Unlike data sets created by the Annotate facility, which contain observations for each graphics element drawn, DSGI does not usually create an observation for each graphics primitive. Only variables created in the DATA step are written to the output data set.

You can output as many observations to the data set as you want. To output these values, you must use the OUTPUT statement. You can also use any other valid SAS DATA step statements in a DSGI DATA step. See *SAS Language Reference: Dictionary* for information about the statements used in the DATA step.

Using SAS/GRAPH Global Statements with DSGI

You can use some SAS/GRAPH global statements with DSGI programs. DSGI recognizes FOOTNOTE, GOPTIONS, and TITLE statements; however, it ignores AXIS, LEGEND, NOTE, PATTERN, and SYMBOL statements.

FOOTNOTE and TITLE statements affect DSGI graphics output the same way as they affect other SAS/GRAPH procedure output. When TITLE and FOOTNOTE statements are used, the output from DSGI statements is placed in the procedure output area. See "Placement of Graphic Elements in the Graphics Output Area" on page 34 for an explanation of how space in graphics output is allocated to titles and footnotes.

Some DSGI functions override the graphics options. The following table lists the DSGI functions that directly override graphics options. For details about the graphics options, see Chapter 9, "Graphics Options and Device Parameters Dictionary," on page 301.

DSGI Function	Graphics Option That Is Overridden
GSET('CBACK', . . .)	CBACK=
GSET('COLREP', . . .)	COLORS=
GSET('DEVICE', . . .)	DEVICE=
GSET('HPOS', . . .)	HPOS=
GSET('HSIZE', . . .)	HSIZE=
GSET('VPOS', . . .)	VPOS=
GSET('VSIZE', . . .)	VSIZE=

DSGI Function	Graphics Option That Is Overridden
GSET('TEXCOLOR', . . .)	CTEXT=
GSET('TEXFONT', . . .)	FTEXT=
GSET('TEXHEIGHT', . . .)	HTEXT=

Operating States

The operating state of DSGI determines which functions and routines may be issued at any point in the DATA step. You can only submit a function or routine when the operating state is appropriate for it. See "How Operating States Control the Order of DSGI Statements" on page 1044 for a discussion of how functions and routines should be ordered within the operating states.

The operating states defined by DSGI are

GKCL   facility closed, the initial state of DSGI. No graphical resources have been allocated.

GKOP   facility open. When DSGI is open, you may check the settings of the attributes.

SGOP   segment open. At this point, graphics output primitives may be generated.

WSAC   workstation active. When the workstation is active, it can receive DSGI statements.

WSOP   workstation open. In this implementation, the graphics catalog, either the default or the one specified through the GSET('CATALOG', . . .)command, is opened or created.

Refer to individual functions and routines in Chapter 32, "DATA Step Graphics Interface Dictionary," on page 1075 for the operating states from which that function or routine can be issued.

The Current Window System

When DSGI draws graphics, it evaluates x and y coordinates in terms of the *current window system*, either a window you have defined or the default window system. Unless you define and activate a different window, DSGI uses the default window system.

The default window system assigns two arbitrary systems of units to the x and y axes. The default window guarantees a range of 0 through 100 in one direction (usually the y direction) and at least 0 through 100 in the other (usually the x direction). The ranges depend on the dimensions of your device. You can use the GASK('WINDOW', . . .)routine to determine the dimensions of your default window system.

You can define the x and y ranges to be any numeric range. For example, you can use − 1000 to +2000 on the x axis and 30 to 35 on the y axis. The units used are arbitrary.

Debugging DSGI Programs

When DSGI encounters an error in a program, it flags the statement in the SAS log and displays a description of the error. (To receive SAS System messages,

GSET('MESSAGE', . . .)must be ON.) The description provides you with an explanation of the error. The description may also provide a return code. If you get a return code, you can refer to "Return Codes for DSGI Routines and Functions" on page 1165 for a description of the error and why it might have occurred.

Some of the most common errors in DSGI programs are

□ syntax errors

□ an invalid number of arguments for the function or routine

□ a function or routine being executed in an operating state that is not correct for the function or routine.

DSGI Graphics Summary

The following sections summarize the functions and routines you can use to create graphics output with DSGI.

DSGI Functions

DSGI provides functions that

□ initialize and terminate DSGI

□ generate graphics elements

□ control the appearance of graphics elements by setting attributes

□ control the overall appearance of the graphics output

□ perform management operations for the catalog

□ control messages issued by DSGI.

Table 31.1 on page 1034 summarizes the types of operations available and the functions used to invoke them. Refer to Chapter 32, "DATA Step Graphics Interface Dictionary," on page 1075 for details about each function.

Table 31.1   DATA Step Graphics Interface Functions

DSGI Operations	Associated Function	Function Description
Bundling Attributes (valid values for *xxx* are FIL, LIN, MAR, and TEX)		
	GSET('ASF', . . .)	sets the aspect source flag of an attribute
	GSET('*xxx*INDEX', . . .)	selects the bundle of attributes to use
	GSET('*xxx*REP', . . .)	assigns attributes to a bundle
Setting Attributes That Affect Graphics Elements		
color index	GSET('COLREF'), . . .)	assigns a color name to color index

DSGI Operations	Associated Function	Function Description
fill area	GSET('FILCOLOR', . . .)	selects the color of the fill area
	GSET('FILSTYLE', . . .)	selects the pattern when FILTYPE is HATCH or PATTERN
	GSET('FILTYPE', . . .)	specifies the type of interior for the fill area
	GSET('HTML', . . .)	specifies the HTML string to invoke when an affected DSGI graphic element in a web page is clicked
line	GSET('LINCOLOR', . . .)	selects the color of the line
	GSET('LINTYPE', . . .)	sets the type of line
	GSET('LINWIDTH', . . .)	specifies the width of the line
marker	GSET('MARCOLOR', . . .)	selects the color of the marker
	GSET('MARSIZE', . . .)	determines the size of the marker
	GSET('MARTYPE', . . .)	sets the type of marker drawn
text	GSET('TEXALIGN', . . .)	specifies horizontal and vertical alignment of text
	GSET('TEXCOLOR', . . .)	selects the color of the text
	GSET('TEXFONT', . . .)	sets the font for the text
	GSET('TEXHEIGHT', . . .)	selects the height of the text
	GSET('TEXPATH', . . .)	determines reading direction of text
	GSET('TEXUP', . . .)	selects the angle of text

Setting Attributes That Affect Entire Graph

	GSET('ASPECT', . . .)	sets the aspect ratio
	GSET('CATALOG', . . .)	selects the catalog to use

DSGI Operations	Associated Function	Function Description
	GSET('CBACK', . . .)	selects the background color
	GSET('DEVICE', . . .)	specifies the output device
	GSET('HPOS', . . .)	sets the number of columns in the graphics output area
	GSET('HSIZE', . . .)	sets the width of the graphics output area in units of inches
	GSET('VPOS', . . .)	sets the number of rows in the graphics output area
	GSET('VSIZE', . . .)	sets the height of the graphics output area in units of inches
Managing Catalogs		
	GRAPH('COPY', . . .)	copies a graph to another entry within the same catalog
	GRAPH('DELETE', . . .)	deletes a graph
	GRAPH('INSERT', . . .)	inserts a previously created graph into the currently open segment
	GRAPH('RENAME', . . .)	renames a graph
Drawing Graphics Elements		
arc	GDRAW('ARC', . . .)	draws a circular arc
bar	GDRAW('BAR', . . .)	draws a rectangle that can be filled
ellipse	GDRAW('ELLIPSE', . . .)	draws an oblong circle that can be filled
elliptical arc	GDRAW('ELLARC', . . .)	draws an elliptical arc
fill area	GDRAW('FILL', . . .)	draws a polygon that can be filled

DSGI Operations	Associated Function	Function Description
line	GDRAW('LINE', . . .)	draws a single line, a series of connected lines, or a dot
marker	GDRAW('MARK', . . .)	draws one or more symbols
pie	GDRAW('PIE', . . .)	draws a pie slice that can be filled
text	GDRAW('TEXT', . . .)	draws a character string
Initializing DSGI		
	GINIT( )	initializes DSGI
	GRAPH('CLEAR', . . .)	opens a segment to receive graphics primitives
Handling Messages		
	GDRAW('MESSAGE', . . .)	prints a message in the SAS log
	GPRINT(*code*)	prints the description of a DSGI error code
	GSET('MESSAGE', . . .)	turns message logging on or off
Ending DSGI		
	GRAPH('UPDATE', . . .)	closes the currently open segment and, optionally, displays it
	GTERM()	ends DSGI
Activating Transformations		
	GET('TRANSNO', . . .)	selects the transformation number of the viewport or window to use
Defining Viewports		
	GSET('CLIP', . . .)	turns clipping on or off
	GSET('VIEWPORT', . . .)	sets the coordinates of the viewport and assigns it a transformation number

DSGI Operations	Associated Function	Function Description
Defining Windows		
	GSET('WINDOW', . . .)	sets the coordinates of the window and assigns it a transformation number

DSGI Routines

DSGI routines return the values set by some of the DSGI functions. Table 31.2 on page 1038 summarizes the types of values that the GASK routines can check. Refer to Chapter 32, "DATA Step Graphics Interface Dictionary," on page 1075 for details about each routine.

Table 31.2   DATA Step Graphics Interface Routines

DSGI Operations	Associated Routine	Routine Description
Checking Attribute Bundles (valid values for *xxx* are FIL, LIN, MAR, and TEX)		
	GASK('ASK', . . .)	returns the aspect source flag of the attribute
	GASK('*xxx*INDEX', . . .)	returns the index of the active bundle
	GASK('*xxx*REP', . . .)	returns the attributes assigned to the bundle
Checking Attribute Settings		
color index	GASK('COLINDEX', . . .)	returns the color indices that currently have colors assigned to them
	GASK('COLREP', . . .)	returns the color name assigned to the color index
fill area	GASK('FILCOLOR', . . .)	returns the color of the fill area
	GASK('FILSTYLE', . . .)	returns the index of the pattern when the FILTYPE is HATCH or PATTERN
	GASK('FILTYPE', . . .)	returns the index of the type of interior

DSGI Operations	Associated Routine	Routine Description
	GASK('HTML', . . .)	finds the HTML string that is in effect when one of the following graphic elements is drawn: bar, ellipse, fill, mark, pie, and text.
line	GASK('LINCOLOR', . . .)	returns the color index of the color of the line
	GASK('LINTYPE', . . .)	returns the index of the type of line
	GASK('LINWIDTH', . . .)	returns the width of the line
marker	GASK('MARCOLOR', . . .)	returns the color index of the color of markers
	GASK('MARSIZE', . . .)	returns the size of markers
	GASK('MARTYPE', . . .)	returns the index of the type of marker drawn
text	GASK('TEXALIGN', . . .)	returns the horizontal and vertical alignment of text
	GASK('TEXCOLOR', . . .)	returns the color index of the color of text
	GASK('TEXEXTENT', . . .)	returns the coordinates of text extent rectangle and the text concatenation point of the character string
	GASK('TEXFONT', . . .)	returns the text font
	GASK('TEXHEIGHT', . . .)	returns the height of text
	GASK('TEXPATH', . . .)	returns the reading direction of text
	GASK('TEXUP', . . .)	returns the character up vector in x vector and y vector

Checking Attributes That Affect Entire Graph

	GASK('ASPECT', . . .)	returns the aspect ratio
	GASK('CATALOG', . . .)	returns the current catalog
	GASK('CBACK', . . .)	returns the background color
	GASK('DEVICE', . . .)	returns the current output device

DSGI Operations	Associated Routine	Routine Description
	GASK('HPOS', . . .)	returns the number of columns in the graphics output area
	GASK('HSIZE', . . .)	returns the width of the graphics output area in units of inches
	GASK('MAXDISP', . . .)	returns the dimensions of maximum display area for the device in meters and pixels
	GASK('VPOS', . . .)	returns the number of rows in the graphics output area
	GASK('VSIZE', . . .)	returns the height of the graphics output area in units of inches
Querying Catalogs		
	GASK('GRAPHLIST', . . .)	returns the names of graphs in the current catalog
	GASK('NUMGRAPH', . . .)	returns the number of graphs in the current catalog
	GASK('OPENGRAPH', . . .)	returns the name of the currently open graph
Checking System Status		
	GASK('STATE', . . .)	returns the current operating state
	GASK('WSACTIVE', . . .)	returns whether or not the workstation is active
	GASK('WSOPEN', . . .)	returns whether or not the workstation is open
Checking Transformation Definitions		
	GASK('TRANS', . . .)	returns the coordinates of the viewport and window associated with the transformation
	GASK('TRANSNO', . . .)	returns the active transformation number
Checking Viewport Definitions		
	GASK('CLIP', . . .)	returns the status of clipping

DSGI Operations	Associated Routine	Routine Description
	GASK('VIEWPORT', . . .)	returns the coordinates of the viewport assigned to the transformation number
Checking Window Definitions		
	GASK('WINDOW', . . .)	returns the coordinates of the window assigned to the transformation number

Creating Simple Graphics with DSGI

Within any DSGI program, you need to follow these basic steps:

1 Initialize DSGI.

The function that initializes DSGI is GINIT(). GINIT() loads the graphics sublibrary, opens a workstation, and activates a workstation.

2 Open a graphics segment.

Before you can submit graphics primitives, you must submit the GRAPH('CLEAR', . . .) function. GRAPH('CLEAR', . . .) opens a graphic segment so that graphics primitives can be submitted.

3 Generate graphics elements.

DSGI can generate arcs, bars, ellipses, elliptical arcs, lines, markers, pie slices, polygons (fill areas), and text. These graphics elements are all produced with the GDRAW function using their associated operator names.

GDRAW functions can only be submitted when a graphics segment is open. Therefore, they must be submitted between the GRAPH('CLEAR', . . .) and GRAPH('UPDATE', . . .) functions.

4 Close the graphics segment.

Once the attribute and graphics statements have been entered, you must submit statements to close the graphics segment and output the graph. The GRAPH('UPDATE', . . .) function closes the graphic segment currently open and, optionally, displays the graphics output.

5 End DSGI.

The GTERM() function ends DSGI by deactivating and closing the workstation, and closing the graphics sublibrary. It frees any memory allocated by DSGI.

Note: You must execute a RUN statement at the end of the DATA step to display the output.

Figure 31.1 on page 1042 outlines the basic steps and shows the functions used to initiate steps 1, 2, 4, and 5. Step 3 can consist of many types of functions. The GDRAW('LINE', . . .)function is used as an example.

Figure 31.1   Basic Steps Used in Creating DSGI Graphics Output

```
data dsname;
                .
                .
                .

        /* Step 1 - initialize DSGI */
      rc=ginit();
                .
                .
                .

        /* Step 2 - open graphics segment */
      rc=graph('clear');
                .
                .
                .

        /* Step 3 - generate graphics elements */
      rc=gdraw('line', 2, 30, 50, 70, 50);
                .
                .
                .

        /* Step 4 - close graphics segment and display output */
      rc=graph('update');
                .
                .
                .

        /* Step 5 - end DSGI */
      rc=gterm();
                .
                .
                .

    run;
```

Notice that there are two pairs of functions that work together within a DSGI DATA step (shown by a and b in Figure 31.1 on page 1042). The first pair, GINIT() and GTERM(), begin and end DSGI. Within the first pair, the second pair, GRAPH('CLEAR', . . .)and GRAPH('UPDATE', . . .)begin and end a graphics segment. You can repeat these pairs within a single DATA step to produce multiple graphics output; however, the relative positions of these functions must be maintained within a DATA step. See "Generating Multiple Graphics Output in One DATA Step" on page 1054 for more information about producing multiple graphics outputs from one DATA step.

The order of these steps is controlled by DSGI operating states. Before any DSGI function or routine can be submitted, the operating state in which that function or routine can be submitted must be active. See "How Operating States Control the Order of DSGI Statements" on page 1044.

Setting Attributes for Graphics Elements

The appearance of the graphics elements is determined by the settings of the attributes. Attributes control such aspects as height of text; text font; and color, size, and width of the graphics element. In addition, the HTML attribute determines whether the element provides a link to another graphic or web page. Attributes are set and reset with GSET functions. GASK routines return the current setting of the attribute specified.

Each graphics primitive is associated with a particular set of attributes. Its appearance or linking capability can only be altered by that set of attributes. Table 31.3 on page 1043 lists the operators used with GDRAW functions to generate graphics elements and the attributes that control them.

Table 31.3 Graphics Output Primitive Functions and Associated Attributes

Graphics Output Primitive	Functions	Associated Attributes
Arc	GDRAW('ARC', . . .)	HTML, LINCOLOR, LININDEX, LINREP, LINTYPE, LINWIDTH
Bar	GDRAW('BAR', . . .)	FILCOLOR, FILINDEX, FILREP, FILSTYLE, FILTYPE, HTML
Ellipse	GDRAW('ELLIPSE', . . .)	FILCOLOR, FILINDEX, FILREP, FILSTYLE, FILTYPE, HTML
Elliptical Arc	GDRAW('ELLARC', . . .)	HTML, LINCOLOR, LININDEX, LINREP, LINTYPE, LINWIDTH
Fill Area	GDRAW('FILL', . . .)	FILCOLOR, FILINDEX, FILREP, FILSTYLE, FILTYPE, HTML
Line	GDRAW('LINE', . . .)	HTML, LINCOLOR, LININDEX, LINREP, LINTYPE, LINWIDTH
Marker	GDRAW('MARK', . . .)	HTML, MARCOLOR, MARINDEX, MARREP, MARSIZE, MARTYPE
Pie	GDRAW('PIE', . . .)	FILCOLOR, FILINDEX, FILREP, FILSTYLE, FILTYPE, HTML
Text	GDRAW('TEXT', . . .)	HTML, TEXALIGN, TEXCOLOR, TEXFONT, TEXHEIGHT, TEXINDEX, TEXPATH, TEXREP, TEXUP

Attribute functions must precede the graphics primitive they control. Once an attribute is set, it controls any associated graphics primitives that follow. If you want to change the setting, you can issue another GSET(*attribute*, . . .)function with the new setting.

If you do not set an attribute before you submit a graphics primitive, DSGI uses the default value for the attribute. Refer to Chapter 32, "DATA Step Graphics Interface Dictionary," on page 1075 for the default values used for each attribute.

How Operating States Control the Order of DSGI Statements

Each DSGI function and routine can only be submitted when certain operating states are active. This restriction affects the order of functions and routines within the DATA step. Generally, the operating states within a DATA step follow this order:

GKCL → WSAC → SGOP → WSAC → GKCL

Functions That Change the Operating State

The functions described earlier in steps 1, 2, 4, and 5 actually control the changes to the operating state. For example, the GINIT() function must be submitted when the operating state is GKCL, the initial state of DSGI. GINIT() then changes the operating state to WSAC. The GRAPH('CLEAR', . . .)function must be submitted when the operating state is WSAC and before any graphics primitives are submitted. The reason it precedes graphics primitives is that it changes the operating state to SGOP, the operating state in which you can submit graphics primitives. The following list shows the change in the operating state due to specific functions:

GINIT()	GKCL → WSAC
GRAPH('CLEAR', . . .)	WSAC → SGOP
GRAPH('UPDATE', . . .)	SGOP → WSAC
GTERM()	WSAC → GKCL

Because these functions change the operating state, you must order all other functions and routines so that the change in operating state is appropriate for the functions and routines that follow. The following program statements show how the operating state changes from step to step in a typical DSGI program. They also summarize the functions and routines that can be submitted under each operating state. The functions that change the operating state are included as actual statements. Refer to "Operating States" on page 1076 for the operating states from which functions and routines can be submitted.

```
data dsname;

        /* GKCL - initial state of DSGI; can execute:      */
        /*   1. GSET functions that set attributes          */
        /*      that affect the entire graphics output      */
        /*   2. some catalog management functions           */
        /*      (some GRAPH functions)                      */

        /* Step 1 - initialize DSGI          */
    rc=ginit();

        /* WSAC - workstation is active; can execute:       */
        /*   1. most GASK routines                          */
        /*   2. some catalog management functions           */
        /*      (some GRAPH functions)                      */
        /*   3. GSET functions that set attributes          */
        /*      and bundles, viewports, windows,            */
```

```
       /*       transformations, and message logging          */

       /* Step 2 - open a graphics segment    */
   rc=graph('clear', 'text');

       /* SGOP - segment open; can execute:              */
       /* 1. any GASK routine                            */
       /* 2. any GDRAW function                          */
       /* 3. some catalog management functions           */
       /*    (some GRAPH functions)                      */
       /* 4. GSET functions that set attributes          */
       /*    and bundles, viewports, windows,            */
       /*    transformations, and message logging        */

       /* Step 3 - execute graphics primitives */
   rc = gdraw('line', 2, 30,50,50,50);

       /* Step 4 - close the graphics segment  */
   rc=graph('update');

       /* WSAC - workstation is active; can execute:     */
       /*  1. most GASK routines                         */
       /*  2. some catalog management functions          */
       /*     (some GRAPH functions)                     */
       /*  3. GSET functions that set attributes         */
       /*     and bundles, viewports, windows,           */
       /*     transformations, and message logging       */

       /* Step 5 - end DSGI */
   rc=gterm();

       /* GKCL - initial state of DSGI          */
   run;
```

Order of Functions and Routines

Functions and routines within each operating state can technically be submitted in any order; however, once an attribute is set, it remains in effect until the end of the DATA step or until you change its value. If you are producing multiple graphics output within the same DATA step, the attributes for one output affect the ones that follow. Attributes are not reset until after the GTERM() function is submitted.

Notice that you can set attributes for the graphics primitives in several places. As long as the functions that set the attributes are executed before the graphics primitives, they will affect the graphics output. If you execute them after a graphics primitive, the primitive is not affected. See "Setting Attributes for Graphics Elements" on page 1042.

The following program statements illustrate a more complex DSGI program that produces Display 31.3 on page 1047 when submitted. Notice that all attributes for a graphics primitive are executed before the graphics primitive. In addition, the GINIT() and GTERM() pairing and the GRAPH('CLEAR') and GRAPH('UPDATE') pairing are maintained within the DATA step. Refer to "Operating States" on page 1076 for the operating states in which each function and routine can be submitted.

```
   /* set the graphics environment */
   goptions reset=global gunit=pct border
         hsize=7 in vsize=5 in
```

```
            targetdevice=pscolor;

      /* execute a DATA step with DSGI */
   data dsname;
         /* initialize SAS/GRAPH software */
         /* to accept DSGI statements      */
      rc=ginit();
      rc=graph('clear');

         /* assign colors to color index */
      rc=gset('colrep', 1, 'blue');
      rc=gset('colrep', 2, 'red');

         /* define and display titles */
      rc=gset('texcolor', 1);
      rc=gset('texfont', 'swissb');
      rc=gset('texheight', 6);
      rc=gdraw('text', 45, 93, 'Simple Graphics Output');

         /* change the height and */
         /* display second title  */
      rc=gset('texheight', 4);
      rc=gdraw('text', 58, 85, 'Created with DSGI');

         /* define and display footnotes */
         /* using same text font and      */
         /* color as defined for titles  */
      rc=gset('texheight', 3);
      rc=gdraw('text', 125, 1, 'GR31N03  ');

         /* define and draw bar */
      rc=gset('lincolor', 2);
      rc=gset('linwidth', 5);
      rc=gdraw('line', 2, 72, 72, 30, 70);
      rc=gdraw('line', 2, 52, 92, 50, 50);

         /* display graph and end DSGI */
      rc=graph('update');
      rc=gterm();
   run;
```

Display 31.3 Simple Graphics Output Generated with DSGI

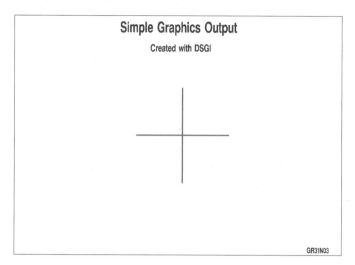

Bundling Attributes

DSGI allows you to bundle attributes. As a result, you can select a group of attribute values rather than having to select each one individually. This feature is useful if you use the same attribute settings over and over within the same DATA step.

To use an attribute bundle, you assign the values of the attributes to a bundle index. When you want to use those attributes for a graphics primitive, you select the bundle rather than set each attribute separately.

Attributes That Can Be Bundled for Each Graphics Primitive

Each graphics primitive has a group of attributes associated with it that can be bundled. Only the attributes in that group can be assigned to the bundle. Table 31.4 on page 1047 shows the attributes that can be bundled for each graphics primitive.

Note: You do not have to use attribute bundles for all graphics primitives if you use a bundle for one. You can define bundles for some graphics primitives and set the attributes individually for others. △

However, if the other graphics primitives are associated with the same attributes you have bundled and you do not want to use the same values, you can use other bundles to set the attributes, or you can set the attributes back to 'INDIVIDUAL'.

Table 31.4 Attributes That Can Be Bundled for Each Graphics Primitive

Graphics Output Primitive	Associated Attributes That Can Be Bundled
GDRAW('ARC', . . .)	LINCOLOR, LINTYPE, LINWIDTH
GDRAW('BAR', . . .)	FILCOLOR, FILSTYLE, FILTYPE
GDRAW('ELLARC', . . .)	LINCOLOR, LINTYPE, LINWIDTH

Graphics Output Primitive	Associated Attributes That Can Be Bundled
GDRAW('ELLIPSE', . . .)	FILCOLOR, FILSTYLE, FILTYPE
GDRAW('FILL', . . .)	FILCOLOR, FILSTYLE, FILTYPE
GDRAW('LINE', . . .)	LINCOLOR, LINTYPE, LINWIDTH
GDRAW('MARK', . . .)	MARCOLOR, MARSIZE, MARTYPE
GDRAW('PIE', . . .)	FILCOLOR, FILSTYLE, FILTYPE
GDRAW('TEXT', . . .)	TEXCOLOR, TEXFONT

Assigning Attributes to a Bundle

To assign values of attributes to a bundle, you must

☐ assign the values to a numeric bundle index with the GSET('*xxx* REP', . . .)function. Each set of attributes that can be bundled uses a separate GSET('*xxx* REP', . . .)function, where *xxx* is the appropriate prefix for the set of attributes to be bundled. Valid values for *xxx* are FIL, LIN, MAR, and TEX.

☐ set the aspect source flag (ASF) of the attributes to 'BUNDLED' before you use the bundled attributes. You can use the GSET('ASF', . . .)function to set the ASF of an attribute. You need to execute a GSET('ASF', . . .)function for each attribute in the bundle.

The following example assigns the text attributes, color, and font, to the bundle indexed by the number 1. As shown in the GSET('TEXREP', . . .)function, the color for the bundle is green, the second color in the COLOR= graphics option. The font for the bundle is the 'ZAPF' font. (See "COLREP" on page 1134 for an explanation of how colors are used in DSGI.)

```
goptions colors=(red green blue);

data dsname;
   .
   .      /* other DATA step statements */
   .

       /* associate the bundle with the index 1 */
   rc=gset('texrep', 1, 2, 'zapf');

   .
   .      /* more statements */
   .

       /* assign the text attributes to a bundle */
   rc=gset('asf', 'texcolor', 'bundled');
   rc=gset('asf', 'texfont', 'bundled');

       /* draw the text */
   rc=gdraw('text', 50, 50, 'Today is the day.');
```

The bundled attributes are used when an associated GDRAW function is executed. If the ASF of an attribute is not set to 'BUNDLED' at the time a GDRAW function is executed, DSGI searches for a value to use in the following order:

1 the current value of the attribute

2 the default value of the attribute.

Selecting a Bundle

Once you have issued the GSET('ASF', . . .)and GSET('*xxx* REP', . . .)functions, you can issue the GSET('*xxx* INDEX', . . .)function to select the bundle. The following statement selects the bundle defined in the previous example:

```
/* invoke the bundle of text attributes */
   rc=gset('texindex', 1);
```

The 1 in this example corresponds to the index number specified in the GSET('TEXREP', . . .)function.

Defining Multiple Bundles for a Graphics Primitive

You can set up more than one bundle for graphics primitives by issuing another GSET('*xxx* REP', . . .)function with a different index number. If you wanted to add a second attribute bundle for text to the previous example, you could issue the following statement:

```
/* define another attribute bundle for text */
   rc=gset('texrep', 2, 3, 'swiss');
```

When you activate the second bundle, the graphics primitives for the text that follows will use the third color, blue, and the SWISS font.

Note: When using a new bundle, you do not need to reissue the GSET('ASF', . . .) functions for the attributes that will be bundled. Once the ASF of an attribute has been set, the setting remains in effect until it is changed. △

How DSGI Selects the Value of an Attribute to Use

Attributes that are bundled override any of the same attributes that are individually set. For example, you assign the line color green, the type 1, and the width 5 to a line bundle with the following statements:

```
goptions colors=(red green blue);
rc=gset('asf', 'lincolor', 'bundled');
rc=gset('asf', 'linwidth', 'bundled');
rc=gset('asf', 'lintype', 'bundled');
rc=gset('linrep', 3, 2, 5, 1);
```

In subsequent statements, you activate the bundle, select other attributes for the line, and then draw a line:

```
/* activate the bundle */
rc=gset('linindex', 3);

   /* select other attributes for the line */
rc=gset('lincolor', 3);
rc=gset('linwidth', 10);
rc=gset('lintype', 4);

   /* draw a line from point (30,50) to (70,50) */
rc=gdraw('line', 2, 30, 70, 50, 50);
```

The color, type, and width associated with the line bundle are used rather than the attributes set just before the GDRAW('LINE', . . .)function was executed. The line that is drawn is green (the second color from the colors list of the COLORS= graphics option), 5 units wide, and solid (line type 1).

During processing, DSGI chooses the value of an attribute using the following logic:

1 Get the index of the active line bundle.

2 Check the ASF of the LINCOLOR attribute. If the ASF is 'INDIVIDUAL', the value selected with GSET('LINCOLOR', . . .) is used; otherwise, the LINCOLOR associated with the bundle index is used.

3 Check the ASF of the LINTYPE attribute. If the ASF is 'INDIVIDUAL', the value selected with GSET('LINTYPE', . . .) is used; otherwise, the LINTYPE associated with the bundle index is used.

4 Check the ASF of the LINWIDTH attribute. If the ASF is 'INDIVIDUAL', the value selected with GSET('LINWIDTH', . . .) is used; otherwise, the LINWIDTH associated with the bundle index is used.

5 Draw the line using the appropriate color, type, and width for the line.

Disassociating an Attribute from a Bundle

To disassociate an attribute from a bundle, use the GSET('ASF', . . .)function to reset the ASF of the attribute to 'INDIVIDUAL'. The following program statements demonstrate how to disassociate the attributes from the text bundle:

```
/* disassociate an attribute from a bundle */
   rc=gset('asf', 'texcolor', 'individual');
   rc=gset('asf', 'texfont', 'individual');
```

Using Viewports and Windows

In DSGI, you can define viewports and windows. Viewports enable you to subdivide the graphics output area and insert existing graphs or draw graphics elements in smaller sections of the graphics output area. Windows define the coordinate system within a viewport and enable you to scale the graph or graphics elements drawn within the viewport.

The default viewport is defined as (0,0) to (1,1) with 1 being 100 percent of the graphics output area. If you do not define a viewport, graphics elements or graphs are drawn using the default.

The default window is defined so that a rectangle drawn from window coordinates (0,0) to (100,100) is square and fills the display in one dimension. The actual dimensions of the default window are device dependent. Use the GASK('WINDOW', . . .) routine to find the exact dimensions of your default window. You can define a window without defining a viewport. The coordinate system of the window is used with the default viewport.

If you define a viewport, you can position it anywhere in the graphics output area. You can define multiple viewports within the graphics output area so that more than one existing graph, part of a graph, or more than one graphics element can be inserted into the graphics output.

Transformations activate both a viewport and the associated window. DSGI maintains 21 (0 through 20) transformations. By default, transformation 0 is active. Transformation 0 always uses the entire graphics output area for the viewport and maps the window coordinates to fill the viewport. The definition of the viewport and window of transformation 0 may not be changed.

By default, the viewports and windows of all the other transformations (1 through 20) are set to the defaults for viewports and windows. If you want to define a different viewport or window, you must select a transformation number between 1 and 20.

You generally follow these steps when defining viewports or windows:

□ Define the viewport or window.

□ Activate the transformation so that the viewport or window is used for the output.

These steps can be submitted in any order; however, if you use a transformation you have not defined, the default viewport and window are used. Once you activate a transformation, the graphics elements drawn by the subsequent DSGI functions are drawn in the viewport and window associated with that transformation.

Defining Viewports

You can define a viewport with the GSET('VIEWPORT', *n*, . . .)function, where *n* is the transformation number of the viewport you are defining. You can also use this function to define multiple viewports, each containing a portion of the graphics output area. You can then place a separate graph, part of a graph, or graphics elements within each viewport.

The following program statements divide the graphics output area into four subareas:

```
/* define the first viewport, indexed by 1 */
rc=gset('viewport', 1, .05, .05, .45, .45);

   /* define the second viewport, indexed by 2 */
rc=gset('viewport', 2, .55, .05, .95, .45);

   /* define the third viewport, indexed by 3 */
rc=gset('viewport', 3, .55, .55, .95, .95);

   /* define the fourth viewport, indexed by 4 */
rc=gset('viewport', 4, .05, .55, .45, .95);
```

Once you define the viewports, you can insert existing graphs or draw graphics elements in each viewport by activating the transformation of that viewport.

Clipping around Viewports

When you use viewports, you also may need to use the clipping feature. Even though you have defined the dimensions of your viewport, it is possible for graphics elements to display past its boundaries. If the graphics elements are too large to fit into the dimensions you have defined, portions of the graphics elements actually display outside of the viewport. To ensure that only the portions of the graphics elements that fit within the dimensions of the viewport display, turn the clipping feature on by using the GSET('CLIP', . . .)function. For details, see "CLIP" on page 1133.

Defining Windows

You can define a window by using the GSET('WINDOW',*n*, . . .)function, where *n* is the transformation number of the window you are defining. If you are defining a window for a viewport you have also defined, *n* must match the transformation number of the viewport.

You can scale the *x* and *y* axes differently for a window. The following program statements scale the axes for each of the four viewports defined earlier in "Defining Viewpoints":

```
/* define the window for viewport 1 */
rc=gset('window', 1, 0, 50, 20, 100);
```

```
    /* define the window for viewport 2 */
rc=gset('window', 2, 0, 40, 20, 90);

    /* define the window for viewport 3 */
rc=gset('window', 3, 10, 25, 45, 100);

    /* define the window for viewport 4 */
rc=gset('window', 4, 0, 0, 100, 100);
```

See "Scaling Graphs by Using Windows" on page 1062 for an example of using windows to scale graphs.

Note: When you define a window for a viewport, the transformation numbers in the GSET('VIEWPORT', . . .)and GSET('WINDOW', . . .)functions must match in order for DSGI to activate them simultaneously. △

Activating Transformations

Once you have defined a viewport or window, you must activate the transformation in order for DSGI to use the viewport or window. To activate the transformation, use the GSET('TRANSNO',*n*, . . .)function where *n* has the same value as *n* in GSET('VIEWPORT',*n*, . . .)or GSET('WINDOW',*n*, . . .).

The following program statements illustrate how to activate the viewports and windows defined in the previous examples:

```
/* define the viewports */
   .
   .
   .
   /* define the windows */
   .
   .
   .
   /* activate the first transformation */
gset('transno', 1);
.
.  /* graphics primitive functions follow */
.
   /* activate the second transformation */
gset('transno', 2);
.
.  /* graphics primitive functions follow */
.
   /* activate the third transformation */
gset('transno', 3);
.
.  /* graphics primitive functions follow */
.
   /* activate the fourth transformation */
gset('transno', 4);
.
.  /* graphics primitive functions follow */
.
```

When you activate these transformations, your display is logically divided into four subareas as shown in Figure 31.2 on page 1053.

Figure 31.2 Graphics Output Area Divided into Four Logical Transformations

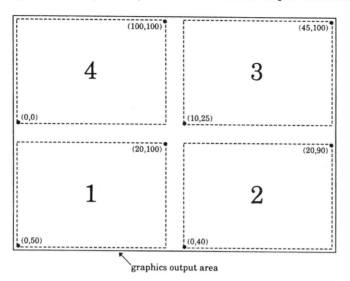

graphics output area

If you want to use the default viewport and window after selecting different ones, execute the GSET('TRANSNO', 0) function to reselect the default transformation for DSGI.

Inserting Existing Graphs into DSGI Graphics Output

You can insert existing graphs into graphics output you are creating. The graph you insert must be in the same catalog in which you are currently working. Follow these steps to insert an existing graph:

1 Use the GSET('CATALOG', . . .)function to set the output catalog to the catalog that contains the existing graph.

   Note: Unless you are using the WORK library, you must have previously defined the libref in a LIBNAME statement or window when using GSET('CATALOG', . . .). △

2 Define a viewport with the dimensions and position of the place in the graphics output where you want to insert the existing graph. GSET('VIEWPORT',*n*, . . .) defines a viewport and GSET('WINDOW',*n*, . . .)defines a window.

3 Define a window as (0,0) to (100,100) so that the inserted graph is not distorted. The graph must have a square area defined to avoid the distortion. If your device does not have a square graphics output area, the window defaults to the units of the device rather than (0,0) to (100,100) and may distort the graph.

4 Activate the transformation number *n*, as defined in the viewport function, and possibly in the window function, using GSET('TRANSNO', *n*, . . .).

5 Use the GRAPH('INSERT', . . .)function with the name of the existing graph.

The following program statements provide an example of including an existing graph in the graphics output being created. The name of the existing graph is 'MAP'. 'LOCAL' points to the library containing the catalog 'MAPCTLG'. The coordinates of the viewport are percentages of the graphics output area. **SAS-data-library** refers to a permanent SAS data library.

Example Code 31.1 Graphics Output Area Divided into Four Logical Transformations

```
libname local 'SAS-data-library';
```

```
      .
      .
      .
         /* select the output catalog to the */
         /* catalog that contains 'map' */
      rc=gset('catalog', 'local', 'mapctlg');
         .
         .
         .


         /* define the viewport to contain the */
         /* existing graph */
      rc=gset('viewport', 1, .25, .45, .75, .9);
      rc=gset('window', 1, 0, 0, 100, 100);

         /* set the transformation number to the one */
         /* defined in the viewport function */
      rc=gset('transno', 1);

         /* insert the existing graph */
      rc=graph('insert', 'map');
```

These statements put the existing graph 'MAP' in the upper half of the graphics output.

Generating Multiple Graphics Output in One DATA Step

You can produce more than one graphics output within the same DATA step. All statements between the GRAPH('CLEAR', . . .)and GRAPH('UPDATE', . . .)functions will produce one graphics output.

Each time the GRAPH('UPDATE', . . .)function is executed, a graph is displayed. After the GTERM() function is executed, no more graphs are displayed for the DATA step. The GINIT() function must be executed again to produce more graphs.

CAUTION:
   Be careful using global SAS/GRAPH statements when you are producing multiple output from within the DATA step. △

If you use global SAS/GRAPH statements when producing multiple output from one DATA step, the last definition of the statements is used for all displays.

Processing DSGI Statements in Loops

You can process DSGI statements in loops to draw a graphics element multiple times in one graphics output or to produce multiple output. If you use loops, you must maintain the GRAPH('CLEAR', . . .)and GRAPH('UPDATE', . . .)pairing within the GINIT() and GTERM() pairing. (See Figure 31.1 on page 1042.) The following program statements illustrate how you can use DSGI statements to produce multiple graphics output for different output devices:

```
data _null_;
   length d1-d5 $ 8;
   input d1-d5;
   array devices{5} d1-d5;
```

```
          .
          .
          .
      do j=1 to 5;
         rc=gset('device', devices{j});
            .
            .
            .
         rc=ginit();
            .
            .
            .
         do i=1 to 5;
            rc=graph('clear');
            rc=gset('filcolor', i);
            rc=gdraw('bar', 45, 45, 65, 65);
            rc=graph('update');
         end;
            .
            .
            .
         rc=gterm();
      end;
      cards;
   tek4105 hp7475 ps qms800 ibm3279
   ;
   run;
```

The inner loop produces five graphs for each device. Each graphics output produced
by the inner loop consists of a bar. The bar uses a different color for each graph. The
outer loop produces all of the graphs for five different devices. A total of 25 graphs is
generated by these loops.

Examples

The following examples show different applications for DSGI and illustrate some of
its features such as defining viewports and windows, inserting existing graphs, angling
text, using GASK routines, enlarging a segment of a graph, and scaling a graph.

These examples use some additional graphics options that may not be used in other
examples in this book. Because the dimensions of the default window vary across
devices, the TARGETDEVICE=, HSIZE=, and VSIZE= graphics options are used to
make the programs more portable. The COLORS= graphics option provides a standard
colors list.

Refer to Chapter 32, "DATA Step Graphics Interface Dictionary," on page 1075 for a
complete description of each of the functions used in the examples.

Vertically Angling Text

This example generates a pie chart with text that changes its angle as you rotate
around the pie. DSGI positions the text by aligning it differently depending on its
location on the pie. In addition, DSGI changes the angle of the text so that it aligns
with the spokes of the pie.

This example illustrates how global statements can be used with DSGI. In this
example, FOOTNOTE and TITLE statements create the footnotes and title for the
graph. The GOPTIONS statement defines general aspects of the graph. The COLORS=

graphics option provides a colors list from which the colors referenced in GSET('*xxx* COLOR', . . .)functions are selected.

The following program statements produce Display 31.4 on page 1057:

```
/* set the graphics environment */
goptions reset=global gunit=pct border
        ftext=swissb htitle=6 htext=3
        colors=(black blue green red)
        hsize=7 in vsize=5 in
        targetdevice=pscolor;

    /* define the footnote and title */
footnote1 j=r 'GR31N04  ';
title1 'Text Up Vector';

    /* execute DATA step with DSGI */
data vector;

        /* prepare SAS/GRAPH software */
        /* to accept DSGI statements   */
    rc=ginit();
    rc=graph('clear');

        /* define and display arc   */
        /* with intersecting lines */
    rc=gset('lincolor', 2);
    rc=gset('linwidth', 5);
    rc=gdraw('arc', 84, 50, 35, 0, 360);
    rc=gdraw('line', 2, 49, 119, 51, 51);
    rc=gdraw('line', 2, 84, 84, 15, 85);

        /* define height of text */
    rc=gset('texheight', 5);

        /* mark 360 degrees on the arc */
        /* using default align          */
    rc=gdraw('text', 121, 50, '0');

        /* set text to align to the right and */
        /* mark 180 degrees on the arc          */
    rc=gset('texalign', 'right', 'normal');
    rc=gdraw('text', 47, 50, '180');

        /* set text to align to the center and */
        /* mark 90 and 270 degrees on the arc  */
    rc=gset('texalign', 'center', 'normal');
    rc=gdraw('text', 84, 87, '90');
    rc=gdraw('text', 84, 9, '270');

        /* reset texalign to normal and          */
        /* display coordinate values or quadrant */
    rc=gset('texalign', 'normal', 'normal');
    rc=gdraw('text', 85, 52, '(0.0, +1.0)');

        /* rotate text using TEXUP and          */
```

```
      /* display coordinate values or quadrant */
   rc=gset('texup', 1.0, 0.0);
   rc=gdraw('text', 85, 49, '(+1.0, 0.0)');

      /* rotate text using TEXUP and            */
      /* display coordinate values or quadrant */
   rc=gset('texup', 0.0, -1.0);
   rc=gdraw('text', 83, 50, '(0.0, -1.0)');

      /* rotate text using TEXUP and            */
      /* display coordinate values or quadrant */
   rc=gset('texup', -1.0, 0.0);
   rc=gdraw('text', 83, 52, '(-1.0, 0.0)');

      /* display graph and end DSGI */
   rc=graph('update');
   rc=gterm();
run;
```

Display 31.4   Text Angled with the GSET('TEXUP', ...) Function

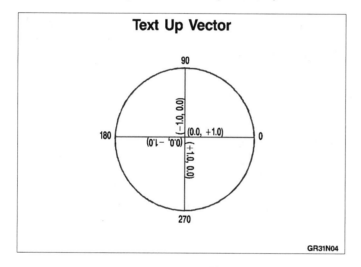

This example illustrates the following features:

☐ The COLORS= graphics option provides a colors table to be used with the GSET('LINCOLOR', . . .)function.

☐ The HSIZE= graphics option provides a standard width for the graphics output area.

☐ The VSIZE= graphics option provides a standard height for the graphics output area.

☐ The TARGETDEVICE= graphics option selects the standard color PostScript driver to use as the target device.

☐ The GINIT() function begins DSGI.

☐ The GRAPH('CLEAR') function sets the graphics environment. Because the function does not specify a name for the catalog entry, DSGI will use the default name 'DSGI'.

☐ The GSET('TEXHEIGHT', . . .), GSET('LINCOLOR', . . .), and GSET('LINWIDTH', . . .)functions set attributes of the graphics primitives. The

COLORS= graphics option provides a colors table for the GSET('LINCOLOR', 2) function to reference. In this example, the color indexed by 2 is used to draw lines. Since no other colors table is explicitly defined with GSET('COLREP', . . .) functions, DSGI looks at the colors list and chooses the color indexed by 2 (the second color in the list) to draw the lines.

□ The GDRAW('ARC', . . .)function draws an empty pie chart. The arguments of the GDRAW('ARC', . . .)function provide the coordinates of the starting point, the radius, and the beginning and ending angles of the arc.

□ The GDRAW('LINE', . . .)function draws a line. It provides the type of line, the coordinates of the beginning point, and the coordinates of the ending point.

□ The GDRAW('TEXT', . . .)function draws the text. It sets the coordinates of the starting point of the text string as well as the text string to be written.

□ The GSET('TEXALIGN', . . .)function aligns text to the center, left, or right of the starting point specified in the GDRAW('TEXT', . . .)function.

□ The GSET('TEXUP', . . .)function determines the angle at which the text is to be written.

□ The GRAPH('UPDATE', . . .)function closes the graphics segment.

□ The GTERM() function ends DSGI.

Changing the Reading Direction of the Text

This example changes the reading direction of text. Notice that the data set name is _NULL_. No data set is created as a result of this DATA step; however, the graphics output is generated. The following program statements produce Display 31.5 on page 1059:

```
   /* set the graphics environment */
goptions reset=global gunit=pct border
        ftext=swissb htitle=6 htext=3
        colors=(black blue green red)
        hsize=7 in vsize=5 in
        targetdevice=pscolor;

   /* define the footnote and title */
footnote1 j=r 'GR31N05  ';
title1 'Text Path';

   /* execute DATA step with DSGI */
data _null_;

     /* prepare SAS/GRAPH software */
     /* to accept DSGI statements   */
   rc=ginit();
   rc=graph('clear');

     /* define height of text */
   rc=gset('texheight', 5);

     /* display first text */
   rc=gdraw('text', 105, 50, 'Right');

     /* change text path so that text reads from */
     /* right to left and display next text      */
   rc=gset('texpath', 'left');
```

```
rc=gdraw('text', 65, 50, 'Left');

    /* change text path so that text reads up */
    /* the display and display next text      */
rc=gset('texpath', 'up');
rc=gdraw('text', 85, 60, 'Up');

    /* change text path so that text reads down */
    /* the display and display next text        */
rc=gset('texpath', 'down');
rc=gdraw('text', 85, 40, 'Down');

    /* display the graph and end DSGI */
rc=graph('update');
rc=gterm();
run;
```

Display 31.5   Reading Direction of the Text Changed with the GSET('TEXPATH', ...) Function

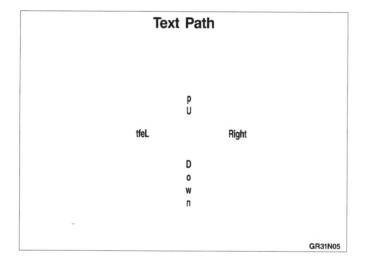

Features not explained earlier in "Vertically Angling Text" are described here:

☐ DATA _NULL_ causes the DATA step to be executed, but no data set is created.

☐ The GSET('TEXPATH', . . .)function changes the direction in which the text reads.

Using Viewports in DSGI

This example uses the GCHART procedure to generate a graph, defines a viewport in which to display it, and inserts the GCHART graph into the graphics output being created by DSGI. Display 31.6 on page 1061 shows the pie chart created by the GCHART procedure. Display 31.7 on page 1062 shows the same pie chart after it has been inserted into a DSGI graph.

```
    /* set the graphics environment */
goptions reset=global gunit=pct border
         ftext=swissb htitle=6 htext=4
         colors=(black blue green red)
         hsize=7 in vsize=7 in
         targetdevice=pscolor;
```

```
   /* create data set TOTALS */
data totals;
   length dept $ 7 site $ 8;
   do year=1996 to 1999;
      do dept='Parts','Repairs','Tools';
         do site='New York','Atlanta','Chicago','Seattle';
            sales=ranuni(97531)*10000+2000;
            output;
         end;
      end;
   end;
run;

   /* define the footnote */
footnote1 h=3 j=r 'GR31N06   ';

   /* generate pie chart from TOTALS */
   /* and create catalog entry PIE    */
proc gchart data=totals;
   format sales dollar8.;
   pie site
       / type=sum
         sumvar=sales
         midpoints='New York' 'Chicago' 'Atlanta' 'Seattle'
         fill=solid
         cfill=green
         coutline=blue
         angle=45
         percent=inside
         value=inside
         slice=outside
         noheading
         name='gr31n06';
run;

   /* define the titles */
title1 'Total Sales';
title2 'For Period 1996-1999';

   /* execute DATA step with DSGI */
data piein;

      /* prepare SAS/GRAPH software */
      /* to accept DSGI statements  */
   rc=ginit();
   rc=graph('clear');

      /* define and activate viewport for inserted graph */
   rc=gset('viewport', 1, .15, .05, .85, .90);
   rc=gset('window', 1, 0, 0, 100, 100);
   rc=gset('transno', 1);
```

```
       /* insert graph created from GCHART procedure */
   rc=graph('insert', 'gr31n06');

       /* display graph and end DSGI */
   rc=graph('update');
   rc=gterm();
run;
```

Display 31.6   Pie Chart Produced with the GCHART Procedure

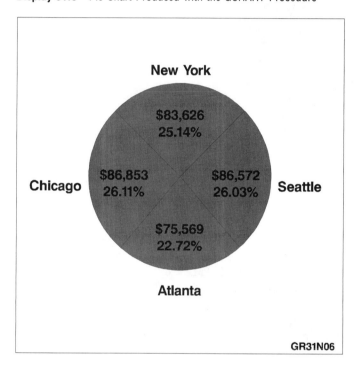

Display 31.7   Pie Chart Inserted into DSGI Graph by Using a Viewport

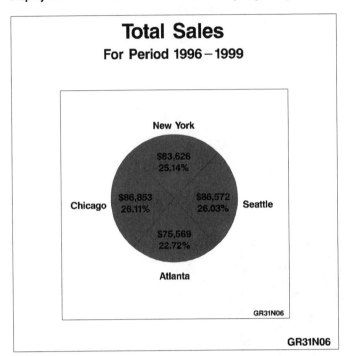

Features not explained in previous examples are described here:

□ A graph can be created by another SAS/GRAPH procedure and inserted into DSGI graphics output. In this case, the NAME= option in the PIE statement of the GCHART procedure names the graph, 'GR31N06', to be inserted.

□ The GSET('VIEWPORT', . . .)function defines the section of the graphics output area into which GR31N06 is inserted. The dimensional ratio of the viewport should match that of the entire graphics output area so that the inserted graph is not distorted.

□ The GSET('WINDOW', . . .)function defines the coordinate system to be used within the viewport. In this example, the coordinates (0,0) to (100,100) are used. These coordinates provide a square area to insert the graph and preserve the aspect ratio of the GCHART graph.

□ The GSET('TRANSNO', . . .)function activates the transformation for the defined viewport and window.

□ The GRAPH('INSERT', . . .)function inserts the existing graph, 'GR31N06', into the one being created with DSGI. If no viewport has been explicitly defined, DSGI inserts the graph into the default viewport, which is the entire graphics output area.

Scaling Graphs by Using Windows

This example uses the GPLOT procedure to generate a plot of AMOUNT*MONTH and store the graph in a permanent catalog. DSGI then scales the graph by defining a window in another DSGI graph and inserting the GPLOT graph into that window. Display 31.8 on page 1064 shows the plot as it is displayed with the GPLOT procedure. Display 31.9 on page 1065 shows how the same plot is displayed when the *x* axis is scaled from 15 to 95 and the *y* axis is scaled from 15 to 75.

```
     /* set the graphics environment */
goptions reset=global gunit=pct border
```

```
             ftext=swissb htitle=6 htext=3
             colors=(black blue green red)
             hsize=7 in vsize=5 in
             targetdevice=pscolor;

   /* create data set EARN, which holds month */
   /* and amount of earnings for that month   */
data earn;
   input month amount;
   datalines;
1 2.1
2 3
3 5
4 6.4
5 9
6 7.2
7 6
8 9.8
9 4.4
10 2.5
11 5.75
12 4.35
;
run;

   /* define the footnote for the first graph */
footnote1 j=r 'GR31N07(a)   ';

   /* define axis and symbol characteristics */
axis1 label=(color=green 'Millions of Dollars')
      order=(1 to 10 by 1)
      value=(color=green);
axis2 label=(color=green 'Months')
      order=(1 to 12 by 1)
      value=(color=green Tick=1 'Jan' Tick=2 'Feb' Tick=3 'Mar'
             Tick=4 'Apr' Tick=5 'May' Tick=6 'Jun'
             Tick=7 'Jul' Tick=8 'Aug' Tick=9 'Sep'
             Tick=10 'Oct' Tick=11 'Nov' Tick=12 'Dec');

symbol value=M font=special height=8 interpol=join
       color=blue width=3;

   /* generate a plot of AMOUNT * MONTH,           */
   /* and store in member GR31N07                  */
proc gplot data=earn;
   plot amount*month
        / haxis=axis2
          vaxis=axis1
          name='gr31n07';
run;

   /* define the footnote and titles for         */
   /* second graph, which will scale output */
footnote1 j=r 'GR31N07(b)   ';
```

```
title1 'XYZ Corporation Annual Earnings';
title2 h=4 'Fiscal Year 1999';

   /* execute DATA step with DSGI using  */
   /* catalog entry created in previous   */
   /* plot, but do not create a data set */
   /* (determined by specifying _NULL_)   */
data _null_;

      /* prepare SAS/GRAPH software */
      /* to accept DSGI statements */
   rc=ginit();
   rc=graph('clear');

      /* define viewport and window for inserted graph */
   rc=gset('viewport', 1, .20, .30, .90, .75);
   rc=gset('window', 1, 15, 15, 95, 75);
   rc=gset('transno', 1);

      /* insert graph previously created */
   rc=graph('insert', 'gr31n07');

      /* display graph and end DSGI */
   rc=graph('update');
   rc=gterm();
run;
```

Display 31.8 Plot Produced with the GPLOT Procedure

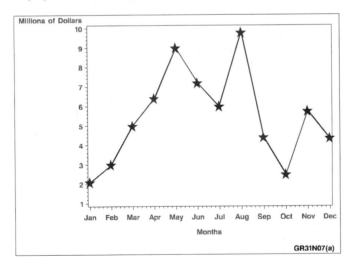

Display 31.9   Plot Scaled by Using a Window in DSGI

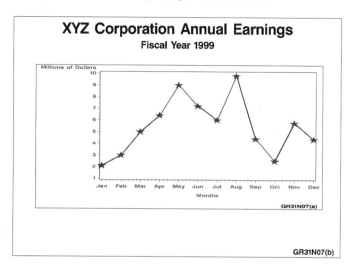

One feature not explained in previous examples is described here:

☐ The GSET('WINDOW', . . .)function scales the plot with respect to the viewport that is defined. The *x* axis is scaled from 15 to 95, and the *y* axis is scaled from 15 to 75. If no viewport were explicitly defined, the window coordinates would be mapped to the default viewport, the entire graphics output area.

Enlarging an Area of a Graph by Using Windows

This example illustrates how you can enlarge a section of a graph by using windows. In the first DATA step, the program statements generate graphics output that contains four pie charts. The second DATA step defines a window that enlarges the bottom-left quadrant of the graphics output and inserts 'GR31N08' into that window. The following program statements produce Display 31.10 on page 1067 from the first DATA step, and Display 31.11 on page 1067 from the second DATA step:

```
    /* set the graphics environment */
goptions reset=global gunit=pct border
         ftext=swissb htext=3
         colors=(black blue green red)
         hsize=7 in vsize=5 in
         targetdevice=pscolor;

    /* define the footnote for the first graph */
footnote1 j=r 'GR31N08(a)  ';

    /* execute DATA step with DSGI */
data plot;

        /* prepare SAS/GRAPH software */
        /* to accept DSGI statements  */
    rc=ginit();
    rc=graph('clear', 'gr31n08');

        /* define and draw first pie chart */
    rc=gset('filcolor', 4);
    rc=gset('filtype', 'solid');
```

```
       rc=gdraw('pie', 30, 75, 22, 0, 360);

         /* define and draw second pie chart */
       rc=gset('filcolor', 1);
       rc=gset('filtype', 'solid');
       rc=gdraw('pie', 30, 25, 22, 0, 360);

         /* define and draw third pie chart */
       rc=gset('filcolor', 3);
       rc=gset('filtype', 'solid');
       rc=gdraw('pie', 90, 75, 22, 0, 360);

         /* define and draw fourth pie chart */
       rc=gset('filcolor', 2);
       rc=gset('filtype', 'solid');
       rc=gdraw('pie', 90, 25, 22, 0, 360);

         /* display graph and end DSGI */
       rc=graph('update');
       rc=gterm();
    run;

         /* define the footnote for the second graph */
    footnote1 j=r 'GR31N08(b)   ';

       /* execute DATA step with DSGI    */
       /* that zooms in on a section of */
       /* the previous graph            */
    data zoom;

         /* prepare SAS/GRAPH software */
         /* to accept DSGI statements  */
       rc=ginit();
       rc=graph('clear');

         /* define and activate a window      */
         /* that will enlarge the lower left */
         /* quadrant of the graph            */
       rc=gset('window', 1, 0, 0, 50, 50);
       rc=gset('transno', 1);

         /* insert the previous graph into */
         /* window 1                       */
       rc=graph('insert', 'gr31n08');

         /* display graph and end DSGI */
       rc=graph('update');
       rc=gterm();
    run;
```

Display 31.10 Four Pie Charts Generated with DSGI

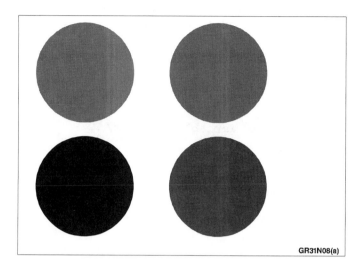

Display 31.11 Area of the Graph Enlarged by Using Windows

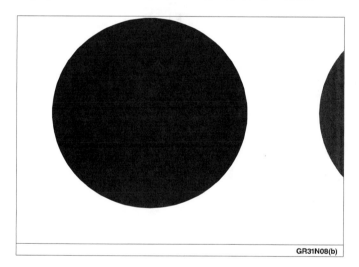

Features not explained in previous examples are described here:

☐ The GSET('WINDOW', . . .)function defines a window into which the graph is inserted. In this example, no viewport is defined, so the window coordinates map to the default viewport, which is the entire graphics output area. The result of using the default viewport is that only the portion of the graph enclosed by the coordinates of the window is displayed.

☐ The GRAPH('INSERT', . . .)function inserts a graph that was previously generated with DSGI. If you want to insert output created by DSGI, the output to be inserted must be closed.

Using GASK Routines in DSGI

This example illustrates how to invoke GASK routines and how to display the returned values in the SAS log and write them to a data set.

This example assigns a predefined color to color index 2 and then invokes a GASK routine to get the name of the color associated with color index 2. The value returned from the GASK call is displayed in the log and written to a data set. Output 31.1 on page 1068 shows how the value appears in the log. Output 31.2 on page 1069 shows how the value appears in the data set in the OUTPUT window.

```
       /* execute DATA step with DSGI */
data routine;

        /* declare character variables used */
        /* in GASK subroutines               */
    length color $ 8;

        /* prepare SAS/GRAPH software */
        /* to accept DSGI statements  */
    rc=ginit();
    rc=graph('clear');

        /* set color for color index 2 */
    rc=gset('colrep', 2, 'orange');

        /* check color associated with color index 2 and */
        /* display the value in the LOG window           */
    call gask('colrep', 2, color, rc);
    put 'Current FILCOLOR =' color;
    output;

        /* end DSGI */
    rc=graph('update');
    rc=gterm();
run;

        /* display the contents of ROUTINE */
proc print data=routine;
run;
```

Output 31.1 Checking the Color Associated with a Particular Color Index

```
3          /* execute DATA step with DSGI */
4      data routine;
5
6          /* declare character variables used */
7          /* in GASK subroutines              */
8      length color $ 8;
9
10         /* prepare SAS/GRAPH software */
11         /* to accept DSGI statements  */
12     rc=ginit();
13     rc=graph('clear');
14
15         /* set color for color index 2 */
16     rc=gset('colrep', 2, 'orange');
17
18         /* check color associated with color index 2 and */
19         /* display the value in the LOG window            */
20     call gask('colrep', 2, color, rc);
21     put 'Current FILCOLOR =' color;
22     output;
23
24         /* end DSGI */
25     rc=graph('update');
26     rc=gterm();
27  run;

Current FILCOLOR =ORANGE
```

Output 31.2   Writing the Value of an Attribute to a Data Set

```
The SAS System                   13:50 Tuesday, December 22, 1998   1

   Obs      color      rc

    1       ORANGE      0
```

Features not explained in previous examples are described here:

□ The GSET('COLREP', . . .)function assigns the predefined color 'ORANGE' to the color index 2.

□ GASK routines check the current value of an attribute. In this example, the GASK('COLREP', . . .)function returns the color associated with color index 2.

□ A PUT statement displays the value of the COLOR argument in the log.

□ An OUTPUT statement writes the value of COLOR to the ROUTINE data set.

□ The GRAPH('UPDATE') function closes the graphics segment.

□ The PRINT procedure displays the contents of the ROUTINE data set.

Generating a Drill-down Graph Using DSGI

This example uses ODS processing with DSGI to generate a drill-down graph. To get the drill-down capability, you use the GSET('HTML',...) function to specify a URL that points to the location of the target output. This HTML string can be used with the following graphic element types drawn in the code *after* the string is set: BAR, ELLIPSE, FILL, MARK, PIE, and TEXT. The example uses a PIE element type.

Note: The example assumes users will access the output through a file system rather than accross the Web, so the HTML string uses a file specification rather than a full URL. For information on bringing SAS/GRAPH output to the Web, see Chapter 5, "Bringing SAS/GRAPH Output to the Web," on page 71. For specific information about drill-down graphs, see "About Drill-down Graphs" on page 90. △

This example also includes a FILENAME statement to allocate an aggregate storage location for the HTML and GIF files produced by the code. You should replace the term *path-to-Web-server* with the location where you want to store the files.

In the example, the ODS HTML statement is used to create a body file named dsgi.htm. When file dsgi.htm is viewed in a Web browser, it displays a solid pie chart, as shown in Display 31.12 on page 1071. To drill down to the graph shown in Display 31.13 on page 1072, click anywhere in the pie chart. This example uses PROC GSLIDE to create the simple graphic that is used for the target output:

```
   /* This is the only line you have to  */
   /* change to run the program. Specify */
   /* a location in your file system.    */
filename odsout 'path-to-Web-server';

   /* close the listing destination */
ods listing close;

   /* set the graphics environment */
goptions reset=global gunit=pct noborder
        ftitle=swissb htitle=6
        ftext=swiss htext=3
        colors=(black blue)
        hsize=5 in vsize=5 in
        device=gif;

   /* define tile and footnote for graph */
title1 'Drill-down Graph';
footnote1 j=l '  Click in pie chart'
         j=r 'GR31N10  ';

ods html body='dsgi.htm'
        path=odsout;

   /* execute DATA step with DSGI */
data _null_;
     /* prepare SAS/GRAPH software */
     /* to accept DSGI statements  */
  rc=ginit();
  rc=graph('clear');
     /* set a value for the html variable */
  rc=gset('html', 'href="blue.htm"');

     /* define and draw a pie chart */
  rc=gset('filcolor', 2);
  rc=gset('filtype', 'solid');
  rc=gdraw('pie', 55, 50, 22, 0, 360);

     /* generate graph and end DSGI */
  rc=graph('update');
  rc=gterm();
```

```
run;

goptions ftext=centb ctext=blue;

   /* open a new body file for the */
   /* target output                */
ods html body='blue.htm'
        path=odsout;

title1;
footnote1;
proc gslide wframe=4
     cframe=blue
     name='blue';
     note height=20;
     note height=10
          justify=center
          'Blue Sky';
run;
quit;

ods html close;
ods listing;
```

Display 31.12   Drill-down Graph Generated with DSGI

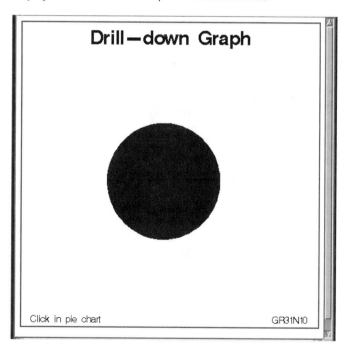

Display 31.13 Target Output for Drill-down Graph

Features not explained in previous examples are described here:

□ FILENAME allocates a storage location for the HTML and GIF files that are produced by the program.

□ To conserve system resources, ODS LISTING CLOSE closes the Listing destination.

□ On the GOPTIONS statement, DEVICE=GIF tells SAS/GRAPH to generate a GIF file for each GRSEG that is created in the code. The GIF files are needed to display the graphics output in a Web browser.

□ On the first ODS HTML statement, BODY= specifies a name for the file that will reference the pie chart that is generated with DSGI. PATH= specifes the output location that was allocated by the FILENAME statement.

□ In the DATA step, the presence of the GSET('HTML',...) function causes SAS/GRAPH to create the pie chart as a drill-down graph. The HTML string *'href="blue.htm"'* will be used as the value for the HREF attribute in the image map that SAS/GRAPH creates for the drill-down capability. The image map will be created in the body file dsgi.htm, because that is the file that references the pie chart. (The target output file blue.htm does not exist yet, but it will be created by the GSLIDE procedure later in the program.)

□ The second ODS HTML file specifies a new body file. Thus, the first body file dsgi.htm is closed, and the new body file blue.htm is opened. File blue.htm is the file that is identified as the target output by the HREF value on the GSET('HTML',...) function.

□ PROC GSLIDE produces the graphic that is used as the target output for the drill-down graph.

□ ODS HTML CLOSE closes the HTML destination, and ODS LISTING opens the Listing destination for subsequent output during the SAS session.

See Also

"Storing Graphics Output in SAS Catalogs" on page 49
  for an explanation of graphics catalogs and catalog entries

Chapter 9, "Graphics Options and Device Parameters Dictionary," on page 301
  for complete information about graphics options

"TITLE, FOOTNOTE, and NOTE Statements" on page 251
  for details of using the TITLE and FOOTNOTE statements

"GOPTIONS Statement" on page 182
  for details of using the GOPTIONS statement

Chapter 10, "The Annotate Data Set," on page 403
  for an explanation of the Annotate facility

Chapter 32, "DATA Step Graphics Interface Dictionary," on page 1075
  for complete information on the functions and routines used with DSGI

SAS Language Reference: Dictionary
  for information about additional functions and statements that can be used in the
  DATA step

CHAPTER

32

DATA Step Graphics Interface Dictionary

Overview

This chapter contains detailed descriptions of each command used in the DATA Step Graphics Interface (DSGI).

The commands are discussed in the following order:

1 utility functions

  □ GINIT

  □ GPRINT

  □ GTERM

2 GASK routines

3 GDRAW functions

4 GRAPH functions

5 GSET functions.

Each routine or function is followed by an alphabetical listing of the operators used with it. For each operator, this chapter provides the statement syntax, other argument definitions, and notes about using the functions and routines, operating states, and return codes. Operating states are summarized in "Operating States" on page 1033.

The syntax for all routines and functions contains the argument *return-code-variable*. This argument must be a numeric variable name and can be a different variable name for each routine.

The *return-code-variable* argument is used to debug DSGI programs. It contains the return code of the routine or function call. If the return code is any value other than 0, the routine or function did not execute properly.

Each routine and function has a different set of possible return codes. The return codes are listed in the heading for the routine or function. Refer to "Return Codes for DSGI Routines and Functions" on page 1165 for an explanation of the return codes.

Operating States

This list summarizes the operating states in DSGI. For a detailed discussion of operating states, see "Operating States" on page 1033.

GKCL   facility closed, initial state of DSGI.

GKOP   facility open. DSGI is open. You may check the settings of attributes.

SGOP   segment open. Graphics output can be generated.

WSAC   workstation active. You can issue DSGI statements.

WSOP   workstation open. The graphics catalog is opened or created.

Utility Functions

Utility functions enable you to initialize a session for DSGI, print error messages, and terminate the session.

GINIT

Initializes DSGI

Operating States: GKCL
Return Codes: 0, 1, 26, 301, 307
Resulting Operating State: WSAC

Syntax

return-code-variable=GINIT();

Description   The GINIT function performs three functions: it readies the library that contains SAS/GRAPH graphics routines, it opens a workstation, and it activates it. A workstation is a Graphics Kernel Standard (GKS) concept. GKS allows for multiple workstations to be open at the same time; however, for DSGI applications, you always use exactly one workstation. This function moves the operating state from GKCL to WSAC.

See Also

GTERM utility function

GPRINT

Prints the specified interface error message

Operating States: All
Return Codes: 0

Syntax

return-code-variable=GPRINT(*code*);

Description   The GPRINT function displays the message that corresponds to the error code entered. You can use this routine if you have disabled automatic error logging but still want to display the message associated with a return code you have received.

Argument Definitions

code   numeric constant or numeric variable name; should be the value of a return code received from some previous function.

See Also

GSET('MESSAGE', . . .)function

GTERM

Terminates DSGI

Operating States: WSAC
Return Codes: 0, 3
Resulting Operating State: GKCL

Syntax

return-code-variable=GTERM();

Description   The GTERM function performs three functions: it deactivates the workstation, closes the workstation, and closes the library that contains SAS/GRAPHroutines. This function should be issued to free memory allocated by DSGI. This function moves the operating state from WSAC to GKCL.

See Also

GINIT utility function

GASK Routines

GASK routines enable you to check the current attribute settings. When you use GASK routines, remember the following:

□ All arguments are required.

□ Most arguments are expressed as variable names. You can use any valid SAS variable name.

□ If character arguments are expressed as character strings, they must be enclosed in quotation marks.

□ All character variable names used as arguments *must* be declared in a previous LENGTH statement.

□ GASK routines do not change the operating state.

□ PUT statements display a value returned by a routine in the SAS log.

□ OUTPUT statements write a value that is returned by a routine to a data set.

ASF

Finds whether an aspect source flag is bundled or separate

Operating States: GKOP, SGOP, WSAC, WSOP

Return Codes: 0, 8

Syntax

CALL GASK('ASF', *attribute, status, return-code-variable*);

Description   The GASK('ASF', . . .)routine returns the aspect source flag (ASF) of a particular attribute. Possible ASF values are BUNDLED (associated with a bundle index) and INDIVIDUAL (separate from a bundle index). GASK('ASF', . . .)returns the default value INDIVIDUAL if you have not set the ASF for an attribute.

Argument Definitions

attribute   character string enclosed in quotes or character variable name with one of the following values:

□ FILCOLOR

□ FILSTYLE

□ FILTYPE

□ LINCOLOR

□ LINTYPE

□ LINWIDTH

□ MARCOLOR

□ MARSIZE

□ MARTYPE

□ TEXCOLOR

□ TEXFONT.

status   character variable name; returns either the value BUNDLED or INDIVIDUAL.

return-code-variable   numeric variable name; returns the return code of the routine call.

See Also

GSET('ASF', . . .)function
GSET('FILCOLOR', . . .)function
GSET('FILSTYLE', . . .)function
GSET('FILTYPE', . . .)function
GSET('LINCOLOR', . . .)function
GSET('LINTYPE', . . .)function
GSET('LINWIDTH', . . .)function
GSET('MARCOLOR', . . .)function
GSET('MARSIZE', . . .)function
GSET('MARTYPE', . . .)function
GSET('TEXCOLOR', . . .)function
GSET('TEXFONT', . . .)function

ASPECT

Finds the aspect ratio

Operating States: All

Return Codes: 0

Syntax

CALL GASK('ASPECT', *aspect, return-code-variable*);

Description   The GASK('ASPECT', . . .)routine returns the current aspect ratio used to draw graphics output. GASK('ASPECT', . . .)searches for the current aspect ratio in the following order:

1 the aspect ratio set with the GSET('ASPECT', . . .)function

2 the ASPECT= graphics option

3 the device's default aspect ratio found in the device entry. For more information about device entries, see Chapter 15, "The GDEVICE Procedure," on page 651.

Argument Definitions

aspect   numeric variable name; returns the aspect ratio.

return-code-variable   numeric variable name; returns the return code of the routine call.

See Also

ASPECT= graphics option (see "ASPECT" on page 305)
GSET('ASPECT', . . .)function

CATALOG

Finds the catalog for the graphs

Operating States: All

Return Codes: 0

Syntax

CALL GASK('CATALOG', *libref, memname, return-code-variable*);

Description The GASK('CATALOG', . . .)routine returns the libref and the name of the current output catalog. GASK('CATALOG', . . .)returns the default catalog, WORK.GSEG, if no other catalog has been specified with the GSET('CATALOG', . . .)function.

Argument Definitions

libref	character variable name; returns the libref of the library in which the current catalog is stored.
memname	character variable name; returns the name of the current output catalog.
return-code-variable	numeric variable name; returns the return code of the routine call.

See Also

GSET('CATALOG', . . .)function
GASK('NUMGRAPH', . . .)routine
GASK('OPENGRAPH', . . .)routine

CBACK

Finds the background color

Operating States: All

Return Codes: 0

Syntax

CALL GASK('CBACK', *cback, return-code-variable*);

Description The GASK('CBACK', . . .)routine returns the current background color. GASK('CBACK', . . .)searches for the current background color in the following order:

1 the background color selected with the GSET('CBACK', . . .)function
2 the CBACK= graphics option
3 the default background color for the device found in the device entry. For more information about device entries, see Chapter 15, "The GDEVICE Procedure," on page 651.

Argument Definitions

cback   character variable name; returns the background color name.

return-code-variable   numeric variable name; returns the return code of the routine call.

See Also

CBACK= graphics option (see "CBACK" on page 309)
GSET('CBACK', . . .)function

CLIP

Finds whether clipping is on or off

Operating States: GKOP, SGOP, WSAC, WSOP
Return Codes: 55, 56

Syntax

CALL GASK('CLIP', *status*);

Description   The GASK('CLIP', . . .)routine checks whether clipping outside of viewports is enabled or disabled. One of the two following messages is displayed when this routine is called:

    NOTE: Clipping is ON.

or

    NOTE: Clipping is OFF.

Clipping is OFF by default.

Argument Definitions

status   numeric variable name; returns the current setting, 55 (ON) or 56 (OFF), for clipping.

See Also

GSET('CLIP', . . .)function

COLINDEX

Finds the color indexes that have colors associated with them

Operating States: SGOP
Return Codes: 0, 4, 86, 87

Syntax

CALL GASK('COLINDEX', *n, index-array, return-code-variable*);

Description   The GASK('COLINDEX', . . .)routine returns the color indexes that currently have colors assigned to them.

Argument Definitions

n   numeric constant or numeric variable name; tells how many color indexes you want returned. If *n* is expressed as a variable, the variable must be initialized. The variable returns the number of colors currently assigned. If *n* is expressed as a constant, it will not return this value.

index-array   list of numeric variables into which the used color index numbers are returned. The list of variable names can be members of an array or OF argument lists (where the arguments are variables). If you are using an array, *index-array* must have been declared as an array. The dimension of the array is determined by the number of color indexes you want returned. Refer to the discussion of ARRAY in *SAS Language Reference: Dictionary* for more information about OF argument lists.

return-code-variable   numeric variable name; returns the return code of the routine call.

See Also

GASK('COLINDEX', . . .)routine
GASK('COLREP', . . .)routine
GSET('COLREP', . . .)function

COLREP

Finds the color name associated with a color index

Operating States: SGOP

Return Codes: 0, 4, 86, 87

Syntax

CALL GASK('COLREP', *color-index, color, return-code-variable*);

Description The GASK('COLREP', . . .)routine returns the predefined SAS color name associated with a color index. GASK('COLREP', . . .)searches for the current color assigned to a color index in the following order:

1 the color selected by the GSET('COLREP', . . .)function.
2 the COLORS= graphics option. If *color-index* is 2, the routine returns the second color from the colors list of the COLORS= graphics option.
3 the device's default colors list found in the device entry. If *color-index* is 2, the routine returns the second color from the default colors list.

See "Predefined SAS Colors" on page 145 for a list of SAS predefined color names.

Argument Definitions

color-index   numeric constant; indicates the color index for which you want to check the color. Valid values are 1 to 256, inclusive.

color   character variable name; returns the color name associated with *color-index*.

return-code-variable   numeric variable name; returns the return code of the routine call.

See Also

GASK('COLINDEX', . . .)routine
GSET('COLREP', . . .)function

DEVICE

Finds the output graphics device

Operating States: All
Return Codes: 0

Syntax

CALL GASK('DEVICE', *device, return-code-variable*);

Description The GASK('DEVICE', . . .)routine returns the current device driver. This routine returns the device driver set by one of the following methods:

□ the GSET('DEVICE', . . .)function
□ the DEVICE= graphics option

□ the device driver you entered in the DEVICE prompt window

□ the device driver you entered in the OPTIONS window.

There is no default value for a device driver. To use DSGI, you must specify a device driver. For more information about setting device drivers, see "Selecting a Device Driver" on page 39.

Argument Definitions

device   character variable name; returns the name of the device driver.

return-code-variable   numeric variable name; returns the return code of the routine call.

See Also

DEVICE= graphics option (see "DEVICE" on page 321)

GSET('DEVICE', . . .)function

FILCOLOR

Finds the color index of the color to be used to draw fill areas

Operating States: GKOP, SGOP, WSAC, WSOP

Return Codes: 0, 8

Syntax

CALL GASK('FILCOLOR', *color-index, return-code-variable*);

Description   The GASK('FILCOLOR', . . .)routine returns the current fill color. If a GSET('FILCOLOR', . . .)function has not been previously submitted, GASK('FILCOLOR', . . .)returns the default value, 1. The color index returned corresponds to a color specification in the following order:

1 the color assigned to a color name with the GSET('COLREP', . . .)function

2 the nth color in the colors list of the COLORS= graphics option

3 the nth color in the device's default colors list found in the device entry.

Argument Definitions

color-index   numeric variable name; returns the color index of the fill color currently selected.

return-code-variable   numeric variable name; returns the return code of the routine call.

See Also

COLORS= graphics option (see "COLORS" on page 314)
GASK('COLREP', . . .)
GSET('COLREP', . . .)
GSET('FILCOLOR', . . .)

FILINDEX

Finds the bundle of fill area attributes that is active

Operating States: GKOP, SGOP, WSAC, WSOP

Return Codes: 0, 8

Syntax

CALL GASK('FILINDEX', *index, return-code-variable*);

Description The GASK('FILINDEX', . . .)routine asks which fill bundle is active. If no fill bundles have been previously defined with GSET('FILREP', . . .)or activated with GSET('FILINDEX', . . .), GASK('FILINDEX', . . .)returns the default value, 1.

Argument Definitions

index	numeric variable name; returns the index of the fill bundle currently selected.
return-code-variable	numeric variable name; returns the return code of the routine call.

See Also

GASK('FILREP', . . .)
GSET('FILREP', . . .)
GSET('FILINDEX', . . .)

FILREP

Finds the fill area attributes associated with a bundle index

Operating States: GKOP, WSOP, WSAC, SGOP

Return Codes: 0, 8, 75, 76

Syntax

CALL GASK ('FILREP', *index, color-index, interior, style-index, return-code-variable*);

Description   The GASK('FILREP', . . .)routine returns the color, type of interior, and fill pattern associated with a specific fill bundle. If the bundle indicated by *index* has not been previously defined with the GSET('FILREP', . . .)function, DSGI issues the following error message:

```
ERROR: A representation for the specified fill area index has
    not been defined on this workstation.
```

Argument Definitions

index   numeric constant or numeric variable name; indicates the fill bundle to check. Valid values are 1 to 20, inclusive. If *index* is expressed as a variable, the variable must be initialized to a value between 1 and 20.

color-index   numeric variable name; returns the color index of the fill color associated with the bundle. The color index that is returned corresponds to a color specification in the following order:

    1 a color index assigned to a color name with the GSET('COLREP', . . .)function
    2 the *n*th color in the colors list of the COLORS= graphics option
    3 the *n*th color in the device's default colors list found in the device entry.

interior   character variable name; returns the style of the interior associated with the bundle index – that is, one of the following values:

    ☐ HATCH
    ☐ HOLLOW
    ☐ PATTERN
    ☐ SOLID.

style-index   numeric variable name; returns the index of the fill pattern associated with the bundle. See the GSET('FILSTYLE', . . .)function on page 1138 for the fill patterns represented by *style-index*.

return-code-   numeric variable name; returns the return code of the routine call.
variable

See Also

COLORS= graphics option (see "COLORS" on page 314)
GASK('FILINDEX', . . .)routine
GSET('COLREP', . . .)function
GSET('FILREP', . . .)function
GSET('FILSTYLE', . . .)function

FILSTYLE

Finds the style of the fill area when FILTYPE is PATTERN or HATCH

Operating States: GKOP, SGOP, WSAC, WSOP

Return Codes: 0, 8

Syntax

CALL GASK('FILSTYLE', *style-index, return-code-variable*);

Description The GASK('FILSTYLE', . . .)routine returns the current fill style of the interior when FILTYPE is PATTERN or HATCH. If no fill style has been previously selected with the GSET('FILSTYLE', . . .)function, GASK('FILSTYLE', . . .)returns the default value, 1.

Argument Definitions

style-index numeric variable name; returns the index of the fill pattern associated with the bundle. See the GSET('FILSTYLE', . . .)function on page 1138 for the interior styles represented by *style-index*.

return-code-variable numeric variable name; returns the return code of the routine call.

See Also

GASK('FILSTYLE', . . .)routine

GSET('FILSTYLE', . . .)function

GSET('FILTYPE', . . .)function

FILTYPE

Finds the type of the interior of the fill area

Operating States: GKOP, SGOP, WSAC, WSOP

Return Codes: 0, 8

Syntax

CALL GASK('FILTYPE', *interior, return-code-variable*);

Description The GASK('FILTYPE', . . .)routine returns the current fill type. If no fill type has been previously selected with the GSET('FILTYPE', . . .)function, GASK('FILTYPE', . . .)returns the default value, HOLLOW.

Argument Definitions

interior character variable name; returns the fill type that is active, that is, one of the following values:

- □ HATCH
- □ HOLLOW
- □ PATTERN
- □ SOLID.

return-code-variable   numeric variable name; returns the return code of the routine call.

See Also

GASK('FILSTYLE', . . .)routine
GSET('FILTYPE', . . .)function

GRAPHLIST

Finds the names of segments in the current catalog

Operating States: GKOP, SGOP, WSAC, WSOP

Return Codes: 0, 8

Syntax

CALL GASK('GRAPHLIST', *n, name-array, return-code-variable*);

Description   The GASK('GRAPHLIST', . . .)routine lists the first *n* names of the graphs that are in the current catalog. If a catalog has not been previously specified with the GRAPH('CATALOG', . . .)function, the routine returns names from the default catalog, WORK.GSEG.

The names returned are any of the following:

- □ those specified in the GRAPH('CLEAR', . . .)function
- □ if the name is omitted from the GRAPH('CLEAR' . . .)function, some form of DSGI: for example, DSGI, DSGI1, or DSGI2.
- □ the name specified in the NAME= option of a graphics procedure
- □ graphs previously created by other graphics procedures and already in the catalog.

Argument Definitions

n   numeric variable name; tells the maximum number of graph names you want returned. If you express *n* as a variable, the variable must be initialized to the maximum number of graph names you want returned.

name-array   list of character variable names into which the graph names will be returned. The list of variable names can be members of an array or OF argument lists (where the arguments are variables). If you are using an array, *name-array* must be declared as an array. The dimension of the array is determined by the number of color indexes you want returned. See the discussion for ARRAY in *SAS Language Reference: Dictionary* for more information about OF argument lists.

return-code-variable   numeric variable names; returns the return code of the routine call.

See Also

GRAPH ('CLEAR', . . .)function

HPOS

Finds the number of columns

Operating States: All
Return Codes: 0

Syntax

CALL GASK('HPOS',*hpos, return-code-variable*);

Description   The GASK('HPOS', . . .)routine returns the number of columns currently in the graphics output area. GASK('HPOS', . . .)searches for the current number of columns in the following order:

1   the value selected in the GSET('HPOS', . . .)function
2   the value of the HPOS= graphics option
3   the device's default HPOS value found in the device entry.

Argument Definitions

hpos   numeric variable name; returns the number of columns in the graphics output area.

return-code-variable   numeric variable name; returns the return code of the routine call.

See Also

GASK('HSIZE', . . .)function
GSET('HPOS', . . .)routine
HPOS= graphics option (see "HPOS" on page 355)

HSIZE

Finds the horizontal dimension of the graphics output area

Operating States: All

Return Codes: 0

Syntax

CALL GASK('HSIZE', *hsize, return-code-variable*);

Description   The GASK('HSIZE', . . .)routine returns the current horizontal dimension, in inches, of the graphics output area. GASK('HSIZE', . . .)searches for the current horizontal dimension in the following order:

1 the value selected in the GSET('HSIZE', . . .)function
2 the value of the HSIZE= graphics option
3 the device's default HSIZE found in the device entry.

Argument Definitions

hsize   numeric variable name; the size of the graphics output area in the *x* dimension (in inches).

return-code-variable   numeric variable name; returns the return code of the routine call.

See Also

GASK('HPOS', . . .)routine
GSET('HSIZE', . . .)function
HSIZE= graphics option (see "HSIZE" on page 356)

HTML

Finds the HTML string that is in effect when one of the following graphic elements is drawn: bar, ellipse, fill, mark, pie, and text.

Operating States: GKOP, SGOP, WSAC, WSOP
Return Codes: 0, 8

Syntax

CALL GASK('HTML', *string, return-code-variable*);

Description   The GASK('HTML', . . .)routine returns the current HTML string. If a GSET('HTML', . . .)function has not been previously submitted, GASK('HTML', . . .)returns the default value, null.

Argument Definitions

string   the HTML string invoked when an affected DSGI graphic element in a web page is clicked.

return-code-variable   numeric variable name; returns the return code of the routine call.

See Also

GDRAW('BAR', . . .)function
GDRAW('ELLIPSE', . . .)function
GDRAW('FILL', . . .)function
GDRAW('MARK', . . .)function
GDRAW('PIE', . . .)function
GDRAW('TEXT', . . .)function
GSET('HTML', . . .)function

LINCOLOR

Finds the current setting of the color to be used to draw lines

Operating States: GKOP, SGOP, WSAC, WSOP
Return Codes: 0, 8

Syntax

CALL GASK('LINCOLOR', *color-index, return-code-variable*);

Description   The GASK('LINCOLOR', . . .)routine returns the current line color. If a GSET('LINCOLOR', . . .)function has not been previously submitted, GASK('LINCOLOR', . . .)returns the default value, 1. The color index returned corresponds to a color specification in the following order:

1   the color specified in a GSET('COLREP', . . .)function
2   the *n*th color in the colors list of the COLORS= graphics option
3   the *n*th color in the device's default colors list.

Argument Definitions

color-index   numeric variable name; returns the color index of the current line color.

return-code-variable   numeric variable name; returns the return code of the routine call.

See Also

COLORS= graphics option (see "COLORS" on page 314)
GASK('COLREP', . . .)routine
GSET('COLREP', . . .)function
GSET('LINCOLOR', . . .)function

LININDEX

Finds the index of the bundle of line attributes

Operating States: GKOP, SGOP, WSAC, WSOP

Return Codes: 0, 8

Syntax

CALL GASK('LININDEX', *index, return-code-variable*);

Description   The GASK('LININDEX', . . .)routine returns the current line bundle. If no line bundles have been previously defined with GSET('LINREP', . . .)or activated with GSET('LININDEX', . . .), GASK('LININDEX', . . .)returns the default value, 1.

Argument Definitions

index	numeric variable name; returns the index of the current line bundle.
return-code-variable	numeric variable name; returns the return code of the routine call.

See Also

GASK('LINREP', . . .)routine
GSET('LININDEX', . . .)function
GSET('LINREP', . . .)function

LINREP

Finds the bundle of line attributes associated with an index

Operating States: GKOP, SGOP, WSAC, WSOP

Return Codes: 0, 8, 60, 61

Syntax

CALL GASK ('LINREP', *index, color-index, width, type, return-code-variable*):

Description   The GASK('LINREP', . . .)routine returns the color, width, and line type associated with a specific line bundle. If the bundle indicated by *index* has not been previously defined with the GSET('LINREP', . . .)function, DSGI issues the following error message:

```
ERROR: A representation for the specified line type index has
    not been defined on this workstation.
```

Argument Definitions

index   numeric constant or numeric variable name; indicates the fill bundle to check. Valid values are 1 to 20, inclusive. If *index* is expressed as a variable, the variable must be initialized to a value between 1 and 20.

color-index   numeric variable name; returns the color index of the fill color associated with the bundle. The color index returned corresponds to a color specification in the following order:

    1 a color index assigned with the GSET('COLREP', . . .)function
    2 the *n*th color in the colors list of the COLORS= graphics option
    3 the *n*th color in the device's default colors list.

width   numeric variable name; returns the line width (in pixels) associated with the bundle.

type   numeric variable name; returns the index of the line type associated with the bundle. Refer to Figure 8.22 on page 249 for representations of the line types.

return-code-variable   numeric variable name; returns the return code of the routine call.

See Also

COLORS= graphics option (see "COLORS" on page 314)
GASK('COLREP', . . .)routine
GASK('LININDEX', . . .)routine
GSET('COLREP', . . .)function
GSET('LINREP', . . .)function

LINTYPE

Finds the line type

Operating States: GKOP, SGOP, WSAC, WSOP
Return Codes: 0, 8

Syntax

CALL GASK('LINTYPE', *type, return-code-variable*);

Description   The GASK('LINTYPE', . . .)routine returns the current line type. If no line type was previously selected with the GSET('LINTYPE', . . .)function, GASK('LINTYPE', . . .)returns the default value, 1.

Argument Definitions

type   numeric variable name; returns the index of the line type currently selected. Refer to Figure 8.22 on page 249 for representations of the line types.

return-code-variable   numeric variable name; returns the return code of the routine call.

See Also

GSET('LINTYPE', . . .)function

LINWIDTH

Finds the line thickness

Operating States: GKOP, SGOP, WSAC, WSOP

Return Codes: 0, 8

Syntax

CALL GASK('LINWIDTH', *width, return-code-variable*);

Description   The GASK('LINWIDTH', . . .)routine returns the current line width. If a line width has not been previously selected with the GSET('LINWIDTH', . . .)function, GASK('LINWIDTH', . . .)returns the default value, 1.

Argument Definitions

width   numeric variable name; returns the current line width (in units of pixels).

return-code-variable   numeric variable name; returns the return code of the routine call.

See Also

GSET('LINWIDTH', . . .)function

MARCOLOR

Finds the color index of the color to be used to draw markers

Operating States: GKOP, SGOP, WSAC, WSOP

Return Codes: 0, 8

Syntax

CALL GASK('MARCOLOR', *color-index, return-code-variable*);

Description   The GASK('MARCOLOR', . . .)routine returns the current marker color. If a GSET('MARCOLOR', . . .)function has not been previously submitted, GASK('MARCOLOR', . . .)returns the default value, 1. The color index returned corresponds to a color specification in the following order:

1 the color selected in a GSET('COLREP', . . .)function
2 the *n*th color in the colors list of the COLORS= graphics option
3 the *n*th color in the device's default colors list.

Argument Definitions

color-index   numeric variable name; returns the color index of the current marker color.

return-code-variable   numeric variable name; returns the return code of the routine call.

See Also

COLORS= graphics option (see "COLORS" on page 314)
GASK('COLREP', . . .)routine
GSET('COLREP', . . .)function
GSET('MARCOLOR', . . .)function

MARINDEX

Finds the index of the bundle of marker attributes currently selected

Operating States: GKOP, SGOP, WSAC, WSOP

Return Codes: 0, 8

Syntax

CALL GASK('MARINDEX', *index, return-code-variable*);

Description   The GASK('MARINDEX', . . .)routine returns the current marker bundle. If no marker bundles have been previously defined with GSET('MARREP', . . .)or activated with GSET('MARINDEX', . . .), GASK('MARINDEX', . . .)returns the default value, 1.

Argument Definitions

index   numeric variable name; returns the index of the marker bundle currently selected.

return-code-variable   numeric variable name; returns the return code of the routine call.

See Also

GASK('MARREP', . . .)routine
GSET('MARINDEX', . . .)function
GSET('MARREP', . . .)function

MARREP

Finds the bundle of marker attributes associated with an index

Operating States: GKOP, SGOP, WSAC, WSOP
Return Codes: 0, 8, 64, 65

Syntax

CALL GASK('MARREP', *index, color-index, size, type, return-code-variable*);

Description   The GASK('MARREP' . . .)routine returns the color, size, and type of marker associated with a specific marker bundle. If the bundle indicated by *index* has not been previously defined with the GSET('MARREP', . . .)function, DSGI issues the following error message:

```
ERROR: A representation for the specified marker index has
     not been defined on this workstation.
```

Argument Definitions

index   numeric constant or numeric variable name; indicates the index of the fill bundle to check. Valid values are 1 to 20, inclusive. If *index* is expressed as a variable, the variable must be initialized to a value between 1 and 20.

color-index	numeric variable name; returns the color index of the fill color associated with the bundle. The color index returned corresponds to a color specification in the following order:

> **1** a color index assigned with the GSET('COLREP', . . .)function
> **2** the *n*th color in the colors list of the COLORS= graphics option
> **3** the *n*th color in the device's default colors list.

size	numeric variable name; returns the marker size in units of the current window system.
type	numeric variable name; the index of the marker type associated with the bundle. See the GSET('MARTYPE', . . .)function on page 1149 for an explanation of the marker indexes.
return-code-variable	numeric variable name; returns the return code of the routine call.

See Also

COLORS= graphics option (see "COLORS" on page 314)

GASK('COLREP', . . .)routine

GSET('COLREP', . . .)function

GSET('MARINDEX', . . .)function

GSET('MARREP', . . .)function

GSET('MARTYPE', . . .)function

MARSIZE

Finds the size of markers

Operating States: GKOP, SGOP, WSAC, WSOP

Return Codes: 0, 8

Syntax

CALL GASK('MARSIZE', *size, return-code-variable*);

Description   The GASK('MARSIZE', . . .)routine returns the current marker size. If no marker size has been previously selected with the GSET('MARSIZE', . . .)function, GASK('MARSIZE', . . .)returns the default value, 1.

Argument Definitions

size	numeric variable name; returns the marker size in units of the current window system.
return-code-variable	numeric variable name; returns the return code of the routine call.

See Also

GSET('MARSIZE', . . .)function

MARTYPE

Finds the kind of markers

Operating States: GKOP, SGOP, WSAC, WSOP

Return Codes: 0, 8

Syntax

CALL GASK('MARTYPE', *type, return-code-variable*);

Description   The GASK('MARTYPE', . . .)routine returns the current marker type. If no marker type has been previously selected with the GSET('MARTYPE', . . .)function, GASK('MARTYPE', . . .)returns the default value, 1.

Argument Definitions

type
numeric variable name; returns the index of the marker type currently selected. See the function GSET('MARTYPE', . . .) on page 1149 for an explanation of the indexes for markers.

return-code-variable
numeric variable name; returns the return code of the routine call.

See Also

GSET('MARTYPE', . . .)function

MAXDISP

Finds the maximum display area size

Operating States: GKOP, SGOP, WSAC, WSOP

Return Codes: 0, 8

Syntax

CALL GASK ('MAXDISP', *units, x-dim, y-dim, x-pixels, y-pixels, return-code-variable*);

Description   The GASK('MAXDISP', . . .)routine returns the dimensions of the maximum display area for the device. This routine is useful when you need to know the maximum display area in order to determine the aspect ratio or to scale a graph.

There is a difference between the maximum display size returned when the operating state is not SGOP and when it is SGOP. The full addressable display area is returned when the operating state is not SGOP, and the display area minus room for titles and footnotes is returned when the operating state is SGOP.

Argument Definitions

units	numeric variable name; returns a 1 to show that *x-dim* and *y-dim* are in meters.
x-dim	numeric variable name; returns the dimension, in meters, in the *x* direction.
y-dim	numeric variable name; returns the dimension, in meters, in the *y* direction.
x-pixels	numeric variable name; returns the number of pixels in the *x* direction.
y-pixels	numeric variable name; returns the number of pixels in the *y* direction.
return-code-variable	numeric variable name; returns the return code of the routine call.

See Also

GASK('HSIZE', . . .)routine

GASK('VSIZE', . . .)routine

GSET('HSIZE', . . .)function

GSET('VSIZE', . . .)function

NUMGRAPH

Finds the number of graphs in the current catalog

Operating States: GKOP, SGOP, WSAC, WSOP

Return Codes: 0, 8

Syntax

CALL GASK('NUMGRAPH', *n, return-code-variable*);

Description   The GASK('NUMGRAPH', . . .)routine returns how many graphs are in the current catalog. The catalog checked is the catalog selected in the GSET('CATALOG', . . .)function, if specified; otherwise, it is the default catalog, WORK.GSEG.

Argument Definitions

n   numeric variable name; returns the number of graphs in the current catalog.

return-code-variable   numeric variable name; returns the return code of the routine call.

See Also

GASK('CATALOG', . . .)routine
GSET('CATALOG', . . .)function

OPENGRAPH

Finds the name of the segment currently open

Operating States: SGOP
Return Codes: 0, 4

Syntax

CALL GASK('OPENGRAPH', *name, return-code-variable*);

Description   The GASK('OPENGRAPH', . . .)routine returns the name of the graph that is currently open.
The name returned is one of the following:

☐ the name specified in the GRAPH('CLEAR', . . .)function

☐ if the name is omitted from the GRAPH('CLEAR', . . .)function, some form of DSGI: for example, DSGI, DSGI1, and DSGI2.

Argument Definitions

name   character variable name; returns the name of the graph that is currently open.

return-code-variable   numeric variable name; returns the return code of the routine call.

See Also

GRAPH('CLEAR', . . .)function

STATE

Finds the current operating state of DSGI

Operating States: All
Return Codes: 0

Syntax

CALL GASK('STATE', *status*);

Description   The GASK('STATE', . . .)routine returns the current operating state of DSGI.

Argument Definitions

status   character variable name; returns one of the following values:

- □ GKCL
- □ GKOP
- □ SGOP
- □ WSAC
- □ WSOP.

See Also

GASK('WSACTIVE', . . .)routine
GASK('WSOPEN', . . .)routine

TEXALIGN

Finds the horizontal and vertical alignment of the text string
Operating States: GKOP, SGOP, WSAC, WSOP
Return Codes: 0, 8

Syntax

CALL GASK('TEXALIGN', *halign, valign, return-code-variable*);

Description   The GASK('TEXALIGN', . . .)routine returns the current horizontal and vertical text alignment. If no values have been previously selected with the GSET('TEXALIGN', . . .)function, GASK('TEXALIGN', . . .)returns the default value NORMAL for both *halign* and *valign*.

Argument Definitions

halign   character variable name; indicates the horizontal alignment set by the GSET('TEXALIGN', . . .)function; returns one of the following values:

- □ CENTER

> □ LEFT
>
> □ NORMAL
>
> □ RIGHT.

valign character variable name; indicates the vertical alignment set by the GSET('TEXALIGN', . . .)function; returns one of the following values:

> □ BASE
>
> □ BOTTOM
>
> □ HALF
>
> □ NORMAL
>
> □ TOP.

return-code-variable numeric variable name; returns the return code of the routine call.

See Also

GASK('TEXPATH', . . .)routine

GASK('TEXUP', . . .)routine

GSET('TEXALIGN', . . .)function

TEXCOLOR

Finds the color index of the color currently selected to draw text strings

Operating States: GKOP, SGOP, WSAC, WSOP

Return Codes: 0, 8

Syntax

CALL GASK('TEXCOLOR', *color-index, return-code-variable*);

Description The GASK('TEXCOLOR', . . .)routine returns the current text color. If a GSET('TEXCOLOR', . . .)function has not been previously submitted, GASK('TEXCOLOR', . . .)returns the default value, 1. The color index returned corresponds to a color specification in the following order:

1 the color specified in a GSET('COLREP', . . .)function

2 the nth color in the colors list of the COLORS= graphics option

3 the nth color in the device's default colors list.

Argument Definitions

color-index numeric variable name; returns the color index of the color used to draw text.

return-code-variable numeric variable name; returns the return code of the routine call.

See Also

COLORS= graphics option (see "COLORS" on page 314)
GASK('COLREP', . . .)routine
GSET('COLREP', . . .)function
GSET('TEXCOLOR', . . .)function

TEXEXTENT

Finds the text extent rectangle and concatenation point for a specified text string

Operating States: SGOP, WSAC, WSOP

Return Codes: 0, 8

Syntax

CALL GASK ('TEXEXTENT', *x, y, string, x-end, y-end, x1, x2, x3, x4, y1, y2, y3, y4, return-code-variable*);

Description   The GASK('TEXEXTENT', . . .)routine returns the text extent rectangle and text concatenation point for a specified text string. All text extent coordinates returned are in units of the current window system. If no text string is specified for *string*, GASK('TEXEXTENT', . . .)does not return values for the other arguments.

The text attributes and bundles affect the values returned by this query. See Figure 32.1 on page 1103 for a diagram of the text extent rectangle (in the figure, *x,y* is always the place where the text string starts).

Figure 32.1   Text Extent Diagram

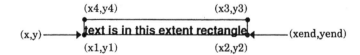

Argument Definitions

x	numeric variable name; *x* coordinates are in units based on the current window system; returns *x* coordinate after justification. The variable used to specify *x* must be initialized.
y	numeric variable name; *y* coordinates are in units based on the current window system; returns *y* coordinate after justification. The variable used to specify *y* must be initialized.
string	character string enclosed in single quotation marks or a character variable name; a set of characters for which the text extent rectangle and text concatenation point are calculated.

x-end	numeric variable name; returns the *x* coordinate of the point at which the next text string may be concatenated.
y-end	numeric variable name; returns the *y* coordinate of the point at which the next text string may be concatenated.
x1, x2, x3, x4, y1, y2, y3, y4	numeric variable names; return the text extent rectangles of the text strings as shown in Figure 32.1 on page 1103.
return-code-variable	numeric variable name; returns the return code of the routine call.

See Also

GASK('WINDOW', . . .)routine

GDRAW('TEXT', . . .)function

TEXFONT

Finds the font used to draw text strings

Operating States: GKOP, SGOP, WSAC, WSOP

Return Codes: 0, 8

Syntax

CALL GASK('TEXFONT', *font, return-code-variable*);

Description   The GASK('TEXFONT' . . .)routine returns the current text font. GASK('TEXFONT', . . .)searches for the current font in the following order:

1 the value selected in the GSET('TEXFONT', . . .)function, if specified

2 the value of the FTEXT= graphics option, if specified

3 the device's default hardware font if the device supports a hardware font

4 the SIMULATE font.

Argument Definitions

font	character variable name; returns the font name.
return-code-variable	numeric variable name; returns the return code of the routine call.

See Also

FTEXT= graphics options in (see "FTEXT" on page 335)

GSET('TEXFONT', . . .)function

TEXHEIGHT

Finds the character height of the text strings

Operating States: GKOP, SGOP, WSAC, WSOP

Return Codes: 0, 8

Syntax

CALL GASK('TEXHEIGHT', *height, return-code-variable*);

Description   The GASK('TEXHEIGHT', . . .)routine returns the current text height.
GASK('TEXHEIGHT', . . .)searches for the current text height in the following order:

1 the value selected in the GSET('TEXHEIGHT', . . .)function, if specified

2 the value of the HTEXT= graphics option, if specified

3 the default text height, 1.

Argument Definitions

height   numeric variable name; returns the character height in units of the
                            current window system.

return-code-   numeric variable name; returns the return code of the routine call.
variable

See Also

GSET('TEXHEIGHT', . . .)function

HTEXT= graphics options (see "HTEXT" on page 357)

TEXINDEX

Finds the index of the bundle of text attributes currently selected

Operating States: GKOP, SGOP, WSAC, WSOP

Return Codes: 0, 8

Syntax

CALL GASK('TEXINDEX', *index, return-code-variable*);

Description   The GASK('TEXINDEX', . . .)routine returns the current text bundle. If no text bundles have been previously defined with GSET('TEXREP', . . .)or activated with GSET('TEXINDEX', . . .), GASK('TEXINDEX', . . .)returns the default value, 1.

Argument Definitions

index   numeric variable name; returns the text bundle index.

return-code-   numeric variable name; returns the return code of the routine call.
variable

See Also

GASK('TEXREP', . . .)routine
GSET('TEXREP', . . .)function
GSET('TEXINDEX', . . .)function

TEXPATH

Finds the direction of the text string

Operating States: GKOP, SGOP, WSAC, WSOP
Return Codes: 0, 8

Syntax

CALL GASK('TEXPATH', *path, return-code-variable*);

Description   The GASK('TEXPATH', . . .)routine returns the current text path (reading direction). If TEXPATH has not been previously selected with the GSET('TEXPATH', . . .)function, GASK('TEXPATH', . . .)returns the default value, RIGHT. See the GSET('TEXPATH', . . .)function on page 1156 for an illustration of text paths.

Argument Definitions

path   character variable name; returns one of the following values:

      □ DOWN

      □ LEFT

      □ RIGHT

      □ UP.

return-code-   numeric variable name; returns the return code of the routine call.
variable

See Also

GASK('TEXALIGN', . . .)routine

GASK('TEXUP', . . .)routine

GSET('TEXPATH', . . .)function

TEXREP

Finds the attribute settings associated with a text bundle

Operating States: GKOP, SGOP, WSAC, WSOP

Return Codes: 0, 8, 68, 69

Syntax

CALL GASK('TEXREP', *index, color-index, font, return-code-variable*);

Description   The GASK('TEXREP', . . .)routine returns the color and font associated with a specific text bundle. If the bundle indicated by *index* has not been previously defined with the GSET('TEXREP', . . .)function, DSGI issues the following error message:

```
ERROR: A representation for the specified text index has
not been defined on this workstation.
```

Argument Definitions

index
numeric constant or numeric variable name; indicates the fill bundle to check. Valid values are 1 to 20, inclusive. If *index* is expressed as a variable, the variable must be initialized to a value between 1 and 20.

color-index
numeric variable name; returns the color index of the fill color associated with the bundle. The color index that is returned corresponds to a color specification in the following order:

1 a color index assigned with the GSET('COLREP', . . .)function
2 the *n*th color in the colors list of the COLORS= graphics option
3 the *n*th color in the device's default colors list.

font
character variable name; returns the text font associated with the bundle.

return-code-variable
numeric variable name; returns the return code of the routine call.

See Also

COLORS= graphics option (see "COLORS" on page 314)
GASK('COLREP', . . .)routine
GSET('COLREP', . . .)function
GSET('TEXREP', . . .)function

TEXUP

Finds the orientation (angle) of the text string

Operating States: GKOP, SGOP, WSAC, WSOP

Return Codes: 0, 8

Syntax

CALL GASK('TEXUP', *up-x, up-y, return-code-variable*);

Description   The GASK('TEXUP', . . .)routine returns the character up vector values. If TEXUP has not been previously selected with the GSET('TEXUP', . . .)function, GASK('TEXUP', . . .)returns the default values for *x* and *y*, 0 and 1. See the GSET('TEXUP', . . .)function on page 1158 for an explanation of the vector values.

Argument Definitions

up-x   numeric variable name; returns the *x* component of the vector.

up-y   numeric variable name; returns the *y* component of the vector.

return-code-variable   numeric variable name; returns the return code of the routine call.

See Also

GASK('TEXALIGN', . . .)routine
GASK('TEXPATH', . . .)routine
GSET('TEXUP', . . .)function

TRANS

Finds the viewport and window coordinates associated with a transformation number

Operating States: GKOP, SGOP, WSAC, WSOP

Return Codes: 0, 8, 50

Syntax

CALL GASK ('TRANS', *n, vllx, vlly, vurx, vury, wllx, wlly, wurx, wury, return-code-variable*);

Description The GASK('TRANS', . . .)routine returns the viewport and window coordinates associated with a particular transformation number. GASK('TRANS', . . .)returns the default coordinates for viewports and windows if other coordinates have not been defined for the transformation specified.

Argument Definitions

n	numeric constant or numeric variable name; indicates the number of the transformation to check. Valid values are 0 to 20, inclusive. If *n* is expressed as a variable, the variable must be initialized to a value between 0 and 20.
vllx	numeric variable name; returns the *x* coordinate of the lower-left viewport corner.
vlly	numeric variable name; returns the *y* coordinate of the lower-left viewport corner.
vurx	numeric variable name; returns the *x* coordinate of the upper-right viewport corner.
vury	numeric variable name; returns the *y* coordinate of the upper-right viewport corner.
wllx	numeric variable name; returns the *x* coordinate of the lower-left window corner.
wlly	numeric variable name; returns the *y* coordinate of the lower-left window corner.
wurx	numeric variable name; returns the *x* coordinate of the upper-right window corner.
wury	numeric variable name; returns the *y* coordinate of the upper-right window corner.
return-code-variable	numeric variable name; returns the return code of the routine call.

See Also

GASK('TRANSNO', . . .)routine
GASK('VIEWPORT', . . .)routine
GASK('WINDOW', . . .)routine
GSET('TRANSNO', . . .)function
GSET('VIEWPORT', . . .)function
GSET('WINDOW', . . .)function

TRANSNO

Finds the number of the transformation to be used

Operating States: GKOP, SGOP, WSAC, WSOP
Return Codes: 0, 8

Syntax

CALL GASK('TRANSNO', *n, return-code-variable*);

Description The GASK('TRANSNO', . . .)routine returns the current transformation. If a transformation has not been previously selected with the GSET('TRANSNO', . . .)function, GASK('TRANSNO', . . .)returns the number of the default transformation, 0.

Argument Definitions

n   numeric variable name; returns the number of the current transformation.

return-code-   numeric variable name; returns the return code of the routine call.
variable

See Also

GASK('TRANS', . . .)
GASK('VIEWPORT', . . .)
GASK('WINDOW', . . .)
GSET('VIEWPORT', . . .)
GSET('WINDOW', . . .)
GSET('TRANSNO', . . .)

VIEWPORT

Finds coordinates of the viewport associated with a transformation number
Operating States: GKOP, SGOP, WSAC, WSOP
Return Codes: 0, 8, 50

Syntax

CALL GASK('VIEWPORT', *n, llx, lly, urx, ury, return-code-variable*);

Description The GASK('VIEWPORT', . . .)routine returns the coordinates of the viewport associated with the specified transformation. If a viewport has not been defined with the GSET('VIEWPORT', . . .)function for the specified transformation, *n*, GASK('VIEWPORT', . . .)returns the default coordinates for the viewport, (0,0) and (1,1).

Argument Definitions

n   numeric constant or numeric variable name; indicates the transformation number assigned to the viewport to check. Valid values are 0 to 20, inclusive. If *n* is expressed as a variable, the variable must be initialized to a value between 0 and 20.

llx   numeric variable name; returns the *x* coordinate of the lower-left corner.

lly   numeric variable name; returns the *y* coordinate of the lower-left corner.

urx   numeric variable name; returns the *x* coordinate of the upper-right corner.

ury   numeric variable name; returns the *y* coordinate of the upper-right corner.

return-code-variable   numeric variable name; returns the return code of the routine call.

See Also

GASK('TRANS', . . .)routine

GASK('TRANSNO', . . .)routine

GASK('WINDOW', . . .)routine

GSET('TRANSNO', . . .)function

GSET('VIEWPORT', . . .)function

GSET('WINDOW', . . .)function

VPOS

Finds the number of rows

Operating States: All

Return Codes: 0

Syntax

CALL GASK('VPOS', *vpos, return-code-variable*);

Description   The GASK('VPOS', . . .)routine returns the current number of rows in the graphics output area. GASK('VPOS', . . .)searches for the current number of rows in the following order:

1 the value selected in the GSET('VPOS', . . .)function

2 the value of the VPOS= graphics option

3 the device's default VPOS value found in the device entry.

Argument Definitions

vpos   numeric variable name; returns the number of rows in the graphics output area.

return-code-variable   numeric variable name; returns the return code of the routine call.

See Also

GASK('HPOS', . . .)routine
GASK('VSIZE', . . .)routine
GSET('VPOS', . . .)function
VPOS= graphics option (see "VPOS" on page 397)

VSIZE

Finds the vertical dimension of the graphics output area

Operating States: All
Return Codes: 0

Syntax

CALL GASK('VSIZE', *vsize, return-code-variable*);

Description   The GASK('VSIZE', . . .)routine returns the current vertical dimension, in inches, of the graphics output area. GASK('VSIZE', . . .)searches for the current vertical dimension in the following order:

1 the value selected in the GSET('VSIZE', . . .)function
2 the value of the VSIZE= graphics option
3 the device's default VSIZE found in the device entry.

Argument Definitions

vsize   numeric variable name; returns the size of the graphics output area in the *y* dimension (in inches).

return-code-variable   numeric variable name; returns the return code of the routine call.

See Also

GASK('HSIZE', . . .)routine
GASK('VPOS', . . .)routine
GSET('VSIZE', . . .)function
VSIZE= graphics option (see "VSIZE" on page 398)

WINDOW

Finds the coordinates of the window associated with a transformation number

Operating States: GKOP, SGOP, WSAC, WSOP
Return Codes: 0, 8, 50

Syntax

CALL GASK('WINDOW', *n, llx, lly, urx, ury, return-code-variable*);

Description The GASK('WINDOW', . . .)routine returns the coordinates of the window associated with the specified transformation number. If no window has been defined with the GSET('WINDOW', . . .)function for transformation *n*, GASK('WINDOW', . . .)returns the default window coordinates, which are device dependent.

Argument Definitions

n	numeric constant or numeric variable name; indicates the transformation number of the window to check. Valid values are 0 to 20, inclusive. If *n* is expressed as a variable, the variable must be initialized to a value between 0 and 20.
llx	numeric variable name; returns the *x* coordinate of the lower-left corner.
lly	numeric variable name; returns the *y* coordinate of the lower-left corner.
urx	numeric variable name; returns the *x* coordinate of the upper-right corner.
ury	numeric variable name; returns the *y* coordinate of the upper-right corner.
return-code-variable	numeric variable name; returns the return code of the routine call.

See Also

GASK('TRANS', . . .)routine
GASK('TRANSNO', . . .)routine
GASK('VIEWPORT', . . .)routine
GSET('TRANSNO', . . .)function
GSET('VIEWPORT', . . .)function
GSET('WINDOW', . . .)function

WSACTIVE

Finds whether the interface is active

Operating States: All
Return Codes: 29, 30

Syntax

CALL GASK('WSACTIVE', *status*);

Description   The GASK('WSACTIVE', . . .)routine asks if the workstation is active. When the workstation is active, you can execute certain DSGI routines and functions.

Argument Definitions

status   numeric variable name; returns either 29 (active) or 30 (inactive).

See Also

GASK('STATE', . . .)routine
GASK('WSOPEN', . . .)routine

WSOPEN

Finds whether the interface is open

Operating States: All
Return Codes: 24, 25

Syntax

CALL GASK('WSOPEN', *status*);

Description   The GASK('WSOPEN', . . .)routine asks if the workstation is open. If a workstation is open, the graphics catalog can be accessed.

Argument Definitions

status   numeric variable name; returns either 24 (open) or 25 (closed).

See Also

GASK('WSACTIVE', . . .)routine
GASK('WSOPEN', . . .)routine

GDRAW Functions

GDRAW functions create graphics elements. Each GDRAW operator is associated with a set of GSET operators that control its attributes. For example, the color, height, and font for the GDRAW('TEXT', . . .)function are controlled by GSET('TEXCOLOR', . . .), GSET('TEXHEIGHT', . . .), and GSET('TEXFONT', . . .), respectively. For a complete list of the attributes associated with each GDRAW function, see Table 31.2 on page 1038. The complete graph is displayed after the GRAPH('UPDATE', . . .)function is submitted.

When using GDRAW functions, remember the following:

□ All arguments must be specified.

□ All arguments are specified as variables or constants. If you express an argument as a variable, the variable must be initialized.

□ All character arguments that are expressed as character strings must be enclosed in quotes.

□ All character variable names used as arguments *must* be declared in a LENGTH statement.

□ All character constants must be enclosed in single or double quotes.

ARC

Draws a circular arc

Operating States: SGOP

Return Codes: 0, 4, 61, 86

Syntax

return-code-variable=GDRAW('ARC', *x, y, radius, start, end*);

Description   The GDRAW('ARC', . . .)function draws a circular arc. The line attributes and bundles affect the appearance of this primitive. See Table 31.2 on page 1038 for a list of these attributes. Figure 32.2 on page 1115 illustrates the arguments used with GDRAW('ARC', . . .).

Figure 32.2   Arguments Used with the GDRAW('ARC', ...) Function

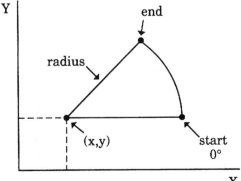

Argument Definitions

x	numeric constant or numeric variable name; specifies the *x* coordinate of the position of the arc on the display; *x* coordinates are in units based on the current window system.
y	numeric constant or numeric variable name; specifies the *y* coordinate of the position of the arc on the display; *y* coordinates are in units based on the current window system;
radius	numeric constant or numeric variable name; the arc radius size is in units based on the current window system.
start	numeric constant or numeric variable name; the starting angle of the arc is in degrees, with 0 degrees at 3 o'clock.
end	numeric constant or numeric variable name; the ending angle of the arc is in degrees, with 0 degrees at 3 o'clock.

See Also

GDRAW('ELLARC', . . .)function

GDRAW('PIE', . . .)function

GSET('LINCOLOR', . . .)function

GSET('LININDEX', . . .)function

GSET('LINREP', . . .)function

GSET('LINTYPE', . . .)function

GSET('LINWIDTH', . . .)function

BAR

Draws a rectangle

Operating States: SGOP

Return Codes: 0, 4, 76, 79, 80, 86

Syntax

return-code-variable=GDRAW('BAR', *x1, y1, x2, y2*);

Description   The GDRAW('BAR', . . .)function draws a rectangular bar whose sides are parallel to the sides of the display area. The fill attributes and bundles affect the appearance of this graphics element. See Table 31.2 on page 1038 for a list of these attributes. Figure 32.3 on page 1117 illustrates the arguments used with GDRAW('BAR', . . .).

Figure 32.3 Points that Draw a Bar

Argument Definitions

x1 numeric constant or numeric variable name; refers to the *x* coordinate of one corner of the bar.

y1 numeric constant or numeric variable name; refers to the *y* coordinate of one corner of the bar.

x2 numeric constant or numeric variable name; refers to the *x* coordinate of the corner of the bar that is diagonally opposite to the corner of (*x1,y1*).

y2 numeric constant or numeric variable name; refers to the *y* coordinate of the corner of the bar that is diagonally opposite to the corner of (*x1,y1*).

See Also

GDRAW('FILL', . . .)function
GSET('FILCOLOR', . . .)function
GSET('FILINDEX', . . .)function
GSET('FILREP', . . .)function
GSET('FILTYPE', . . .)function
GSET('FILSTYLE', . . .)function
GSET('HTML', . . .)function

ELLARC

Draws an elliptical arc

Operating States: SGOP

Return Codes: 0, 4, 61, 86

Syntax

return-code-variable =GDRAW('ELLARC', *x, y, major, minor, start, end, angle*);

Description   The GDRAW('ELLARC', . . .)function draws a hollow section of an ellipse. The line attributes and bundles affect the appearance of this primitive. See

Table 31.2 on page 1038 for a list of these attributes. Figure 32.4 on page 1118 illustrates the arguments used with GDRAW('ELLARC', . . .)and GDRAW('ELLIPSE', . . .).

Figure 32.4   Arguments Used with GDRAW('ELLARC',...) function and GDRAW('ELLIPSE',...) function

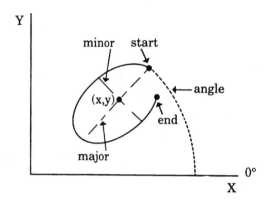

Argument Definitions

x	numeric constant or numeric variable name; *x* coordinates are in units based on the current window system.
y	numeric constant or numeric variable name; *y* coordinates are in units based on the current window system.
major	numeric constant or numeric variable name; the major axis lengths for the elliptical arc.
minor	numeric constant or numeric variable name; the minor axis lengths for the elliptical arc.
start	numeric constant or numeric variable name; the starting angle from the major axis, in degrees, for the elliptical arc with 0 degrees beginning at the major axis.
end	numeric constant or numeric variable name; the ending angle from the major axis, in degrees, for the elliptical arc with 0 degrees at 3 o'clock.
angle	numeric constant or numeric variable name; the angle that the major axis of the elliptical arc has to 0 degrees (with 0 degrees at 3 o'clock).

See Also

GDRAW('ELLIPSE', . . .)function

GSET('LINCOLOR', . . .)function

GSET('LINTYPE', . . .)function

GSET('LINWIDTH', . . .)function

GSET('LINREP', . . .)function

GSET('LININDEX', . . .)function

ELLIPSE

Draws an ellipse

Operating States: SGOP

Return Codes: 0, 4, 76, 79, 80, 86

Syntax

return-code-variable =GDRAW('ELLIPSE', *x, y, major, minor, start, end, angle*);

Description The GDRAW('ELLIPSE', . . .)function draws a filled section of an ellipse. The fill attributes and bundles affect the appearance of this primitive. See Table 31.2 on page 1038 for a list of these attributes. Figure 32.4 on page 1118 illustrates the arguments used with GDRAW('ELLARC', . . .)and GDRAW('ELLIPSE', . . .).

Argument Definitions

x	numeric constant or numeric variable name; the *x* coordinate of the position of the ellipse on the display.
y	numeric constant or numeric variable name; the *y* coordinate of the position of the ellipse on the display.
major	numeric constant or numeric variable name; the major axis length for the ellipse.
minor	numeric constant or numeric variable name; the minor axis length for the ellipse.
start	numeric constant or numeric variable name; the starting angle for the ellipse from the major axis, with 0 degrees beginning at the major axis.
end	numeric constant or numeric variable name; the ending angle for the ellipse from the major axis, with 0 degrees at 3 o'clock.
angle	numeric constant or numeric variable name; the angle that the major axis of the ellipse has to 0 degrees, with 0 degrees at 3 o'clock.

See Also

GDRAW('ELLARC', . . .)function
GSET('FILCOLOR', . . .)function
GSET('FILINDEX', . . .)function
GSET('FILREP', . . .)function
GSET('FILTYPE', . . .)function
GSET('FILWIDTH', . . .)function
GSET('HTML', . . .)function

FILL

Draws a filled area

Operating States: SGOP

Return Codes: 0, 4, 76, 79, 80, 86, 100, 301

Syntax

return-code-variable=GDRAW('FILL', *n, x-values, y-values*);

Description   The GDRAW('ILL' . . .)function draws a filled polygon. The fill attributes and bundles affect the appearance of this primitive. See Table 31.2 on page 1038 for a list of these attributes.

Note: All of the *x* coordinates are listed in the function first, followed by the *y* coordinates. This primitive takes the first *n* values and stores them as *x* coordinates. The next *n* values are stored as *y* coordinates. △

Argument Definitions

n   numeric constant or numeric variable name; the number of vertices (*x* and *y* pairs) in the polygon. You can specify a missing value (.) for *n*. If *n* is missing, the number of vertices is computed from the number of *x* and *y* arguments.

x-values   list of numeric constants, variables, or OF arguments that describe the *x* coordinates for the vertices in units based on the current window system.

y-values   list of numeric constants, variables, or OF arguments that describe the *y* coordinates for the vertices in units based on the current window system.

See Also

GDRAW('BAR', . . .)function
GSET('FILCOLOR', . . .)function
GSET('FILINDEX', . . .)function
GSET('FILREP', . . .)function
GSET('FILTYPE', . . .)function
GSET('FILSTYLE', . . .)function
GSET('HTML', . . .)function

LINE

Draws a polyline

Operating States: SGOP

Return Codes: 0, 4, 61, 86, 100, 301

Syntax

return-code-variable=GDRAW('LINE', *n, x-values, y-values*);

Description   The GDRAW('LINE' . . .)function draws one line, a series of connected lines, or a dot. The line attributes and bundles affect the appearance of this primitive. See Table 31.2 on page 1038 for a list of these attributes.

Note: All of the *x* coordinates are listed in the function first, followed by the *y* coordinates. This primitive takes the first *n* values and stores them as *x* coordinates and the next *n* values and stores them as *y* coordinates. △

Argument Definitions

n   numeric constant or numeric variable name; the number of vertices (*x* and *y* pairs) in the polygon. You can specify a missing value (.) for *n*. If *n* is missing, the number of vertices is computed from the number of *x* and *y* pairs.

x-values   list of numeric constants, variables, or OF arguments that describe the *x* coordinates for the vertices in units based on the current window system.

y-values   list of numeric constants, variables, or OF argument lists that describe the *y* coordinates for the vertices in units based on the current window system.

See Also

GSET('LINCOLOR', . . .)function
GSET('LININDEX', . . .)function
GSET('LINREP', . . .)function
GSET('LINTYPE', . . .)function
GSET('LINWIDTH', . . .)function

MARK

Draws a polymarker

Operating States: SGOP

Return Codes: 0, 4, 65, 86, 100, 301

Syntax

return-code-variable=GDRAW ('MARK', *n, x-values, y-values*);

Description The GDRAW('MARK', . . .)function draws a series of symbols. The marker attributes and bundles affect the appearance of this primitive. See Table 31.2 on page 1038 for a list of these attributes. Refer to the GSET('MARTYPE', . . .)function on page 1149 for a list of symbols that you can draw with GDRAW('MARK', . . .).

Note: All of the *x* coordinates are listed in the function first, followed by the *y* coordinates. This primitive takes the first *n* values and stores them as *x* coordinates and the next *n* values and stores them as *y* coordinates. △

Argument Definitions

n	numeric constant or numeric variable name; the number of times the symbol is drawn. You can specify a missing value (.) for *n*. If *n* is missing, the number of vertices is calculated from the number of *x* and *y* pairs.
x-values	list of numeric constants, variables, or OF arguments that describe the *x* coordinates of the symbols in units based on the current window system.
y-values	list of numeric constants, variables, or OF arguments that describe the *y* coordinates of the symbols in units based on the current window system.

See Also

GDRAW('TEXT', . . .)function
GSET('HTML', . . .)function
GSET('MARCOLOR', . . .)function
GSET('MARINDEX', . . .)function
GSET('MARREP', . . .)function
GSET('MARTYPE', . . .)function
GSET('MARWIDTH', . . .)function

MESSAGE

Prints a message in the SAS log

Operating States: All

Return Codes: 0

Syntax

return-code-variable=GDRAW('MESSAGE', *message*);

Description The GDRAW('MESSAGE', . . .)function prints a message in the SAS log. This function may be used for debugging applications or for printing custom messages for your application.

Argument Definitions

message   character string enclosed in quotes or character variable name; the text to be printed in the log.

See Also

GSET('MESSAGE', . . .)function
GPRINT('*code*') utility function

PIE

Draws a filled circle or section of a filled circle

Operating States: SGOP

Return Codes: 0, 4, 76, 79, 80, 86

Syntax

return-code-variable=GDRAW('PIE', *x, y, radius, start, end*);

Description   The GDRAW('PIE', . . .)function draws a filled section of a circular arc. The fill attributes and bundles affect the appearance of this primitive. See Table 31.2 on page 1038 for a list of these attributes.

Argument Definitions

x   numeric constant or numeric variable name; *x* coordinates are in units based on the current window system.

y   numeric constant or numeric variable name; *y* coordinates are in units based on the current window system.

radius   numeric constant or numeric variable name; the pie radius size in units based on the current window system.

start   numeric constant or numeric variable name; the starting angle of the pie, with 0 degrees at 3 o'clock on the unit circle.

end   numeric constant or numeric variable name; the ending angle of the pie, with 0 degrees at 3 o'clock on the unit circle.

See Also

GDRAW('ARC', . . .)function
GSET('FILCOLOR', . . .)function
GSET('FILINDEX', . . .)function
GSET('FILREP', . . .)function
GSET('FILTYPE', . . .)function
GSET('FILSTYLE', . . .)function
GSET('HTML', . . .)function

TEXT

Draws a text string

Operating States: SGOP
Return Codes: 0, 4, 69, 86

Syntax

return-code-variable=GDRAW('TEXT', *x, y, string*);

Description   The GDRAW('TEXT', . . .)function draws a text string. The text attributes and bundles affect the appearance of this primitive. See Table 31.2 on page 1038 for a list of these attributes.

Argument Definitions

x   numeric constant or numeric variable name; *x* coordinates are in units based on the current window system.

y   numeric constant or numeric variable name; *y* coordinates are in units based on the current window system.

string   character string enclosed in quotes or character variable name; a set of characters to be drawn on the output beginning at position (*x,y*).

See Also

GDRAW('MARK', . . .)function
GSET('HTML', . . .)function
GSET('TEXCOLOR', . . .)function
GSET('TEXINDEX', . . .)function
GSET('TEXREP', . . .)function
GSET('TEXTYPE', . . .)function
GSET('TEXHEIGHT', . . .)function

GRAPH Functions

GRAPH functions perform library management tasks from within the DATA Step Graphics Interface. These functions can only be performed on one catalog at a time. They cannot be performed across catalogs. For example, you cannot copy a graph from one catalog to another.

When using GRAPH functions, remember the following:

□ All arguments are specified as variables or constants. If you express an argument as a variable, the variable must be initialized.

□ All character arguments expressed as character strings must be enclosed in quotes.

□ All character variable names used as arguments *must* be declared in a LENGTH statement.

□ All character constants must be enclosed in single or double quotes.

CLEAR

Opens a graphics segment for output

Operating States: WSAC
Return Codes: 0, 3, 301, 302
Resulting Operating State: SGOP

Syntax

return-code-variable=GRAPH ('CLEAR'<, *name*> <, *des*><, *byline*>);

Description   The GRAPH('CLEAR', . . .)function opens a graphics segment for output in the current catalog. The first parameter, 'CLEAR', is the only required one. The values of *name*, *des*, and *byline* are displayed in catalog listings and in catalog information in the GREPLAY procedure.

If the name specified is an existing graph, DSGI will suffix the name with a number. For example, if PIE is chosen for the name and it already exists, DSGI will name the output PIE1; the next time the code is submitted, DSGI names the output PIE2, and so forth.

This function moves the operating state from WSAC to SGOP.

Argument Definitions

name   character string enclosed in quotes or character variable name; gives a name to the graph to be opened. If *name* is not specified, DSGI assigns the graph a name that is some form of DSGI: for example, DSGI, DSGI1, and DSGI2.

des   character string enclosed in quotes or character variable name; gives a description to the graph to be opened. If *des* is not specified, DSGI assigns the following description to the catalog entry: Graph from DATA Step Graphics Interface.

by-line   character string enclosed in quotes or character variable name; gives another line of description for the graph. The byline appears under the titles on the graph. DSGI does not provide a default byline.

See Also

GASK('OPENGRAPH', . . .)routine
GRAPH('UPDATE', . . .)function

COPY

Copies a graph

Operating States: GKOP, WSOP, WSAC, SGOP

Return Codes: 0, 8, 307

Syntax

return-code-variable=GRAPH('COPY', *name, new-name*);

Description   The GRAPH('COPY', . . .)function copies a graph to another catalog entry. The graph to be copied must be closed and be in the current catalog. You cannot copy from one catalog to another. The new graph will also be in the current catalog.

Argument Definitions

name   character string enclosed in quotes or character variable name; name of the graph to be copied.

new-name   character string enclosed in quotes or character variable name; name of the graph to be created.

See Also

GASK('CATALOG', . . .)routine
GRAPH('DELETE', . . .)function
GRAPH('INSERT', . . .)function
GSET('CATALOG', . . .)function

DELETE

Deletes a graph

Operating States: GKOP, SGOP, WSAC, WSOP

Return Codes: 0, 4, 8, 307

Syntax

return-code-variable=GRAPH('DELETE', *name*);

Description   The GRAPH('DELETE', . . .)function deletes a graph in the current catalog. The graph does not have to be closed to be deleted.

Argument Definitions

name   character string enclosed in quotes or character variable name; the name of the graph to delete.

See Also

GASK('CATALOG', . . .)routine
GRAPH('COPY', . . .)function
GSET('CATALOG', . . .)function

INSERT

Inserts a previously created segment into the currently open graph

Operating States: SGOP

Return Codes: 0, 4, 302, 307

Syntax

return-code-variable=GRAPH('INSERT', *name*);

Description   The GRAPH('INSERT', . . .)function inserts a graph into the currently open graph. The graph to be inserted must be closed and be in the current catalog.

Argument Definitions

name   character string enclosed in quotes or character variable name; the name of a graph to be inserted.

See Also

GASK('CATALOG', . . .)routine
GRAPH('COPY', . . .)function
GSET('CATALOG', . . .)function

RENAME

Renames a graph

Operating States: GKOP, SGOP, WSAC, WSOP
Return Codes: 0, 8, 307

Syntax

return-code-variable=GRAPH('RENAME', *name, new-name*);

Description   The GRAPH('RENAME', . . .)function renames a graph. The graph to be renamed must be in the current catalog and be closed.

Argument Definitions

name   character string enclosed in quotes or character variable name; the name of the closed graph that is to be changed.

new-name   character string enclosed in quotes or character variable name; the new name for the graph.

See Also

GASK('CATALOG', . . .)routine
GRAPH('INSERT', . . .)function
GSET('CATALOG', . . .)function

UPDATE

Completes the currently open graph and (optionally) displays it

Operating States: SGOP
Return Codes: 0, 4
Resulting Operating State: WSAC

Syntax

return-code-variable=GRAPH('UPDATE' <, *'show'*>);

Description The GRAPH('UPDATE', . . .)function closes the graph currently open and displays it. DSGI operates in buffered mode, so the picture is never displayed until this function is called.

This function can be called only once for the currently open graph. Therefore, you cannot incrementally build a graph; however, you can close the currently open graph and later insert it into another graph within the same DATA step.

This function moves the operating state from SGOP to WSAC.

Argument Definitions

show　　　　character string, optional; valid values are SHOW and NOSHOW. If SHOW is specified, the graph is displayed. If NOSHOW is specified, the graph is closed and not displayed.

See Also

GRAPH('CLEAR', . . .)function

GSET Functions

GSET functions allow you to set attributes for the graphics elements. Some GSET functions set the attributes for a subset of graphics primitives. For example, attributes prefixed by FIL control the appearance of the graphics primitives GDRAW('BAR', . . .), GDRAW('ELLIPSE', . . .), GDRAW('FILL', . . .), and GDRAW('PIE', . . .). See Table 31.2 on page 1038 for a complete list of the attributes that control the appearance of the graphics primitives.

Some GSET functions affect the appearance of the entire graphics output. For example, GSET('HPOS', . . .)and GSET('VPOS', . . .)set the number of columns and rows for the output. See each GSET function for the aspect of the graphics output that it controls.

When using GSET functions, remember the following:

☐ All arguments must be specified.

☐ All arguments are specified as variables or constants. If you express an argument as a variable, the variable must be initialized.

☐ All character arguments that are expressed as character strings must be enclosed in quotation marks.

☐ All character variable names used as arguments *must* be declared in a LENGTH statement.

☐ All character constants must be enclosed in single or double quotation marks.

ASF

Specifies an aspect source flag to bundle or separate attributes

Operating States: GKOP, SGOP, WSAC, WSOP

Return Codes: 0, 8

Default Value: INDIVIDUAL

Syntax

return-code-variable=GSET('ASF', *attribute, status*);

Description   The GSET('ASF', . . .)function sets an attribute's aspect source flag (ASF) so that it can be used in a bundle (BUNDLED) or individually (INDIVIDUAL).

If an attribute's ASF is set to 'BUNDLED', it cannot be used outside of a bundle. It must be defined in a GSET('*xxx*REP', . . .)function and activated with a GSET('*xxx*INDEX', . . .)function, where *xxx* can have one of the following values: FIL, LIN, MAR, TEX.

If an attribute's ASF is set to 'INDIVIDUAL', it cannot be used with a bundle. In this case, the attribute is set with a GSET('*attribute*', . . .). The values of *attribute* are listed in "Argument Definitions."

Argument Definitions

attribute   character string enclosed in quotes or character variable name with one of the following values:

☐ FILCOLOR

☐ FILSTYLE

☐ FILTYPE

☐ LINCOLOR

☐ LINTYPE

☐ LINWIDTH

☐ MARCOLOR

☐ MARSIZE

☐ MARTYPE

    □ TEXCOLOR

    □ TEXFONT.

status   character string enclosed in quotation marks or character variable name; accepts either the value BUNDLED or INDIVIDUAL.

See Also

GASK('ASF', . . .)routine

GSET('FILCOLOR', . . .)function

GSET('FILSTYLE', . . .)function

GSET('FILTYPE', . . .)function

GSET('LINCOLOR', . . .)function

GSET('LINTYPE', . . .)function

GSET('LINWIDTH', . . .)function

GSET('MARCOLOR', . . .)function

GSET('MARSIZE', . . .)function

GSET('MARTYPE', . . .)function

GSET('TEXCOLOR', . . .)function

GSET('TEXFONT', . . .)function

ASPECT

Specifies the aspect ratio

Operating States: GKCL

Return Codes: 0, 1, 90, 307

Default Value: 0.0

Syntax

return-code-variable=GSET('ASPECT', *aspect*);

Description   The GSET('ASPECT', . . .)function sets the aspect ratio used to draw graphics output. GSET('ASPECT', . . .)affects only pies, arcs, and software text.

Argument Definitions

aspect   numeric constant or numeric variable name; specifies the aspect ratio and cannot be less than 0.

See Also

ASPECT= graphics option (see "ASPECT" on page 305)
GASK('ASPECT', . . .)routine

CATALOG

Specifies the catalog for the graphs

Operating States: GKCL

Return Codes: 0, 1

Default Values: *libref* = WORK, *catalog-name*=GSEG

Syntax

return-code-variable=GSET('CATALOG', *libref, catalog-name*);

Description   The GSET('CATALOG', . . .)function makes the specified catalog the current catalog in which to store graphs generated with DSGI. GSET('CATALOG', . . .)creates the catalog if it does not exist.

The values of *libref* and *catalog-name* cannot exceed eight characters. The number of characters allowed for a catalog name varies across operating environments; see the SAS companion for your operating system. *Libref* should have been defined through the LIBNAME statement.

Argument Definitions

libref   character string enclosed in quotation marks or character variable name; points to the library that contains the catalog.

catalog-name   character string enclosed in quotation marks or character variable name; specifies the catalog name to be used.

See Also

GASK('CATALOG', . . .)routine
GASK('GRAPHLIST', . . .)routine
GASK('NUMGRAPH', . . .)routine

CBACK

Specifies the background color

Operating States: GKCL

Return Codes: 0, 1

Default Value: 1. CBACK= graphics option, if specified; 2. device's default background color.

Syntax

return-code-variable=GSET('CBACK', *cback*);

Description The GSET('CBACK', . . .)function sets the background color. GSET('CBACK', . . .)has the same effect as the CBACK= graphics option.

Argument Definitions

cback character string enclosed in quotation marks or character variable name; can contain any predefined SAS color name. See "Predefined SAS Colors" on page 145 for a list of predefined SAS color names.

See Also

CBACK= graphics option (see "CBACK" on page 309)

GASK('CBACK', . . .)routine

CLIP

Specifies whether clipping is on or off

Operating States: GKOP, SGOP, WSAC, WSOP

Return Codes: 0

Default Value: OFF

Syntax

return-code-variable=GSET('CLIP', *status*);

Description The GSET('CLIP', . . .)function activates or suppresses clipping around the current viewport.

Argument Definitions

status character string enclosed in quotation marks or character variable name; valid values are ON and OFF. When ON is used, the graphics elements outside of the specified viewport are not displayed. If you turn clipping OFF, the graphics elements outside of the defined viewport are displayed.

See Also

GASK('CLIP', . . .)routine
GASK('VIEWPORT', . . .)routine
GSET('VIEWPORT', . . .)function

COLREP

Associates a color name with a certain color index

Operating States: SGOP
Return Codes: 0, 4, 86
Default Values: 1. colors list of COLORS= graphics option; 2. device's default colors list

---

Syntax

return-code-variable=GSET('COLREP', *color-index, color*);

Description The GSET('COLREP', . . .)function associates a predefined SAS color name with a color index. Many of the GASK routines and GSET functions use *color-index* as an argument.

If this function is not used, DSGI searches for a color specification in the following order:

1 the *n*th color in the colors list of the COLORS= graphics option

2 the *n*th color in the device's default colors list.

Argument Definitions

color-index   numeric constant or numeric variable name; a number from 1 to 256 that identifies a color.

color   character string enclosed in quotation marks or character variable name; a predefined SAS color name. See "Predefined SAS Colors" on page 145 for a list of predefined SAS color names.

See Also

COLORS= graphics option (see "COLORS" on page 314)
GASK('COLINDEX', . . .)routine
GASK('COLREP', . . .)routine

DEVICE

Specifies the output graphics device

Operating States: GKCL

Return Codes: 0, 1

Default Value: 1. DEVICE= graphics option, if specified; 2. value entered in DEVICE prompt window; 3. value entered in OPTIONS window

Syntax

return-code-variable=GSET('DEVICE', *device*);

Description   The GSET('DEVICE', . . .)function selects the device driver.

Argument Definitions

device   character string enclosed in quotation marks or character variable name; the name of the driver you will be using. *Device* must match one of the device entries in the SASHELP.DEVICES catalog or one of your personal device catalogs, GDEVICE0.DEVICES through GDEVICE9.DEVICES. Refer to "About Device Catalogs" on page 652 for more information about catalogs that store device entries.

See Also

DEVICE= graphics option (see "DEVICE" on page 321)

GASK('DEVICE', . . .)routine

FILCOLOR

Specifies the color index of the color used to draw fill areas

Operating States: GKOP, SGOP, WSAC, WSOP

Return Codes: 0, 8, 85

Default Value: 1

Syntax

return-code-variable=GSET('FILCOLOR', *color-index*);

Description   The GSET('FILCOLOR', . . .)function selects the color index of the color used to draw fill areas. The aspect source flag (ASF) of FILCOLOR must be set to 'INDIVIDUAL' for this attribute to be used outside of a fill bundle.

DSGI searches for a color to assign to the index in the following order:

1 the color specified for the index in a GSET('COLREP', . . .)function

2 the *n*th color in the colors list of the COLORS= graphics option

3 the *n*th color in the device's default colors list found in the device entry.

Argument Definitions

color-index   numeric constant or numeric variable name; indicates the index of
                            the color to be used. Valid values are 1 to 256, inclusive.

See Also

COLORS= graphics option (see "COLORS" on page 314)
GSET('ASF', . . .)routine
GSET('COLREP', . . .)function
GASK('FILCOLOR', . . .)function
GSET('FILREP', . . .)function

FILINDEX

Specifies the index of the bundle of fill area attributes

Operating States: GKOP, SGOP, WSAC, WSOP
Return Codes: 0, 8, 75
Default Value: 1

Syntax

return-code-variable=GSET('FILINDEX', *index*);

Description   The GSET('FILINDEX', . . .)function activates a particular fill bundle.
The aspect source flag (ASF) for FILCOLOR, FILSTYLE, and FILTYPE must be set to
'BUNDLED' before the associated GDRAW function is executed if you want the bundled
values to be used when the affected graphics element is drawn.

Argument Definitions

index   numeric constant or numeric variable name; specifies the index
                      number of the fill bundle. Valid values are 1 to 20, inclusive.

See Also

GASK('FILINDEX', . . .)routine
GSET('ASF', . . .)function
GSET('FILREP', . . .)function

FILREP

Associates a bundle of fill attributes with an index

Operating States: GKOP, SGOP, WSAC, WSOP

Return Codes: 0, 8, 75, 78, 85

Default Value: none

Syntax

return-code-variable =*GSET*('FILREP', *index, color-index, interior, style-index*);

Description   The GSET('FILREP', . . .)function assigns a color, type of interior, and style of the interior to a specific fill bundle. The aspect source flags for FILCOLOR, FILTYPE, and FILSTYLE must be set to 'BUNDLED' before the associated GDRAW function is executed if you want the bundled values to be used when the affected graphics element is drawn.

Argument Definitions

index   numeric constant or numeric variable name; indicates the index to be used with the bundle. Valid values are 1 to 20, inclusive. If *index* is expressed as a variable, the variable name must be initialized to a value between 1 and 20.

color-index   numeric constant or numeric variable name; indicates the index of the color to be used. Valid values are 1 to 256, inclusive. The color index should represent one of the following:

    □ a color index assigned with the GSET('COLREP', . . .)function

    □ the *n*th color in the colors list of the COLORS= graphics option

    □ the *n*th color in the device's default colors list.

interior   character string enclosed in quotation marks or character variable name; indicates the type of interior. Valid values are

    □ HATCH

    □ HOLLOW

    □ PATTERN

    □ SOLID.

style-index   numeric constant or numeric variable name; indicates the index of the style to be used. Valid values are 1 to 15, inclusive, when FILTYPE is PATTERN, or 1 to 60, inclusive, when FILTYPE is HATCH. See the GSET('FILSTYLE', . . .)function on page 1138 for a table of the patterns used for each style index. If *interior* is HOLLOW or SOLID, *style-index* is ignored.

See Also

GASK('FILREP', . . .)routine
GSET('ASF', . . .)function
GSET('COLREP', . . .)function
GSET('FILCOLOR', . . .)function
GSET('FILINDEX', . . .)function
GSET('FILSTYLE', . . .)function
GSET('FILTYPE', . . .)function

FILSTYLE

Specifies the style of the interior of the fill area when the FILTYPE is PATTERN or HATCH

Operating State: GKOP, SGOP, WSAC, WSOP
Return Codes: 0, 8, 78
Default Value: 1

Syntax

return-code-variable=GSET('FILSTYLE', *style-index*);

Description   The GSET('FILSTYLE', . . .)function activates a particular fill pattern when FILTYPE is specified as either PATTERN or HATCH. The aspect source flag (ASF) must be set to 'INDIVIDUAL' for this attribute to be used outside of a fill bundle.

Table 32.1   Style Index Table

Value	PATTERN	HATCH	Value	PATTERN	HATCH
1	X1	M1X	31		M3N045
2	X2	M1X030	32		M3N060
3	X3	M1X045	33		M3N090
4	X4	M1X060	34		M3N120
5	X5	M1N	35		M3N135
6	L1	M1N030	36		M3N150
7	L2	M1N045	37		M4X
8	L3	M1N060	38		M4X030
9	L4	M1N090	39		M4X045
10	L5	M1N120	40		M4X060
11	R1	M1N135	41		M4N
12	R2	M1N150	42		M4N030

Value	PATTERN	HATCH	Value	PATTERN	HATCH
13	R3	M2X	43		M4N045
14	R4	M2X030	44		M4N060
15	R5	M2X045	45		M4N090
16		M2X060	46		M4N120
17		M2N	47		M4N135
18		M2N030	48		M4N150
19		M2N045	49		M5X
20		M2N060	50		M5X030
21		M2N090	51		M5X045
22		M2N120	52		M5X060
23		M2N135	53		M5N
24		M2N150	54		M5N030
25		M3X	55		M5N045
26		M3X030	56		M5N060
27		M3X045	57		M5N090
28		M3X060	58		M5N120
29		M3N	59		M5N135
30		M3N030	60		M5N150

Argument Definitions

style-index   numeric constant or numeric variable name. Valid values are 1 to 15, inclusive, when FILTYPE is PATTERN, or 1 to 60, inclusive, when FILTYPE is HATCH. See Table 31.1 on page 1034 for value specifications.

See Also

GASK('FILSTYLE', . . .)routine
GSET('ASF', . . .)function
GSET('FILREP', . . .)function
GSET('FILTYPE', . . .)function

FILTYPE

Specifies the type of the interior of the fill area

Operating States: GKOP, SGOP, WSAC, WSOP
Return Codes: 0, 8, 78
Default Value: HOLLOW

Syntax

return-code-variable=GSET('FILTYPE', *interior*);

Description   The GSET('FILTYPE', . . .)function selects a particular type of interior fill. If FILTYPE is set to HATCH or PATTERN, the GSET('FILSTYLE', . . .)function determines the type of hatch or pattern fill used. The aspect source flag (ASF) for FILTYPE must be set to 'INDIVIDUAL' for this attribute to be used outside of a fill bundle.

Argument Definitions

interior   character string or character variable name; indicates the type of interior fill. Valid values are

- □ HATCH
- □ HOLLOW
- □ PATTERN
- □ SOLID.

See Also

GSET('ASF', . . .)function
GSET('FILREP', . . .)function
GSET('FILSTYLE', . . .)function

HPOS

Specifies the number of columns

Operating States: GKCL
Return Codes: 0, 1, 90, 307
Default Value: 1. HPOS= graphics option, if specified; 2. device's default HPOS setting

Syntax

return-code-variable=GSET('HPOS', *hpos*);

Description   The GSET('HPOS', . . .)function sets the number of columns in the graphics output area. GSET('HPOS', . . .)has the same effect as the HPOS= graphics option. See "HPOS" on page 355 for more information. You can reset the HPOS value by submitting one of the following statements:

```
goptions reset=goptions;
goptions reset=all;

goptions hpos=0;
```

Argument Definitions

hpos   numeric constant or numeric variable name; specifies the number of
                            horizontal columns; must be greater than 0.

See Also

GASK('HPOS', . . .)routine
GSET('HSIZE', . . .)function
GSET('VPOS', . . .)function
HPOS= graphics option (see "HPOS" on page 355)

HSIZE

Specifies the horizontal dimension of the graphics output area

Operating States: GKCL
Return Codes: 0, 1, 90, 307
Default Value: 1. HSIZE= graphics option, if specified; 2. HSIZE device parameter

Syntax

return-code-variable=GSET('HSIZE', *hsize*);

Description   The GSET('HSIZE', . . .)function sets the horizontal dimension, in
inches, of the graphics output area. GSET('HSIZE', . . .)affects the dimensions of the
default window. You can reset the HSIZE value by submitting one of the following
statements:

```
goptions reset=goptions;
goptions reset=all;

goptions hsize=0;
```

Argument Definitions

hsize   numeric constant or numeric variable name; specifies the horizontal
                            dimension, in inches, of the graphics output area; must be greater
                            than 0.

See Also

GASK('HSIZE', . . .)routine
GSET('HPOS', . . .)function
GSET('VSIZE', . . .)function
HSIZE= graphics option (see "HSIZE" on page 356)

HTML

Specifies the HTML string to invoke when an affected DSGI graphic element in a web page is clicked

Operating States: GKOP, SGOP, WSAC, WSOP
Return Codes: 0, 8
Default Value: null

Syntax

return-code-variable=GSET('HTML', '*string*');

Description The GSET('HTML', . . .)function sets the HTML string to invoke when an affected DSGI graphic element in a web page is clicked. The HTML string is used with ODS processing to create a drill-down graph. The string value is used as the value for the HREF= attribute in the image map that implements the drill-down capability.

The value for *string* must be *href=* followed by a valid URL that is specified in double quotation marks, as in

```
rc = GSET('HTML', 'HREF="http://www.sas.com/"');
```

The HTML string can be used by any of the following graphic element types drawn in the code: BAR, ELLIPSE, FILL, MARK, PIE, and TEXT. The string applies to all of these element types that are drawn *after* the string is set. To change the HTML string, set a new value. To turn off the HTML string, specify a null string:

```
rc = GSET('HTML', '');
```

For more information on drill-down graphs, see "About Drill-down Graphs" on page 90. For an example of how to use DSGI to generate a drill-down graph, see "Generating a Drill-down Graph Using DSGI" on page 1069.

Argument Definitions

string   the HTML string. The string must be enclosed in single quotation marks and must begin with *href=* followed by a URL that is enclosed in double quotation marks.

See Also

GASK('HTML', . . .)function
GDRAW('BAR', . . .)function
GDRAW('ELLIPSE', . . .)function
GDRAW('FILL', . . .)function
GDRAW('MARK', . . .)function
GDRAW('PIE', . . .)function
GDRAW('TEXT', . . .)function

LINCOLOR

Specifies the color index of the color used to draw lines

Operating States: GKOP, SGOP, WSAC, WSOP
Return Codes: 0, 8, 85
Default Value: 1

Syntax

return-code-variable=GSET('LINCOLOR', *color-index*);

Description   The GSET('LINCOLOR', . . .)function selects the index of the color used
to draw lines. The aspect source flag (ASF) for LINCOLOR must be set to
'INDIVIDUAL' for this attribute to be used outside of a line bundle.
DSGI searches for a color specification in the following order:

1 the color specified for the index in a GSET('COLREP', . . .)function
2 the nth color in the colors list of the COLORS= graphics option
3 the nth color in the device's default colors list found in the device entry.

Argument Definitions

color-index   numeric constant or numeric variable name; indicates the index of
the color to use. Valid values are 1 to 256, inclusive.

See Also

COLORS= graphics option (see "COLORS" on page 314)
GASK('LINCOLOR', . . .)routine
GSET('ASF', . . .)function
GSET('COLREP', . . .)function
GSET('LINREP', . . .)function

LININDEX

Specifies the index of the bundle of line attributes

Operating States: GKOP, SGOP, WSAC, WSOP
Return Codes: 0, 8, 60
Default Value: 1

Syntax

return-code-variable=GSET('LININDEX', *index*);

Description   The GSET('LININDEX', . . .)function activates a particular line bundle. The aspect source flags (ASF) of LINCOLOR, LINTYPE, and LINWIDTH must be set to 'BUNDLED' before the associated GDRAW function is executed if you want the bundled values to be used when the affected graphics element is drawn.

Argument Definitions

index   numeric constant or numeric variable name; indicates the index of
                                        the bundle to activate. Valid values are 1 to 20, inclusive.

See Also

GASK('LININDEX', . . .)routine
GSET('ASF', . . .)function
GSET('LINREP', . . .)function

LINREP

Associates a bundle of line attributes with an index

Operating States: GKOP, SGOP, WSAC, WSOP
Return Codes: 0, 8, 60, 62, 85, 90
Default Value: none

Syntax

return-code-variable=GSET ('LINREP',*index, color-index, width, type*);

Description   The GSET('LINREP', . . .)function assigns a color, width, and line type to a specific line bundle. The aspect source flags (ASF) for LINCOLOR, LINWIDTH, and LINTYPE must be set to 'BUNDLED' before the associated GDRAW function is executed if you want the bundled values to be used when the affected graphics element is drawn.

Argument Definitions

index   numeric constant or numeric variable name; indicates the number
                                        for the bundle to use as an index. Valid values are 1 and 20,
                                        inclusive. If *index* is expressed as a variable, the variable must be
                                        initialized to a value between 1 and 20.

color-index   numeric constant or numeric variable name; specifies the index of the color to use. Valid values are 1 to 256, inclusive. The color index should represent one of the following:

□ a color index assigned with the GSET('COLREP', . . .)function

□ the *n*th color in the colors list of the COLORS= graphics option

□ the *n*th color in the device's default colors list.

width   numeric constant or numeric variable name; indicates the width of the line; must be greater than 0.

type   numeric constant or numeric variable name; indicates the type of line. Valid values are 1 to 46, inclusive. See Figure 8.22 on page 249 for representations of the different line types.

See Also

GSET('ASF', . . .)function

GSET('COLREP', . . .)function

GSET('LINCOLOR', . . .)function

GSET('LININDEX', . . .)function

GSET('LINREP', . . .)function

GSET('LINTYPE', . . .)function

GSET('LINWIDTH', . . .)function

LINTYPE

Specifies the line type

Operating States: GKOP, SGOP, WSAC, WSOP

Return Codes: 0, 8, 62

Default Value: 1

Syntax

return-code-variable=GSET('LINTYPE', *type*);

Description   The GSET('LINTYPE', . . .)function selects a line type. See Figure 8.22 on page 249 for representations of the different line types. The aspect source flag (ASF) for LINTYPE must be set to 'INDIVIDUAL' for this attribute to be used outside of a line bundle.

Argument Definitions

type   numeric constant or numeric variable name; indicates the type of line to use. Valid values are 1 to 46, inclusive.

See Also

GASK('LINTYPE', . . .)routine

GSET('ASF', . . .)function

GSET('LINREP', . . .)function

LINWIDTH

Specifies the thickness of the line

Operating States: GKOP, SGOP, WSAC, WSOP

Return Codes: 0, 8, 90

Default Value: 1

Syntax

return-code-variable=GSET('LINWIDTH', *width*);

Description   The GSET('LINWIDTH', . . .)function selects a line width in units of pixels. The aspect source flag (ASF) for LINWIDTH must be set to 'INDIVIDUAL' for this attribute to be used outside of a line bundle.

Argument Definitions

width   numeric constant or numeric variable name; specifies the width of the line in pixels; must be greater than 0.

See Also

GASK('LINWIDTH', . . .)routine

GSET('ASF', . . .)function

GSET('LINREP', . . .)function

MARCOLOR

Specifies the color index of the color used to draw markers

Operating States: GKOP, SGOP, WSAC, WSOP

Return Codes: 0, 8, 85

Default Value: 1

Syntax

return-code-variable=GSET('MARCOLOR', *color-index*);

Description   The GSET('MARCOLOR', . . .)function selects the color index of the color used to draw markers. The aspect source flag (ASF) of MARCOLOR must be set to 'INDIVIDUAL' for this attribute to be used outside of a marker bundle.
   DSGI searches for a color specification in the following order:

1   the color specified for the index in a GSET('COLREP', . . .)function

2   the *n*th color in the colors list of the COLORS= graphics option

3   the *n*th color in the device's default colors list found in the device entry.

Argument Definitions

color-index   numeric constant or numeric variable name; indicates the index of the color to use. Valid values are 1 to 256, inclusive.

See Also

COLORS= graphics option (see "COLORS" on page 314)

GASK('MARCOLOR', . . .)routine

GSET('ASF', . . .)function

GSET('COLREP', . . .)function

GSET('MARREP', . . .)function

MARINDEX

Specifies the index of the bundle of marker attributes

Operating States: GKOP, SGOP, WSAC, WSOP

Return Codes: 0, 8, 64

Default Value: 1

Syntax

return-code-variable=GSET('MARINDEX', *index*);

Description   The GSET('MARINDEX', . . .)function activates the marker bundle indicated by *index*. The aspect source flag (ASF) for MARCOLOR, MARTYPE, and MARSIZE must be set to 'BUNDLED' before the GDRAW('MARK', . . .)function is executed if you want the bundled values to be used when the marker is drawn.

Argument Definitions

index   numeric constant or numeric variable name; the number of the bundle to activate. Valid values are 1 to 20, inclusive.

See Also

GASK('MARINDEX', . . .)routine

GSET('ASF', . . .)function

GSET('MARREP', . . .)function

MARREP

Associates a bundle of marker attributes with an index

Operating States: GKOP, SGOP, WSAC, WSOP

Return Codes: 0, 8, 64, 66, 85, 90

Default Value: none

Syntax

return-code-variable=GSET ('MARREP',*index, color-index, size, type*);

Description   The GSET('MARREP', . . .)function assigns a color, size, and type of marker to a specific marker bundle. The aspect source flag (ASF) of MARCOLOR, MARSIZE, and MARTYPE must be set to 'BUNDLED' before the GDRAW('MARK', . . .)function is executed if you want the bundled values to be used when the marker is drawn.

Argument Definitions

index	numeric constant or numeric variable name; defines the bundle index number. Valid values are 1 to 20, inclusive.
color-index	numeric constant or numeric variable name; indicates the color index of the color to use. Valid values are 1 to 256, inclusive. The color index should represent one of the following:

       □ a color index assigned to a color name with the GSET('COLREP', . . .)function

       □ the *n*th color in the colors list of the COLORS= graphics option

       □ the *n*th color in the device's default colors list.

size	numeric constant or numeric variable name; indicates the size of the marker in units of the current window system; must be greater than 0.
type	numeric constant or numeric variable name; specifies the type of marker to use; valid values are 1 to 67, inclusive. See Table 32.2 on page 1150 for a table of the symbols used for each marker type.

See Also

GSET('ASF', . . .)function
GSET('COLREP', . . .)function
GSET('MARCOLOR', . . .)function
GSET('MARINDEX', . . .)function
GSET('MARREP', . . .)function
GSET('MARSIZE', . . .)function
GSET('MARTYPE', . . .)function

MARSIZE

Selects the size of markers

Operating States: GKOP, SGOP, WSAC, WSOP
Return Codes: 0, 8, 90
Default Value: 1

Syntax

return-code-variable=GSET('MARSIZE', *size*);

Description   The GSET('MARSIZE', . . .)function sets the marker size in units of the current window system. The aspect source flag (ASF) of MARSIZE must be set to 'INDIVIDUAL' for this attribute to be used outside of a marker bundle.

Argument Definitions

size   numeric constant or numeric variable name; indicates the size of the
                      marker in units of the current window system; must be greater than
                      0.

See Also

GASK('MARSIZE', . . .)routine
GSET('ASF', . . .)function
GSET('MARREP', . . .)function

MARTYPE

Selects the kind of markers

Operating States: GKOP, SGOP, WSAC, WSOP

Return Codes: 0, 8, 66

Default Value: 1

Syntax

return-code-variable=GSET('MARTYPE', *type*);

Description   The GSET('MARTYPE', . . .)function determines the type of marker drawn. See Figure 8.21 on page 243 for representations of the symbols described in Table 32.2 on page 1150. The aspect source flag (ASF) of MARTYPE must be set to 'INDIVIDUAL' for this attribute to be used outside of a marker bundle.

Table 32.2   Symbol Indexes Used with DSGI

Values and Markers					
1	plus	24	K	46	9
2	x	25	L	47	lozenge
3	star	26	M	48	spade
4	square	27	N	49	heart
5	diamond	28	O	50	diamond
6	triangle	29	P	51	club
7	hash	30	Q	52	shamrock
8	Y	31	R	53	fleur-de-lis
9	Z	32	S	54	star
10	paw	33	T	55	sun
11	point	34	U	56	Mercury
12	dot	35	V	57	Venus
13	circle	36	W	58	Earth
14	A	37	0	59	Mars
15	B	38	1	60	Jupiter
16	C	39	2	61	Saturn
17	D	40	3	62	Uranus
18	E	41	4	63	Neptune
19	F	42	5	64	Pluto
20	G	43	6	65	moon
21	H	44	7	66	comet

Values and Markers					
22	I	45	8	67	asterisk
23	J				

Argument Definitions

type numeric constant or numeric variable name; indicates the index of the marker to draw. Valid values are 1 to 67, inclusive. See Table 32.2 on page 1150 for value specifications.

See Also

GASK('MARTYPE', . . .)routine

GSET('ASF', . . .)function

GSET('MARREP', . . .)function

MESSAGE

Specifies whether the interface error message system is enabled or disabled

Operating States: All

Return Codes: 0

Default Value: ON

Syntax

return-code-variable=GSET('MESSAGE', *status*);

Description   The GSET('MESSAGE', . . .)function activates or suppresses automatic error logging.

Argument Definitions

status character string enclosed in quotation marks or character variable name; indicates whether messages should be displayed. Valid values are ON and OFF. When ON is used, messages are automatically generated by the DSGI based on the return code from the function. If you set MESSAGE to OFF, no messages are automatically printed. You may choose to do this if you want to print custom messages for your application or decide which error message you want printed.

See Also

GDRAW('MESSAGE', . . .)function

GPRINT('*code*') utility function

TEXALIGN

Specifies the horizontal and vertical alignment of the text string

Operating States: GKOP, SGOP, WSAC, WSOP

Return Codes: 0, 8

Default values: *halign*=NORMAL, *valign*=NORMAL

Syntax

return-code-variable=GSET('TEXALIGN', *halign, valign*);

Description   The GSET('TEXALIGN', . . .)function sets a particular type of horizontal and vertical alignment for text strings. Figure 32.5 on page 1152 illustrates *halign*.

Figure 32.5   Halign Values

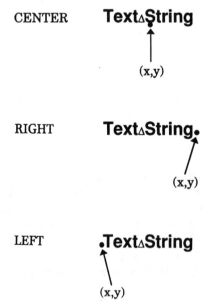

Figure 32.6 on page 1153 illustrates *valign*.

Figure 32.6 Valign Values

Argument Definitions

halign   character string enclosed in quotation marks or character variable name. Valid values are

CENTER

LEFT

NORMAL (the natural alignment based on the text path); alignment is chosen according to the following logic:

1 If TEXPATH is 'RIGHT', then NORMAL is 'LEFT'.
2 Otherwise, if TEXPATH is 'LEFT', then NORMAL is 'RIGHT'.
3 Otherwise, the text string is centered.

RIGHT.

valign   character string enclosed in quotation marks or character variable name. Valid values are

BASE (alignment based on the baseline of the text string)

BOTTOM (alignment based on the bottom of the text string)

HALF (alignment based on the vertical midpoint of the string)

NORMAL (natural alignment based on the text path); alignment is chosen according to the following logic:

1 If TEXPATH is 'RIGHT' or TEXPATH is 'LEFT', then NORMAL is 'BASE'.
2 Otherwise, if TEXPATH is 'UP', then NORMAL is 'BOTTOM'.
3 Otherwise, if TEXPATH is 'DOWN', then NORMAL is 'TOP'.

TOP (alignment based on the top of the string).

See Also

GASK('TEXALIGN', . . .)routine
GDRAW('TEXT', . . .)function
GSET('TEXPATH', . . .)function
GSET('TEXUP', . . .)function

TEXCOLOR

Specifies the color index of the color used to draw text strings

Operating States: GKOP, SGOP, WSAC, WSOP

Return Codes: 0, 8, 85

Default Value: 1

Syntax

return-code-variable=GSET('TEXCOLOR', *color-index*);

Description   The GSET('TEXCOLOR', . . .)function selects the color for text. The aspect source flag (ASF) of TEXCOLOR must be set to 'INDIVIDUAL' for this attribute to be used outside of a text bundle.

The value of GSET('TEXCOLOR', . . .)can be used in a text bundle. See the GSET('TEXREP', . . .)function on page 1157 for information on how to define a text bundle.

DSGI searches for a color specification in the following order:

1   the color specified for the index in a GSET('COLREP', . . .)function

2   the *n*th color from the colors list of the COLORS= graphics option

3   the *n*th color in the device's default colors list found in the device entry.

Argument Definitions

color-index   numeric constant or numeric variable name; indicates the color index of the color to be used. Valid values are 1 to 256, inclusive.

See Also

COLORS= graphics option (see "COLORS" on page 314)

GASK('TEXCOLOR', . . .)routine

GSET('ASF', . . .)function

GSET('COLREP', . . .)function

GSET('TEXREP', . . .)function

TEXFONT

Specifies the font used to draw text strings

Operating States: GKOP, SGOP, WSAC, WSOP

Return Codes: 0, 8

Default values: 1. FTEXT= graphics option, if specified; 2. hardware font, if possible; 3. SIMULATE font

Syntax

return-code-variable=GSET('TEXFONT', *font*);

Description   The GSET('TEXFONT', . . .)function selects a SAS/GRAPH font for the text. The aspect source flag (ASF) of TEXFONT must be set to 'INDIVIDUAL' for this attribute to be used outside of a text bundle. See "Font Lists" on page 131 for a list of valid SAS/GRAPH fonts. You may also use fonts you have created using the GFONT procedure.

Argument Definitions

font   character string enclosed in quotation marks or character variable name; the name of a font that can be accessed by SAS/GRAPH software. If you want to use the hardware font, submit

```
rc=gset('texfont', ' ');
```

When DSGI is used with long font names, the font name must be in double quotation marks that are embedded in single quotation marks, as in "'HW font name'".

See Also

FTEXT= graphics options (see "FTEXT" on page 335)
GASK('TEXFONT', . . .)routine
GSET('ASF', . . .)function
GSET('TEXREP', . . .)function

TEXHEIGHT

Specifies the character height of the text string

Operating States: GKOP, SGOP, WSAC, WSOP
Return Codes: 0, 8, 73
Default Value: 1. HTEXT= graphics option, if specified; 2. 1 unit

Syntax

return-code-variable=GSET('TEXHEIGHT', *height*);

Description   The GSET('TEXHEIGHT', . . .)function sets the height for text. GSET('TEXHEIGHT', . . .)affects text the same way as the HTEXT= graphics option.

Argument Definitions

height   numeric constant or numeric variable name; indicates height in units based on the current window system; must be greater than 0.

See Also

GASK('TEXHEIGHT', . . .)routine

HTEXT= graphics options (see "HTEXT" on page 357)

TEXINDEX

Specifies the index of the bundle of text attributes

Operating States: GKOP, SGOP, WSAC, WSOP

Return Codes: 0, 8, 68

Default Value: 1

Syntax

return-code-variable=GSET('TEXINDEX', *index*);

Description   The GSET('TEXINDEX', . . .)function activates the text bundle
indicated by *index*. The aspect source flag (ASF) for TEXCOLOR and TEXFONT must
be set to 'BUNDLED' before the GDRAW('TEXT', . . .)function is executed if you want
the bundled values to be used when the text is drawn.

Argument Definitions

index   numeric constant or numeric variable name; indicates the number of
                        the bundle to activate. Valid values are 1 to 20, inclusive.

See Also

GASK('TEXINDEX', . . .)routine

GSET('ASF', . . .)function

GSET('TEXREP', . . .)function

TEXPATH

Specifies the direction of the text string

Operating States: GKOP, SGOP, WSAC, WSOP

Return Codes: 0, 8

Default Value: RIGHT

Syntax

return-code-variable=GSET('TEXPATH', *path*);

Description   The GSET('TEXPATH', . . .)function selects a particular type of text path. Text path determines the direction in which the text string reads. Figure 32.7 on page 1157 illustrates the text paths that can be used with DSGI.

Figure 32.7   TEXPATH Values

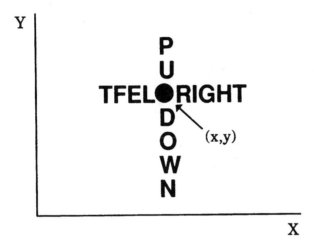

Argument Definitions

path   character string enclosed in quotation marks or character variable name; specifies the direction in which the text will read. Valid values are

□ DOWN

□ LEFT

□ RIGHT

□ UP.

See Also

GASK('TEXPATH', . . .)routine

GDRAW('TEXT', . . .)function

GSET('TEXALIGN', . . .)function

GSET('TEXUP', . . .)function

TEXREP

Associates a bundle of text attributes with an index

Operating States: GKOP, SGOP, WSAC, WSOP

Return Codes: 0, 8, 68, 85

Default Value: none

Syntax

return-code-variable=GSET ('TEXREP',*index, color-index, font*);

Description   The GSET('TEXREP', . . .)function assigns a color and font to a particular text bundle. The aspect source flags (ASF) of TEXCOLOR and TEXFONT must be set to 'BUNDLED' before the GDRAW('TEXT', . . .)function is executed if you want the bundled values to be used when the text is drawn.

Argument Definitions

index   numeric constant or numeric variable name; specifies the number to use as an index for the bundle; valid values are 1 to 20, inclusive. If *index* is expressed as a variable, the variable must be initialized to a value between 1 and 20.

color-index   numeric constant or numeric variable name; indicates the color to use; valid values are 1 to 256, inclusive. The color index should represent one of the following:

□ a color index assigned with the GSET('COLREP', . . .)function

□ the *n*th color in the colors list of the COLORS= graphics option

□ the *n*th color in the device's default colors list.

font   character string enclosed in quotation marks or character variable name; names the font to use with the bundle. See "Font Lists" on page 131 for a list of valid SAS/GRAPH fonts. You may also use fonts you have created using the GFONT procedure.

See Also

COLORS= graphics option (see "COLORS" on page 314)

GASK('TEXREP', . . .)routine

GSET('ASF', . . .)function

GSET('COLREP', . . .)function

GSET('TEXINDEX', . . .)function

TEXUP

Specifies the orientation (angle) of the text string

Operating States: GKOP, SGOP, WSAC, WSOP

Return Codes: 0, 8, 74

Default Values: *upx*=0, *upy*=1

Syntax

return-code-variable=GSET('TEXUP',*upx, upy*);

Description   The GSET('TEXUP', . . .)function sets the angle of the text string. DSGI uses the values of character up vectors to determine the angle of a text string. The character up vector has two components, *upx* and *upy*, that describe the angle at which the text string is placed. The angle is calculated with the following formula:

```
angle=atan(upx/upy)
```

Effectively, when DSGI is calculating the angle for the text, it uses *upx* and *upy* as forces that are pushing the string toward an angle. The natural angle of text in the *upx* direction is toward the 6 o'clock position. In the *upy* direction, text naturally angles at the 3 o'clock position. If *upx* is greater than *upy*, the text is angled toward 6 o'clock. If *upy* is greater than *upx*, the text is angled toward 3 o'clock. Figure 32.8 on page 1159 shows the angle of text when the values for *upx* and *upy* are (0.0, 1.0) and (1.0, 0.0).

Figure 32.8   Natural Angle of Text

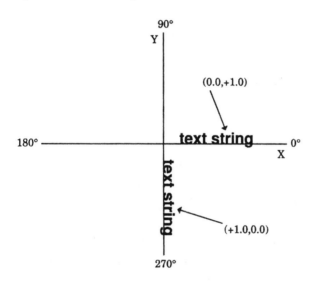

As you change the values of *upx* and *upy*, the coordinate that has the highest value is taken as the angle, and the lowest value as the offset. Figure 32.9 on page 1160 shows the angle of text when the character up vector values (+1.0, +0.5) are used.

Figure 32.9   Varying the Angle of Text

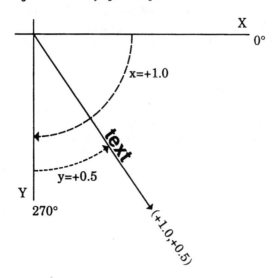

You can use the following macro to convert angles measured in degrees to character up vectors:

```
%macro angle(x);
  if  mod(&x, 180)=90 then do;
     if mod(&x,270) = 0 then
        xup = 1.0;
     else
        xup = -1.0;
     rc = gset('texup', xup, 0.0);
     end;
  else do;
     b = mod(&x, 360);
     /* adjust y vector for 2nd and 3rd quadrants */
     if b > 90 and b lt 270 then
       yup = -1.0;
     else
       yup = 1.0;
     a=&x*1.7453292519943300e-002;
     xup = tan(-a);
     /* adjust x vector for 3rd quadrant */
     if b > 180 and b le 270 then
       xup = -xup;
     rc = gset('texup', xup, yup);
     end;
  %mend angle;

data _null_;
  rc = ginit();
  rc = graph('clear', 'angle');
  rc = gset('texalign', 'left', 'base');
  rc = gset('texheight', 5);
  rc = gset('texfont', 'swissl');
  %angle(180);
  rc = gdraw('text', 50, 50, '180');
  %angle(80);
```

```
rc = gdraw('text', 50, 50, '80');
%angle(600);
rc = gdraw('text', 50, 50, '600');
rc = graph('update');
rc = gterm();
run;
```

Argument Definitions

upx　　　　　　numeric constant or numeric variable name; if *upy* is 0, *upx* cannot be 0.

upy　　　　　　numeric constant or numeric variable name; if *upx* is 0, *upy* cannot be 0.

See Also

GASK('TEXUP', . . .)routine

GDRAW('TEXT', . . .)function

GSET('TEXALIGN', . . .)function

GSET('TEXPATH', . . .)function

TRANSNO

Specifies the number of the transformation to be used

Operating States:　　GKOP, SGOP, WSAC, WSOP

Return Codes:　　0, 8, 50

Default Value:　　0

Syntax

return-code-variable=GSET('TRANSNO', *n*);

Description　　The GSET('TRANSNO', . . .)function activates the viewport and/or window you have defined for the specified transformation number. If you have not defined both a viewport and window for a transformation, the default is used for the one missing.

You can select 0 as the active transformation, but you cannot define a viewport or window for that transformation number. A transformation of 0 activates the default viewport, (0,0) to (1,1), and window, which is device dependent.

Argument Definitions

n　　　　　　numeric constant or numeric variable name; indicates the viewport and/or window to activate; should correspond to the *n* used in the GSET('VIEWPORT', . . .)and/or GSET('WINDOW', . . .)functions. Valid values are 0 to 20, inclusive.

See Also

GASK('TRANS', . . .)routine
GASK('TRANSNO', . . .)routine
GASK('VIEWPORT', . . .)routine
GASK('WINDOW', . . .)routine
GSET('VIEWPORT', . . .)function
GSET('WINDOW', . . .)function

VIEWPORT

Associates a viewport with a transformation number

Operating States: GKOP, SGOP, WSAC, WSOP
Return Codes: 0, 8, 50, 51, 52
Default Values: $llx=0$, $lly=0$, $urx=1$, $ury=1$

Syntax

return-code-variable=GSET('VIEWPORT', *n, llx, lly, urx, ury*);

Description   The GSET('VIEWPORT', . . .)function defines a viewport and associates it with the transformation number, *n*. See the GSET('TRANSNO', . . .)function on page 1161 for information on how to activate the viewport. See the GSET('WINDOW', . . .)function on page 1164 for information on how to define a window to be used within the viewport.

Argument Definitions

n	numeric constant or numeric variable name; specifies the transformation number of the viewport. Valid values are 1 to 20, inclusive.
llx	numeric constant or numeric variable name; defines the *x* component of the lower-left corner of the viewport; must not exceed the value of *urx*; cannot be less than 0. Units are based on percent of the graphics output area.
lly	numeric constant or numeric variable name; defines the *y* component of the lower-left corner of the viewport; must not exceed the value of *ury*; cannot be less than 0. Units are based on percent of the graphics output area.
urx	numeric constant or numeric variable name; defines the *x* component of the upper-right corner of the viewport; cannot be greater than 1. Units are based on percent of the graphics output area.
ury	numeric constant or numeric variable name; defines the *y* component of the upper-right corner of the viewport; cannot be greater than 1. Units are based on percent of the graphics output area.

See Also

GASK('VIEWPORT', . . .)routine
GSET('WINDOW', . . .)function
GSET('TRANSNO', . . .)function
GASK('TRANSNO', . . .)routine
GASK('TRANS', . . .)routine
GASK('WINDOW', . . .)routine

VPOS

Specifies the number of rows

Operating States: GKCL
Return Codes: 0, 1, 90, 307
Default Values: 1. VPOS=graphics option, if specified; 2. device's default VPOS value

Syntax

return-code-variable=GSET('VPOS', *vpos*);

Description The GSET('VPOS', . . .)function sets the number of rows in the graphics output area. GSET('VPOS', . . .)has the same effect on graphics output as the VPOS= graphics option.
  You can reset the VPOS value by submitting one of the following statements:

```
goptions reset=goptions;
goptions reset=all;

goptions vpos=0;
```

Argument Definitions

vpos   numeric constant or numeric variable name; specifies the number of rows in the graphics output area; must be greater than 0.

See Also

GASK('VPOS', . . .)routine
GSET('HPOS', . . .)function
GSET('VSIZE', . . .)function
VPOS= graphics option (see "VPOS" on page 397)

VSIZE

Specifies the vertical dimension of the graphics output area

Operating States: GKCL

Return Codes: 0, 1, 90, 307

Default Values: 1. VSIZE= graphics option, if specified; 2. device's default VSIZE value

Syntax

return-code-variable=GSET('VSIZE', *vsize*);

Description The GSET('VSIZE', . . .)function sets the vertical dimension, in inches, of the graphics output area. GSET('VSIZE', . . .)affects the dimensions of the default window.

You can reset the VSIZE value by submitting one of the following statements:

```
goptions reset=goptions;
goptions reset=all;
goptions vsize=0;
```

Argument Definitions

vsize   numeric constant or numeric variable name; indicates the vertical dimension for the graph in inches; must be greater than 0.

See Also

GASK('VSIZE', . . .)routine

GSET('HSIZE', . . .)function

GSET('VPOS', . . .)function

VSIZE= graphics option (see "VSIZE" on page 398)

WINDOW

Associates a window with a transformation number

Operating States: GKOP, SGOP, WSAC, WSOP

Return Codes: 0, 8, 50, 51

Default Values: *llx*=0, *lly*=0; *urx* and *ury* are device dependent

Syntax

return-code-variable=GSET ('WINDOW', *n, llx, lly, urx, ury*);

Description The GSET('WINDOW', . . .)function defines a window and associates it with a transformation number. See the GSET('TRANSNO', . . .)function on page 1161 for information on how to activate a window. See the GSET('VIEWPORT', . . .)function on page 1162 for information on how to define a viewport for a window.

Argument Definitions

n   numeric constant or numeric variable name; specifies the transformation number of the window. Valid values are 1 to 20, inclusive.

llx   numeric constant or numeric variable name; defines the *x* component of the lower-left corner of the window; must not exceed the value of *urx*. Units are based on percent of the active viewport.

lly   numeric constant or numeric variable name; defines the *y* component of the lower-left corner of the window; must not exceed the value of *ury*. Units are based on percent of the active viewport.

urx   numeric constant or numeric variable name; defines the *x* component of the upper-right corner of the window. Units are based on percent of the active viewport.

ury   numeric constant or numeric variable name; defines the *y* component of the upper-right corner of the window. Units are based on percent of the active viewport.

See Also

GASK('TRANS', . . .)routine

GASK('TRANSNO', . . .)routine

GASK('VIEWPORT', . . .)routine

GASK('WINDOW', . . .)routine

GSET('TRANSNO', . . .)function

GSET('VIEWPORT', . . .)function

Return Codes for DSGI Routines and Functions

0   Function completed successfully.

1   DATA Step Graphics Interface should be in GKCL state; the statement is out of place within the DATA step.

3   DATA Step Graphics Interface should be in WSAC state; the statement is out of place within the DATA step.

4   DATA Step Graphics Interface should be in SGOP state; the statement is out of place within the DATA step.

7   DATA Step Graphics Interface should be in WSOP, WSAC, or SGOP state; the statement is out of place within the DATA step.

8   DATA Step Graphics Interface should be in GKOP, WSOP, WSAC, or SGOP state; the statement is out of place within the DATA step.

24   Workstation is open.

25   Workstation is not open.

26	Workstation cannot be opened.
29	Workstation is active.
30	Workstation is not active.
50	Invalid transformation number; transformation numbers must be in the range 0 to 20; viewports and windows cannot be defined for transformation 0.
51	Transformation is not a well-defined rectangle; transformations must have coordinates for four vertices.
52	Viewport coordinates are out of range; coordinates must be within dimensions of graphics output area for the device.
55	Clipping is on.
56	Clipping is off.
60	Bad line index; index numbers must be in the range 1 to 20.
61	No bundle defined for the line index; a GSET('LINREP', . . .)function has not been submitted for the referenced line index.
62	Line type is less than or equal to 0 or greater than 46; type must be in the range 1 to 46.
64	Invalid marker index; index numbers must be in the range 1 to 20.
65	No bundle defined for the polymarker index; a GSET('MARREP', . . .)function has not been submitted for the referenced marker index.
66	Marker type is less than or equal to 0 or greater than 67; type must be in the range 1 to 67.
68	Invalid text index; index numbers must be in the range 1 to 20.
69	No bundle defined for the text index; a GSET('TEXREP', . . .)function has not been submitted for the referenced text index.
73	Character height is less than or equal to 0; height must be greater than 0.
74	Both components of the character up vector are 0; both X and Y of a character up vector cannot be 0.
75	Invalid fill index; index numbers must be in the range 1 to 20.
76	No bundle defined for the fill index; a GSET('FILREP', . . .)function has not been submitted for the referenced fill index.
78	Style index is less than or equal to 0 or greater than 60; style indexes must be in the range of 1 to 60.
86	Invalid color index; color index is out of the range 1 to 256 or is not numeric.
87	No color name defined for the color index
90	Value is less than 0; value must be greater than or equal to 0.
301	Out of memory; your workstation does not have enough memory to generate the graph.
302	Out of room for graph; your device cannot display the size of the graph.

307   Error occurred in program library management; a GRAPH function
             did not execute properly.

See Also

Chapter 3, "Device Drivers," on page 37
   for information about specifying device drivers.

Chapter 9, "Graphics Options and Device Parameters Dictionary," on page 301
   for descriptions of graphics options and device parameters

Chapter 6, "SAS/GRAPH Fonts," on page 125
   for information about the fonts available in SAS/GRAPH software

Chapter 7, "SAS/GRAPH Colors," on page 139
   for information about specifying colors in SAS/GRAPH programs

"GOPTIONS Statement" on page 182
   for an explanation of setting graphics options with the GOPTIONS statement

"PATTERN Statement" on page 211
   for information about specifying patterns with DSGI

"SYMBOL Statement" on page 226
   for representations of the markers that can be used with DSGI

Chapter 31, "The DATA Step Graphics Interface," on page 1027
   for a complete explanation of using DSGI statements to produce graphs

Chapter 15, "The GDEVICE Procedure," on page 651
   for information about device entries

The discussion for ARRAY in *SAS Language Reference: Dictionary*
   for an explanation of OF argument lists

References

Enderle, G.; Kansy, K.; and Pfaff, G. (1985), *Computer Graphics Programming: GKS–The Graphics Standard* Springer-Verlag New York, Inc.

Glossary

absolute coordinates
coordinates measured from the origin of the coordinate system. In two-dimensional graphs, the origin is (0,0). In three-dimensional graphs, the origin is (0,0,0). See also relative coordinates.

aspect ratio
the ratio of width to height (that is, width divided by height) in an output area such as a display, plotter, or film recorder. In SAS/GRAPH software, the ASPECT= graphics option simulates a change in the aspect ratio of the display, causing fonts and circles to be compressed horizontally or vertically or both.

axis
a one-dimensional line representing the zero point on a scale used to plot values of *x*,*y*, or *z* coordinates. In SAS/GRAPH software, in two dimensions, the X axis represents the horizontal plane, and the Y axis represents the vertical plane. In three dimensions, the X axis represents width, the Y axis represents depth, and the Z axis represents height. See also Cartesian coordinate system. The term *axis* may also refer collectively to the axis line, the major and minor tick marks, the major tick mark values, and the axis label.

axis area
an area bounded by axes. In SAS/GRAPH software, this area may be enclosed by an axis frame. See also frame.

baseline
in a font, the imaginary line upon which the characters rest.

block map
a three-dimensional map that uses blocks of varying heights to represent the value of a variable for each map area.

border
in SAS/GRAPH software, the line drawn around the entire graphics output area. This area includes the title and footnote areas as well as the procedure output area. See also frame.

boundary
in the GMAP procedure, a separating line or point that distinguishes between two or more unit areas or segments.

BY group

all observations with the same values for all BY variables.

BY-group processing

the process of using the BY statement to process observations that are ordered, grouped, or indexed according to the values of one or more variables. Many SAS procedures and the DATA step support BY-group processing.

BY variable

a variable named in a BY statement whose values define groups of observations to process.

Cartesian coordinate system

the two- or three-dimensional coordinate system in which perpendicular axes meet at the origin (0,0) or (0,0,0). Typically, Cartesian coordinate axes are called X, Y, and Z. See also axis.

Cartesian coordinates

values that locate a point in two- or three-dimensional space. Each value represents units measured along an X, Y, or Z axis. See also Cartesian coordinate system.

capline

the highest point of a normal uppercase letter. In some fonts, the capline may be above the top of the letter to allow room for an accent.

catalog

See SAS catalog.

catalog entry

See entry type and SAS catalog entry.

cell

a unit of measure defined by the number of rows and the number of columns in the graphics output area. See also aspect ratio.

CGM

an abbreviation for computer graphics metafile. A CGM is a graphics output file written in the internationally recognized format for describing computer graphics images. This standardization allows any image in a CGM to be imported and exported among different systems without error or distortion.

character string

one or more alphanumeric or other keyboard characters or both.

character value

a value that can contain alphabetic characters, numeric characters 0 through 9, and other special characters. See also character variable.

character variable

a variable whose values can consist of alphabetic and special characters as well as numeric characters.

chart

a graph in which graphics elements (bars, pie slices, and so on) show the magnitude of a statistic. The graphics elements can represent one data value or a range of data values.

chart statistic

the statistical value calculated for the chart variable: frequency, cumulative frequency, percentage, cumulative percentage, sum, or mean.

chart variable

a variable in the input data set whose values are categories of data represented by bars, blocks, slices, or spines.

choropleth map

a two-dimensional map that uses color and fill pattern combinations to represent different categories or levels of magnitude.

class variable

in some SAS procedures, a variable used to group, or classify, data. Class variables can be character or numeric. Class variables can have continuous values, but they typically have a few discrete values that define the classifications of the variable.

classification variable

See class variable.

CMYK

a color-coding scheme that specifies a color in terms of levels of cyan, magenta, yellow, and black components. The levels of each component range from 0 to 255. See also HLS, HSV, and RGB.

color map

a table that is used to translate the original colors in graphics output to different colors when replaying graphics output using the GREPLAY procedure. The table is contained in a catalog entry.

color, predefined

one of the set of colors for which SAS/GRAPH software defines and recognizes names, for example, BLACK, BLUE, and CYAN.

color, user-defined

a color expressed in CMYK, HLS, HSV, RGB, or gray-scale format. See also CMYK, HLS, HSV, RGB, and gray scale.

colors list

the list of foreground colors available for the graphics output. The colors list is either the default list established from the device entry or the list established from the colors specified with the COLORS= graphics option.

computer graphics metafile

See CGM.

confidence limits

the upper and lower values of a confidence interval. There is a percentage of confidence (typically 95%) that the true value of the parameter being estimated lies within the interval.

contour plot

a three-variable plot that uses line styles or patterns to represent levels of magnitude of z corresponding to x and y coordinates.

coordinate system

the context in which to interpret coordinates. Coordinate systems vary according to their origin, limits, and units. See also Cartesian coordinate system.

coordinates

the values representing the location of a data point or a graphics element along the X, Y, and Z axes. Coordinate values are measured from the origin of the coordinate system.

data area

the portion of the graphics output area in which data values are displayed. In the Annotate facility, the data area defines a coordinate system. In plots and bar charts, the data area is bounded by axes; in choropleth maps, the data area is bounded by the edge of the unit areas. See also graphics output area, procedure output area, and coordinate system.

data value

a unit of character or numeric information in a SAS data set. A data value represents one variable in an observation. In the rectangular structure of a SAS data set, intersection of a row and a column.

date value

See SAS date value.

default

(1) The setting of a value, parameter, or argument used by the SAS System if the user does not specify a setting.

(2) the value, parameter, or option setting used by the SAS System if the user specifies no particular setting.

density value

a value assigned to each observation in a map data set reflecting the amount of detail (resolution) contributed by the observation.

dependent variable

a variable whose value is determined by the value of another variable or set of variables.

device driver

a routine that generates the specific machine-language commands needed to display graphics output on a particular device. SAS/GRAPH device drivers take device-independent graphics information produced by SAS/GRAPH procedures and create the commands required to produce the graph on the particular device.

device entry

a SAS catalog entry that stores the values of device parameters (or the characteristics) that are used with a particular output device.

device map

a catalog entry used to convert the SAS/GRAPH internal encoding for one or more characters to the device-specific encoding needed to display the character(s) in hardware text on a particular graphics output device. See also hardware character set.

device parameter

a value in a device entry that defines a default behavior or characteristic of a device driver. Some device parameters can be overridden by graphics options. See also graphics option.

display

the area of the monitor that displays what the software presents to you.

display manager

See SAS Display Manager System.

entry type

a characteristic of a SAS catalog entry that identifies its structure and attributes to the SAS System. When you create an entry, the SAS System automatically assigns the entry type as part of the name.

export

to put a SAS catalog entry containing graphics output into a format that can be moved to another software product.

fileref

a name temporarily assigned to an external file or to an aggregate storage location that identifies it to the SAS System. You assign a fileref with a FILENAME statement or with an operating system command.

fill pattern

a design of parallel or crosshatched lines, solid colors, or empty space used to fill an area in a graph.

font

a complete set of all the characters of the same design and style. The characters in a font can be figures or symbols as well as alphanumeric characters. See also type style.

font maximum

in the GFONT procedure, the highest vertical coordinate in a font.

font minimum

in the GFONT procedure, the lowest vertical coordinate in a font.

font units

in the GFONT procedure, units defined by the range of coordinates specified in the font data set. For example, a font in which the vertical coordinates range from 10 to 100 has 90 font units.

font, hardware

a font stored in an output device. See also font, software.

font, software

a font in which the characters are drawn by graphics software. See also font, hardware.

format

an instruction the SAS System uses to display or write each value of a variable. Some formats are supplied by SAS software. Other formats can be written by the user with the FORMAT procedure in base SAS software or with SAS/TOOLKIT software.

frame

a box enclosing a group of graphics elements. In GSLIDE procedure output, the frame encloses the procedure output area. In GPLOT, GCHART, and GCONTOUR procedure output, the frame encloses the axis area. In a legend, the frame encloses the legend label and entries. See also border.

global statement

a SAS statement that you can specify anywhere in a SAS program.

graph

a visual representation of data showing the variation of a variable in comparison to one or more other variables.

graphics element

a discrete visual part of a picture. For example, a bar in a chart and a plot's axis label are both graphics elements.

graphics device

See graphics output device.

graphics option

a value specified in a GOPTIONS statement that controls some attribute of the graphics output. The values specified remain in effect only for the duration of the SAS session. Some graphics options override device parameters.

graphics output

output from a graphics program that can be stored as a catalog entry of type GRSEG, or as a graphics stream file. Graphics output can be displayed or printed on a graphics output device. See also graphics output device and graphics stream file (GSF).

graphics output area

the area of a graphics output device where the graphics output is displayed or drawn. Typically, the graphics output area occupies the full drawing area of the device, but the dimensions of the graphics output area can be changed with graphics options or device parameters. See also procedure output area and graphics output device.

graphics output device

any terminal, printer, or other output device capable of displaying or producing graphics output. See also graphics output.

graphics stream file (GSF)

a file containing device-dependent graphics commands from a SAS/GRAPH device driver. This file can be sent to a graphics device or to other software packages.

gray scale

a color-coding scheme that specifies a color in terms of gray components. Gray-scale color codes are commonly used with some laser printers and PostScript devices.

grid request

in the G3GRID procedure, the request specified in a GRID statement that identifies the horizontal variables that identify the x-y plane and one or more z variables for the interpolation.

group variable

a variable in the input data set used to categorize chart variable values into groups.

GSF

See graphics stream file (GSF).

HLS

a color-coding scheme that specifies a color in terms of its hue, lightness, and saturation components. Hue is the color, lightness is the percentage of white, and saturation is the attribute of a color that determines its relative strength and its departure from gray. Lightness and saturation added to the hue produce a specific shade. See also CMYK, HSV, and RGB.

HSV (or HSB)

a color-coding scheme that specifies a color in terms of its hue, saturation, and value (or brightness) components. Hue is the color, saturation is the attribute of a color that determines its relative strength and its departure from gray, and value or brightness is its departure from black. See also CMYK, HLS, and RGB.

identification variable

a variable common to both the map data set and the response data set that the GMAP procedure uses to associate each pair of map coordinates and each response value with a unique map area.

import

(1) to read a computer graphics metafile (CGM) and store the graphics output in a SAS catalog. Use the GIMPORT procedure to import the CGM. (2) to restore a SAS transport file to its original form (a SAS data library, a SAS catalog, or a SAS data set) in the format appropriate to the host operating system. Use the CIMPORT procedure to import a SAS transport file created by the CPORT procedure.

independent variable

a variable that does not depend on the value of another variable; in a two-dimensional plot, the independent variable is usually plotted on the x (horizontal) axis.

interpolate

to estimate values between two or more known values.

justify

to position text in relation to the left or right margin or the center of the line.

key map

a SAS catalog entry used to translate the codes generated by the keys on a keyboard into their corresponding SAS/GRAPH internal character encoding. See also device map.

label

(1) in the AXIS and LEGEND statements and GPLOT and GCHART procedures, the text that names the variable associated with an axis, a legend, or a bubble in a bubble plot. By default, this text is the name of a variable or of a label previously assigned with a LABEL statement. The text of a label also can be specified with the LABEL= option. (2) in special cases of pie charts and star charts in the GCHART procedure, the midpoint value and the value of the chart statistic for a slice or spine. (3) in the Annotate facility, the text displayed by the LABEL function or macro.

latitude

the angular measure between the equator and the circle of parallel on which a point lies.

legend

refers collectively to the legend value, the legend value description, the legend label, and the legend frame.

libref

the name temporarily associated with a SAS data library. For example, in the name SASUSERS.ACCOUNTS, the name SASUSER is the libref. You assign a libref with a LIBNAME statement or with operating system control language. See also first-level name.

longitude

the angular measure between the reference meridian and the plane intersecting both poles and a point. The reference meridian, called the prime meridian, is assigned a longitude of 0, and other longitude values are measured from there in appropriate angular units (degrees or radians, for example).

major tick marks

the points on an axis that mark the major divisions of the axis scale. See also minor tick marks.

map

a graphic representation of an area, often a geographic area, but also any other area of any size. See also device map and key map.

map area

a polygon or group of polygons on a map, for example, a state, province, or country. In a map data set, a map area consists of all the observations with the same values for the identification variable or variables. A map area and a unit area are the same things. See also identification variable.

map data set

a SAS data set that contains information the GMAP procedure uses to draw a map. Each observation contains variables whose values are the x,y coordinates of a point on the boundary of a map area, and an identification variable whose value identifies the map area to which the point belongs.

meridian

an imaginary circle of constant longitude around the surface of the earth perpendicular to the equator. See also parallel.

midpoint

a value that represents one data value or the middle of a range of data values. When a midpoint represents a range of values, the algorithm used to calculate it depends on the procedure.

minor tick marks

the divisions of the axis scale that fall between major tick marks. See also major tick marks.

needle plot

a plot in which a vertical line connects each data point to the horizontal axis (two dimensions) or the horizontal plane (three dimensions).

numeric variable

a variable that can contain only numeric values. By default, the SAS System stores all numeric variables in floating-point representation.

observation

a row in a SAS data set. An observation is a collection of data values associated with a single entity, such as a customer or state. Each observation contains one data value for each variable. See also variable.

offset

(1) in a legend, the distance between the edge of the legend or the edge of the legend frame and the axis frame or the border surrounding the graphics output area. (2) on an axis, the distance from the origin to either the first major tick mark or the midpoint of the first bar, or the distance from the last major tickmark or the midpoint of the last bar to the end of the axis.

origin

(1) in a three-dimensional coordinate system, the point at which the X, Y, and Z axes intersect, defined by the coordinates (0,0,0). In a two-dimensional coordinate system, the point at which the X and Y axes intersect, defined by the coordinates (0,0). (2) in the AXIS statement, the origin is the point at which the axis line begins (the left end of the horizontal axis or the bottom of the vertical axis). In the LEGEND statement, the origin is the location of the lower-left corner of the legend. (3) in the graphics output area, the lower-left corner.

palette

the range of colors that can be generated on a graphics device. See also colors list.

panel

in the GREPLAY procedure, a part of the template in which one or more pictures can be displayed. A template can contain one or more panels.

parallel

an imaginary circle of constant latitude around the surface of the earth parallel to the equator. See also meridian.

pattern type

the set of fill patterns that are valid for a particular type of graph. The PATTERN statement supports three pattern types: bar and block patterns, map and plot patterns, and pie and star patterns. See also fill pattern.

pen mounts

on a pen plotter, the holders for the drawing pens.

pie chart

a chart made up of a circle divided by radial lines used to display the relative contribution of each part to the whole.

plot
> a graph showing the relationship between variables. The coordinates of each point on the graph represent the values you plot. See also coordinates.

plot line
> the line joining the data points in a plot.

plotter
> a class of graphics devices that typically use pens to draw hardcopy output.

polygon
> a closed, geometric figure bounded by lines or arcs. Polygons can be filled in to represent a surface.

polygon font
> a font in which the characters are drawn with enclosed areas that can be filled or empty. See also stroked font.

prism map
> a three-dimensional map that uses prisms (polyhedrons with two parallel surfaces) of varying height to indicate the ordinal magnitude of a response variable.

procedure output area
> the portion of the graphics output area where the output from a graphics procedure is displayed. See also graphics output area and data area.

projection
> a two-dimensional map representation of unit areas on the surface of a sphere, for example, geographic regions on the surface of the Earth.

regression analysis
> an analysis of the nature of the relationship between two or more variables, expressed as a mathematical function. On a scatter plot, this relationship is diagrammed as a line drawn through data points. A straight line indicates simple regression; a curve indicates a higher-order regression.

relative coordinates
> the coordinates measured from a point other than the origin, usually the endpoint of the last graphics element drawn. See also absolute coordinates.

relative move
> a move that repositions the graphics element by a specified distance from its current location. See also absolute move.

replay
> to display graphics output that is stored in a catalog entry.

response data set
> a SAS data set the GMAP procedure uses that contains data values associated with map areas and one or more identification variables. See also identification variable, response values, and response variable.

response levels
> the individual values or ranges of values into which the GMAP or GCHART procedure divides the response variable. See also midpoint.

response values
> values of a response variable that the GMAP procedure represents on a map as different pattern/color combinations, or as raised map areas (prisms), spikes, or blocks of different heights. The GCHART procedure represents response values as bars, slices, spines, or blocks. See also midpoint.

response variable

the SAS data set variable in a response data set the GMAP procedure uses that contains data values associated with a map area. Response variables used by the GCHART procedure contain data values associated with bars, slices, spines, or blocks. See also chart variable, response data set, response levels, and response values.

RGB

a color-coding scheme that specifies a color in terms of levels of red, green, and blue components. The levels of each component range from 0 to 255. See also CMYK, HLS, and HSV.

rotate

in the graphics editor, to turn a graphics object about its axis.

RUN group

in SAS procedures, a set of statements ending with a RUN statement.

SAS catalog

a SAS file that stores many different kinds of information in smaller units called catalog entries. A single SAS catalog can contain several different types of catalog entries.

SAS catalog entry

a separate storage unit within a SAS catalog. Each entry has an entry type that identifies its purpose to the SAS System. See also entry type.

SAS data library

a collection of one or more SAS files that are recognized by the SAS System and that are referenced and stored as a unit. Each file is a member of the library.

SAS data set

descriptor information and its related data values organized as a table of observations and variables that can be processed by the SAS System. A SAS data set can be either a SAS data file or a SAS data view.

SAS date value

an integer representing a date in the SAS System. The integer represents the number of days between January 1, 1960, and another specified date. (For example, the SAS date value 366 represents the calendar date January 1, 1961.)

SAS Display Manager System

an interactive, windowing interface to SAS System software. Display manager commands can be issued by typing them on the command line, pressing function keys, or selecting items from the PMENU facility. Within one session, many different tasks can be accomplished, including preparing and submitting programs, viewing and printing results, and debugging and resubmitting programs.

scatter plot

a two- or three-dimensional plot showing the joint variation of two (or three) variables from a group of observations. The coordinates of each point in the plot correspond to the data values for a single observation.

segment

in the GMAP procedure, a polygon that is a part of a unit area consisting of more than one polygon. For example, consider a map of Hawaii. The representation of the single unit area (the state) consists of a group of individual segments (the islands), each of which is a separate polygon. In the GFONT procedure, a segment is a single continuous line that forms part of all of a character or symbol.

software font

See font, software.

spine

a line on a star chart used to represent the relative value of the chart statistic for a midpoint. Spines are drawn outward from the center of the chart.

spline

a method of interpolation in which a smooth line or surface connects data points.

standard deviation

a statistical measure of the variability of a group of data values. This measure, which is the most widely used measure of the dispersion of a frequency distribution, is equal to the positive square root of the variance.

string

See character string.

stroked font

a font in which the characters are drawn with discrete line segments or circular arcs. See also polygon font.

subgroup variable

the variable in the input data set for a chart that is used to proportionally fill areas of the bars or blocks on the chart.

summary variable

a variable in an input data set whose values the GCHART procedure totals or averages to produce the sum or mean statistics, respectively.

surface map

a three-dimensional map that uses spikes of varying heights to indicate levels of relative magnitude.

surface plot

a three-dimensional graph that displays a grid-like surface formed by the values of the vertical (Z) variable plotted on a plane specified by the X and Y variables.

template

in the GREPLAY procedure, a framework that enables you to display one or more pictures on a page.

text string

See character string.

tilt angle

the measure in degrees from the horizontal axis to the major axis of an object.

type style

a typeface design and its variations, for example, Swiss, Swiss Bold, and Swiss Italic. See also font.

unit area

See map area.

user-definable colors

the colors that can be defined using SAS color names, or CMYK (cyan, magenta, yellow, black), RGB (red, green, blue), HLS (hue, lightness, saturation), HSV (hue, saturation, value), or gray-scale color equivalents.

value

the text that labels a major tick mark on an axis. Also, in a legend, a value is a line, bar, or shape that the legend explains.

variable

a column in a SAS data set. A variable is a set of data values that describe a given characteristic across all observations. See also macro variable.

variable type

the classification of a variable as either numeric or character. Type is an attribute of SAS variables.

WORK data library

the SAS data library automatically defined by the SAS System at the beginning of each SAS session or SAS job. It contains SAS files that are temporary by default. When the libref USER is not defined, the SAS System uses WORK as the default library for SAS files created with one-level names.

X axis

in a two-dimensional plot, the horizontal axis. In a three-dimensional plot, the X axis is the axis perpendicular to the Y-Z plane.

Y axis

in a two-dimensional plot, the vertical axis. In a three-dimensional plot, the Y axis is the axis perpendicular to the X-Z plane.

Z axis

in a three-dimensional plot, the axis perpendicular to the X-Y plane.

ndex